Children in Changing Worlds

Children live in rapidly changing times that require them to constantly adapt to new economic, social, and cultural conditions. In this book, a distinguished, interdisciplinary group of scholars explores the issues faced by children in contemporary societies, such as discrimination in school and neighborhoods, the emergence of new family forms, the availability of new communication technologies, and economic hardship, as well as the stresses associated with immigration, war, and famine. The book applies a historical, cultural, and life-course developmental framework for understanding the factors that affect how children adjust to these challenges, and offers a new perspective on how changing historical circumstances alter children's developmental outcomes. It is ideal for researchers and graduate students in developmental and educational psychology or the sociology and anthropology of childhood.

ROSS D. PARKE is Distinguished Professor of Psychology Emeritus and former Director of the Center for Family Studies at the University of California, Riverside, USA. He has received awards for his research from both the American Psychological Association (G. Stanley Hall Award) and the Society for Research in Child Development (Distinguished Scientific Contribution to Child Development).

GLEN H. ELDER, JR. is Howard W. Odum Distinguished Research Professor of Sociology and a fellow in the Carolina Population Center at the University of North Carolina at Chapel Hill, USA. He is a member of the American Academy of Arts and Sciences and a former president of the Society for Research in Child Development.

Children in Changing Worlds

Sociocultural and Temporal Perspectives

Edited by

Ross D. Parke
University of California, Riverside

Glen H. Elder, Jr.
University of North Carolina at Chapel Hill

CAMBRIDGE
UNIVERSITY PRESS

CAMBRIDGE
UNIVERSITY PRESS

University Printing House, Cambridge CB2 8BS, United Kingdom

One Liberty Plaza, 20th Floor, New York, NY 10006, USA

477 Williamstown Road, Port Melbourne, VIC 3207, Australia

314–321, 3rd Floor, Plot 3, Splendor Forum, Jasola District Centre, New Delhi – 110025, India

79 Anson Road, #06-04/06, Singapore 079906

Cambridge University Press is part of the University of Cambridge.

It furthers the University's mission by disseminating knowledge in the pursuit of education, learning, and research at the highest international levels of excellence.

www.cambridge.org
Information on this title: www.cambridge.org/9781108417105
DOI: 10.1017/9781108264846

© Cambridge University Press 2019

First published 2019

Printed in the United Kingdom by TJ International Ltd, Padstow Cornwall

A catalogue record for this publication is available from the British Library.

Library of Congress Cataloging-in-Publication Data
Names: Parke, Ross D., editor. | Elder, Glen H., Jr., editor.
Title: Children in changing worlds : sociocultural and temporal perspectives / edited by Ross D. Parke, Glen H. Elder Jr.
Description: New York: Cambridge University Press, 2019. |
Includes bibliographical references and index.
Identifiers: LCCN 2019000706| ISBN 9781108417105 (hardback) |
ISBN 9781108404464 (paperback)
Subjects: LCSH: Children – United States – Social conditions. |
Children – United States – History – 20th century. |
Child development – United States – History – 20th century.
Classification: LCC HQ792.U5 C4317 2017 | DDC 305.230973–dc23
LC record available at https://lccn.loc.gov/2019000706

ISBN 978-1-108-41710-5 Hardback
ISBN 978-1-108-40446-4 Paperback

Contents

Part III   Social, Legal, and Technological Change: Impact on Children

Part IV   Views of the Interdisciplinary Dialogue: From Developmental Science and Sociology

List of Figures

Contributor Biographies

JULIUS ANASTASIO is a doctoral student at Tufts University Department of Child Study and Human Development. Anastasio was educated at Cornell and Northeastern University, with an educational focus on developmental interventions during early and middle childhood. He was previously an evaluator at the National Institute of Child Health Quality, and has worked in various positions within diverse urban school settings. Anastasio is a co-author of *Learning and Attention Disorders in Adolescence and Adulthood: assessment and treatment* (2nd edn).

MARC H. BORNSTEIN is associated with the National Institute of Child Health and Human Development and the Institute for Fiscal Studies, London. His PhD is from Yale University, and he previously taught at Princeton University and New York University. Bornstein was a J. S. Guggenheim Foundation fellow, and he received a Research Career Development Award from the National Institute of Child Health and Human Development. He also received the C. S. Ford Cross-Cultural Research Award from the Human Relations Area Files, the Boyd McCandless Young Scientist Award, and the G. Stanley Hall Award from the American Psychological Association, a United States PHS Superior Service Award from the National Institutes of Health, awards from the Japan Society for the Promotion of Science and the American Mensa Education & Research Foundation, the Arnold Resell Prize from the Theodor Hellbrügge Foundation, an award of merit from the National Institutes of Health, the Distinguished International Contributions to Child Development Award, and the Distinguished Scientific Contributions to Child Development Award from the Society for Research in Child Development, and honorary doctorates from the University of Padua and University of Trento. Bornstein is Editor Emeritus of *Child Development* and Founding Editor of *Parenting: Science and Practice*.

JOHN BYNNER is Emeritus Professor of Social Sciences in Education at the UCL London Institute of Education. He was past Director of the Centre for Longitudinal Studies, Co-Director of the Wider Benefits of Learning Research Centre and Founder Director of the National Research and Development Centre for Adult Literacy and Numeracy. He was first Executive Editor of the international journal, *Longitudinal and Life Course Studies*, and was Foundation Chair of the Society for Longitudinal and Life Course Studies. His educational career included the Universities of Bristol and London and a Fulbright fellowship at University of Michigan. Most recent books are, with Mike Wadsworth, *A Companion to Life Course Studies* and with Ingrid Schoon, *Young People's Development and the Great Recession*.

MARTHA J. COX is Professor Emerita of Psychology and Neuroscience at the University of North Carolina–Chapel Hill. She received her PhD from the University of Virginia. Cox is known for her longitudinal studies of families and children and for her methodological contributions to the analysis of family interactions. She was one of the investigators of the NICHD-funded Family Life Project, a program project investigating the development of children in poor, rural settings. She was one of 10 principal investigators in the NICHD Study of Early Child Care, a groundbreaking study of children from birth through high school, considering children's development within family, child-care, and school settings. She was Principal Investigator of the NSF-funded North Carolina Child Development Research Collaborative. She also directed the NICHD-funded Carolina Consortium on Human Development.

ROBERT CROSNOE is the Rapoport Centennial Professor of Liberal Arts at the University of Texas at Austin, where he is Chair of the Department of Sociology and a faculty member in the Department of Psychology (by courtesy) and Population Research Center. Prior to this, he received a PhD in Sociology from Stanford University and completed a post-doctoral fellowship at the University of North Carolina at Chapel Hill. Crosnoe's research considers the connections among health, child/adolescent development, and education and the contributions of these connections to socioeconomic and immigration-related inequalities in American society. He is Co-Director of the Interdisciplinary Collaborative on Development in Context, President of the Society for Research on Adolescence, and a member of the Governing Council of the Council on Contemporary Families.

VERONIQUE DUPÉRÉ is Associate Professor in Educational Psychology (École de psychoéducation) at the Université de Montréal, Canada. She has received early career awards from Quebec's Health Research Fund and the Université de Montréal Public Health Research Institute. Her work focuses on children and adolescent development in contrasted contexts, and on preventive approaches aimed at reducing educational gaps between children and youth living in disadvantaged communities and their more advantaged peers. She has authored or co-authored dozens of publications in education and developmental psychology, including in journals such as *Review of Educational Research and Child Development*.

GLEN H. ELDER, JR. is the Howard W. Odum Distinguished Research Professor, Department of Sociology and Fellow in the Carolina Population Center of the University of North Carolina–Chapel Hill. He was educated at the Universities of Penn State, Kent State, and North Carolina–Chapel Hill where he received his doctorate with a major in sociology and a minor in psychology. He has served on the faculties of UC-Berkeley, Cornell, and North Carolina–Chapel Hill. His initial research appointment at the Berkeley Institute of Human Development during the 1960s led to work with pioneer longitudinal samples that drew upon historical, sociological, and psychological perspectives in studies of the life course, leading to the publication of *Children of the Great Depression* (1974; 1999). Other books on the life course (authored, co-authored, or edited) include *Life Course Dynamics: Trajectories and Transitions* (1985), *Children in Time and Place* (1993), and *Children of the Land: Adversity and Success in Rural America* (2000). Senior Scientist awards in support of the investigator came from NIMH (1995–2000) and the Spencer Foundation (2000–5). He is a member of the American Academy of Arts and Sciences and is past President of the Society for Research in Child Development.

CYNTHIA GARCÍA COLL is Visiting Professor at the University of Puerto Rico, after spending 30 years as Professor at Brown University. García Coll was educated at the Universities of Puerto Rico, University of Florida, and Harvard University. She has been Editor of *Developmental Psychology* and is currently Editor of *Child Development*. Her scholarship has been in the interplay of culture and sources of oppression (poverty, discrimination, etc.) in developmental processes and outcomes. She is the author with Amy Marks of *Immigrant Stories*, and editor of many books and special issues on immigrant and minority populations.

PATRICIA M. GREENFIELD received her PhD from Harvard University and is Distinguished Professor of Psychology at UCLA, where she is a member of the Developmental Psychology group. Her central theoretical and research interest is in the relationship between culture and human development. She is a member of the American Academy of Arts and Sciences and a recipient of the American Association for the Advancement of Science Award for Behavioral Science Research, the APA Urie Bronfenbrenner Award for Lifetime Contribution to Developmental Psychology in the Service of Science and Society, and the SRCD award for Distinguished Contributions to Cultural and Contextual Factors in Child Development. She has also received teaching awards from UCLA and APA. Her books include *Mind and Media: The Effects of Television, Video Games, and Computers* (1984). She co-edited (with R. R. Cocking) *Interacting with Video* (1996) and *Cross-Cultural Roots of Minority Child Development* (1994). She also directs Children's Digital Media Center at Los Angeles, which researches the developmental implications of Instagram, Facebook, YouTube, and other technologies. Recent projects include studying social change, culture, and human development in Israel, China, Mexico, and the United States.

TAMA LEVENTHAL is Professor in the Eliot-Pearson Department of Child Study and Human Development at Tufts University. She is a developmental psychologist who has spent her career in policy and applied academic settings. She received her doctorate from Teachers College, Columbia University. Her primary research focus is the role of neighborhood contexts in the lives of children, youth, and families; related work centers housing. She was Co-Editor of the *Handbook of Child Psychology and Developmental Science: Volume 4: Ecological Settings and Processes in Developmental Systems* and is Associate Editor of the *Journal of Research on Adolescence* and *Applied Developmental Science*. Leventhal was formerly a US Department of Housing and Urban Development Postdoctoral Urban Scholar, a William T. Grant Scholar, and a Foundation for Child Development Changing Faces of America's Children Young Scholar. She was Co-Director of the MacArthur Network on Housing and Families with Children and is currently Co-Director of the Housing and Children's Healthy Development study. She has been Co-Investigator on most of the leading neighborhood studies and Adolescence Investigator for Phase IV of the NICHD Study of Child Care and Youth Development.

AMY K. MARKS is Associate Professor and Chair of the Psychology Department at Suffolk University. She received her undergraduate degree at Cornell University, and completed her doctoral studies at Brown University. Her areas of research include immigrant youth development, the effects of discrimination on child and adolescent health and well-being, and contextual risk/protective processes among minority youth. Her books include: *Transitions: The development of immigrant children* (2015), *The Immigrant Paradox in Children and Adolescents: Is becoming American a developmental risk?* (2012), and *Immigrant Stories: Ethnicity and academics in middle childhood* (2009). She was awarded the Society for the Study of Human Development Early Career Award (2017) and a Jacobs Foundation Young Scholar Award (2009) for her research on developmental risk/resilience processes, academics, and ethnic/racial identity among immigrant youth.

ANN S. MASTEN is Regents Professor and Irving B. Harris Professor of Child Development at the University of Minnesota, Twin Cities. Masten completed her undergraduate degree at Smith College and her PhD in Psychology at the University of Minnesota, and her clinical psychology internship at UCLA. She joined the faculty at the Institute of Child Development at Minnesota in 1986, where she has remained for her career, serving as Director 1999–2005. Masten studies risk and resilience in children, youth, and families faced with trauma, war, disaster, homelessness, migration, and other adversities. She is past President of the Society for Research in Child Development and Division 7 (Developmental) of the American Psychological Association (APA). She is a 2014 recipient of APA's Urie Bronfenbrenner Award for Lifetime Contributions to Developmental Psychology in the Service of Science and Society. She is the author of more than 200 publications, including the book *Ordinary Magic: Resilience in children* (2014). She regularly teaches a mass open online course on *Resilience in Children Exposed to Trauma, Disaster and War: Global perspectives* that has reached participants from more than 170 countries.

JEYLAN T. MORTIMER is Professor of Sociology at the University of Minnesota. After receiving her doctorate from the University of Michigan, she joined the Minnesota faculty and subsequently co-founded and directed the Life Course Center from 1986 to 2006. She is past President of three sections of the American Sociological Association: Aging and the Life Course, Children and Youth, and Social Psychology. Mortimer is Principal Investigator of the three-generation longitudinal Youth Development Study and co-editor of the *Handbook of the Life Course* (Vols. 1 and 2). She has made important contributions to the understanding of adolescent work, the transition to adulthood, and the process of attainment. She is currently studying generational change in achievement orientations and the dynamics of intergenerational transmission and reciprocity.

FROSSO MOTTI-STEFANIDI is Professor of Psychology at the National and Kapodistrian University of Athens (NKUA), Greece. She received her PhD from the Institute of Child Development, University of Minnesota, USA. She is recipient of the Distinguished International Alumni Award from the College of Education and Human Development of the University of Minnesota. She is a Fellow of the Association for Psychological Science. She has served as Chair of the Department of Psychology at NKUA, as President of the European Association for Developmental Psychology, and as President of the European Association of Personality Psychology. She is currently serving as a member of the Governing Council of the Society for Research in Child Development. Her research has focused on the study of immigrant youth adaptation and well-being. With international colleagues, she has developed the Athena Studies of Resilient Adaptation longitudinal project that focuses on immigrant youth adaptation, development, and acculturation. She is author of two books in Greek, and of over 150 papers and chapters in journals and edited books in Greek and English. Recently, she co-edited, together with Katariina Salmela-Aro, University of Helsinki, Finland, a special issue for *European Psychologist* titled: "Youth and Migration: What Promotes and What Challenges Their Integration."

ROSS D. PARKE is Distinguished Professor of Psychology Emeritus and past Director of the Center for Family Studies at the University of California, Riverside. Parke was educated at the Universities of Toronto and Waterloo and previously was affiliated with the Universities of Wisconsin and Illinois and the Fels Research Institute. He is past President of Division 7, the Developmental Psychology Division of the American Psychological Association and of the Society for Research in Child Development. He has received awards for his research from both APA (G. Stanley Hall Award for contributions to Developmental Psychology) and SRCD (Distinguished Scientific Contributions to Child Development Award). He has been Editor of *Developmental Psychology* and *Journal of Family Psychology* and Associate Editor of *Child Development*. Parke is author of *Fathers, Fatherhood* (1996) and *Future Families: Diverse forms, rich possibilities* (2013), and co-author of *Throwaway Dads* (1999) and of *Child Psychology: A contemporary viewpoint* (2008).

HAYLEY A. RAHL-BRIGMAN completed a Bachelor of Science in Psychology at Carnegie Mellon University and is enrolled in the PhD program in Child Psychology-Developmental Psychopathology and Clinical Science program at the University of Minnesota. Her research focuses on resilience, social competence, and parenting. She has published on resilience of children in military families, children involved in the criminal justice and child protection systems, and children exposed to conflict, terror, disaster, and immigration.

INGRID SCHOON is Professor of Human Development and Social Policy at University College London, Institute of Education and holds a Research Professorship at the Social Science Centre in Berlin. She is currently President of the Society for Longitudinal and Lifecourse Studies. Her research is guided by a social ecological-developmental approach, mapping human development over time and in context using longitudinal data, such as the British Cohort Data. She has published widely, including a monograph on *Risk and Resilience* (2006), co-edited books on *Transitions from School to Work: Globalisation, individualisation, and patterns of diversity* (2009) with Rainer K. Silbereisen, *Gender Differences in Aspirations and Attainment: A longitudinal perspective* (2014) with Jacquelynne Eccles, and *Young People's Development and the Great Recession: Uncertain transitions and precarious futures* (2017) with John Bynner – all published by Cambridge University Press.

G. ALICE WOOLVERTON is a PhD student in clinical psychology at Suffolk University, where she is a member of the Youth Development in Context Laboratory. Woolverton was previously educated at Amherst College and Boston University and was affiliated with Boston Children's Hospital. Her research and clinical interests focus on youth identity development processes, risk and resilience factors, acculturation, and mixed qualitative and quantitative research methods.

Preface

All books have historical roots and antecedents, and the current volume is no different. Over a quarter of a century ago, *Children in Time and Place: Developmental and Historical Insights* (1993) was published under the editorship of an interdisciplinary trio of scholars. Glen H. Elder, Jr., a sociologist, John Modell, a historian, and Ross D. Parke, a developmental psychologist, led a group of scholars who in this volume argued that an interdisciplinary approach to the study of children's development would broaden and enrich our understanding of children's lives. This first volume sought to promote a view of human development in social-historical context by urging co-authors from development science and history to join their distinctive perspectives in their respective chapters.

At that time, we argued that developmentalists neglected social-historical temporality, whereas historians seldom viewed historical effects across the lives of people. It was recognized that the life course theoretical perspective, in which the lives of children and their family patterns are traced over time and place, provided an often neglected temporal perspective on changes in children's lives. The earlier volume highlighted how these issues were being addressed by different sets of scholars. The assembled group of historians, sociologists, and psychologists collectively argued for and illustrated these principles of historical change, and the need for a contextualized view of development. Our goal was to bring these viewpoints together in a coherent theoretical argument within a single volume.

While our initial effort was partially successful, as the collaborative chapters and commentaries suggest, this earlier volume is best viewed as a promissory note and an invitation to surmount the obstacles to serious interdisciplinary dialogue. As Zuckerman (1993) observed, it was not enough to treat context "merely as an appeal for the provision of a prologue," in which the historical antecedents of a current issue are outlined without a serious effort to probe the meaning of the historical context in shaping the lives of the individuals and families. The earlier volume should be viewed as an opening salvo in the effort to achieve a true appreciation of the role of historically informed contextual analysis, but it is by no means a definitive statement of this position. At the same time, there was reason for optimism since there were examples that showed the path to achieving this goal. Social historian John Modell (1989) explored the transition from adolescence to adulthood. In his volume *Into One's Own: From Youth to Adulthood in the United States, 1920–1975*, Modell revealed the ways that the changing work and educational norms and advances in the availability of cars together altered the experience of adolescence across time. Similarly, historian Tamara Hareven (1982) in Family Time and Industrial Time showed how historically based shifts in the means of industrial production transformed work as well as family patterns for both adults and children.

In the ensuing years, on the social science side this argument gained wide recognition in part through the writings of Urie Bronfebrenner, who argued for a contextual theoretical approach to child development research in his 1979 volume *The Ecology of Human Development by Nature and Design*. In this book and in later writings he outlined an ecological theory of development that focuses on the multiple systems, from the most immediate (the family or peer group) to the most remote (culture and society's values and laws), in which children are embedded and how these systems are linked. Guided in part by this social ecological perspective, over the past 25 years there has been remarkable progress in achieving the goal of a contextualized and historically informed view of development that was imagined in the earlier volume.

The current volume can best be viewed as a progress report that documents the changing lives of children in changing worlds by providing examples of the ways in which context and history shape child and adult developmental trajectories. As a whole, this volume reflects advances in both theory and methodology that have been achieved over the past several decades.

Part I

Theoretical and Methodological Approaches:
A Cross-Disciplinary Challenge

1   Theoretical Orientation, Methodological Advances, and a Guide to the Volume

Ross D. Parke and Glen H. Elder, Jr.

As noted in the preface, the underlying message of the original volume *Children in Time and Place: Developmental and Historical Insights* stressed the importance of recognizing that children's development is best understood when placed in a specific historical and life course developmental context. The current formulation updates this perspective by focusing more explicitly on the socio-cultural aspects as well.

In this opening chapter we provide a chronology of the relatively recent recognition that an understanding of children's lives across time requires that context in terms of historical time and place also needs to consider culture. Early efforts often failed to recognize this fundamental premise and instead studied children out of context. The emergence of the life course perspective with its recognition of the centrality of changing historical contexts as necessary for an adequate understanding of children's development was a major step forward in theorizing about children's development. Moreover in the past several decades, the life course perspective has also evolved and now recognizes the role of both individual and collective agency in shaping both individual outcomes and those at other levels of analysis (Elder, 1998; Elder et al., 2015). Moreover, as prior work has long recognized (Elder, 1974, 1999) it is increasingly accepted that secular changes co-occur and often come as a package. For example war, famine, migration, and economic hardship generally operate together. We also underscore the increasing appreciation of cross disciplinary dialogue as necessary for understanding issues such as children's genetic influences and how they are constrained in their expression by historical and environmental factors.

Recent Secular Changes

To set the stage for this volume it is worthwhile briefly noting the recent secular changes that have occurred in both North America and in other parts of the world. These changes have been at various levels of society, including social-demographic, economic, cultural beliefs and norms.

A variety of demographic shifts have occurred over the past several decades.

First, the changing racial/ethnic composition of our society due to changing birth rates and patterns of immigration has shifted many societies from homogeneous on race and ethnicity to a much more mixed ethnic composition. This is particularly evident in the USA where Asian, Latino, and African-American ethnic/racial groups are quickly outpacing Caucasians in their patterns of growth. Similarly, in Europe and Australia, due in part to immigration patterns, there is movement toward more racially and ethnically diverse societies.

A second shift has been the growing levels of economic inequality between rich and poor members of society, which is increasingly divided by social class and has resulted in increasingly "diverging destinies" (McLanahan, 2004) for rich and poor. These inequalities are reflected in a variety of contexts from treatment by legal and court systems, to neighborhood conditions and access to occupational and educational opportunities.

Third, work patterns have shifted from permanent, stable employment to a pattern of less stable and temporary employment, a trend that is especially likely to affect those at the bottom of the economic ladder. Accompanying these changes are shifts toward more automation and the decline in work opportunities, especially for unskilled and less educated workers. A major change has been the shift toward more women in the workplace and the subsequent re-organization of family responsibilities between mothers and fathers.

Fourth, with the advent of new technologies, telecommuting and other forms of distance-based interactions have become more common. Nor have the effects of technological advances been limited to the workplace. New means of communication are producing major changes in the ways we relate and communicate with each other.

Fifth, another demographic shift has entailed the uncoupling of life course transitions. With marriage in decline and cohabitation on the rise, the transition to parenthood is increasingly taking place outside of marriage. And with advances in the new reproductive technology, opportunities for parenthood have expanded to include single individuals, infertile couples as well as gay and lesbian couples, which represents a further uncoupling of reproduction from social institutions such as marriage. Another change is the delay in the timing of entry into either marriage or parenthood with a related shift to more time in formal education. The period of economic dependence on parental economic support has expanded with the increase of boomerang young adults who often return home after completion of formal education.

Sixth, amidst these demographic shifts there has been changing and more positive attitudes and norms concerning patterns of social relations such as same-sex marriage. In addition to these broad changes, there have been more discrete crises that have occurred that merit our attention such as the Great Recession of 2008 and the effects of unrest in Europe and the Middle East that have prompted an increase in the flow of refugees. Our goal is to address some of these recent social changes in the chapters that follow.

Theoretical Advances

Since the original volume, several other theoretical strands have entered the discourse, especially with continued recognition and elaboration of Bronfenbrenner's bio-ecological perspective. It provides a rich language for describing the contexts in which children's development takes place and through which historical effects may be expressed (Bronfenbrenner & Morris, 2006). Related theoretical frameworks such as Relational Developmental systems approaches (Lerner & Overton, 2008; Overton, 2015) have emerged as guides as well. The acceptance of bio-ecological models has resulted in studies of children in which multiple levels of contextual influences are examined. For example, parental relationships with school systems are often examined to better understand this type of cross context influence on children's academic progress (Crosnoe, this volume; Hill & Torres, 2010).

Others examine the links between court decisions concerning post-divorce custody and child outcomes and how changes in legal opinion concerning custody alter children's outcomes (Fabricius et al., 2010). Similarly, studies of the effects of recent supreme court decisions (Obergefell v. Hodges) concerning the recognition of same-sex marriage on family formation and societal attitudes concerning same-sex unions are further examples of this cross context inquiry (Gates & Brown, 2015; Masci & Motel, 2015; Parke, this volume). Links between religious institutions and religious practice and child and adolescent outcomes have been stimulated by this theoretical focus on contexts of development (Elder & Conger, 2000; Holden & Williamson, 2014). Studies of the links among neighborhood characteristics, family child-rearing practices (Leventhal & Brooks-Gunn, 2000; Leventhal et al., this volume) and child outcomes as well as the links between social networks and child well-being (Belle & Benenson, 2014) are other examples of how this multi-level bio-ecological theory has expanded both the contexts that are examined but in addition illuminated the ways in which these levels of context mutually influence each other.

Similarly, there has been an increasing recognition that development is not solely governed by universal principles, but is constrained and informed by cultural contextual factors as well. This Vygotskian-inspired recognition of cultural embeddedness is now firmly entrenched as a necessary aspect of the theoretical developmental dialogue (Rogoff, 2003; Greenfield, this volume). Recent theoretical advances include combining Bronfenbrenner's bio-ecological notions as well as Vygotskian advances in our understanding of the role of cultural factors in understanding development with a historical life course perspective. This cultural awareness is reflected in a general movement away from a strictly western view of development by recognizing both cultural variations in other countries but also the variations that exist within our own country.

In recent years there has been a burst of activity documenting how cultural contexts in other countries shape the trajectories of children's development. For example, compared to the USA, adolescents in China and Japan spend less time with peers and their parents play a more prominent role in their daily lives (Chen, Chung et al., 2011; Rothbaum et al., 2000). Another difference reflected in peer relationships is the particular types of social behavior that the culture values. In traditional Chinese culture, shyness and sensitivity are valued and are believed to reflect accomplishment, maturity, and understanding (Chen et al., 2006, 2009). Similarly there has been increased recognition of intra-country variations based on ethnic origins. For example, in the USA Latino children are more family-oriented and less influenced by their peers than US children and their parents often directly discourage peer interactions (Ladd, 2005; Schneider, 2000).

At the same time there is a growing appreciation that historical shifts in other countries and our own country can significantly modify the ways in which children relate to their peers. As Chinese culture shifts toward a more market-oriented economic model, children's social values, which guide children's peer relationships, are changing. Although Chinese elementary school children accepted peers' shyness as a positive characteristic in 1990, they did not do so in 2002. Instead assertiveness and self-direction were more highly valued attributes in their peers among these later cohorts of children, which are values more aligned with a more competitive economic climate. To illustrate the dynamic nature of social change, it is noteworthy that in rural areas of China shyness is still associated with better social and psychological adjustment and with peer relationships in children (Chen, Wang et al., 2011). This pattern of behavior observed in rural areas will likely change as economic transformation expands from urban to rural areas. A similar pattern of historically bound change is evident among immigrant populations in the USA as well. As a result of acculturation and adaptation to their new country, many Latino children and adolescents become less family-oriented and more peer-oriented. This retreat from traditional Latino values and increased embrace of mainstream American values is often associated with increases in delinquency and poorer academic outcomes, a phenomenon termed the immigrant paradox (Garcia-Coll & Marks, 2012; Marks et al., this volume). Similarly Mexican-American women's child-rearing attitudes shift toward a more egalitarian stance as a result of acculturation (Parke et al., 2004). As these examples illustrate, we need to consider both cultural contexts and historical changes in secular domains of society.

Finally, there has been an increasing focus not merely on describing social change and its effects on child and adult outcomes, but on exploration of the processes that underlie and possibly account for these changes. Processes that account for or modify these change-based effects are evident throughout these chapters. Just as the descriptive enterprise has benefited from bio-social ecological perspectives with their emphasis on multiple levels of analysis, so has the process-based phase of this endeavor. Investigators are now identifying explanatory processes at multiple levels. For example, Marks and colleagues (this volume) adopt an integrative risk and resilience model for understanding the development and adaptation of immigrant origin children and youth in which macro-level influences such as national policies and conditions are recognized along with microsystem factors such as neighborhoods and social networks and individual coping strategies (Suarez-Orozco, Motti-Stefanidi, Marks & Katsiaficas, 2018). Similarly, Masten et al. adopt a similar risk-resilience approach in which multiple levels of influence are operative and explanatory processes are suggestive at each level and these can modify the effects of the stress-related change on children's adaptation.

In these examples and others in this volume, there is recognition of both individual variability in how particular people respond to these change events, and appreciation of the circumstances that can either ameliorate or worsen the impact of change. Not only are processes associated with macro-level institutional policies being recognized (refugee services, unemployment and retraining programs), but variations in individual capacities for dealing with challenges associated with change such as self-regulation abilities and coping strategies (see Schoon & Brynner and Crosnoe for institutional level examples and Elder & Cox, Masten et al., and Marks et al. for examples of individual level processes). Moreover, these processes are no longer viewed as influences imposed on passive individuals, communities or societies but actors at various levels through the exercise of individual as well as collective agency shape their own destinies (Bandura, 2000; Elder, 1998). It is also evident that recognition of a systems-level theoretical analysis implies that the success or failure of processes at one level will have a cascade effect on other domains and levels of adaptation (see Masten et al., this volume).

One of the most important advances in our search for processes to explain change-related outcomes has come from the success achieved by both the biological and social sciences in better understanding the role of biological factors (hormones to genetics) in development and adaptation. Just as multi-level environmental contexts are recognized, there is a similar recognition of the multi-level organization of biological contexts as influences on developmental outcomes as well. These levels include genes, epigenetic influences, hormones, autonomic reactivity, homeostatic functions, and biological insults (illness, physical trauma, premature birth) (Feldman, 2019). For example, the genomic revolution has underscored the essential "contextual contribution of social environments" in understanding gene-environment effects across the developmental life course of children and parents (Rutter, 2006). Even genetic and biomarker influences cannot be understood without knowledge of their historical and situational/cultural context (Caspi et al., 2003; Rutter, 2006; Plomin, 2012).

In a well-known study of 1000 young adults, Caspi and colleagues (2003) found that a genetic predisposition for depression resulted in depressive symptoms only when the person had experienced numerous life stressors during the previous few years and had been abused in childhood. They found a significant interaction between a genotype (a genetic predisposition for depression) and a stressful environment, which underscores the importance of recognizing the environmental context as a factor affecting genetic expression. Other examples of this type of gene x environment interaction are available for genetic predisposition for aggression (Brendgen et al., 2011) and drug use (Brody et al., 2009). Similarly, brain imaging studies of humans show more neural activity in the amygdala in response to fearful events for people with a depressive gene (Heinz et al., 2005), an example of the interplay between genetic and neural levels of analysis. Evidence of neurological shifts during the transition to parenthood is another example of the interplay across levels of analysis. For example, when researchers used fMRI (scans of brain activity) to examine the brains of mothers as they listen to their babies cry, they found that the brain areas associated with emotional regulation, planning and decision making showed increased activity – possibly as a way to prepare the mother for the tasks and responsibilities of parenting

(Lorberbaum et al., 1999). Fathers show similar patterns of neural activity in response to infant cries (Seifritz et al., 2003).

These studies suggest that the neural context is another level of analysis that is involved in our efforts to understand parental behavior. Recent work underscores the importance of hormonal level influences on both child and adult behavior patterns and illustrates the interplay between environmental contexts and the development of hormones, which in turn alter development. Children who were reared in Russian or Romanian orphanages before being adopted by US families were less responsive to their adoptive parents than non-institutionalized children reared by their biological parents. Part of the reason for these differences in social responsiveness is the fact that the levels of the hormone oxytocin (often termed the love hormone) were lower in the institutionally reared toddlers. Instead, during social interactions, these infants showed heightened levels of the stress-sensitive hormone cortisol, which is associated with lower levels of emotional regulatory ability (Wismer Fries et al., 2005; see also Masten et al., this volume).

This work provides another example of the ways in which child rearing contexts (home vs. institution) alters hormone development and in turn alters children's ability to development satisfactory social relationships with their caregivers. And parenting is altered by hormones as well. Recent studies of fathers indicate that during the transition to parenthood, men experience a decrease in testosterone, which in turn makes them more sensitive to infant cues such as cries. However, this outcome is evident especially if the father was highly involved as a socially supportive source for his partner during the pregnancy, which again suggests the interplay across biological and social contexts (Storey et al., 2000; see also Parke, 2013 and this volume).

Increased Recognition of the Value of Interdisciplinary Approaches

The unique and overlapping theoretical perspectives of historians, historically-oriented social scientists (anthropologists, sociologists, and developmental psychologists) are highlighted and the value gained by combining these diverse disciplines is emphasized by all contributors to this volume. The authors cover a range of disciplines such as sociology (Crosnoe, Elder), economics (Elder; Schoon & Bynner), cross-cultural studies (Greenfield, Masten), ethnic studies (Marks et al.), demography (Crosnoe), ecologically oriented developmental science (Cox, Leventhal et al., Parke) and biologically oriented developmental scholars (Cox, Greenfield, Masten et al.). To adequately address issues of historical change and its impact on children, many disciplinary perspectives are necessary.

Methodological Advances

Finally, we examine the unique methodologies offered by a variety of disciplines and make a case for how the integration of these methods will enrich our efforts to better understand children's lives across time as presented in the chapters of this volume. A wide range of methods and research designs are used which represents the increasingly diverse set of methodological approaches currently being employed across disciplines which focus on understanding social change. A plethora of methods is now a common approach to assessing social change with both qualitative and quantitative measurement assessments and a variety of designs often being used together to provide an enriched profile of changing patterns.

To capture historical change, longitudinal methods have been and continue to be the design of choice, although cross-sectional designs to enable in-depth exploration of an outcome associated with a social change such as shifts in school organization or class size (see Crosnoe, this volume). The use of cross-time designs range from classical long term longitudinal studies such as Elder' s *Children of the Great Depression* (1974) study in which participants are tracked across wide spans of time that, in turn, capture major periods of secular change such as economic downturn and recovery as well as later events such as World War II (Elder & Cox, this volume). Shorter-term longitudinal designs, which involve assessments before and after briefer social changes, such as the recent studies of the Great Recession (Schoon & Brynner, this volume) or the Midwest farm crisis in the USA (Conger et al., 1994; Elder & Conger, 2000). A major advance in increasing our confidence in the causal factors underlying change has been the use of natural field experimental designs in which naturally occurring change such as the introduction of television into a community and the effects of this social change are monitored across time in comparison with communities who did not experience such changes (MacBeth, 1996; Greenfield, this volume).

Field experimental studies in which a social change is designed and engineered by the investigator is also an increasingly common and powerful approach to assessing the causal links between social change and outcomes. Early experimental field studies of the effects of various forms of TV content (prosocial vs. aggressive) were useful strategies for documenting the impact of TV content on children's social behavior (Friedrich & Stein, 1973; Greenfield, this volume). The Moving to Opportunity project in which families were provided housing in less poor neighborhoods is an example of a field experimental approach (Gennetian et al., 2012) to the assessment of neighborhood contextual effects on children's development. Similarly, recent field experimental studies in Ethiopia examined the effect of computers distributed to 10- to 15-year-olds on abstract reasoning compared to children without access to computers (Hansen et al., 2012). Other approaches include quasi-experimental studies, such as the provision of housing vouchers without constraints on where families would re-locate (Rabinovitz & Rosenbaum, 2000), represent still another way to assess social change on child and family outcomes.

Considerable statistical advances have been made to minimize the impact of selection effects, which often make correlational studies difficult to interpret. As Leventhal et al. (this volume) argues, "These approaches range from regression analyses that control for individual and family background characteristics related to neighborhood selection (e.g., family income, parent education, race/ethnicity) to more rigorous analytic strategies such as propensity score matching, instrumental variable analysis, or fixed effects" (p. 17).

Sampling strategies have expanded as well. While national surveys such as the National Longitudinal Survey of Youth continue to be widely used strategies to assess social change, especially by sociologists and demographers (Brown, 2017), these approaches are increasingly used by other social scientists such as developmental psychologists as well (Friedman, 2007). And other large-scale databases are frequently used to assess the effects of social change in a variety of countries such as the UK (British Household Panel Study and the UK Household Longitudinal Study), the USA (Panel Study of Income Dynamics), and Germany (German Socio-Economic Panel Study), as well as national longitudinal cohort studies, including the US National Longitudinal Study of Youth, the US Monitoring the Future, and the European Union Statistics on Income and Living Conditions. Oversampling minorities is a common strategy used to assess ethnic variations in response to social change. Clearly we have made major progress in assessing change with respectable generalizability by this movement away from small-scale samples to representative samples.

As several contributors demonstrate, mixed methods are often used in which qualitative strategies such as focus groups, content analyses of media based exchanges between children (Turkle, 2011; see Greenfield, this volume) are combined with observational strategies (Parke, this volume) and in-depth ethnographic work (Edin & Nelson, 2013).

Finally biological measures are increasingly used as part of the assessment battery including genetic analyses, hormonal indices, and neurological assessments (EEG, fMRI) of brain functioning (see Masten et al., and Greenfield this volume).For example, the stress associated with social change such as immigration or war-induced displacement is often indexed by hormonal assessments such as cortisol levels (Masten et al., this volume) as are the stress-linked effects of chronic poverty (Elder & Cox, this volume).

A Theoretical Orientation to this Volume

To reflect these theoretical advances, the organizing theme of this volume notes that children's development should be viewed in terms of three intersecting perspectives as outlined in Figure 1.1 – (1) historical/temporal, which addresses change and continuity across historical or secular time; (2) a developmental or age-graded life course perspective, which addresses age change-life course transitions and trajectories; and (3) a social/cultural-ecology perspective. This perspective captures the significant advances in both our conceptualization of the important processes underlying development and our theoretical recognition and conceptualization of the cultural and ecological factors that have been made over the past 20 years. Our goal is to challenge social scientists (developmental psychologists, education scholars, sociologists, historians, and anthropologists) to recognize the value of this multi-factor approach.

The three perspectives are contextual on different levels. This is illustrated by the relation between cognitive development and schooling. It links development to a schooling trajectory, but this trajectory may not be embedded in a particular historical change of children's lives. The descriptor "historical" may refer only to a situation and not to temporality. The historical-temporal perspective represents the macro or more distal level compared to the developmental life course level of the individual. The social-cultural ecology dimension and historical change dimension refer to the change in school organization from state or country policy. In the extreme case the introduction of formal schooling into a country (i.e., Mexico or Central American rural areas) that previously did not provide formal instruction would represent a cultural shift. In combination, the framework is multi-level – the developmental life course of children embedded in a temporal context of historical time, place, and culture.

As noted above, the theme of the original *Children in Time and Place* volume, which underscored the importance of recognizing that children's development is best understood in specific historical and life course developmental contexts, remains valid and relevant to contemporary dialogue. However, in the current volume we expand and update this

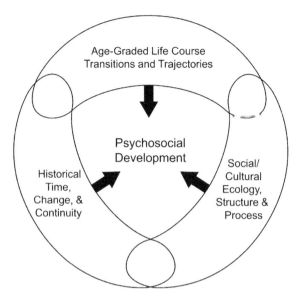

Figure 1.1 Contextual perspectives

perspective by focusing on the socio-cultural context as well. This revised theoretical framework served as a guide for authors and co-authors of each chapter to work together in linking these three perspectives. To achieve this integrative goal and to reflect the inherently interdisciplinary nature of this enterprise, the contributors to the volume include culturally and contextually oriented developmental psychologists, sociologists, and education and policy scholars who are versed in a developmental life course perspective.

As noted above, many new issues such as economic upheavals, war, famine, and subsequent increases in immigration, which are best understood through a life course developmental, historical, and socio-cultural ecology lens have emerged over the past two decades and merit examination using this three-factor framework. Not only are there shifts and transitions in the lives of immigrants who have been forced to relocate, but they also face the demands of navigating the challenges of new cultural contexts in their new country. Changes in the treatment of racial and ethnic minorities by educational and legal institutions can best be understood through a historically, situationally and culturally sensitive approach. Altered family forms have introduced new contexts for children that can be better appreciated within this interdisciplinary framework as can the recent advances in communication technology that have altered children's relationships with their peers and their often separated relatives. By a fresh examination of these contemporary concerns within a temporal framework (historical and developmental life course), and a bio-socio-cultural perspective, we show the contribution of this approach to an understanding of children's development in the midst of a rapidly changing world. In each chapter we consider the changing historical and socio-cultural context and how these shifting environments help us better understand children's outcomes, transitions, and trajectories.

Overview of the Volume

Chapter 2 When Societal Events Occur in Lives: Developmental Linkages and Turning Points (Elder & Cox)

In this chapter sociologist Glen Elder and developmental psychologist Martha Cox examine how the timing of societal events plays a major role in shaping lives through developmental processes. These authors focus on how two such events in historical proximity dramatically altered the lives of California children who were born at opposite ends of the 1920s: 1920–21 and 1928–29, the Great Depression of the 1930s followed by World War II (1941–45), and the Korean War (1950–53). They employ insights from both the cohort historical life course and developmental science, including recent work on developmental neuro-science, to understand the life-long impact of exposure to events that occur at different times in life, and the mechanisms through which these exposures may influence development, as well as experiences that may provide turning points in development. Finally, this chapter illustrates the move to a greater focus on process by a review of recent work on the links between poverty, stress, and biological regulatory processes.

Chapter 3 Entering Adulthood in the Great Recession: A Tale of Three Countries (Schoon & Bynner)

In this chapter Ingrid Schoon, a human developmental and policy scholar, and John Bynner, an education specialist, examine the effects of the 2008 worldwide recession on children and families using recent data from the USA, the UK, and Germany. By addressing this recent eco-nomic downturn and comparing it to the effects of economic downturns of the 1930s, the historical role of shifting government economic policies and safety net structures in buffering the impact of economic stress is illustrated. Comparisons across these three countries underscore how culturally informed values and policies shape the outcomes of these economic disruptions for children and families.

Chapter 4 Developmental Risk and Resilience in the Context of Devastation and Forced Migration (Masten, Motti-Stefanidi & Rahl-Brigman)

In many parts of the world, including Central America, Europe, the Middle East, and Africa there have been major economic challenges due to war and famines. In this chapter American developmental psychologists Ann Masten and Hayley Rohl, in collaboration with Greek developmentalist Frosso Motti-Stefanidi, examine the effects of these disruptions on children's lives associated with mass migration from war-torn regions to other parts of the world with greater economic and educational opportunities. They provide a dynamic risk–resilience theoretical framework to guide their chapter. The impact of the original culture on how children cope in a new and unfamiliar culture underscores the importance of a cultural perspective in understanding the relative success and failure of these challenges.

Chapter 5 Children's Migratory Paths Between Cultures: The Effects of Migration Experiences on the Adjustment of Children and Families (Marks, Woolverton, & García Coll)

In this chapter, developmental psychologists Amy Marks, Alice Woolverton, and Cynthia García Coll examine the effects of immigration and acculturation on children in different historical periods. Their chapter illustrates how shifting historical contexts and policies facilitate or disrupt the process of integration into a host culture. The case of the migration from Mexico to the USA is highlighted. They document the shift from a historical view (30 years ago) where the main focus was acculturation and assimilation into the host culture with fewer adherences to the values and traditions of the culture of origin to a current bi-cultural view. According to this contemporary perspective, immigration is a bi-cultural process whereby the customs and traditions of the culture of origin co-exist alongside the traditions and cultural norms of the host culture.

Chapter 6 Education in Historical and Cultural Perspective (Crosnoe)

The domain of education has undergone dramatic shifts over the past several decades. The dramatic restructuring and globalization of the economy over the last several decades have greatly increased the life-long benefits of higher education in the United States and many other developed countries, which in turn has created downward pressure on earlier stages of the educational systems in such societies. In the context of the rapidly diversifying populations being served by these systems, the increasingly cumulative and differentiated nature of their academic curricula has consequences for the academic progress and educational attainment of individual youth, but also for socioeconomic, racial/ethnic, and other kinds of disparities in youth outcomes. In this chapter, sociologist Robert Crosnoe examines this changing system and what it means for young people by describing economic restructuring, its effects on returns to higher education and curricular differentiation, and what these effects mean for inequality in a globalizing and diversifying world. In addition he examines different kinds of policy and programmatic responses to inequality in a changing educational context. The goal is to consider the ways that developmentally informed, culturally responsive, and multi-level solutions can be developed to help promote equality of opportunity and educational equity.

Chapter 7 The Urban World of Minority and Majority Children (Leventhal, Anastasio, & Dupéré)

The goal of this chapter is to address how urban dynamics at the neighborhood level are linked to children's development. To do so, developmental psychologists Tama Leventhal, Julius Anastasio, and Veronique Dupéré review trends in the spatial concentration of poverty and inequality in the United States in recent decades under the guidance of a Relational Developmental Systems framework. Then, they turn to theoretical models describing how local communities, with a focus on urban settings, influence children's development. They critically examine methodological issues, followed by an overview of empirical studies linking neighborhood socioeconomic conditions and children's development, with emphasis on their educational, behavioral, and socioemotional outcomes. In closing, they discuss implications for policy and practice and note future issues that merit attention.

Chapter 8 Changing Family Forms: The Implications for Children's Development (Parke)

Using a life course framework and an interdisciplinary perspective, developmental psychologist Ross Parke examines how recent demographic, historical, legal, and medical changes have reshaped family forms and, in turn, signal a historical departure from the prominence of the nuclear family form as the cultural ideal. He examines how children are affected by growing up in these new family forms, including divorced, cohabiting, single parent families as well as same gender parent families and children in families formed through the assistance of new reproductive technologies. The lag between social change in family forms and social policy is emphasized.

Chapter 9 Communication Technologies and Social Transformation: Their Impact on Human Development (Greenfield)

Patricia Greenfield, a cross-culturally oriented developmental psychologist, focuses on the effects of new forms of communication and entertainment technology (e.g., the internet, cell phones, twitter, Instagram) on children's social lives and academic progress. The role of culture in this social change is noted by comparisons across cultures with and without access to new technological advances as well as by historically sensitive analyses, which involve comparisons of how children distribute time before and after the introduction of new technologies. The author provides an integrative model of technology-related change, which underscores how multiple levels of analysis from individual to community to society and culture are necessary to understand these patterns of change.

Chapter 10 A Developmentalist's Viewpoint: "It's About Time!" Ecological Systems, Transaction, and Specificity as Key Developmental Principles in Children's Changing Worlds (Bornstein)

Developmental psychologist Marc Bornstein, who has a history of cross-disciplinary and cross-cultural collaboration and a broad appreciation of the value of interdisciplinary dialogue about children, offers a developmentalist's perspective on the issues raised in this volume and his sense of the remaining challenges for this area of inquiry.

Chapter 11 A Sociologist's Perspective: The Historical Specificity of Development and Resilience in the Face of Increasingly Ominous Futures (Mortimer)

Sociologist Jeylan Mortimer is well versed on cross-time and life course perspectives as well as the developmental implications of changing cultural contexts. She provides a sociological perspective on the issues addressed in this volume as well as a glance at the future of this enterprise. In her commentary she highlights the main themes of the volume and addresses important but neglected topics that require our attention in the future, such as the effects of climate change on children, adults, and society.

References

Bandura, A. (2000). Exercise of human agency through collective efficacy. *Current Directions in Psychological Science, 9,* 75–78.

Belle, D. & Benenson, J. (2014). Children's social networks and well-being. In A. Ben-Arieh, F. Casas, I. Frones, & J. E. Korbin (Eds.), *Handbook of Child Well-Being, Vol. 2: Theories, Methods, and Policies in Global Perspective* (pp. 1335–1363). New York: Springer.

Brendgen, M., Boivin, M., Dionne, G., Barker, E. D., Vitaro, F., Girard, A., & Pérusse, D. (2011). Gene–environment processes linking aggression, peer victimization, and the teacher–child relationship. *Child Development, 82,* 2021–2036.

Brody, G. H., Beach, S. R. H., Philibert, R. A., Chen, Y.-F., Lei, M.-K., Murry, V. M., & Chen, Y. (2009). Parenting moderates a genetic vulnerability factor on longitudinal increases in youths' substance use. *Journal of Consulting and Clinical Psychology, 77,* 1–11.

Bronfenbrenner, U. & Morris, P. A. (2006). The bioecological model of human development. In R. M. Lerner & W. Damon (Eds.), *Handbook of Child Psychology* (6th ed., Vol. 1, pp. 793–828). Hoboken, NJ: Wiley.

Brown, S. L. (2017). *Families in America.* Berkeley, CA: University of California Press.

Caspi, A., Sugden, K., Moffitt, T. E., Taylor, A., Craig, I. W., Harrington, H., ... Poulton, R. (2003). Influence of life stress on depression: Moderation by a polymorphism in the 5-HTT gene. *Science, 301,* 386–389.

Chen, X., Chung, J., Lechcier-Kimel, R., & French, D. (2011). Culture and social development. In P. K. Smith & C. Hart (Eds.), *The Wiley-Blackwell Handbook of Childhood Social Development* (2nd ed., pp. 141–160). Oxford, UK: Wiley-Blackwell.

Chen, X., DeSouza, A., Chen, H., & Wang, L. (2006). Reticent behavior and experiences in peer interactions in Canadian and Chinese children. *Developmental Psychology, 42,* 656–665.

Chen, X., Wang, L., & Cao, R. (2011). Shyness-sensitivity and unsociability in rural Chinese children: Relations with social, school, and psychological adjustment. *Child Development, 82,* 1531–1543.

Chen, X., Wang, L., Cao, R., & Wang, Z. (2009). Shyness-sensitivity and social, school, and psychological adjustment in rural migrant and urban children in China. *Child Development, 80,* 1499–1513.

Conger, R. D. & Elder, G. H., Jr. (1994). (In collaboration with Frederick O. Lorenz, Ronald L. Simons, & Les B. Whitbeck.) *Families in Troubled Times: Adapting to change in rural America.* Hawthorne, NY: Aldine.

Edin, K. & Nelson, T. J. (2013). *Doing the Best I Can: Fatherhood in the inner city.* Berkeley, CA: University of California Press.

Elder, G. H., Jr. (1974). *Children of the Great Depression: Social change in life experience.* Chicago: University of Chicago Press.

(1998). The life course as developmental theory. *Child Development, 69,* 1–12.

(1999). *Children of the Great Depression: Social change in life experience,* 25th anniversary expanded edition. Boulder, CO: Westview Press.

Elder, G. H., Jr. & Conger, R. (2000). *Children of the Land: Adversity and success in rural America.* Chicago: University of Chicago Press.

Elder, G. H., Shanahan, M. J., & Jennings, J. A. (2015). Human development in time and place. In M. H. Bornstein & T. Leventhal (Eds.) & R. M. Lerner (Editor-in-Chief), *Handbook of Child Psychology and Developmental Science, Vol. 4: Ecological Settings and Processes in Developmental Systems* (7th ed., pp. 6–54). Hoboken, NJ: Wiley.

Fabricius, W. V., Braver, S. L., Diaz, P., & Velez, C. E. (2010). Custody and parenting time: Links to family relationships and well-being after divorce. In M. E. Lamb (Ed.). *Role of the Father in Child Development* (5th ed., pp. 245–289). New York: John Wiley & Sons.

Feldman, R. (2019). Hormonal bases of parenting. In M. Bornstein (Ed.), *Handbook of Parenting* (3rd ed., pp. 26–32). New York: Routledge.

Friedman, S. L. (2007). Finding treasure: Data sharing and secondary analysis in developmental science. In S. L. Friedman (Guest editor). New findings from secondary data analysis: Results from the NICHD Study of Early Child Care and Youth Development. *Journal of Applied Developmental Psychology, 28*(5–6), 381–560.

Friedrich, L. K. & Stein, A. H. (1973). Aggressive and prosocial television programs and the natural behavior of preschool children. *Monographs of the Society for Research in Child Development, 38*(4), Serial No. 151.

Garcia Coll, C. & Marks, A. K. (Eds.) (2012). *The Immigrant Paradox in Children and Adolescents: Is Becoming American a Developmental Risk?* Washington, DC: American Psychological Association.

Gates, G. J. & Brown, T. N. T. (2015). *Marriage and Same-Sex Couples after Obergefell.* Los Angeles, CA: Williams Institute, UCLA School of Law.

Gennetian, L. A., Sanbonmatsu, L., Katz, L. F., Kling, J. R., Sciandra, M., Ludwig, J., ... Kessler, R. (2012). The long-term effects of moving to opportunity on youth outcomes. *Cityscape, 14*(2), 137–167.

Hansen, N., Koudenburg, N., Hiersemann, R., Tellegen, P. J., Kocsev, M., & Postmes, T. (2012). Laptop usage affects abstract reasoning of children in the developing world. *Computers in Education, 59,* 989–1000.

Heinz, A., Braus, D. F., Smolka, M. N., Wrase, J., Puls, I., Hermann, D., ... Büchel, C. (2005). Amygdala-prefrontal coupling depends on a genetic variation of the serotonin transporter. *Nature Neuroscience, 8,* 20–21.

Hill, N. E. & Torres, K. A. (2010). Negotiating the American Dream: The paradox of aspirations and achievement among Latino students and engagement between their families and schools. *Journal of Social Issues, 66*(1), 95–112.

Holden, G. W. & Williamson, P. A. (2014). Religion and child well-being. In A. Ben-Arieh, F. Casas, I. Frones, & J. E. Korbin (Eds.), *Handbook of Child Well-Being, Vol. 2: Theories, Methods, and Policies in Global Perspective* (pp. 1137–1169). New York: Springer.

Ladd, G. W. (2005). *Children's Peer Relationships and Social Competence: A century of progress.* New Haven, CT: Yale University Press.

Lerner, R. M. & Overton, W. F. (2008). Exemplifying the integrations of the relational developmental system. *Journal of Adolescent Research, 23*(3), 245–255.

Leventhal, T. & Brooks-Gunn, J. (2000). The neighborhoods they live in: Effects of neighborhood residence on child and adolescent outcomes. *Psychological Bulletin, 126*(2), 309–337.

Lorberbaum, J. P., Newman, J. D., Dubno, J. R., Horwitz, A. R., Nahas, Z., Teneback, C. C., ... George, M. S. (1999). The feasibility of using fMRI to study mothers responding to infant cries. *Depression and Anxiety, 10*, 99–104.

MacBeth, T. M. (Ed., 1996). *Tuning in to Young Viewers: Social science perspectives on television.* Thousand Oaks, CA: Sage.

Masci, D. & Motel, S. (2015). 5 Facts about same sex marriage. Pew Research Centre: www.pewresearch.org/facttank/2015, August 5.

McLanahan, S. (2004). Diverging destinies: How children fare under the second demographic transition. *Demography, 41*(4), 607–627.

Overton, W. F. (2015). Processes, relations, and relational-developmental-systems. In W. F. Overton & P. C. M. Molenaar (Eds.) & R. M. Lerner (Editor-in-Chief), *Handbook of Child Psychology and Developmental Psychology* (Vol. 1, 7th ed.). Hoboken, NJ: Wiley.

Parke, R. D. (2013). *Future Families: Diverse forms, rich possibilities.* Malden, MA: Wiley Blackwell.

Parke, R. D., Coltrane, S., Duffy, S., Buriel, R., Dennis, J., Powers, J., ... Widaman, K. F. (2004). Economic stress, parenting, and child adjustment in Mexican American and European American families. *Child Development, 75*(6), 1632–1656.

Plomin, R. (2012). Child development and molecular genetics: 14 years later. *Child Development, 83*, 104–120.

Rogoff, B. (2003). *The Cultural Nature of Human Development.* New York: Oxford University Press.

Rothbaum, F., Pott, M., Azuma, H., Miyake, K., & Weisz, J. (2000). The development of close relationships in Japan and the United States: Paths of symbiotic harmony and generative tension. *Child Development, 71*, 1121–1142.

Rubinowitz, L. S. & Rosenbaum, J. E. (2000). *Crossing the Class and Color Lines: From public housing to white suburbia.* Chicago: University of Chicago Press.

Rutter, M. (2006). *Genes and Behavior.* New York: Blackwell.

Schneider, B. (2000). *Friends and Enemies: Peer relations in childhood.* London: Arnold.

Seifritz, E., Esposito, F., Neuhoff, J., Lüthi, A., Mustovic, H. et al. (2003). Differential sex-independent amygdala response to infant crying and laughing in parents versus nonparents. *Biological Psychiatry, 54*, 1367–1375.

Storey, A. E., Walsh, C. J., Quinton, R. L., & Wynne-Edwards, K. E. (2000). Hormonal correlates of paternal responsiveness in new and expectant fathers. *Evolution and Human Behavior, 21*, 79–95.

Suárez-Orozco, C., Motti-Stefanidi, F., Marks, A., & Katsiaficas, D. (2018). An integrative risk and resilience model for understanding the adaptation of immigrant origin children and youth. *American Psychologist, 73*(6), 781–796.

Turkle, S. (2011). *Alone Together: Why we expect more from technology and less from each other.* New York: Basic Books.

Wismer Fries, A. B., Ziegler, T. E., Kurian, J. R., Jacoris, S. & Pollak, S. D. (2005). Early experience in humans is associated with changes in neuropeptides critical for regulating social behavior. *Proceedings of the National Academy of Sciences, 102,* 17237–17240.

Part II

Historical and Life Course Transitions:
Economic and Demographic Change

.

2   When Societal Events Occur in Lives: Developmental Linkages and Turning Points

Glen H. Elder, Jr. and Martha J. Cox

The timing of societal events plays a major role in shaping lives through developmental processes. In this chapter, we focus on how two such events in historical proximity dramatically altered the lives of California children who were born at opposite ends of the 1920s: 1920–21 and 1928–29, the Great Depression of the 1930s followed by World War II (1941–45) and the Korean War (1950–53). We employ insights from both the cohort historical life course and developmental science including recent work on developmental neuroscience to understand the life-long impact of exposure to events that occur at different times in life, and the mechanisms through which these exposures may influence development, as well as experiences that may provide turning points in development.

Work by Elder (1974/99) showed that the impact of these national crises exposed the young to widespread hardship, social disruption, and stressful change. The Depression's unemployment and heavy income losses led to prolonged deprivation for families and their children. These hardships were soon followed by the extraordinary demands and dislocation of a booming wartime economy with abundant job opportunities as well as the uncertainties of military duty abroad for family members and friends. The negative effects of such change were sometimes coupled with positive outcomes. For example, the Depression's misfortunes brought families together for assistance and the young frequently found themselves with work to do in the household and in assisting neighbors.

Older children assumed adult-like responsibilities and became more essential in doing household chores, in caring for younger siblings, and in preparing meals. Some covered their school and clothing costs with earnings from paid jobs. With the onset of World War II, children of all ages were mobilized to assist in the war effort by collecting newspapers from neighboring families, and by working with local scout troops to collect scrap metal. In small towns, children delivered household goods and groceries. As older brothers completed high school, they soon entered the pool of qualified recruits for military duty.

The personal impact of such events varied by gender and age at exposure to the change, such as a heavy income loss during the economic depression. Children of pre-school age were especially vulnerable to disruptive change, especially the young boys who lacked a supportive father and the maternal protection and nurturance that young girls enjoyed. Older youth spent more time outside the household, joining activities with friends on school projects and community social functions. There were risks associated with this independence, especially during the war when the long work hours of parents created "empty households" and a lack of parental attention and supervision. Age or life stage during exposure to the stresses of change tended to produce both risks and a developmental challenge, with notable variations by gender.

The opportunity to explore the impact of this social change on children at very different points in their young lives emerged in the early twentieth century when California children with contrasting birth years in the 1920s became members of longitudinal studies. We turn to the launching of these cohorts, separated by approximately eight to nine years. And then we focus on the differential timing of their experiences in the Great Depression, followed by World War II and the Korean War. We also consider how the observations from this work on the lives of children in the Great Depression stimulated later research on child development, adversity, and income loss and to what extent that research has extended and confirmed the observations reported here by suggesting mechanisms or processes implicated in the effects on development of exposure to hardship, social disruption, and stressful change.

The opportunity to explore the impact of this social change on children at very different points in their young lives emerged in the early twentieth century when California children with contrasting birth years in the 1920s became members of longitudinal studies. We turn to the launching of these cohorts, separated by approximately eight to nine years. And then we focus on the differential timing of their experiences in the Great Depression, followed by World War II and the Korean War.

In the years since these studies were conducted, major advances have been made in the developmental science of adversity in children's lives. We consider how observations on the lives of children in the Great Depression stimulated later developmental and developmental neuroscience research on child development, adversity, and income loss and the extent that research has confirmed and extended the observations reported here. An important question in developmental science has been whether early childhood is an especially vulnerable time for exposure to the stressful environments of both poverty and the family loss of income.[1]

Encountering the Same Historical Event at Different Life Stages

The opportunity for such a study occurred when the University of California at Berkeley established a research institute in 1928 to study child development under the direction of Herbert R. Stolz, MD. Its evolving mission became a study of children "the long way" by using samples of children who would be observed over time, from childhood into the adult years. With life span development as a framework, the original institute of child welfare eventually acquired a more appropriate name, the Institute of Human Development.

Jean Macfarlane, a recent PhD of Berkeley's Department of Psychology, was invited to direct the Berkeley Guidance Study (1971), beginning with approximately 240 children who were born in 1928–29. Data collection began in 1930–31 when the children were approximately 18 months old. Another Institute study, the Oakland Adolescent Study, focused on adolescence and was launched in 1932 by Harold E. Jones, a developmental psychologist. The sample included some 200 adolescents who were born in 1920–21 and grew up in the northeastern sector of Oakland. When the adolescents were followed into adulthood, the project was renamed the Oakland Growth Study.

It should be noted that an age difference between children in different birth cohorts only involves one of the ways we can think of a comparison between children of different ages – an inter-cohort perspective. We could also compare the historical experience of children who are siblings in the same family. This line of work is known as studies of birth order, a field of research (Dunn & Plomin, 1990) that consistently shows first born children to be more achievement oriented and conscientious than the later born. But this research focus is seldom linked to the assessment of cohort effects. In any case, a within-family design was not possible with the Berkeley and Oakland studies – neither study systematically collected data on siblings from the same family.

---

[1] This chapter refers to studies of economic deprivation as measured by a significant loss of family income often resulting from unemployment; and to developmental neuroscience studies of family poverty (income below the poverty line). We recognize that the effects may differ, and that a drastic loss of family income may result in income below the poverty line. This family change occurred among Oakland middle and working class families in the Great Depression (Elder, 1974–99).

The Oakland and Berkeley cohorts were distinguished by different historical pathways from adolescence into adulthood. But their "comparative potential" was not recognized at the time. In fact, the studies addressed different questions, and they remained independent lines of research over 35 years, up to the 1970s. The comparative potential was first explored when a young sociologist from the University of North Carolina (Glen Elder) joined the Institute research staff in 1962 to work with the Oakland Adolescent Study and began thinking of this sample of adolescents as subject to the collapse of the economy and its impact on their families and lives.

Guided by the cohort research of demographers (Ryder, 1965) and the developmental literature, he developed a study of the Oakland children as "Children of the Great Depression." Some of the families were members of deprived families while others were spared such hardship. He assessed the impact of such hardship in the middle and working class, but realized that he would need eventually to come up with a cohort comparison of children who were "born at a different time" to more fully understand the Depression's life-long impact. In theory, children of different ages during the worst years of the Depression would have been influenced in different ways. This comparison was also considered essential for assessing the impact of subsequent wars – World War II and the Korean War. From the evidence at hand, we had good reason to expect differential effects of Depression hard times and war among young people who differed significantly in life stage as well as gender.

Consistent with the life stage of the Oakland cohort's exposure to economic hardship in the 1930s, family deprivation did not significantly or adversely affect the lives of boys in adolescence (Elder, 1974/99). The cohort's life stage minimized exposure to the most adverse effects of the Depression. The adolescents were well beyond the risks of the dependency years and they were too young to be exposed to the perils of a depressed labor market. But the picture changed among the Oakland girls from deprived families. They experienced the years of physical maturity without attractive clothing or shoes, and were obligated to assist their mothers in the household. They felt shunned by their classmates and were in fact excluded from their groups and social activities. In middle age, they remembered this time as their "worst time" of life.

We expected the younger boys and girls to be more exposed to the negative effects of deprivation and disruption, especially those of preschool age. In the case of the young boys, family deprivation exposed them to the probable loss of a supportive father and a harmonious family.

By contrast, the young girls were typically protected from the harshness of such families by a nurturing and protective mother.

With birth years at the opposite end of the 1920s (1928–29), the Berkeley sample became Elder's best chance for a comparative cohort of children. Our focus in this comparison, then, is on what we can learn from the different timing of the Berkeley cohort's experience in the Depression's economic collapse followed by the impact of adolescence and young adulthood in World War II and the Korean War. We compared this sequence to the Oakland cohort's encounter with the Depression and World War II.

The proximity of World War II to the Depression years of the 1930s meant that the Oakland children of the Great Depression became young men and women on the home and war fronts of World War II. Three out of five members of the Oakland cohort were exposed to a heavy income loss in the 1930s and nine out of ten of these young men eventually served in the Armed Forces. In the Berkeley cohort, by contrast, two out of five of the young children grew up in families troubled by hard times during the Depression, and nearly three-fourths of the young men served in the military. They were teenagers on the home front of World War II before military duty. The cohort's range of military service spans the last year of World War II and extends well into the Korean War of the early 1950s.

The age difference between the Oakland and Berkeley children is only one such difference among others in families. For example, the Oakland and Berkeley families were headed by mothers and fathers of different ages, who were also likely to experience different historical outcomes in this rapidly changing world. From this perspective, the family can be viewed as "a meeting ground for members of different cohorts," and their interwoven sets of linked lives (Elder, Modell, & Parke, 1993, p. 14). This whole-family perspective adds complexity to family life in rapidly changing circumstances. However, our focus on the life stage of children and their gender in a changing world remains the key issue for understanding the developmental effects of Depression hardship and America at war.

We turn now to an in-depth examination of life stage "cohort and gender differences" in the Depression experience, followed by the hardship effects that the Berkeley young men carried into military service. We also ask how the personal impact of hard times among the Berkeley women influenced their wartime experience with employment, education, and marriage. Were the enduring effects of their Depression experience enhanced in such "wartime" transitions when waves of veterans returned in the post-war era?

Children of the Great Depression: Older vs. Younger

Across the Depression decade of the 1930s, three modes of adaptation distinguished deprived families in the Oakland and Berkeley cohorts from families that were spared such hardship: changes in the family economy, in family relationships, and in level of social and psychological stress. For both cohorts, Oakland and Berkeley, income loss during the early 1930s increased indebtedness as savings diminished, as well as the curtailment and postponement of expenditures, more family labor in place of funds for services and goods; and greater reliance on the earnings of women and older children.

Changes in family relationships stemmed from fathers' loss of earnings, leading to their withdrawal from family roles. Economic loss increased the relative power and emotional significance of mother vis-à-vis father for boys as well as for girls. Lastly, economic deprivation heightened parental irritability, the likelihood of marital conflicts, arbitrary and inconsistent discipline of children, and the risk of fathers' behavioral impairment through heavy drinking, demoralization, and health disabilities.

Both age and gender status differentiated the household experience of the Oakland and Berkeley study members in ways that produced contrasting pathways into adulthood. The Oakland boys in deprived families were old enough to earn money on jobs in the community that helped to pay for their clothes and cover school expenses. They also provided assistance around the house and yard. Exposure to work roles enhanced their vocational development, contributing to a more crystallized perspective on their occupational future. The Oakland girls in hard-pressed families became the right arm of their mothers, caring for younger siblings, cleaning house, and assisting with the preparation of meals. This domestic role limited their involvement with peers as did the lack of attractive clothes for social activities during adolescence. In mid-life, they recalled this time as one of the worst periods of their lives.

By comparison, young boys in the Berkeley cohort experienced the most severe phase of the Depression crisis during their preschool years when they were most dependent on family nurturance and vulnerable to family instability, emotional strain, and family conflicts. Hardship came early in their lives and persisted during most of the 1930s. In many working class families, hardship continued up to the war years and even to their departure from high school and home. Consequently, the Berkeley boys from deprived homes were relatively unsuccessful in school and in adolescence they were less hopeful, self-directed, and con-fident about their future than were youth who were spared such hardship. Nevertheless, from young adulthood to mid-life, the men from deprived families achieved noteworthy developmental gains in self-esteem and assertiveness, though not sufficient to erase completely the inadequacies of their early years.

Much of this description of the family life of the Berkeley boys applies as well to girls in these families, except that they were protected by mothers from the punitive actions of frustrated fathers and from more general family stresses. Mother typically projected the image of a strong, caring parent. In contrast to boys in hard-pressed families, the girls fared well in school through adolescence and emerged with a positive self-image. The greater vulnerability of the Berkeley boys is consistent with other findings showing that family stressors are most pathogenic for males in early childhood (e.g., Rutter & Madge, 1976).

But why did the older Oakland boys fare so well in their transitions to adolescence and young adulthood? Part of the answer centers on their family and community roles under deprived and stressful circumstances. These were least exposed to the negative dynamics of family life in the Depression. They were also more likely to acquire jobs outside the home to aid their financially troubled families. More of the Depression era was lived outside the stresses of their hard-pressed families. Conditions of this sort enhanced their social and family independence and reduced their exposure to conflict and the turmoil of their home.

Recent Studies of Economic Loss and Deprivation and Pathways from Early Experience

The contrast of the lives of the Berkeley and Oakland children, particularly the boys, has been important in guiding subsequent study of children in poverty and adversity to understand how these conditions may impact children of different ages. Much of the later research has been correlational and often cross-sectional with limited ability to infer causality. The "natural or quasi experiment" of the Great Depression and subsequent war in which families and children were differentially influenced by events not of their own making, allowed for inferences that most research on income and early child development has found it more difficult to make (Duncan, Magnuson & Votruba-Drzal, 2017). However, there have been several long-term longitudinal studies of children and families in poverty and adversity, and these studies have attempted to institute controls that allow for some confidence in inference about direction of effects by isolating poverty as important in setting in motion a cascade of events in the lives of children and their families.

An important question has been whether adversity early in childhood has more negative effects on development than later adversity. There is significant support in these studies, for example, for the assertion that low family income in early and middle childhood shows a greater association with poor school achievement and lower educational attainment for children than does low income during adolescence (Duncan et al., 2017; Huston & Bentley, 2010) as suggested by Elder's original work on children of the Great Depression. Analyses from two nationally representative longitudinal studies (Duncan et al., 2017; Votruba-Drzal, 2006) suggested that low family income at birth through age 5 was more strongly associated with the child's eventual educational attainment and achievement than low income after age 5.

Findings regarding behavioral adjustment are less clear on the potential greater harm of early poverty and deprivation versus later, with both early and late poverty associated with such outcomes as externalizing problems in behavior (Duncan et al., 2017; Huston & Bentley, 2010) and with one major longitudinal study finding a greater impact on behavioral adjustment when low income occurred after age 4 as compared to before (NICHD Early Childcare Research Network, 2005). The research over the last decades has made clear that the pathways from economic stress to children's outcomes are likely complex in that pathways may be different at different ages as well as for different outcomes (Cox, Mills-Koonce, Propper, & Gariepy, 2010; Huston & Bentley, 2010). However, the hypothesis of increased risk for poor outcome when poverty is experienced at young ages as opposed to later ages continues to be one major focus of research.

Early Experience of Poverty: The Search for Mechanisms

Why would we expect early experience with poverty and deprivation to have a different outcome than exposure to poverty at later ages and what might these different pathways involve? The idea of a persistent role of early experience in development has been a source of debate for many decades (see Clark & Clark, 1976). The case has been made that child behavioral, physiological, and neural systems relevant to self-regulatory control are developing early, and that these self-regulatory systems are foundational for a number of later aspects of competent development (Blair, 2002; Calkins & Bell, 2015; Thompson, 2015). Moreover, recent advances in neuroscience have provided new impetus to consider that there may be heightened susceptibility to environmental disadvantage in early life (Tottenham & Sheridan, 2010).

The questions are complex, because as Sroufe (2009) notes, whether an effect of early experience is found depends on what specific early experiences occur and what specific outcomes are considered. Further, Sroufe notes, the effects can be both direct and indirect, can interact with other factors, and even direct effects are probabilistic. Indirect effects may be quite complex in that the child's experiences may initiate a chain of events, alter the organism in some way, or promote the impact of later experience. Explicating these various pathways is the subject of ongoing research effort with much of the work focused on the impact of poverty on mediating factors of family relationships and parenting as Elder's work suggested, because it is expected that for the very young child, experiences in interaction with the caregiver are critical to establishing early self-regulatory systems that support the development of many aspects of later competence (Dozier, Roben, & Hoye, 2015; Leerkes & Parade, 2015).

Two major theories have guided much of the work on economic deprivation: Economic or Family Investment Theory and Family Stress Theory (Huston & Bentley, 2010). Family Investment Theory emphasizes resources available to poor children and includes not only the material or economic resources, but also the parent's skills and abilities and time spent with children, and the interactions of children with parents and other people as important to the child's development (Huston & Bentley, 2010). The idea that the financial resources and resources of time and attention that parents have in order to provide children with stimulation and advantageous activities that promote intellectual and academic development has significant support in the literature (Bornstein & Bradley, 2003; Bradley & Corwyn, 2002).

However, it is Family Stress Theory that more closely follows Elder's observations and emphasizes the influence of poverty and economic stress on parent psychological stress and cascading effects on marital conflict and parenting including lower parental warmth, sensitivity, and support, and greater harshness and control of children that are expected to lead to poor outcomes for children (Conger & Elder, 1994; Huston & Bentley, 2010; McLoyd, 1998). The development of Family Stress Theory was influenced by Elder's observations from the Great Depression that economic loss and deprivation were associated with changes in family relationships. These changes that Elder noted included heightened irritability in parents, increased likelihood of marital conflict, less effective support and discipline of children, and increased mental health symptoms in parents, particularly in fathers, who Elder noted sometimes withdrew from family roles in response to loss of earnings.

A number of studies over the last three decades suggest that parenting and family relationships are important mechanisms through which poverty influences child development (Brody, Murry, Kim & Brown, 2002;

Conger & Elder, 1994; Gershoff, Aber, Raver, & Lennon, 2007; McLoyd, 1990; 1998; Mistry, Vandewater, Huston, McLoyd, 2002; Vernon-Feagans, Cox, & the Family Life Project Investigators, 2013). Although much of that work has focused on adolescence, a current ongoing study of children in poverty, The Family Life Project (FLP, Vernon-Feagans et al., 2013), was begun at the child's birth and has followed a representative sample of children and their families in six poor rural counties of the rural south and Appalachia currently into their preadolescent years. A major focus has been on the way in which family relationships are associated with poverty and disadvantage. Particularly of concern has been the association of poverty and disadvantage with parent's sensitivity and support of young children as well as on parent's irritability, hostility, and intrusive control in parent–child interactions (Vernon-Feagans et al., 2013). This concern stems from the fact that early childhood appears to be an important developmental phase for basic skills in regulating emotion, attention, and physiological stress response systems, and that these qualities of parenting support the competent development of these systems (Blair, 2002; Calkins & Bell, 2010; Ursache, Blair, & Raver, 2012; Vernon-Feagans et al., 2013).

Sensitivity and support as well as harshness and intrusive control in early parenting have been found in many studies to predict important early outcomes in children including emotional self-regulation, social competence, and aspects of early cognitive control, including executive function (EF), an aspect of cognition involving the volitional control of thinking in purposeful goal-directed activities (Blair, 2002; Ursache et al., 2012). The expectation is that by helping the very young child regulate their emotions and focus their attention on interactive activities, parents support the development of attentional and emotional regulatory control and the regulation of stress reactivity and that these foundational regulatory skills support the development of the EF cognitive control processes, which in turn support the child's readiness for academic work and self-management in classrooms and with peers (Blair, 2002; Calkins & Marcovitch, 2010; Ursache et al., 2012).

In the Family Life Project, mothers and fathers were observed individually in dyadic play interactions with their young children at regular intervals over the first years of their child's life to assess the extent to which parents in the play interaction sensitively and supportively followed their children's lead, attended to their emotional cues and indications of interest, and helped their very young children stay emotionally regulated and maintain interest in the play activities. Parents were also observed for the extent to which they showed negative, hostile behavior toward their children and demonstrated intrusive control of the child's behavior, thus potentially undermining the child's developing sense of their own efficacy and agency in regulating emotion and directing attention. It was expected that these qualities of interactions would underlie the child's development of regulated behavior and appropriate responsiveness to others and that stressful economic conditions for parents would negatively impact the parent's sensitive/supportive or hostile/intrusive responses to the child. Thus, variation in these qualities of parenting was expected to mediate the association between poverty and regulatory outcomes (Blair, Granger, Willoughby, Mills-Koonce, Cox, & Greenberg, 2011; Vernon-Feagans et al., 2013).

Much of this work builds upon research with animals showing that early experience is important in developing the brain's regulation of stress and emotion systems. Gunnar (2016) is recognized for her work using findings on the neurobiology of stress and development in animals to test hypotheses about how adverse experiences and care in early human development affects child physical and mental health. Her research has influenced researchers trying to understand how early adverse experiences are related to the child's physiological response to stress and how that stress response is related to aspects of the child's cognitive development, particularly EF (Blair et al., 2011).

Early adversity related to poverty is physiologically stressful (Evans, 2003; Shonkoff, Boyce, & McEwen, 2009), and chronically high stress hormones levels can influence the neural circuitry associated with the regulation of emotional and physiological responses as well as the circuitry associated with EF (Blair et al., 2011). Resting levels of the stress hormone cortisol, the end product of activity in the hypothalamic-pituitary-adrenal (HPA) axis is related in both animals and humans to behavioral reactivity to and poor regulation of stress and with difficulty in complex learning tasks (Holmes & Wellman, 2009; Meaney, 2001). In two papers, Blair and colleagues (Blair et al., 2008; Blair et al., 2011), using FLP data, tested the associations of poverty with early maternal care and child stress physiology as mediators of an association of poverty with early EF. They (Blair et al., 2008) initially found that as predicted sensitive supportive parenting in infancy was associated with better infant cortisol regulation (lower basal levels of cortisol and greater cortisol reactivity to emotional arousal at age 7 and 15 months). In a follow-up report explicitly testing the role of poverty in this cascade, Blair et al. (2011) found that level of salivary cortisol measured at child ages 7, 15, and 24 months was significantly higher in children in poverty and partially mediated the effects of higher poverty and less sensitive/supportive maternal parenting on child poorer cognitive abilities at age 3.

One of the challenges long recognized by poverty researchers is that it has been difficult in most studies, even those that follow children and families longitudinally, to isolate the adverse effects of poverty or income loss on children's development from the many other negative environmental exposures that children who grow up in poverty are more likely to experience (Evans, 2004). Because these risk exposures are not readily separated from each other, many studies have used an index of cumulative risk to represent the extent to which the child and family are exposed to adverse environmental experiences (Evans, Li, & Whipple, 2013; Gutman, Sameroff, & Cole, 2003; Vernon-Feagan, et al., 2013). This approach has been important in documenting the impact of poverty and its associated risks with child outcomes and demonstrating pathways to outcome from cumulative risk. However, a recent critique of this approach has come from McLaughlin, Sheridan, and colleagues (McLaughlin & Lambert, 2017; McLaughlin & Sheridan, 2016; Sheridan, Peverill, Finn, & McLaughlin, 2017) who maintain, as others have before them, that a cumulative risk approach may mask different impacts of aspects of risk associated with poverty that may have different effects on child development and that the focus on the regulation of stress response systems may be too narrow as a central mechanism associated with later outcomes. Instead they see a central role for learning mechanisms as mediators.

They suggest that an important distinction should be made between deprivation and threat, and that deprivation and threat are associated with distinct neurocognitive consequences (McLaughlin & Sheridan, 2016; Sheridan et al., 2017). Experiences involving harm or threat of harm included observing community violence or interparental conflict or violence or being the object of parenting that threatens or leads to harm while deprivation experiences involve an absence of expected inputs from the environment (McLaughlin & Sheridan, 2016). McLaughlin and Sheridan (2016) further suggest that emotional-learning processes, including fear and reward learning, are central mechanisms linking adversity and developmental outcomes and note that atypical reward learning has been observed in children exposed to deprivation (institutional rearing and neglect) as well as disruptions in neural circuitry that supports reward learning.

Clearly, there is much more to understand about the associations of adversity on children's development, and continuing progress in developmental neuroscience is likely to provide some important insights into why early childhood may be a vulnerable time for exposure to the stresses of poverty. Techniques of neuroimaging that link timing of adverse childhood experiences to differences in neural structure and function, a process of "biologically embedding" adversity, hold the potential to help us understand ways that early experiences influence future development (Tottenham & Sheridan, 2010). This work suggests that early childhood may be a time of great susceptibility to environmental stress, but it also recognizes that the effects of adversity will vary as a function of developmental timing in that not all neural structures follow the same developmental trajectory, and some structures will be more affected at early ages than others, and thus effects will vary as a function of outcome measured and timing of measurement (Tottenham & Sheridan, 2010).

Beyond Early Experience: The Importance of Environmental Turning Points

Neural systems related to higher order cognitive function show plasticity in response to environmental experiences well into maturity, and thus changes in environmental conditions can alter children's trajectories significantly (Blair, 2002). This observation is relevant to the issues that we address next in that a major finding of the Berkeley and Oakland studies was that the disruptions of the Great Depression and subsequent wars provided many potential "turning points" in the development of youth. A key question related to intervention approaches concerns understanding when turning points in development may occur and how changes in environment may result in new trajectories in the child's development at these points. Gunnar (2016) notes that many periods beyond early life likely are times when defense and stress systems are open to recalibration by environmental experience, and that puberty might be such a period.

Elder and his colleagues were also concerned with the issue of turning points, and in looking for a more complete explanation of why some individuals took very different paths after initial adversity, they turned to entry into higher education, the stabilizing influence of marriage, and military service as important forces. Of these, military service proved to be the most powerful force in turning lives around for the Oakland and Berkeley men. It opened the door to college through the GI Bill along with job training and access to housing, so we turn to this experience and its developmental change processes.

Military Service as a Turning Point

Turning points in life refer to the process by which life course trajectories are altered or redirected – for example, a life trajectory may be changed from cumulative disadvantages to a pathway of opportunity. Among young men of the Great Depression, many were liberated from the barriers of socioeconomic disadvantage by opportunity through military service and its links to higher education and rewarding employment.

The Oakland cohort of young men from middle and working class families left high school just prior to America's entry into World War II, and nine out of ten entered the Armed Forces. Three out of four young men in the Berkeley cohort also entered the Armed Forces between the last years of World War II and the end of the Korean War. They grew up in a culture shaped by America at war, one that greatly valued the young men who served in its Armed Forces. But both cohorts shared the prominence of military service in their young adult transition, with its major consequences for other choices that typically occur in this formative time of life.

The service experience of the two cohorts and wars had long-term implications across the life course. War mobilization promoted social independence, a broadened range of knowledge and experience, legitimated a time out from age-graded careers and their ever-present expectations, and provided greater access to educational and work-life achievement. Lastly, the timetable of entry into the military was critical to the turning point benefits, such as whether entry occurred out of high school or much later.

Entry into the service meant separation from family influences and a measure of social independence coupled with the establishment of new social relationships. Induction "knifed-off" (Brotz & Wilson, 1946) the recruit's past, such as family history and a troubled education. Basic training fostered peer equality and comradeship among recruits by separating them from their pasts. It provided new identities (except where race was concerned), called for uniform dress and appearance, minimized privacy, and viewed the relevance of performance in terms of group achievement or failure. An Oakland veteran stressed "the unforgiving environment" in which the consequences of personal failure were felt by the entire unit.

Another feature of military experience is the extent to which service time represents a clear-cut break with the conventional expectations of an age-graded career – a time out or moratorium from "adult-like" responsibilities. Military duty provides a legitimate time out from educational, work, and family pressures in a structured environment. As a rule, one's presence in the military is not questioned, and neither is the lack of career progress or work plans resulting from being in the service. The very act of military service provides adequate justification for not conforming with age-related expectations of career development. Indeed, Stouffer and his associates in The American Soldier (1949, p. 572) noted that for many soldiers in World War II, "perhaps for a majority, the break caused by military service [meant] a chance to evaluate where they had gotten and to reconsider where they were going." For individuals deprived of job opportunities and the normally expected transition into careers, the service provided a temporary respite from the uncertain and even desperate search for employment.

Especially among young men from deprived circumstances, military service and its situational imperatives provided a way out of poverty by promoting independence, new ideas and role models. It offered a legitimate time out for those who were unsure of the course to follow in life. For the economically deprived, who lacked self-direction and a sense of adequacy, military service offered developmental alternatives to the life course charted by their families, such as separation from mother's control through involvement in a masculine culture and the opportunity to sort things out in ways that bolster self-confidence, resolve, and goal setting. Some of these themes appear in life reviews. The break from a painful family situation is a recurring theme (Elder, 1987). An Oakland veteran recalled that he "finally realized what was happening and broke away." He entered the Navy. Another described the time he joined the Army at 18 as the end of his mother's domination and the beginning of independence.

Several Oakland veterans recalled the novel and rewarding experience of mastering military tasks, acquiring new skills in the military, and of doing something well and on their own. Across this challenging time in the Armed Forces, we see a contrast between descriptions of self before and after leaving the service, from the implication of being "such a flop" in adolescence – "I couldn't do anything" – to the claim that from "the day I went into the service, I was almost on my own ... figured out my own situation and went on from there."

Another feature of military service during World War II entailed a broadened range of perspectives and social knowledge. Mobilization increased the scope of awareness of oneself and others through an expanded range of social experiences, such as encountering new people and places that could promote greater tolerance of social diversity. Willard Waller (1940, p. 14) once likened the population mixing of World War II to "stirring soup; people are thrown together who have never seen one another before and will never see one another again."

Out of this experience may come greater awareness of self and others, and an expanded range of interactional experiences with their behavioral models, and possibly a greater tolerance of diversity. A veteran interviewed after World War II in a study by Robert Havighurst and co-authors (1951, p. 188) spoke about the incredible diversity of his acquaintances in the service and their influence on his views. As he put it, the experience "sort of opens up your horizons ... You start thinking in broader terms than you did before."

The impact of entry into the military hinged on its "timing in their lives." It was less whether they entered the military than when they entered. The earlier young men entered the military after high school, the greater their prospects for access to post-service benefits from the 1944 GI Bill (Mettler, 2005), from access to federal support of a college education to job training support, and loans for the purchase of housing. Early entrants in the Oakland cohort (before the age of 21) were most likely to come from lower status families and those hard-hit by the Great Depression (Elder, 1987).

And consistent with expectations, they were more apt to benefit from college support through the GI Bill. Over half completed higher education after leaving the service. This support dropped off significantly for later entrants – for entrants at age 21 or older. Most noteworthy, any disadvantage effect associated with early entry (poor scholarship, lack of self-confidence) faded to insignificance by mid-life in educational and occupational standing, owing in large measure to their higher education and employment training through the GI Bill.

In addition, early entry to the Armed Forces proved to be far less stressful for men's social relationships than later entry. Typically, the early entrants in the Oakland cohort were not engaged or married when they entered the service, and few had jobs of career significance. Looking back on the timing of their military service, most of the early entrants thought it was "just about right." From all perspectives, early mobilization was a timely age at which to enter the war. It was timely in terms of "maximizing benefits and minimizing costs" in men's lives (Elder, 1987, p. 467). These men were four times more likely to claim that their lives had been enhanced through military service.

By contrast, the men who joined the military at a later age were likely to have established their adult careers at the time. As a result, they experienced major costs and setbacks from the service as well as painful family pressures from the disruption of family relationships and the hardship of prolonged separations. Among aspects of the service that produced dissatisfaction with military experience, late entry turned out to be far more important than even exposure to combat. Three-fourths of the Oakland men who entered the service at a later age regarded this stressful time table (relative to marriage/family) as the primary source of "their dissatisfaction with time of entry" compared to a third of the early entrants. They were too old at departure from the service to benefit from the GI Bill on college support.

The Berkeley Cohort: Coming of Age in World War II

The Oakland cohort's service occurred during the greatest mass mobilization of American Armed Forces, "during World War II," a time when the Berkeley youth were teenagers. The local culture of this mobilization in San Francisco and Oakland conveyed a powerful impression to the minds and military aspirations of the young men in the Berkeley cohort who were coming to the end of their adolescent years.

When they entered high school, the culture of the community and region was defined by symbols and activities of an unprepared nation rapidly mobilizing for war (Elder, 1986). Signs of mobilization and consciousness-raising were everywhere in Berkeley and the San Francisco area, including a local radio series entitled "My War." It dramatized "the wartime contributions of every man, woman, and child on the home front." Children at Saturday matinee movies saw war's horrific reality through newsreels of atrocities along the eastern front in Poland. Troop trains from nearby army bases were constantly moving through Oakland, as shipping moved in and out of San Francisco Bay, passing under the newly constructed Bay Bridge.

Families worked victory gardens on vacant plots – over 40,000 were reported in the East Bay area during 1943. The energetic role of young people in the war effort and their acquired sense of significance were documented by the seemingly endless collection drives for fats, wastepaper, scrap metal, and even milkweed pods. During the summer months, older youth responded to urgent calls for assistance in the harvesting of fruits and nuts on nearby farms and ranches.

The "War" became the most popular conversational topic with peers, outranking girls, school, parents, and the "things I want." As military events began to shift in favor of the United States and the Allies, Berkeley boys were asked what they most often talked about with friends. The list included aspects of popular culture (such as movies), relations with girls, family and school affairs, and war items – the war in general, the armed service one would choose, the new defense workers and their families, and post-war planning. Over half the boys claimed that they often talked about the war with other boys, and the preferred branch of military service was only slightly less popular as a topic. For many, a major concern was getting into the armed forces underage.

These preferences anticipate the boys' "future life course" and reflect disadvantages that extend back to the Great Depression. Nearly three-fourths eventually served in the Armed Forces, and those who found the war an especially salient experience were likely to join up at the first opportunity, frequently during the last months of World War II. Early joiners entered the service before age 21; and the later entrants, at age 21 or older. Nearly 70 percent of the early joiners selected at least one military occupation on a "things to be" inventory in 1943–44, as did half of the late joiners. Fewer than 40 percent of the youth who never served also chose a military occupation during their high school career in World War II. Conversation on this topic shows corresponding differences between these groups.

Frequent conversations with friends about military roles during World War II were linked to disadvantages of one kind or another, such as low family status, Depression hardship, poor high school grades, and feelings of personal inadequacy. As in the Oakland cohort, it is noteworthy that a background of disadvantage was more relevant to the timing of military service than to entry itself. In both cohorts, the greater the Depression-caused disadvantage, the earlier the military induction. The Berkeley males who entered the service early turned out to be the most disadvantaged group in their cohort. They were most likely to have grown up in hard-pressed families during the 1930s, and their school performance was less than promising. And they were also less goal-oriented, confident, and assertive than other adolescents.

But was this cumulative disadvantage a serious handicap for their post-war lives? To answer this question, we distinguish again between veterans who entered the service relatively early or late. On family disadvantage, the early entrants resemble the Berkeley men who did not enter the service at all. However, they ended up with a more successful record in education – 70 percent completed at least some college, compared with 58 percent of the non-veterans. For most early joiners, the GI Bill made college possible and a reality.

Consider the life of a young man from a deprived family in the 1930s. He came from a working-class family and expressed a positive attitude toward the military during World War II. He listed a variety of attractive military occupations, but becoming a Marine was his primary goal. As his mother said at the time, "He'll be a Marine regardless of what I want him to be." He followed through on this objective by quitting high school at age 17 and persuading his parents to let him join the Marines under age. After a four-year stint in the Middle East he returned to civilian life, launched an apprenticeship in printing, using the resources of the GI Bill, and married his high school sweetheart. Another young man, with similar aspirations for military service, followed suit by dropping out of high school to join the Navy. After the service, he joined the Naval air reserve and earned his high school diploma. Eventually, his fascination with flying led to enrollment in a university electrical engineering program on the GI Bill.

Some Berkeley veterans did not go on to higher education with the GI Bill, owing to one of the following considerations. First, military service did not reinforce or increase the college aspirations of all men. Some with strong vocational aspirations (e.g., electricians), for example, entered corresponding jobs after demobilization. Second, the experience of combat left some men psychologically and physically impaired, while other veterans experienced an accumulation of health problems that discouraged the needed effort. Third, some men who returned to heavy responsibilities were discouraged from entering or completing their higher education. In many cases, they did not receive support from wives, children, and parents that would enable them to take advantage of the GI Bill. The time for personal and family sacrifice had passed.

The first decade after military service for the early entrants proved to be a difficult time in life for many, reflected by an evolving disorderly work life of numerous changes in job and employer, and even change in line of work. But by age 40, stabilization of their work life had occurred, providing suggestive evidence that military service was a turning point in their life course. Those who entered the service early ranked higher on occupational status than the non-veterans. The two groups were evenly matched on social position in 1929, although the early entrants were far more likely to come from hard-pressed families in the 1930s, by a difference of three to one. In addition, marital stability had become a distinctive feature of their lives. Three out of four had stable marriages. This compared favorably with the marriage stability of the later entrants who enjoyed higher occupational status.

More notably, we even find an increasing similarity up to the middle years in the occupational rank of early and late entrants, despite their markedly different backgrounds and educational attainment. For example, slightly more than half of the late entrants became college graduates, compared to a third of the early joiners. But status differences associated with this educational disparity tended to diminish as they moved into middle age. Supportive marital relations may have played a significant role, but they may also reflect important personality changes.

Developmental advances over the life course are suggestive, from an ineffectual pattern of behavior in adolescence to greater mastery and self-direction during the middle years. Consider a comparison of the early entrants and non-veterans on four measures of psychological functioning in adolescence and at mid-life (approximately age 40, Elder, 1986, p. 243): self-inadequacy, goal orientation, social competence, and submissiveness. The content of each measure is identical for the two periods. In general, the data point to a convergence of psychological functioning by mid-life, with veterans who joined the service early showing a pronounced shift toward greater competence. Nevertheless, these men still had not completely closed the gap with the non-veterans; at mid-life they ranked slightly lower in all domains.

The years beyond the age of 30 appear to have been good ones for the early entrants in terms of greater psychological well-being. In fact, their 40-year follow-up indicates that they tended to consider this time of life as the very best time, especially when compared to their troubled war-time adolescence. Half of the mid-life men from deprived families looked back on these early years as the "very worst time" of their life – a time of confusion, insecurity, and inadequacy (Elder & Rockwell, 1979, p. 295).

The origin of these self-perceptions may date back to harsh mistreatment at the hands of their frustrated fathers during the pre-school years of Depression hardship and family turmoil, an experience that left them unable to cope with the insecurities of the war years. Unstable ranks on psychological health are more common for the men who entered the service at a young age than for the non-veterans on both goal orientation and social competence. Neither of these dimensions shows continuity from adolescence to the age of 40. The apparent developmental gains of the early entrants are matched by their perception of the change we obtained during a follow-up in 1985.

The men were asked if their military service had made a difference in their lives and, if so, what the difference amounted to up to the middle years. At the time, they were entering their 50s, a life stage over two decades removed from the Korean War. In line with the objective evidence of life improvement, the early joiners were more likely than the late entrants to report a positive influence (94% vs. 62%). When asked to explain this positive outcome, they tended to cite "a maturing experience," "developed character," and "greater educational opportunity."

Disadvantaged men from the Berkeley cohort who entered the service as soon as they could tended to rise above the limitations of their background. They achieved a significant level of personal growth from Depression adolescence to middle age, consistent with their work life accomplishments and marital stability. Was military service a key factor or would growth have occurred even outside this institution? A precise answer to this question is not possible with the data at hand. However, we can say that the military experience (without reference to combat) was conducive to the personal growth of men who seemed to have so little to look forward to from the vantage point of their adolescence.

Military service may have enhanced life opportunities by enabling men in the Berkeley cohort to use their personal resources to good effect in education, work, and family. Motivation is part of the explanation, along with personal qualities that veterans frequently cited as benefits of their service experience. Especially prominent among these qualities are self-discipline, the ability to cope with adversity, and skill in managing people and their relationships. Such qualities were most likely to be put to a test in the lives of these children of the Great Depression. They had to use all they had to be successful in life. Neither a quality education nor a rewarding job was a given for this cohort.

Building on this account, we assumed that military service was more predictive of occupational achievement among men from deprived families than among the non-deprived and, further, that the service effect occurred primarily through higher education. To put these ideas to a test, Elder and Caspi (1990) set up the same prediction equation for men from deprived and non-deprived backgrounds, with childhood IQ and military service as antecedents of mid-life occupational status. This analysis indicates that military service had a significant effect only among the deprived in the Berkeley cohort, whereas IQ was generally predictive in both groups. In addition, the service effect occurred primarily through higher education. With education in the model for men from deprived families, military service no longer had any effect on adult occupational status.

These results suggest that some economically deprived men in the Berkeley cohort escaped "the cycle of disadvantage" by entering military service and, if not mobilized, they did so through their own intellectual ability. By contrast, the attainment of men from non-deprived homes most clearly hinge on their own cognitive abilities. Military service in young adulthood neither aided nor hindered their life success, in large part because these veterans generally entered military service later in life, typically after college.

Many years after the Great Depression and World War II, the director emeritus of the Berkeley Guidance Study, Jean Macfarlane (1963, p. 338) offered some reflections on the lives of the Berkeley men that summarize in many respects the "turnaround" that we observe in the life course of the Berkeley veterans who grew up in deprived families. She concludes that some of the Berkeley boys turned out to be more stable and effective adults than any members of the research team, with differing theoretical biases, had predicted. Most noteworthy were the number of men whose poor scholastic records "completely belie the creative intelligence demands of their present position."

These reflections are not scientifically based observations by any means, but they are remarkably attuned to the results we have presented. Macfarlane sought explanations for the disparity between early experience and the adult life course in the psyche and proximal world of the individual. First, she noted a common failure to recognize the maturation value of hardship experiences. As she put it, "We have learned that no one becomes mature without living through the pains and confusions of maturing experiences" (1971, p. 341).

Second, she criticized an insufficient appreciation of experiences in late adolescence and early adulthood, including the potential of later events, for altering life trajectories. As she noted, the Berkeley boys did not achieve a sense of ego identity and strength until later situations "forced them or presented an opportunity to them to fulfill a role that gave them a sense of worth" (p. 341). Thus, the developmental gains may be associated with departure from home and community, changes that provide an opportunity to "work through early confusions and inhibitions."

Indeed, historical experiences of the transition to young adulthood offer promising explanations for the disparity between early deprivation and adult fulfillment among the Berkeley men as "children of the Great Depression." After a decade of Depression hardship, these teenagers experienced full-scale mobilization in World War II, followed at a short distance by the Korean War and post-war affluence. Paradoxically, the experience of industrial mobilization for World War II and the Korean War converged in ways that improved the life chances of veterans who grew up in the midst of family hardship during the Great Depression. It did so by transforming the Depression's legacy of disadvantage in placing them on a more promising path to health and rewarding opportunity.

Military service and higher education emerged in the lives of the Berkeley men as events that turned their lives around by enabling them to surmount childhood disadvantages in the 1930s. Another cohort of males who were born in Boston during the years of 1925–30 adds significance to this set of findings. Two sociologists, Robert Sampson and John Laub (1996), drew upon life records (1940–65) from a study by Sheldon Glueck and Eleanor Glueck (1930) of 500 delinquent boys of European-American origins who grew up in poverty areas of the city. They were matched with non-delinquents from the city schools. Seven out of ten of the men entered the Armed Forces during World War II. They typically entered before the age of 21 and served for more than two years including time in training and under arrest.

The delinquent boys had a much longer history of antisocial events, and were less apt to obtain in-service training and veterans' benefits from the GI Bill. Even so, they were more likely to profit from military service over their life course, when compared to the controls and this trajectory was especially the case for men who entered the service at an early age. In-service training, overseas duty, and veteran benefits for both education and housing markedly enhanced the job stability of men with an antisocial past, especially when they entered the service at a young age.

The benefits of the GI Bill, educational, occupational, and economic, were not restricted to college attendance. Indeed, the evidence suggests that the benefits of the GI Bill were due in part to the opportunity to complete high school and enroll in trade schools. A third of the veterans enrolled in craft, trade or industrial courses. The authors (1996, p. 349) conclude that veterans from disadvantaged backgrounds used the GI Bill less "to mimic the middle-class ideal of going to college than to finish high school or trade school and improve their technical skills to position themselves for long-term advancement in the labor market." This broader application did also apply to some of the Oakland and Berkeley veterans from the working class, but college-going remained the goal of most of these veterans.

Another relevant event of significance for changing the trajectory of young men's lives in constructive ways is marriage. Lee Robins (1966) underscores the support a spouse provides by enabling young men to overcome problem behaviors in the transition to adulthood, and we find similar benefits of wife support in the lives of the Berkeley and Oakland veterans of World War II and the Korean War (Elder & Clipp, 1988). Mobilization frequently brought the veterans in these cohorts together with their prospective wives on military bases or in hospitals; in some cases, the likelihood of wartime separation led to hasty or early marriages. But for the men who had lost confidence and hope in their future, an optimistic and loving wife could turn their sorrowful outlook toward greater vitality.

From another angle, we find that young women in the Berkeley cohort frequently managed to escape the legacy of hard times through marriage to a young man of potential. Economic hardship during the 1930s accelerated the transition to adult family roles among women from the middle class, as expressed in marriage and childbearing. The women who entered but did not finish college were more likely than the college graduates and postgraduates to meet their husband in school (55 vs. 31%), to leave college for marriage and for the labor force (Bennett & Elder, 1979). Veterans with GI benefits were prominent among their husbands. The enhanced level of higher education achieved by World War II veterans enabled more of them to marry up by meeting and marrying women with at least some college education (cf. Larsen et al., 2015). These educational benefits also were frequently carried over to the educational achievement of the veteran's offspring (Mettler, 2005).

Up to this point, military service during World War II and the Korean War has been portrayed as a developmental change agent in the lives of young men from the Oakland and Berkeley cohorts who grew up during the Great Depression of the 1930s. In part, it became such a change agent by providing a path to all forms of advanced education. For the parents of these "Children of the Great Depression," the soaring economy of war mobilization provided a stunning upswing toward full employment and much higher wages and salaries. In the United States, the income level of families in 1939 increased by a factor of three by 1944.

To tell how this change influenced both parents and children of a more disadvantaged working class, we turn to the workforce of the Amoskeag textile mills in Manchester, New Hampshire. The mills were forced to close during the worst years of the Depression. A study by Tamara Hareven (1982) of the children's cohort of mill families include extensive open-ended interviews obtained between 1980 and 1983 as well as demographic, career, and migration histories based on the interviews and other vital records. Data on the children were linked to the parents, thus making comparisons across the generations possible.

"The Truly Disadvantaged": Their Path to Opportunity in Wartime

The closing of the Amoskeag Mills deprived entire families of jobs and tore many of these families apart, as their members wandered around New England or returned to Quebec in search of work. The blow of unemployment on Manchester's laborers was particularly severe, because these immigrant workers had already been deprived through low wages and the ups and downs typical of the textile industry prior to the Great Depression. The first opportunity for relief in Manchester came with the arrival of war industries and military induction, following the United States' entry into World War II.

The war effort united community members with a new sense of a common purpose and a commitment to the joint effort for survival. Sons and daughters who had left in search of jobs outside Manchester returned to find employment in the new industries mushrooming in the city. A new feeling of hope overcame the sense of despair and loss of purpose in the wake of the shutdown. The first stage of Manchester's recovery during the war involved the opening of war-production factories in the empty buildings of the Amoskeag Mills – a sweater factory for the military, a rubber plant for producing rafts and life jackets, a metal factory that made bullets, and a parachute factory. These industries restored the beat of life and activity into the desolate mill yard with recruited workers of all ages, male and female.

Teenage boys and girls, and even their older siblings were elated by the sudden return of opportunity for good jobs with the growth of war industries: "And they paid well," reminisced one of the young mill workers who had remained unemployed after the devastating shutdown. Manchester youth who had been wandering around in parts of New Hampshire and New England, working on occasional, temporary jobs, began to return home and start regular employment at unprecedented high wages. For the city's young men, the industrial mobilization for war lifted them out of the impoverished world they had experienced in the Depression.

The change occurred in two stages. First, war industries provided employment, some of which involved learning new skills. These opportunities benefited the entire community and provided employment for young and older women as well. Second, the war produced new opportunities for workers in nearby communities and nearby shipyards. These developments produced great excitement in the community. As a former shipyard worker recalled, "You could make yourself three to four hundred a week, no problem at all. Big money! My father was working for $54 a week for a job he had all his life. I told him 'Quit it Pa! Quit it. Come down to the shipyard and we will get you in there.'"

Manchester's young men and women, born between 1920 and 1924, were members of the cohort that came to work when there was no work (Hughes, 1971, p. 124). They became the "lost generation" of the Great Depression, the children of the Amoskeag Mills shutdown. As they were growing up, their parents dreamt that they would escape mill work by graduating from high school and entering "middle-class" occupations. But the decline and shutdown of the mills during the Great Depression set this cohort's progression into the middle class back by one generation. They were unable to escape blue-collar occupations, but felt fortunate to have a chance to return to or enter such occupations once the war industries opened in the city. Those who went to work in such industries before military service felt for the first time a sense of self-respect as workers and enjoyed the kind of sociability with fellow workers that their parents had enjoyed in the Amoskeag Mills. They had missed that experience entirely because of the mill shutdown and the Great Depression.

Married men in this cohort were soon recruited into the military along with the single men, and this prompted more married women to seek employment in the booming war industries. And Manchester parents of daughters with young children and men in the military were known to have provided childcare and assistance with meals whenever possible and desirable. In another version of such assistance a woman in the 1920–24 cohort supported her young children and elderly mother-in-law through employment in an armaments factory and later on by work in a factory making sweaters for the army. "I was the only one who could cut army sweaters, 50 dozen a day, by hand."

One member of the cohort obtained a wartime job with Pratt-Whitney Aircraft and then served in the Navy until the war's end, followed by a career in family business. Military service offered the young men in Manchester an escape from unwanted parental and societal pressures to attend college or obtain steady work. As in the case of the Oakland and Berkeley men, it provided a moratorium from the normative expectation that they move through orderly transitions, such as graduating from high school and embarking on a continuous, stable work life or with higher education or technical training. The war gave them a good reason for delaying such steps. For other young men, military service provided an escape from oppressive working conditions.

The men in Manchester who entered the Armed Forces during World War II without a high school degree were more likely to acquire training in a skill during their service career that opened up related job training and work–life advances in the post-war economy than to pursue a college degree. This is the life story of a number of veterans in the 1920–24 cohort. Lacking a high-school diploma, one of the vets with service in the Navy noted that, "work was very hard to get in Manchester before the war." In fact, he thought it was "the hardest time in his life." Trained as a radio operator in the Navy, he concluded that this training "made my subsequent advancement as an electrical technician possible." From this work he decided to use the GI Bill for training in the repair of electrical motors, leading eventually to his work as a turbine tester for General Electric (GE).

In the city of Manchester's working class, a full understanding of men's ability to take advantage of the challenges and opportunities provided by the war-boom economy and the armed forces during the Second World War depended on the support of family members on the home front. The back-up services family members provided by caring for young children and older relatives were crucial not only for the family's survival but also for the servicemen's ability to concentrate on resettling when they returned. The post-war careers of the Manchester cohorts of war-industry workers and veterans can be understood only by taking family configurations, needs, and supports into consideration. Some returnees from the military entered their relatives' businesses and many found employment through relatives and friends. Some returning service personnel acquired a house with the assistance of relatives who helped them with the purchase of one. Mutual assistance by kin was a tradition in Manchester's working class.

General Discussion

American children in birth cohorts of the 1920s lived out their lives during a time marked by unparalleled "ups and downs" of economic and social change, from the urban prosperity of the 1920s to the economic depression of the 1930s, followed by World War II (1940–45), a global war of immense proportion in which America became an "Arsenal of Democracy" and in doing so generated unimagined prosperity up to the mid-1970s. This chapter explored the proposition for these cohorts that "the impact of this trajectory of change" varied according to their life stage at the time, especially for males. How old were they when they encountered such change?

We focused mainly on two birth cohorts, the Oakland cohort of 1920–21 and the Berkeley cohort of 1928–29. The members of each cohort belonged to longitudinal studies at the Institute of Human Development, the University of California, Berkeley (originally known as the Institute of Child Welfare). Both studies were launched just before the most severe phase of the Great Depression. The Oakland cohort encountered Depression hard times when the children were old enough to assume a helping role in the household, and yet, were too young to experience the difficulties of being on their own in a depressed labor market. By contrast, the Berkeley children in the preschool years were wholly dependent on parents in a very stressful time. The deprivation was especially pronounced for young boys who lacked support from their father.

Ordinarily one might assume that this childhood risk would be expressed in the adult lives of the two cohorts. However, their world changed significantly when the country entered World War ll in 1941. The Oakland boys were in their 20s and virtually all were soon in the Armed Forces. The Berkeley cohort was entering the teenage years surrounded by the symbols and pressures of wartime. Their feelings of insecurity from hard times became more pronounced during the war, but they also began entering the Armed Forces during the last months of the war in the Pacific.

As in the Great Depression, timing made a difference on the effects of entry into the service. But contrary to the experience of hard times, the most beneficial time for entry into the military was early rather than late. The military entrants' life stage made a significant difference for both cohorts. The children of Depression hard times benefited more from the service by entering at the earliest possible time, giving them a better chance to benefit from the federal government's GI program that offered veterans access to educational, occupational, and housing benefits. As a result, by mid-life the deprived Berkeley men had closed the achievement gap with men from non-deprived families. In the two cohorts of young men, the early entrants were less likely to be married with children and therefore did not have the problems with separation and family support that other veterans had experienced. Young women's lives were also powerfully influenced by the Great Depression and World War II, but they were often contingent on the experiences of these men.

Contrasts between the hardship of Depression life and the benefits of both war industry and serving in the armed forces were most pronounced in communities of the truly disadvantaged, as vividly depicted by Tamara Hareven's account of the closing of the Amoskeag textile mills in Manchester, New Hampshire, during the Great Depression and the troubled future of the former mill workers across the war years. Unlike the Berkeley and Oakland cohorts of veterans, who gained federal support for higher education, the Manchester veterans more often ended up with manufacturing jobs, employment in the trades, and even small businesses.

Do these findings about turning points from the Great Depression and the WWII years share common ground with contemporary opportunities for "turning points" for youth and young adults in our country? Edin and Kissane (2010) note that the literature is consistent in showing that a change in employment is the critical predictor for slipping into poverty, while returns to school are the most common "trigger for entry onto the mobility ladder" (Edin & Kissane, 2010, p. 464). At the current time (Spring, 2018), the nation has seen consistent job growth over the last several years and has reached an unemployment rate of 3.9 percent (Bureau of Labor Statistics, US Department of Labor, 2018), yet consideration of the newest data suggests that the share of men who are without work during the prime working years (aged 25–54) has nearly tripled over the last 50 years, and the rise is highest in the eastern parts of the American Heartland from Mississippi to Michigan, leading to suggestions that the country needs "placed-based" employment policies (Austin, Glaeser, & Summers, Spring 2018).

The data cited in this report by Austin and colleagues (Spring, 2018) for the Brookings Institute point to education as playing a significant role, along with the decline of manufacturing jobs, in a divide between more educated male workers who are benefiting from the modern economy and their less educated male peers. The authors of the report assert that there is a large social cost of non-employment as it is a strong predictor of unhappiness, suicide, and opioid use for men aged 25–54. The findings of turning points for youth and young adults negatively affected by the high unemployment rates of the Great Depression would suggest that employment policy and educational opportunity, whether in colleges or trade schools, could be used to address this alarming situation. As we go forward as a nation in trying to solve our contemporary problems, it is wise to look to lessons from our past.

References

Austin, B., Glaeser, E. & Summers, L. (Spring, 2018). Saving the heart-land: Place-based policies in 21st century America. Brookings Papers on Economic Activity (BPEA) Conference Draft, Brookings Institute.

Bennett, S. K. & Elder, G. H., Jr. (1979). Women's work in the family economy: A study of Depression hardship in women's lives. *Journal of Family History*, 4(2), 153–176.

Blair, C. (2002). School readiness: Integrating cognition and emotion in a neurobiological conceptualization of children's functioning at school entry. *American Psychologist*, 57(2), 111–127.

Blair, C., Granger, D. A., Kivlighan, K. T., Mills-Koonce, R., Willoughby, M., Greenberg, M. T., & the FLP Investigators (2008). Maternal and child contributions to cortisol response to emotional arousal in young children from low-income, rural communities. *Developmental Psychology*, *44*, 1095–1109.

Blair, B., Granger, D. A., Willoughby, M., Mills-Koonce, R., Cox, M., Greenberg, M. T., Fortunato, C., & the FLP Investigators (2011). Salivary cortisol mediates effects of poverty and parenting on executive functions in early childhood. *Child Development*, *82*(6), 1970–1984.

Bornstein, M. H. & Bradley, R. H., eds. (2003). *Socioeconomic Status, Parenting, and Child Development.* Mahwah, NJ: Erlbaum.

Bradley, R. H. & Corwyn, R. F. (2002). Socioeconomic status and child develop-ment. *Annual Review of Psychology*, *53*, 371–399.

Brody, G. H., Murry, V. M., Kim, S., & Brown, A. C. (2002). Longitudinal pathways to competence and psychological adjustment among African American children living in rural single-parent households. *Child Development*, *73*(5), 1505–1516.

Brotz, H. & Wilson, E. (1946). Characteristics of military society. *American Journal of Sociology*, *51*, 371–375.

Bureau of Labor Statistics, US Department of Labor (2018). www.bls.gov/news .release/pdf/empsit.pdf

Calkins, S. D. & Bell, M. A.(Ed.) (2010). *Child Development at the Intersection of Emotion and Cognition.* Washington, DC: American Psychological Association.

Calkins, S. D. & Marcovitch, S. (2010). Emotion regulation and executive functioning in early development: Integrated mechanisms of control supporting adaptive functioning. In S. D. Calkins & M. A. Bell (Eds.),

Child Development at the Intersection of Emotion and Cognition (pp. 37–58). Washington, DC: American Psychological Association.

Clarke, A. M. & Clarke, A. (1976). *Early Experience: Myth and evidence.* London: Open Books.

Conger, R. D. & Elder, G. H., Jr. (1994). *Families in Troubled Times: Adapting to change in rural America.* New York: A. de Gruyter.

Cox, M. J., Mills-Koonce, R., Propper, C., & Gariepy, J. L. (2010). Systems theory and cascades in developmental psychopathology. *Development and Psychopathology, 22,* 497–506.

Dozier, M., Roben, C. K. P., & Hoye, J. R. (2015). Adversity in early social relationships. In S. D. Calkins (Ed.), *Handbook of Infant Biopsychosocial Development* (pp. 336–358). New York: Guilford Press.

Duncan, G. J., Magnuson, K., & Votruba-Drzal, E. (2017). Moving beyond correlations in assessing the consequences of poverty. *Annual Review of Psychology, 68,* 413–434.

Dunn, J. & Plomin, R. (1990). *Separate Lives: Why siblings are so different.* New York: Basic Books.

Edin, K. & Kissane, R. J. (2010). Poverty and the American family: A decade in review. *Journal of Marriage and the Family, 72,* 460–479.

Elder, G. H., Jr. (1974/99). *Children of the Great Depression: Social change in life experience.* Boulder, CO: Westview Press (originally published by University of Chicago Press).

(1986). Military times and turning points in men's lives. *Developmental Psychology, 22*(2), 233–245.

(1987). War mobilization and the life course: A cohort of World War II veterans. *Sociological Forum, 2*(3), 449–472.

Elder, G. H., Jr. & Clipp, E. C. (1988). Wartime losses and social bonding: Influences across 40 years in men's lives. *Psychiatry, 51,* 177–198.

Elder, G. H., Jr. & Hareven, T. K. (1993). Rising above life's disadvantage: From the Great Depression to war. G. H. Elder, Jr., J. Modell, & R. D. Parke (eds.) *Children in Time and Place: Developmental and Historical Insights* (pp. 47–72). New York: Cambridge University Press.

Elder, G. H., Jr., Modell, J., & Parke, R. D. (eds.) (1993). *Children in Time and Place: Developmental and historical insights.* New York: Cambridge University Press.

Elder, G. H., Jr. & Rockwell, R. C. (1979). Economic depression and postwar opportunity in men's lives: A study of life patterns and health. In R. Simmons (ed.), *Research in Community and mental health.* (Vol. 1, pp. 249–303). Greenwich, CT: JAI Press.

Evans, G. W. (2003). A multimethodological analysis of cumulative risk and allostatic load among rural children. *Developmental Psychology, 39,* 924–933.

(2004). The environment of childhood poverty. *American Psychologist, 59,* 77–92.

Evans, G. W., Li, D., & Whipple, S. S. (2013). Cumulative risk and child development. *Psychological Bulletin, 139,* 1342–1396.

Gershoff, E. T., Aber, J. L., Raver, C. C., & Lennon, M. C. (2007). Income is not enough: Incorporating material hardship into models of income associations with parenting and child development. *Child Development, 78,* 70–95.

Glueck, S. & Glueck, E. (1930). *500 Criminal Careers*. New York: A. A. Knopf

Gunnar, M. R. (2016). Early life stress: What is the human chapter of the mammalian story? *Child Development Perspectives, 10*(3), 178–183.

Gutman, L. M., Sameroff, A. J., & Cole, R. (2003). Academic growth curve trajectories from 1st grade to 12th grade: Effects of multiple social risk factors and preschool child factors., *Developmental Psychology, 39*(4), 777–790.

Hareven, T. K. (1982). *Family Time and Industrial Time: The relationship between the family and work in a New England industrial town*. Cambridge: Cambridge University Press.

Havighurst, R. J., et al. (1951). *The American Veteran Back Home*. New York: Longmans, Green.

Holmes, A. & Wellman, C. L. (2009). Stress-induced prefrontal reorganization and executive dysfunction in rodents. *Neuroscience Biobehavioral Review, 33*(6), 773–783.

Huston, A. C. & Bentley, A. C. (2010). Human development in societal context. *Annual Review of Psychology, 61*, 411–437.

Larsen, M. F. et al. (2015). War and marriage: Assortative mating and the World War II GI Bill. *Demography, 52*, 1431–1461.

Leerkes, E. M. & Parade, S. H. (2015). A psychobiological perspective on emotional development within the family context. In S. D. Calkins (Ed.), *Handbook of Infant Biopsychosocial Development* (pp. 206–231). New York: Guilford Press.

Macfarlane, J. W. (1963). From infancy to adulthood. *Childhood Education, 39*, 336–342.

(1971). Perspectives on personality consistency and change from the Guidance Study. In M. C. Jones et al. (eds.), *The Course of Human Development: Selected papers from the Longitudinal Studies, Institute of Human Development, the University of California, Berkeley* (pp. 410–415). Waltham, MA: Xerox College Publishing.

McLaughlin, K. A. & Lambert, H. K. (2017). Child trauma exposure and psychopathology: Mechanisms of risk and resilience. *Current Opinion in Psychology, 14*, 29–34.

McLaughlin, K. A. & Sheridan, M. A. (2016). Beyond cumulative risk: A dimensional approach to childhood adversity. *Current Directions in Psychological Science, 25*, 239–245.

McLoyd, V. C. (1990). The impact of economic hardship on black families and children: Psychological distress, parenting, and socioemotional development. *Child Development, 61*(2), 311–346.

(1998). Socioeconomic disadvantage and child development. *American Psychologist, 53*, 185–204.

Meaney, M. J. (2001). Maternal care, gene expression, and the transmission of individual differences in stress reactivity across generations. *Annual Review of Neuroscience, 24*, 1161–1192.

Mettler, S. (2005). *Soldiers to Citizens: The GI Bill and the making of the greatest generation*. New York: Oxford University.

Mistry, R. S., Vandewater, E. A., Huston, A. C., & McLoyd, V. C. (2002). Economic well-being and children's social adjustment: The role of family process in an ethnically diverse low-income sample. *Child Development, 73*(3), 935–951.

NICHD Early Child Care Research Network (2005). Duration and developmental timing of poverty and children's cognitive and social development from birth through third grade. *Child Development, 76*, 795–810.

Robins, L. N. (1966). *Deviant Children Grown Up: A sociological and psychiatric study of sociopathic personality*. Baltimore, MD: Williams & Wilkins.

Rutter, M. & Madge, N. (1976). *Cycles of Disadvantage: A review of research*. London: Heinemann.

Ryder, N. B. (1965). The cohort as a concept in the study of social change. *American Sociological Review, 30*, 843–861.

Sampson, R. J. & Laub, J. H. (1996). Socioeconomic achievement in the life course of disadvantaged men: Military service as a turning point, circa 1940–1965. *American Sociological Review, 61*(3), 347–367.

Sheridan, M. A., Peverill, M., Finn, A. S., & McLaughlin, K. A. (2017). Dimensions of childhood adversity have distinct associations with neural systems underlying executive functioning. *Development and Psychopathology, 29*, 1777–1794.

Shonkoff, J. P., Boyce, W. T., & McEwen, B. S. (2009). Neuroscience, molecular biology, and the childhood roots of health disparities: Building a new framework for health promotion and disease prevention. *Journal of the American Medical Association, 301*, 2252–2259.

Sroufe, L. A., Coffino, B., & Carlson, E. A. (2009) Conceptualizing the role of early experience: Lessons from the Minnesota longitudinal study. *Developmental Review, 30*, 36–51.

Stouffer, S. A. et al. (1949). *The American Soldier: Combat and its aftermath, Vol. 2: Studies in Social Psychology in World War II*. Princeton University Press.

Thompson, R. A. (2015). Relationships, regulation, and early development. In R. M. Lerner (Ed.) *Handbook of Child Psychology and Developmental Science, Vol. 3: Social and Emotional Development* (7th ed., pp. 201–246). New York: Wiley.

Tottenham, N. & Sheridan, M. A. (2010). A review of adversity, the amygdala, and the hippocampus: a consideration of developmental timing. *Frontiers in Human Neuroscience, 3*, Article 68, 1–18.

Ursache, A., Blair, C., & Raver, C. C. (2012). The promotion of self-regulation as a means of enhancing school readiness and early achievement in children at risk for school failure. *Child Development Perspectives, 6*(2), 122–128.

Vernon-Feagans, L., Cox, M., & The Family Life Project Key Investigators. (2013). The Family Life Project: An epidemiological and developmental study of young children living in poor rural communities. *Society for Research in Child Development Monographs, 78*(5), 1–150.

Votruba-Drzal, E. (2006). Economic disparities in middle childhood development: Does income matter? *Developmental Psychology, 42*(6), 1154–1167.

Wilson, W. J. (1987). *The Truly Disadvantaged: The inner city, the underclass, and public policy*. Chicago: University of Chicago Press.

Waller, W. W. (1940). *War and the Family*. New York: Dryden Press.

3   Entering Adulthood in the Great Recession: A Tale of Three Countries

Ingrid Schoon and John Bynner

Young people on the cusp of independent adulthood are entering a make-or-break period in their lives in which external shocks have the potential to create diverging destinies. Such an external shock occurred in 2007/8 when a global economic downturn devastated the world financial markets as well as the banking and real estate industries, producing a tidal wave of economic consequences for employment and living standards that have rightly come to be described as the "Great Recession" (Bell & Blanchflower, 2011).

Although the Great Recession officially ended ten years ago, its impact is still affecting the opportunities and life chances of young people. In particular, there might be long-term scaring effects, i.e., long-term effects of not making a successful transition into paid employment, especially if conditions for young people do not improve. Employment opportunities have dramatically declined in the aftermath of the recession, and compared to older workers young people (aged 16 to 24 years) were hit especially hard. In 2017 the global youth unemployment rate was 13.1 percent – the same as at the crisis peak in 2011 and 2013, despite a slight recovery between 2014–2016 (ILO, 2017). There are, however, considerable variations in youth unemployment across countries, pointing to the crucial role of institutional leverage in buffering the recession effects. Figure 3.1 gives the trends in youth unemployment between 2000 and 2017 for the USA, the UK, Germany, Europe, and OECD average. It also shows the time lag in response.

While the overall effects of the Great Recession on employment outcomes are well documented (Bell & Blanchflower, 2011; Danzinger, 2013) there has been less attention to variations within and between countries and the diverse challenges and opportunities facing young people in navigating a changing social context. In this chapter we consider these variations in more detail, reviewing evidence collected for a three country study assessing the impact of the 2007/8 recession on young people coming of age in the UK, the USA, and in Germany (Schoon & Bynner, 2017). We adopt a life course perspective asking to what extent

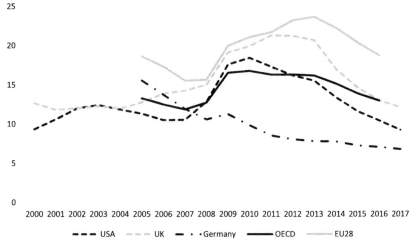

Figure 3.1 Youth unemployment rate (age 16–24) in OECD countries between 2000 and 2017
Source: OECD Data (2018)

the changing socio-cultural conditions influence young people's lives. In particular we ask whether the recession has transformed or merely accelerated pre-existing trends towards prolonged youth transitions, and examine variations in how societal institutions have responded in trying to support young people making the transition from school to work.

The choice of countries was motivated by their shared status as developed economies with distinctive features of their labor markets – contrasting the neo-liberal deregulatory framework of the US and Britain with the corporatist and socially protective framework of Germany. This differentiation is reflected further in the quite different cultural assumptions and institutional structures for managing youth transitions, ranging from a focus on high school graduation in the US, multiple pathways in Britain, to the occupation- and employment-focused apprenticeship system of Germany.

Another important factor was the existence of comparable national household panels and other longitudinal datasets supplying the evidence base on which to found enquiry. The use of longitudinal data from a range of cross-national sources is central to the research undertaken. In particular, the findings stem from data collected for the household panel studies in the UK (British Household Panel Study and the UK Household Longitudinal Study), the USA (Panel Study of Income Dynamics), and Germany (German Socio-Economic Panel Study), as well as national longitudinal cohort studies, including the US National Longitudinal Study of Youth, the US Monitoring the Future, and the European Union Statistics on Income and Living Conditions. Using longitudinal data enabled the comparison of youth transitions before and after the onset of the 2007/8 Great Recession, contrasting the experiences of different age cohorts.

The 2007/8 Great Recession: A Global Crisis

The 2007/8 Great Recession started in the USA with the Lehman Brothers filing for bankruptcy, followed by the collapse of the housing market then much of the rest of the investment banking system. It was characterized by large market losses and drops in employment and wealth (Grusky, Western, & Wimer, 2012) spreading globally as countries interconnected national banking systems collapsed and governments were compelled to draw on taxation revenue to shore them up. Despite these measures, the recession was unavoidable.

Although the USA faced only a moderate decrease in GDP, unemployment increased, reaching an exceptionally high level, especially among young people. However, mainly through the continued injection of large quantities of public funding, euphemistically called "quantitative easing," recovery was achieved and has been maintained since. The price to be paid was austerity budgeting achieved by cuts in government spending and much tougher labor market conditions, the brunt of which were experienced by young people – especially when confronting entry to the labor market.

In contrast, Germany was slower to enter into, and quicker to emerge, from the Great Recession, reflecting its stable banking and housing sectors and more socially protective labor market. At the time of the 2007/8 downturn Germany saw a strong, but short decline in GDP, with unemployment rates even falling below the pre-recession level after a quick economic recovery. However, during the past 20 years Germany has experienced the strongest increase in economic inequality and poverty among the Organisation for Economic Development countries (Groh-Samberg, 2007; OECD, 2008). This was chiefly because of the sharp increase in low-wage and precarious employment since the mid- to late 1990s, especially among young people (e.g., Carlin & Soskice, 2009), and through labor market de-regulation and introduction of welfare reforms during 2004/5 (Blossfeld, 2017; Groh-Samberg & Wise, 2017) following the fall of the Berlin Wall in 1989 and German reunification.

Britain stands in between, with a similar strong recession-produced decline in GDP, but slower recovery than in Germany. Because of its relatively weak employment regulations, the labor market in Britain reacted rapidly to the economic crisis: the unemployment rate rose sharply within a few months and there was an even steeper increase in the 'underemployment' rate, where a person wants to work more hours than is stated under their current employment contract (Walling & Clancy, 2010), or where a highly skilled person is working in low paying or low skill jobs. Countering this trend, since 2013 the economy has been recovering – but because of the reliance on such areas as housing, the recovery's sustainability has been questioned (see Ashton, 2017). Moreover, as in Germany there has been an increase in self-employment, which accounts for nearly three quarters of the overall growth in employment since 2008 (D'Arcy & Gardiner, 2014), insecure jobs including major expansion of "zero hours contracts" and the growth of precarious employment (Bloodworth, 2018; Standing, 2011).

A Life Course Approach

Inspired by Glen Elder's seminal work on *Children of the Great Depression* we set out to learn from obvious parallels between the economic catastrophe of the 1930s and the 2007/8 banking crisis and "Great Recession" that followed (Schoon & Bynner, 2017). Accordingly a life course approach was adopted. Key themes of life course research comprise the role of historical time, socio-cultural influences, the timing of events, the importance of social relationships, and individual agency (Elder, Shanahan, & Jennings, 2015). Human lives are understood to be shaped by ongoing interactions between a developing individual and a changing socio-historical context and are embedded within specific geographical locations characterized by distinct socio-cultural conditions, institutional regulations, and policies. We thus embarked on the comparative analysis of how the socio-historical and cultural context shape individual experiences of young people making the transition to independent adulthood.

Within a life course approach the transition to adulthood can be considered as a status passage in the institutionalized life course (Shanahan, 2000). It involves multiple and inter-related social role changes across the "big five" role transitions, i.e., completion of full-time education, entry into paid employment, leaving the parental home, and the step into family formation and parenthood (Settersten, 2007). Transitions are embedded in longer-term social trajectories, which give them meaning and a distinctive direction (Elder et al., 2015).

The transition to adulthood is guided by age-related legal norms such as minimum school leaving, working hours restrictions and age at marriage, as well as population-based norms and informal expectations regarding appropriate ages for the completion of education, leaving the family home and becoming a parent, and the sequencing and combination of these roles (Billari & Liefbroer, 2010; Buchmann & Kriesi, 2011; Neugarten, 1996). These norms and expectations, or "scripts of life" (Buchmann, 1989), can vary by gender, ethnicity, and social class – they vary by cultural contexts and are also highly responsive to social change. For example, in Germany compulsory school leaving age is 18 and the minimum employment age is 15; in the USA compulsory school leaving age and employment age varies by individual states; in the UK compulsory school leaving age was 16 until 2012. England and Wales raised the compulsory engagement in education age from age 16 to age 17 in 2013 and to age 18 in 2015 to render young people more competitive in the global labor market. In addition, there are country-specific variations in how access to and progression through the education system and into the labor market are regulated by institutions, and to what extent young people are protected from the effects of a global financial melt-down. We will discuss these variations in more detail later. For now, we note that to fully comprehend the multiple influences shaping young people's lives it is necessary to consider the historical and contextual circumstances during which the transition is made, where it takes place (cultural factors), and timing effects, for example, the age at which the recession was experienced.

Lives are lived in a changing social context. In our analysis we investigated current challenges and trends, contrasting them with pre-existing, longer-term trends. For example, the trend towards extended transitions arose in the 1970s as a result of labor market transformations and increasing demand for skilled labor, resulting in extended education participation coupled with prolonged dependency on family resources (Ashton & Bynner, 2011; Bynner, 2001; Furlong & Cartmel, 2007; Jones, 2009b; Settersten & Ray, 2010; Shanahan, 2000). In our analysis, we thus aimed to separate out the "crisis effects" of the current recession from pre-existing trends towards a prolonged entry into adulthood. A key question in this context is whether the Great Recession did speed up or slow down present trends towards a general prolongation of youth transitions. To answer this question it was necessary to draw on longitudinal data, comparing experiences of different age cohorts making the transition to adulthood before and after the onset of the 2007/8 Great Recession. In particular we focused on different age cohorts reaching adulthood between 2000 and 2012, following their development over time. The analysis covered a wide age range (ages 16 to 35 years), including those who were in their teens and early 20s when the recession hit, as well as those who were in their mid-20s at the onset of the recession.

We also took into account age-dependent influences. In Glen Elder's pioneering study the long-time effects of the Great Depression were less severe for young men who were already adolescents when the Great Depression hit, compared to those who were still children. The older boys were already involved in adult life-tasks within the family economy and did aspire to become autonomous adults, while younger boys were less hopeful, less self-directed and less confident about their future. Likewise, in the more recent study (Schoon & Bynner, 2017) we noted that the timing of the recession effects mattered. For example, while younger cohorts experienced increased difficulties in gaining entry to the labor market, older cohorts were at an increased risk of insecure and temporary employment. However, while the psychological well-being of adolescents appeared to be relatively unaffected by the Great Recession (Pförtner, Elgar, Rathmann, & Richter, 2017), older cohorts (aged 18 to 25) were more vulnerable to its psychological impact (Cavanagh, 2017). Our findings thus suggest a shift in the critical time window with younger children maybe being better protected by their families or institutional structures than young adults.

In the following we summarize what we have learned from the comparison of country-specific experiences of young people before and after the 2007/8 Recession. We discuss the evidence in the light of key themes of contemporary youth research and point to intersections with life course theory, focusing on socio-cultural aspects and temporal patterns in youth transitions. We then consider the role of social institutions in buffering the effects of the economic downturn and discuss implications of our findings for policies directed at young people in times of a rapidly changing social world.

Youth Transitions in Times of Social Change

The social context plays a crucial role in shaping the lives of young people, influencing the opportunities and challenges they are facing. Moreover, the transition to adulthood is set in a changing socio-historical context, which includes newly emerging structural forces impacting on and contributing to variations in individual life courses. Key processes describing the linkages of individual lives to a changing social context are conceptualized in terms of (de)standardization, individualization, stratification, and precaritization, which we consider next.

De-standardization of Youth Transitions

It has been argued that since the 1970s transitions into adulthood have become de-standardized, i.e., more variable and protracted, and less uniform (Beck, 1992; Buchmann, 1989; Giddens, 1991). De-standardization refers to the timing and the sequencing in which youth transitions tend to occur (Buchmann & Kriesi, 2011; Macmillan, 2005; Shanahan, 2000). Up to the 1960s transition experiences of young people have been characterized by a normative linear timetable of events, characterized by completion of full-time education, entry into the labor market, partnership formation, and parenthood (Buchmann, 1989; Neugarten, 1996), although some authors have doubted whether post-war transitions were as straightforward as the argument suggests (Goodwin & O'Connor, 2005).

Empirical evidence suggests that since the early 1970s the average age of leaving full-time education and entering primary employment has been pushed back from the late teens to the middle 20s in most Western societies – with consequences for the achievement of other adult statuses including traditional markers of adulthood such as long term partnership commitments, marriage, and parenthood, which are now commonly postponed to the late 20s and even the early 30s (Billari & Liefbroer, 2010; Buchmann & Kriesi, 2011; Shanahan, 2000). Delay in the timing of one transition impacts on the timing of others, reflecting path dependency of transitions. For example, between 1970 and 1998/2000 the mean age at first birth in the UK increased from 24.7 to 27.2 years (Neels, Murphy, NíBhrolcháin, & Beaujouan, 2017), and in the USA from 21.4 to 24.9 years (Mathews & Brady, 2002). In the UK about 27 percent of this change can be accounted for by the increase in time spent in education (Neels et al., 2017).

Moreover, transitions have become more variable and complex in form, as for example reflected in the "uncoupling," or increasing disassociation of transitions, such as the linkage between marriage and fertility, the increasing proportion of births to non-married parents and a greater incidence of partnership formation not associated with family formation (Billari & Liefbroer, 2010; Kiernan, 2008; Lyons-Amos & Schoon, 2017).

More generally, employment opportunities in most Western countries have changed considerably since the 1970s, following the introduction of new technologies, the disappearance of manual jobs especially in manufacturing, and the increasing participation of women in higher education and in the labor market (Blossfeld, Klijzing, Mills, & Kurz, 2005;

Müller & Gangl, 2003; Schoon & Silbereisen, 2009). Furthermore in most developed countries, fueled by technological transformation and the collapse of manufacturing employment there has been a growth of white collar, high tech, and service jobs accompanied by a "deskilling" of many of those employed in what had been until then skilled occupations. Currently there are increasing concerns regarding advances in automation and digitalization and the risk that a substantial share of jobs is at risk of computerization, with low qualified workers likely to carry the brunt of the adjustment costs leading to rising inequality (Arntz, Gregory, & Zierahn, 2016).

Other major features of the new labor market included a growing proportion of full-time employees with fixed-term, temporary, and zero hour contracts and a shift towards more precarious working arrangements and low pay (Ashton, 2017; Bloodworth, 2018; Standing, 2011), arising from increased outsourcing of jobs such as cleaning and care work to private agencies. Young people have been hit particularly hard by these changes, as unemployment and flexible employment among the young (i.e., 16- to 24-year-olds) was generally higher than average (Blossfeld et al., 2005; Furlong & Cartmel, 1997; Schoon & Silbereisen, 2009; Settersten, Furstenberg, & Rumbaut, 2005).

For young people this means that it takes longer to achieve financial autonomy and prolonged dependence on their parents for support (Wightman., Schoeni, Patrick, & Schulenberg, 2017). Configurations of young adult statuses lacking full financial autonomy and independence challenge the very basis of adult identity as traditionally understood – "citizenship by proxy" as Jones and Wallace (1992) described it. Moreover, transitions became increasingly reversible indicating a shift from linear passages to yo-yo movements (Walther, 2009), such as returning to education after early school leaving, or moving back in with one's parents when employment prospects faltered (especially relevant for young men).

The findings from our three-country study suggests that the impact of the Great Recession on the timing and sequencing of youth transitions was less transformative than reinforcing pre-existing trends towards extended and more complex transitions. For example, using data from multiple age cohorts of young adults participating in the US National Longitudinal Study of Youth 79-Young Adult cohort, Crosnoe & Smith (2017) show that transitions into new social roles have slowed down during the Great Recession, with higher education enrolment being the least affected and family formation the most affected status (see also Lyons-Amos & Schoon, 2017).

The findings thus suggest a defensive strategy with persisting levels of education enrolment even when the labor market deteriorates. This is in accordance with the "substitution effect" argument, i.e., that long-term investments in education are assumed to be stimulated or maintained by a current shortage of (well-paid) jobs (Crosnoe & Smith, 2017; Mont'Alva, Mortimer, & Kirkpatrick Johnson, 2017). However, participation in full-time education among 16- to 25-year-olds across Europe and the USA increased only slightly, suggesting that for some young people the reduction of both state and family budgets made it more difficult to stay on in education, which would be in line with the "income effect" argument, i.e., short-term needs are assumed to surpass long-term investments (such as participating in extended education), especially among the more disadvantaged. The findings presented by Crosnoe and Smith (2017), and Lyons-Amos and Schoon (2017) supply evidence supporting both effects (income versus substitution), depending on social location, with a greater tendency towards substitution effects among those from a relative advantaged background and income effects more common among the more disadvantaged youths.

In addition, the link between educational credentials and labor market outcomes has loosened (Green & Pensiero, 2017) and young people, including graduates, need longer to find employment (Blossfeld, 2017; Iacovou, 2017). However, young people with a degree-level qualification were generally more likely to secure jobs and to earn more than those without them (Blossfeld, 2017; Vuolo, Mortimer, & Staff, 2016; Wightman et al., 2017). Generally, the findings suggest that the percentage of young people in full-time employment decreased, and the rate of unemployment or the experience of not being in education, employment, or training (NEET) increased (Crosnoe & Smith, 2017; Groh-Samberg & Wise, 2017; Iacovou, 2017; Schoon & Lyons-Amos, 2016), pointing to more precarious employment opportunities. In addition, in the USA most of the traditional (mainly part-time) teenage jobs had vanished and the number of job starters with fixed term contracts had increased (Staff, Ramirez, & Cundiff, 2017). Reduced employment opportunities, in turn, were associated with postponement of child-bearing, suggesting a reduced desire to commit to life-altering and non-reversible transitions in times of economic uncertainty (Crosnoe & Smith, 2017; Lyons-Amos & Schoon, 2017).

In interpreting these findings, one has to take into account that there are significant variations in these patterns by social background, highlighting the importance of disentangling aggregate statistics. For instance, those enrolled in education may also be economically active; in particular those from less privileged backgrounds, and therefore may be classified as either employed or unemployed (Bell & Blanchflower, 2011). Moreover, the identification of NEET often also confusingly includes young mothers, apparently denying that caring for small children can be an occupation in its own right. In addition, the recession effects were not homogeneous across outcomes, and depended on constellations of achieved adult status positions a person had already achieved, prior transitions experiences, and challenges and opportunities in the wider socio-historical context.

Individualization and "Bounded" Agency

The observation of the de-standardization and diversification of transition experiences has led to the assumption of an increasing individualization of youth transitions. Indeed the terms de-standardization and individualization are often used interchangeably. Yet, while de-standardization refers to the demographic component of social change, individualization concerns its ideational aspect (Brückner & Mayer, 2005). The phenomenon of individualization, first formulated in Ulrich Beck's 1986 book *Risk Society* (English translation first published in 1992), is based on the hypothesis that since the 1970s individual behavior has become less bound by traditional norms and values and sources of collective identity such as class, gender, and ethnicity. Instead, Beck argued that life is increasingly a "reflexive" or self-steered phenomenon, governed by risks that have to be circumvented; that is to say "something you must largely accomplish yourself." The life course is thus considered more of a "project" that individuals themselves construct, i.e., an expression of their individual agency.

The assertion that individuals are now free to choose their destination has, however, been questioned, as there is persisting evidence of unequal access to educational and career opportunities (Bynner, 2001; Furlong & Cartmel, 2007; Heinz, 2009; Schoon & Lyons-Amos, 2016). Social change has affected all young people – but not all in the same way. There is a differentiation of transition pathways across different social groups in the population, and the preparation for adulthood has been elongated, especially for those who can afford to invest in their education. The notion of "structured" or "bounded" agency stresses the interaction between individual agency and social structure as a basis for understanding young people's current situation (Evans, 2002; Furlong & Cartmel, 2007; Shanahan, 2000). For example, young women's destinations in the labor market compared with those of young men may reflect both individual choices (agency) and discrimination against women in the job opportunities open to them (structure), with significant shifts between cohorts. In other words, individualization (and de-standardization for that matter) is contextualized by the persistent variations in social background, age, gender, and migration status that accompany it.

Social stratification adds to the contextualization of individualization, describing structurally driven patterns of inequality within and between different age cohorts and their consequences for life course outcomes (Elder et al., 2015). In the broadest sense, stratification refers to any differentiation of a population into groups sharing common characteristics, which may also reflect power, hierarchy, and inequality. Social class, education, gender, locality (including country), ethnicity, religion, and disability are the most obvious stratifiers. For example, young people from relatively privileged backgrounds and high status socioeconomic backgrounds tend to have more ambitious education and career aspirations than their less privileged peers and are more likely to embark on extended transitions, marked by participation in higher education and delayed entry into employment and family formation (Crosnoe & Smith, 2017; Mortimer, Kirkpatrick Johnson, & Mont'Alva, 2017; Schoon & Lyons-Amos, 2016, 2017). They are also more likely to attend highly selective colleges and universities, enhancing their employment prospects. In contrast, less privileged young people are more work-oriented and likely to experience the traditional accelerated transition, characterized by early school leaving, precipitate labor market participation, and early family formation. There are, however, variations in the timing of transitions by country, as shown by Iacovou (2017), Crosnoe and Smith (2017), Groh-Samberg and Wise (2017), and Blossfeld (2017), with relatively protracted youth transitions in Germany and the USA and accelerated transitions in the UK. This points to the importance of institutional leverage, which we will discuss later.

The findings of our three-country study suggest that structural constraints, such as economic turbulence and hardship can undermine achievement orientation of young people, their intrinsic motivation, and work values (Mortimer, Zhang, Hussemann, & Wu, 2014; Mortimer et al., 2017; Schoon, 2014), and increased feelings of uncertainty. For example, there is a focus on short-term projects and solutions instead of medium to long-term planning and delayed gratification (Leccardi, 2017). However, young people reacted to the experience of economic hardship in different ways, depending on their parents' education and history of unemployment, as well as parents' own achievement-related attitudes (Mortimer et al., 2017). This suggests that parents' resources can to some extent protect their children from the risks of economic troubles many years later.

Moreover, young people in northern European countries, where the welfare state still provides significant support, were considerably more optimistic and had a more positive outlook to the future than those in southern Europe, which provides little support for young people

(Leccardi, 2017). The study by Leccardi also shows that young people in the US likewise tend to be more optimistic and hang onto the idea of the "American Dream," in their case, however based on their considerable confidence in meritocratic principles, i.e., the belief that they can make it given their skill and effort (see also Shane & Heckhausen, 2017).

The findings suggest that individual response to economic adversity depends to a large degree on family socio-economic resources, available institutional support and cultural values. However, even in situations of grave economic hardship young people try to maintain efforts to exert control over their lives. There is evidence of resilience and the experience of adversity was countered by many young people with a sense of optimism that opportunities were available or would emerge in the future (Leccardi, 2017). This included the anticipation of a fulfilling life achieved in other ways besides that of the traditional occupational career, or moving to another country in search of better prospects.

Young people are not passively exposed to external events and strive to be in charge of their own destiny. They are guided by the assumption that a better life is possible and that individual efforts and capabilities will be rewarded. However, the findings also suggest disillusion with government performance, in particular among young people in countries with the highest levels of youth unemployment (Janmaat, 2017). This more critical evaluation is also reflected in the growing concern that the American Dream is evaporating (Putnam, 2015) and that it is becoming increasingly more difficult for young people to achieve their ambitions of moving up the social ladder, or even to maintain their status. Indeed, current cohorts of young people are more likely to experience downward social mobility than previous cohorts, i.e., they will not achieve the same relative social position as their parents (Goldthorpe, 2016).

Precaritization and the Marginalization of Young Workers

The issue of precaritization takes stratification and individualization a stage further by pointing to the emergence of new relationships with the labor market for a growing "marginalized" minority spanning traditional class and education levels. The change is reflected in the growth of temporary poorly paid casual employment, "zero-hour" contracts and internships, a "gig economy" characterized by short term contracts, shift work, and lack of workers' basic rights such as cover for illness or holidays. Beset continually by income and other forms of insecurity, such individuals are largely bypassed by the traditional means of achieving solidarity and support through others in the same situation by mechanisms such as occupational identity or trade union membership. As Standing (2011) argues, for this group entry to employment bears no semblance to beginning a career – it is more a means of survival by accepting anything the labor market offers.

Our findings demonstrate increasing precaritization, i.e., a growing section of the youth population encountered low paid temporary jobs and unemployment and difficulties in making key transitions, heightening the risk of exclusion from prospects in the mainstream economy (Blossfeld, 2017; Green & Pensiero, 2017; Groh-Samberg & Wise, 2017; Wightman et al., 2017). Such a trend, though longstanding, was intensified by the Great Recession.

A particularly striking feature of precarious and potentially exploitative employment, is its growing presence in all countries (Bloodworth, 2018; Standing 2016). The apparent success of Germany in staving off, with the help of legislation, unemployment during and after the Great Recession, was bought at the price of job protection for the "insider" section of the workforce, i.e., those with permanent employment contracts (Blossfeld, 2017; Groh-Samberg & Wise, 2017). At the same time the "outsider" section, i.e., the unemployed and temporary workers, comprising in large numbers the poorly qualified, often minorities and immigrants, swelled the ranks of the precariat. This trend is also reflected in the increasing number of young people being "not in education, employment or training" (NEET), especially in younger cohorts (Groh-Samberg & Wise, 2017; Schoon & Lyons-Amos, 2016) who are at an increased risk of entering the precariat. Such individuals tend to leave education at the minimum age, usually without any or only low level qualifications and then, subsequently, spend a significant proportion of their time occupationally inactive. NEET status may of course be a voluntary lifestyle choice among those who could continue education or vocational preparation but choose not to. Most frequently, however, NEET signals the manifestation of a "trajectory of disadvantage" (Bynner & Parsons, 2002, 2007) to which the Great Recession added reinforcement.

Moreover, precariat status has spread increasingly from the mainly traditional working class unskilled segment of the workforce where it began (Standing, 2011). It can now be found across the educational achievement spectrum to the middle reaches of the skilled manual and non-manual sectors and even the graduate sector. Hence the Great Recession had a significant role in contributing to the growth of the precariat.

The Role of Social Institutions

There are considerable national variations in the extent to which young people were affected by the economic changes, pointing to the crucial role of social institutions and variations in "institutional filters" regulating and channelling access to education and to the labor market (Ashton, 2017; Green & Pensiero, 2017; Iacovou, 2017). Social institutions are a key factor in managing the transition from school to work and in buffering the effects of economic shocks at labor market entry. National policies, educational institutions, and labor market regulations did make a big difference in the way the Great Recession affected youth transitions (Ashton, 2017; Mont'Alvao et al., 2017; Green & Pensiero, 2017; Groh-Samberg & Wise, 2017).

Transition Systems

The origins of concurrent trends lay in the technological transformation of industry and globalization and their implications for the nature of work and the occupational structure (Ashton, 2017). In response to the changing opportunity structures, college and university enrollment has increased, driven by the expectation shared by young people and their parents that a college degree is the prerequisite for a career or at least for securing employment in the knowledge economy (Schoon & Mortimer, 2017). Public opinion, business, and governments also subscribe to the belief that a higher education certificate or degree will protect against precarious life course transitions (Putnam, 2015). There are, however, considerable variations across countries in how this protection is realized – which we examine next.

In the USA the transition pathways are largely defined by an education system with a substantial segment of private providers, a flexible labor market, and failed national programs for improving vocational and technical training (Ashton, 2017). The guiding belief is that individuals are responsible for their career decisions and have to accumulate the necessary resources for managing life course transitions *(individualization)*. The young people who do not succeed in their transition to the labor market tend to be regarded as low achievers, lacking initiative, and the requisite skills. This belief contributes to neglecting the economic and political causes of a failing transition system for the lower class, concentrated in the US case among African-American and Hispanic youth, a disproportionate number of whom, compared with other G12 countries, are incarcerated (Carson, 2014).

The policy principle under which the whole system operates is that the state provides a framework ostensibly of equal opportunity and does not compensate for individual resource deficits. Moreover, rather than boost state institutions to help young people withstand the recession's damaging effects on the transition process, the response was reduced state funding for them and increased tuition fees, mitigated to a small degree by federal support for low-income students (loans and grants). As argued by Danzinger (2013) in a *Special Issue* of the *Annals of the American Academy for Political and Social Science*, the focus was on relieving, in the adult population, severe poverty, hunger, and on providing shelter and income through tax measures. In consequence, more high school graduates opted for the less expensive community college degree, a shorter two-year or three year program and better connections with the local/regional employers than the university four-year degree. For low-income high school graduates the decision to take this pathway can be seen as a considered reaction to the long-term trend of a vanishing youth labor market which, as Staff et al. (2017) point out, used to be a way of gaining work experience, to acquire social skills, and build connections with potential employers. The jobs that used to be available to teenagers increasingly became the only means of employment for young adults whose needs gave priority access to them. As the contributions by Crosnoe and Smith (2017) and Mont'Avalo et al. (2017) suggest, the Great Recession did not dramatically change this situation, but at the same time the high school curriculum became more demanding and more young people entered the post-high school academic route.

The UK (with distinctive variations in Scotland) is characterized by a centralized education system, a deregulated labor market with a large segment of low-skilled and non-standard jobs, and chequered attempts to establish a vocational training system (Wolf, 2011, 2016). The long standing tradition of five-year apprenticeships in mostly male-dominated occupations, such as the various branches of engineering, was dismissed as "time serving" by the Thatcher government of the 1980s. Such apprenticeships were replaced first by "youth training schemes" and then by "The New Modern Apprenticeship" comprising a one-year (foundation) and a three-year (advanced) apprenticeship directed at all school leavers. Accreditation was offered at different levels through the new National Vocational Qualifications (NVQs). More recently, maybe as a response to the Great Recession and/or the increased compulsory education leaving age (which was raised from age 16 to 17 in 2013 and to 18 in 2015), government policy was directed at building the apprenticeship system further, including an increase in the number of certification levels and training hours. Indeed, a new "T-level" system, which will be implemented in 2019, intends to overhaul how technical education is taught and administered, aiming to put vocational training on an equal footing with academic work – and improve Britain's levels of productivity, which currently lag behind the United States and Germany.

Currently the UK apprenticeship system attracts well below one-fifth of the age cohort aged 18 or younger, while half of the new apprentices are in fact in their early 20s. However, the poor quality of much of the work-based training available to teenagers, and low credibility of the certification arising from it, has yet to convince employers and families that apprenticeship is a high value alternative to staying on in education (Wolf, 2011, 2016). For young people not planning to go to university the Further Education (FE) colleges provide the main post compulsory education route for gaining vocational qualifications or making good previous poor school performance by also offering an alternative route to academic qualifications needed for going to university. But more generally, as in the USA, young people and parents do not regard a vocational training pathway as a promising option, nor it seems does the government. There were cuts in public funding of the Further Education Colleges and major increases of university tuition fees.

In Germany the diverse education and training (VET) institutions are a component of a social market economy that includes free education. Governance is achieved through a "social partnership" comprising local government, employers' organizations, and trade unions in maintaining and reforming the apprenticeship pathway, with a direct link to the employment system. The system resides in a strongly established "training culture" targeted at supplying an occupational identity to trainees and providing the basis of employability and citizenship in the German state.

Unlike the comprehensive secondary education system prevalent in the USA and the UK, the German educational system is highly structured, involving basically a three-class system that divides students into three different career tracks: (1) *Gymnasium* for students headed for university, (2) *Realschule* for students headed for white-collar positions, and (3) *Hauptschule* for the bottom tier, generally aimed at the trades and blue-collar jobs. By the age of 10 most pupils in Germany are selected into one of these three educational tracks. Students on the vocational track generally attend a Berufsschule, which combines academic study with an apprenticeship (Dual System), and usually offers a two- or three-year course of study. For those who were unsuccessful in obtaining an apprenticeship or who dropped out (up to 10 percent of the youth population), there is the option to enter the state-funded "transition system," which provides training in preparation for entering an apprenticeship. These places do not lead to vocational certification and are generally filled by those with the lowest school-leaving certificate from the Hauptschule, those with no qualifications, and those from migration backgrounds.

At the other end of the educational spectrum, there is – in addition to traditional Bachelor's, Master's, and state examination degree programs – the option to combine a degree program with vocational training (Dual Studies). Dual Study programs include a component of practical experience, and students have to sign a contract with a company. The training then usually takes place at two separate locations: on the company's premises and at the higher education institution. Successful graduates of both the vocational and the Dual Studies training program are certified in a certain trade or industrial field, facilitating a relatively smooth school to work transition into specific occupations. Enrollment to Dual Studies and universities has been growing in the past decade, as a response to the employment uncertainty created by the Great Recession.

Germany has been building its Dual System of vocational training for more than a century and has maintained its institutional set-up across changes of government. Although the system is still popular, there are a growing number of upper level school graduates who opt for university studies and the upper occupational segments of the labor market instead. The attractiveness of varied education and training (VET) in the crafts and manufacturing is declining and there is a move towards high-end apprenticeships in business and IT. Moreover, as Blossfeld (2017) shows, the Great Recession prolonged the duration of young people's job search in Germany: before the Great Recession 40 percent found a job within two months; afterwards only 25 percent did so. Yet, generally young people in Germany were more likely to avoid experiences of unemployment than those coming of age in the US, the UK, or the OECD average (see Figure 3.1).

In summary, the findings suggest that characteristics of the transition system played a crucial role in mediating the effects of the economic downturn. The institutional mechanisms that young people can use to improve their starting position in the competition for good jobs and a successful transition to independent adulthood have been stabilized in Germany by policy initiatives that sustain employment. For example, during the economic downturn the state-funded apprenticeship and transition system provided a shelter from unemployment. In addition the German government reduced employee and employer unemployment insurance, subsidized short-time working, increased staffing in the public employment service and provided funding for training (Ashton, 2017; Groh-Samberg & Wise, 2017). Employers hung on to their skilled workers, which included those who had already enrolled in apprenticeships or Dual studies. Crucially the findings suggest that close links between the education system and employers facilitated a relative smooth transition into the labor market. In the USA and the UK, in contrast, successful labor market integration for young adults is limited by market forces.

Welfare Regimes and Family Support

The impact of economic instability and uncertainty on young people's lives is significantly influenced by the welfare state. Modern countries have created different welfare regimes that imply different national ideologies about social solidarity, i.e., the degree to which individuals, or families, can uphold a socially acceptable standard of living independently of market participation (Esping-Anderson, 1990). While the USA and the UK are generally viewed as a liberal welfare regime, Germany is often identified as an example of a corporatist or conservative welfare regime (Blossfeld et al., 2005). Liberal welfare regimes are characterized by passive labor-market policies, moderate support for underprivileged people, and relatively limited public-sector employment. The liberal welfare states are built on the idea that a free market allows individuals to realize their potential, regardless of the pre-existing social hierarchies. Corporatist welfare regimes, such as in Germany, in contrast, are concerned with maintaining order and status. They are not so much designed to promote employment opportunities, job mobility, and full employment, but aim to ensure that workers who leave employment because of job loss, disability or due to early retirement are protected against serious decline in living standards. They provide relatively more generous benefits based upon principles of insurance contributions, i.e., benefits are linked to the contributions paid by wage-earners to the national insurance schemes, thereby preserving pre-existing status differentials in society. Whereas liberal regimes exhibit more inequality with respect to indicators such as income, Gini co-efficient or housing patterns, they are more socially inclusive than corporatist regimes regarding educational participation and post-primary completion rates (Beblavý, Thum, & Veselkova, 2011).

In response to the Great Recession, costly bank bailouts, tax cuts, and other stimulus measures drained the public purse, resulting in drastic austerity measures. For example, in both the USA and the UK, the contraction of state budgets led to a decrease in state financial support for public and non-profit institutions, which in turn, led to higher tuition fees for students (Mont'Alva et al., 2017). In the USA, spending on the main social safety net programs, including means-tested and social insurance programs, increased during the Great Recession, but was focused on relieving severe poverty, hunger, and homelessness in the adult population (Danzinger, 2013). This was, however, associated with the danger of increased inequality at the bottom end of the income distribution and enhanced risks for long-term unemployment. Regarding support for young people, there was a shift in funding sources from state subsidies to federally funded loans and grants as well as private payments from students and their families. For example, the federal funded Pell grant program, designed to support low-income students through college, became more widely available (Mont'Alva et al., 2017), buffering against increasing tuition costs and helping to increase enrolment.

In the UK, universities had to absorb a 40 percent cut to their budgets, leading to an unprecedented increase in university tuition fees in England, rising from about £3000 to £9000 per year since 2012. In addition, the Employment and Support Allowance (income-replacement benefit for individuals unable to work because of a health condition or disability based on national insurance contributions) has been shortened. Young recipients can no longer renew their claims after one year, and special contribution mechanisms for young people have been removed (van Kersbergen, Vis, & Hemerijck, 2012). Moreover, those younger than 20 (or under 25 if in education or training) can no longer access the Employment Support Allowance without meeting contribution conditions. Moreover, the 2012 Welfare Reform Act replaces various means-tested benefits with a new Universal Credit, which introduces a maximum cap to the amounts that can be received from benefits, and cuts to several benefits, including the Disability Living Allowance.

In Germany, austerity measures were less severe, and participation in higher education is free or involves minimal contributions. However, the limited-term supplementary unemployment benefit for students has been removed, and generally welfare costs are contained by implementing existing rules more strictly. It has, however, to be kept in mind, that Germany had already introduced major reforms of its social welfare system in 2004/5 as a response to socio-economic pressures arising from the German reunification, which included high levels of unemployment (Blossfeld, 2017; Groh-Samberg & Wise, 2017).

Generally, at a time of reduced public financial assistance there is the expectation that parents will carry the additional burden and support their children in the transition to independent adulthood. Young people need the support of their parents if they are to achieve in education and employment. Evidence from the US suggests, that the financial support that parents provided to their children did fall on average during the Great Recession (similar to past recessions), but nonetheless remained responsive to young people's needs (Wightman et al., 2017). Indeed, intergenerational solidarity increased with the trend towards prolonged postsecondary education enrolment – which requires paying tuition fees. At a time of reduced public financial assistance, family support was seen as the vital means of economic survival and coping with ever escalating inflation of prices, especially regarding tuition fees and increasing housing costs. There are, however, also many young people who do not have access to family based financial resources and support.

Moreover, there is no legislation or generally accepted legal framework regarding the timeframe for parental responsibility (Jones, 2009). Belief systems, i.e., parental support for extended education, rather than legal frameworks act as a resource to help families to negotiate matters of dependence and support. However, there is a social cost associated with the assumption that there is a consensus about the value of extended education and parental obligation. Increased hardship places considerable strain on family relationships, as parents might refuse to accept prolonged responsibility for their children, or children questioning their parent's authority. For example Glen Elder's study on *Children of the Great Depression* (1974/99) demonstrated that the success and misfortune of a family is shared through its members. The life course principle of "linked lives" emphasizes that lives are lived interdependently, that individual experiences are connected to the lives of significant others in the family, the community, at school, and in the work place. Social relationships, in particular family support, including emotional support and financial backing as well as encouragement and advice, are generally significant factors in shaping young people's lives.

Yet the importance of parents in young people's lives is affected by socio-economic change. For example, in Elder's study, children's perception of the relative influence of mother and fathers was affected by economic hardship. In particular fathers who lost heavily in the Great Depression in terms of employment and income, were generally perceived as less powerful in family affairs than mothers. Likewise, current findings suggest that the experience of hardship undermined feelings of closeness, producing conflict with parents. Evidence from the German Family Panel (Pairfam) suggests that in the aftermath of the Great Recession the role of fathers was particularly affected (Walper & Friedrich, 2017), with unemployment impacting negatively on their children's relationships with them, especially among boys.

Conclusions

In this chapter, the effects of the worldwide 2007/8 recession on young people at the cusp of making the transition to adulthood are considered using data from the USA, the UK, and Germany. Asking if the 2007/8 recession has transformed or merely accelerated pre-existing trends, the role of shifting government economic policies and safety net structures in buffering the impact of economic stress can be illustrated. Comparisons across the three countries underscores how culturally distinct values and policies shape the outcomes of economic disruptions for families and their children. Socio-cultural systems provide the "blue print" for social lives, bestow laws, rules and regulations, informing attitudes and beliefs, and one's outlook to the future.

The life course principles considered at the beginning of the chapter provide a good basis for considering the processes involved. That is to say in Shanahans' (2000) terms, the transition to adulthood is a key "status passage" in the longitudinal trajectories from which the life course is constructed. The trajectories established early on in life take on a more distinct shape during adolescence when choices are made and decisions regarding education, the labor market, leaving home, partnership, family formation, and citizenship begin to firm up.

We see the *timing and sequencing* of transitions – also referred to as *de-standardization* – extending and complicating further in all three countries in the aftermath of the recession. Such changes accompany processes of *individualization,* the need to rely on the mobilization of individual resources. Extended transitions, in the absence of institutional financial assistance, imply prolonged dependence and reliance on family support. As a consequence, one's own financial independence and full personal autonomy remains continually postponed. Those without family resources become increasingly marginalized. Even when in employment – regardless of qualification – young people are often relegated to the category of the "outsider" (i.e., those on fixed or zero hour contracts) as opposed to "insiders" (i.e., those with full job security) in an ever-more volatile labor market. We thus seem to be observing a reconfiguration of the traditional class structure now defined, as Standing (2011) claims by the growth of a *precariat.*

Hence, we conclude that the consequences of the Great Recession hit young people in all these respects in the three countries examined here, forcing them to come to terms with insecure and low-income employment and changing labor market opportunities. However, the Great Recession did not bring about a radical transformation of transition systems; the financial crisis was not an instance of a "creative destruction" as Joseph Schumpeter (1942/75) would call it. Secular economic trends in education and labor markets were not basically changed, but rather reinforced and accelerated. Nonetheless, the recession effects presented new obstacles to entering and sustaining employment within the adult labor market. In particular, the increasing precaritization of employment and marginalization of growing sections of the youth population, including graduates, is a major concern.

The effects of the Great Recession on young people varied substantially between the UK, the USA, and Germany, pointing to the crucial role of social institutions in buffering the impact of an economic downturn. The process of becoming adult is shaped by social institutions, relationships (linked lives), and events that occur at the local and the national level. Progressive and dynamic institutions can both mediate and moderate pressures from the external economy, thus supplying the essential protection that the coming generations need in optimizing life chances and avoiding exclusion.

At times when there is exceptional economic strain, the institutions concerned with managing the education and training system of any country become the key agents of social policy concerned with ensuring not only the immediate but also the long-term welfare of its citizenry – a prerequisite for social cohesion. In particular, close bridges between the education system and the labor market play an important role in buffering the negative effect of the recession on employment prospects (Green & Pensiero, 2017; Mont'Alva et al., 2017). This responsibility does not begin and end with the youth transition but needs to apply throughout the life course to secure the social, occupational, and economic outcomes embodied in the capability that individual citizens, their families, and society need. Lifelong learning managed through social partnerships is the means of building the political commitment to bring it about.

Focusing on just three countries has the advantage of bringing specific country difference in comparable economic and socio-political contexts more easily to light, thus controlling for some confounders while capitalizing on readily available research resources for the analysis reported. However, we see this study as a first stage in a much wider process of country comparisons which is needed to identify the wider range of recession effects on youth transitions across the European Union and globally. We also need a longer time window of observation. This would enable the analysis of changes in opportunity due to the growing right-wing populism that brings with it more openly expressed prejudice against "outsiders" and minority groups, and increasing nationalism, such as the "Brexit" movement.

Future analysis should include comparison with the countries in Southern Europe that were dramatically affected by the global financial and EURO crises. The economies of Greece, Spain, Portugal, and Italy could not recover and had youth unemployment rates above 40 percent at the beginning of 2016. Moreover, the economic and political situation in Southern/Latin America (Brazil and Mexico) has become worse. Brazil struggles with its worst recession since the Great Depression of the 1930s, resulting from falling world market prices for oil and mineral resources and corruption in government. East and South Asia report lower rates of youth unemployment, yet they use different metrics, and there are great regional variations.

"Corporatist" countries such as Germany, Austria, and Switzerland as well as the Nordic and Benelux countries generally had a better crisis management than most others, based on a stable system of social inclusion. However, even in these countries labor market entrants were offered mostly temporary contracts in the wake of the Great Recession. These contracts may be stepping stones to a career if they offer work experience and decent wages, but a downward path of exclusion if they do not. Such labor market and socio-structural shifts present institutional challenges to ensuring all young people have an effective and fulfilling adulthood. Leaving them without the support they need to forge their pathways to independence and prosperity will have implications for generations to come. Young people of today are the parents of tomorrow's children and also have to feed the pensions of the older generation. Their welfare and pathways to independence has to be a central policy concern.

References

Arntz, M., Gregory, T., & Zierahn, U. (2016). The risk of automation for jobs in OECD countries: A comparative analysis. *OECD Social, Employment and Migration Working Papers, No. 189, OECD Publishing, Paris. http://dx.doi.org/ 10.1787/5jlz9h56dvq7-en*

Ashton, D. (2017). Globalization and its impact on the political, economic, and labor market aspects of the youth transition. In I. Schoon & J. Bynner (Eds.), *Young People's Development and the Great Recession: Uncertain transitions and precarious futures* (pp. 25–51). Cambridge: Cambridge University Press.

Ashton, D. & Bynner, J. (2011). Labour market, employment and skills. In M. E. J. Wadsworth & J. Bynner (Eds.), *A Companion to Life Course Studies: The social and historical context of the British birth cohort studies.* London: Routledge.

Beblavý, M., Thum, A.-E., & Veselkova, M. (2011). Education policy and welfare regimes in OECD countries: Social stratification and equal opportunity in education. *CEPS Working Document No. 357. http://aei.pitt.edu/33008/1/WD_ 357_Beblavy_Thum__Veselkova.pdf?*

Bell, D. N. F. & Blanchflower, D. G. (2011). Young people and the Great Recession. *Oxford Review of Economic Policy, 27*(2), 241–267. doi:10.1093/ oxrep/grr011

Billari, F. C. & Liefbroer, A. C. (2010). Towards a new pattern of transition to adulthood? *Advances in Life Course Research, 15*(2–3), 59–75. doi:10.1016/ j.alcr.2010.10.003

Bloodworth, J. (2018). *Hired: Six months undercover in low-wage Britain.* London: Atlantic Books.

Blossfeld, H. P., Klijzing, E., Mills, M., & Kurz, K. (Eds.). (2005). *Globalization, Uncertainty and Youth in Society.* London: Routledge.

Blossfeld, P. (2017). Labour market entry in Germany before and after the financial crisis: An analysis of duration of labor market entry, quality of first job and fixed-term employment. In I. Schoon & J. Bynner (Eds.), *Young People's*

Development and the Great Recession: Uncertain transitions and precarious futures (pp. 208–232). Cambridge: Cambridge University Press.

Brückner, H. & Mayer, K. U. (2005). De-standardization of the life course: What does it mean? And if it means anything, whether it actually took place? *Advances in Life Course Research, 9,* 27–53.

Buchmann, M. C. (1989). *The Script of Life in Modern Society: Entry into adulthood in a changing world.* Chicago: Chicago University Press.

Buchmann, M. C. & Kriesi, I. (2011). Transition to adulthood in Europe. *Annual Review of Sociology, 37,* 481–503.

Bynner, J. (2001). British youth transitions in comparative perspective. *Journal of Youth Studies, 4*(1), 5–23.

Bynner, J. & Parsons, S. (2002). Social exclusion and the transition from school to work: The case of young people not in education, employment, or training (NEET). *Journal of Vocational Behavior, 60*(2), 289–309.

Carson, E. A. (2014). *Prisoners in 2013.* Revised in September 2014. US Department of Justice, Bulletin. *NCJ* 247282.

Cavanagh, S. (2017). Impact of the Great Recession on young adult health: The significance of social class. In I. Schoon & J. Bynner (Eds.), *Young People's Development and the Great Recession: Uncertain transitions and precarious futures* (pp. 425–444). Cambridge: Cambridge University Press.

Crosnoe, R. & Smith, C. (2017). Structural advantages, personal capacities and young adult functioning during the Great Recession. In I. Schoon & J. Bynner (Eds.), *Young People's Development and the Great Recession: Uncertain transitions and precarious futures* (pp. 129–153). Cambridge: Cambridge University Press.

Danzinger, S. (2013). Evaluating the effects of the recession. *Annals of the American Academy of Political and Social Science, 650,* 6–24.

Elder, G. H. (1999). *Children of the Great Depression: Social change in life experience* (25th Anniversary Edition). Boulder, CO: Westview Press (Originally published in 1974, University of Chicago Press).

Elder, G. H., Shanahan, M. J., & Jennings, J. A. (2015). Human development in time and place. In M. H. Bornstein & L. T. Leventhal (Eds.), *Ecological Settings and Processes in Developmental Systems* (Vol. 4, pp. 6–54). Hoboken, NJ: Wiley.

Esping-Anderson, G. (1990). *The Three Worlds of Welfare Capitalism.* Princeton: Princeton University Press.

Evans, K. (2002). Taking control of their lives? Agency in young adult transitions in England and the New Germany. *Journal of Youth Studies, 5,* 245–271.

Furlong, A. & Cartmel, F. (2007). *Young People and Social Change* (2nd ed.). Buckingham: Open University Press.

Goldthorpe, J. H. (2016). Social class mobility in modern Britain: Changing structure, constant process. *Journal of the British Academy, 4,* 89–111. doi:10.5871/jba/004.089

Goodwin, J. & O'Connor, H. (2005). Exploring complex transitions: Looking back at the "golden age" of from school to work. *Sociology, 39*(2), 201–220.

Green, A. & Pensiero, N. (2017). Comparative perspectives: Education and training system effects on youth transitions and opportunities. In I. Schoon & J. Bynner (Eds.), *Young People's Development and the Great Recession: Uncertain transitions and precarious futures* (pp. 75–100). Cambridge: Cambridge University Press.

Groh-Samberg, O. & Wise, R. (2017). Education and employment transitions in Germany before and after the financial crisis. In I. Schoon & J. Bynner (Eds.), *Young People's Development and the Great Recession: Uncertain transitions and precarious futures* (pp. 177–207). Cambridge: Cambridge University Press.

Grusky, D., Western, B., & Wimer, C. (2012). *The Great Recession*. New York: Russel Sage.

Heinz, W. R. (2009). Structure and agency in transition research. *Journal of Education and Work. Special issue: Continuity and change in 40 years of school to work transitions, 22,* 391–404.

Iacovou, M. (2017). Young people's experiences of employment and unemployment across Europe: Evidence from the EU-SILC. In I. Schoon & J. Bynner (Eds.), *Young People's Development and the Great Recession: Uncertain transitions and precarious futures* (pp. 103–128). Cambridge: Cambridge University Press.

ILO (2017). Global employment trends for youth 2017: Paths to a better working future. International Labour Organization. www.ilo.org/wcmsp5/groups/public/---dgreports/---dcomm/---publ/documents/publication/wcms_598669.pdf

Janmaat, J. G. (2017). The impact of the recession on young people's satisfaction with democratic politics. In I. Schoon & J. Bynner (Eds.), *Young People's Development and the Great Recession: Uncertain transitions and precarious futures* (pp. 372–400). Cambridge: Cambridge University Press.

Jones, G. (2009). From paradigm to paradox: Parental support and transitions to independence. In I. Schoon & K. R. Silbereisen (Eds.), *Transitions from School to Work: Globalisation, individualisation, and patterns of diversity* (pp. 145–164). Cambridge: Cambridge University Press.

Kiernan, K. (2008). Marriage and cohabitation. *European Journal of Population-Revue Europeenne De Demographie, 24*(3), 341–342. doi:10.1007/s10680-008-9154-x

Leccardi, C. (2017). The recession, young people, and their relationship with the future. In I. Schoon & J. Bynner (Eds.), *Young People's Development and the Great Recession: Uncertain transitions and precarious futures* (pp. 348–371). Cambridge: Cambridge University Press.

Lyons-Amos, M. & Schoon, I. (2017). Employment and family transitions in the UK: Trends before and after the Great Recession. In I. Schoon & J. Bynner (Eds.), *Young People's Development and the Great Recession: Uncertain transitions and precarious futures* (pp. 297–317). Cambridge: Cambridge University Press.

Macmillan, R. (Ed.) (2005). *The Structure of the Life Course: Standardized? Individualized? Differentiated?* Amsterdam: Elsevier.

Mathews, T. J. & Brady, E. H. (2002). National vital statistics reports. www.cdc.gov/nchs/data/nvsr/nvsr51/nvsr51_01.pdf. *51*(1)

Mont'Alva, A., Mortimer, J., & Kirkpatrick Johnson, M. (2017). The Great Recession and youth labor market outcomes in international perspective. In I. Schoon & J. Bynner (Eds.), *Young People's Development and the*

Great Recession: Uncertain transitions and precarious futures (pp. 52–74). Cambridge: Cambridge University Press.

Mortimer, J., Kirkpatrick Johnson, M., & Mont'Alva, A. (2017). Economic recession and youth achievement orientations. In I. Schoon & J. Bynner (Eds.), *Young People's Development and the Great Recession: Uncertain transitions and precarious futures* (pp. 321–347). Cambridge: Cambridge University Press.

Mortimer, J., Zhang, L., Hussemann, J., & Wu, C.-Y. (2014). Parental economic hardship and children's achievement orientations. *Longitudinal and Life Course Studies, 5,* 105–128.

Müller, W. & Gangl, M. (Eds.). (2003). *Transitions from Education to Work in Europe: The integration of youth into EU labour markets.* Oxford: Oxford University Press.

Neels, K., Murphy, M., NíBhrolcháin, M., & Beaujouan, É. (2017). Rising educational participation and the trend to later childbearing. *Population and Development Review, 43*(4), 667–693. doi:10.111/padr.12112

Neugarten, D. (1996). *The Meanings of Age: Selected papers of Bernice Neugarten* Chicago: University of Chicago Press.

OECD. (2008). Growing unequal? Income distribution and poverty in OECD countries. Retrieved from www.oecd.org/els/social/inequality

Pförtner, T.-K., Elgar, F. J., Rathmann, K., & Richter, M. (2017). The Great Recession, health, and health inequalities of adolescents in North America, Europe, and Israel. In I. Schoon & J. Bynner (Eds.), *Young People's Development and the Great Recession: Uncertain transitions and precarious futures* (pp. 401–424). Cambridge: Cambridge University Press.

Schoon, I. (2007). Adaptations to changing times: Agency in context. *International Journal of Psychology, 42*(2), 94–101. doi:10.1080/00207590600991252

(2014). Parental worklessness and the experience of NEET among their offspring: Evidence from the Longitudinal Study of Young People in England (LSYPE). *Longitudinal and Life Course Studies, 6*(6), 129–150.

Schoon, I. & Bynner, J. (Eds.). (2017). *Young People's Development and the Great Recession: Uncertain transitions and precarious futures.* Cambridge: Cambridge University Press.

Schoon, I. & Lyons-Amos, M. (2016). Diverse pathways in becoming an adult: The role of structure, agency and context. *Research in Social Stratification and Mobility, 46,* 11–20. doi:10.1016/j.rssm.2016.02.008

(2017). A socio-ecological model of agency: The role of structure and agency in shaping education and employment transitions in England. *Longitudinal and Life Course Studies, 8*(1), 35–56. doi:10.14301/llcs.v8i1.404

Schoon, I. & Mortimer, J. (2017). Youth and the Great Recession: Are values, achievement orientation and outlook to the future affected? *International Journal of Psychology, 52*(1), 1–8. doi:10.1002/ijop.12400

Schoon, I. & Silbereisen, K. R. (Eds.). (2009). *Transitions from School to Work: Globalisation, individualisation, and patterns of diversity.* New York: Cambridge University Press.

Settersten, R. A. (2007). The new landscape of adult life: Road maps, signposts, and speed lines *Research in Human Development, 4,* 239–252.

Settersten, R. A. Furstenberg, F. F., & Rumbaut, R. G. (2005). *On the Frontier of Adulthood: Theory, research, and public policy*. Chicago, IL; London: University of Chicago Press.

Settersten, R. A. & Ray, B. (2010). What's going on with young people today? The long and twisting path to adulthood. *Future of Children, 20*(1), 19–41.

Shanahan, M. J. (2000). Pathways to adulthood in changing societies: Variability and mechanisms in life course perspective. *Annual Review of Sociology, 26*, 667–692.

Shane, J. & Heckhausen, J. (2017). It's only a dream if you wake up: Young adults' achievement expectations, opportunities, and meritocratic beliefs. *International Journal of Psychology, 52*(1), 40–48. doi:10.1002/ijop.12408

Staff, J., Ramirez, N., & Cundiff, K. (2017). The vanishing teenage worker in the United States. In I. Schoon & J. Bynner (Eds.), *Young People's Development and the Great Recession: Uncertain transitions and precarious futures* (pp. 154–176). Cambridge: Cambridge University Press.

Standing, G. (2011). *The Precariat: The new dangerous class*. London: Bloomsbury.

van Kersbergen, K., Vis, B., & Hemerijck, A. (2012). The Great Recession and welfare state reform: Is retrenchment really the only game left in town? *Social Policy and Administration, 48*(7), 883–904. doi:10.1111/spol.12063

Vuolo, M., Mortimer, J. T., & Staff, J. (2016). The value of educational degrees in turbulent economic times: Evidence from the Youth Development Study. *Social Science Research, 57*, 233–252. doi:10.1016/j.ssresearch.2015.12.014

Walling, A. & Clancy, G. (2010). Underemployment in the UK labour market. *Economic & Labour Market Review, 4*(2), 16–24.

Walper, S. & Friedrich, S. (2017). Impact of the recession on family dynamics and youth well-being: Findings from the German Family Panel (Pairfam). In I. Schoon & J. Bynner (Eds.), *Young People's Development and the Great Recession: Uncertain transitions and precarious futures* (pp. 269–296). Cambridge: Cambridge University Press.

Walther, A. (2009). "It was not my choice, you know?" Young people's subjective views and decision-making processes in biographical transitions. In I. Schoon & R. K. Silbereisen (Eds.), *Transitions from School to Work: Globalisation, individualisation, and patterns of diversity* (pp. 121–144). New York: Cambridge University Press.

Wightman., P., Schoeni, R. F., Patrick, M. E., & Schulenberg, J. E. (2017). Transitioning to adulthood in the wake of the Great Recession: Family context and consequences. In I. Schoon & J. Bynner (Eds.), *Young People's Development and the Great Recession: Uncertain transitions and precarious futures* (pp. 235–268). Cambridge: Cambridge University Press.

Wolf, A. (2011). *Review of vocational education. The Wolf Report*. Department of Education. www.gov.uk/government/uploads/system/uploads/attachment_data/file/180504/DFE-00031-2011.pdf

(2016). Remaking tertiary education: Can we create a system that is fair and fit for purpose? *Education Policy Institute*. http://epi.org.uk/wp-content/uploads/2016/11/remaking-tertiary-education-web.pdf

4 Developmental Risk and Resilience in the Context of Devastation and Forced Migration

Ann S. Masten, Frosso Motti-Stefanidi,
and Hayley A. Rahl-Brigman

Introduction

Unprecedented numbers of children and families displaced by conflict, famine, and natural disasters in the twenty-first century are fleeing for safety and a better life. The United Nations High Commission on Refugees (UNHCR, 2018) reported in their annual Global Trends report that forced displacement reached record numbers in 2017, at 68.5 million. The average number of people newly displaced per day set a record. In 2017, over 16 million new refugees were displaced and the majority of all refugees were hosted by very low-income countries with few resources. Over half of the refugee population worldwide are children. Moreover, many refugees and migrants originate from countries in the Global South that are not only low-income but also more susceptible to devastating political and ecological disasters. While most refugees are displaced within their own countries, large numbers flee to neighboring countries and a portion of those subsequently seek refuge in developed countries that offer economic opportunities as well as asylum.

The current number of refugees worldwide is overwhelming resources in destination countries, creating challenges for both immigrants and receiving societies (Motti-Stefanidi, 2017). Many displaced children have experienced chronic and acute trauma related to severe violence, persecution, starvation, disease, disruptions in education, separation from parents and homes, and loss of family members and friends (Fazel, Reed, Panter-Brick, & Stein, 2012; Masten, 2014a; Masten, Narayan, Silverman, & Osofsky, 2015; Motti-Stefanidi, 2017). Consequently, there is global interest in understanding the impact of forced displacement on development, with the goal of informing policies and practices to mitigate the risks to children threatened by the adversities of war or disaster and to promote the healthy development of child and adolescent refugees. Successful adaptation and positive developmental outcomes of immigrant children and youth are vitally important for receiving societies as well as immigrant children and youth (Motti-Stefanidi & Masten, 2017).

In this chapter, we review theory and evidence on risk, challenges, and resilience of children in situations of conflict, terror, and disaster that lead families with children and unaccompanied minors to flee for their lives and undertake the many challenges of migration. The adaptive challenges faced by young refugees and their families highlight the interplay of developmental, cultural, sociological, and historical perspectives on the adaptation of children to the devastating consequences of conflict, disaster, and migration. In the first section, we discuss models of risk and resilience that have evolved since World War II, focusing on contemporary models of resilience grounded in developmental systems theory. In the following sections, we review the evidence on risk, adaptation, and protective processes for the adjustment and future development of young people displaced by life-threatening community-level crises. Subsequently, issues and controversies for research are discussed, including ethical, methodological, and practical issues. We close with conclusions about progress in this literature, emerging themes, implications for intervention, and directions for future research.

Models of Adaptation and Development in the Context of Severe Adversity

Concerns about the welfare of children exposed to the adversities that accompany economic, political, and natural disasters have a long history (Elder, 1999; Elder & Cox, this volume; Garmezy, 1983; Masten, 2014a, b; Masten et al., 2015). World War II motivated influential child clinicians, including Anna Freud, to reflect and take action to address the consequences of war-related trauma, separation, and loss on child development. Freud published a book on children in war (Freud & Burlingham, 1943), and also treated numerous child victims of war trauma, including children liberated from concentration camps. Research on the effects of war trauma on child development was limited at the time, but already suggested striking variability in effects on individual children depending on the nature and severity of their war experiences, caregiving situation, and resources (Garmezy, 1983).

During the 1950s and 1960s, important longitudinal studies of risk were initiated by multiple investigators who were aiming to elucidate the childhood causes of mental health problems and antisocial behavior in human development (Obradović, Shaffer, & Masten, 2012; Watt, Anthony, Wynne, & Rolf, 1984; Werner & Smith, 1982). This body of work underscored the marked variation in life course trajectories among children who experienced traumatic events or high levels of cumulative adversity and led to systematic research on resilience in children (Masten, 2014a, b).

Five decades of research on risk and resilience ensued, including studies of children exposed to war, disaster, displacement, and migration, as well as maltreatment, economic crisis, family dissolution, community violence, and extreme poverty (Luthar, 2006; Masten, 2014b; Masten & Cicchetti, 2016). Influential models of adaptation to adversity emerged and evolved as evidence and theory accumulated (Masten & Cicchetti, 2016).

Defining Resilience

Over the years, the definition of "resilience" in the context of adverse childhood experiences evolved, although the focus of research remained centered on understanding the variations in response and adaptation, both short term and long term, observed among children who experienced significant challenges (Masten, Best, & Garmezy, 1990; Masten & Cicchetti, 2016). Scholars differed in their conceptual and operational definitions of resilience as an outcome (doing well despite adversity), a process (adapting well to adversity), or an ability (to adapt to adversity). With time and engagement by multiple disciplines in research on resilience, particularly in the context of major calamities, support has grown for a systems definition that is scalable across levels of analysis, integrates various definitions, and has portability across disciplines (Masten, 2014a, b). Systems function in ways that encompass the varying conceptualizations of resilience emphasizing outcomes, processes, or capabilities. In addition, large-scale calamities, such as war and disaster, disturb or destroy multiple systems that sustain human life and healthy development. A strong case can be made that preparing for such threats and fostering recovery requires a dynamic systems perspective as well as integrated knowledge from multiple disciplines (Masten, 2014a; Masten et al., 2015; Vindevogel, 2017).

As a result of this shift, contemporary models of risk and resilience in the context of mass-trauma events and migration reflect the growing dominance of developmental systems theory and contextual approaches that situate development in cultural and historical context (Bronfenbrenner & Morris, 2006; Elder, 1999; Masten, 2014a; Masten et al., 2015; Motti-Stefanidi, 2018; Theron, Liebenberg, & Ungar, 2015; Tol, Song, & Jordans, 2013). Masten & Cicchetti (2016) identified major themes comprising a developmental systems perspective on resilience. Fundamental to this perspective are the following core ideas with implications for conceptualizing resilience.

First, development emerges from continuous interactions that span multiple levels of the developing organism (at many levels of genetic, neurobiological, psychological, and behavioral function) as well as the many other socioecological and environmental systems in which the developing organism is embedded (family, friendships, educational, cultural, healthcare, ecological, and many other interconnected systems). Resilience of an individual will depend on interactions among many systems over time. As a result, resilience will be dynamic, changing over time, and also distributed across multiple systems that extend beyond the individual person.

Second, judgments about adaptive function and conclusions about "how well development is proceeding" will depend on the current sociocultural and historical context and expectations for children over the course of development within these contexts. Viewing adaptive function and development in light of sociocultural and historical context has profound implications for judging adaptive successes of children and youth who migrate into cultures or societies very different from their contexts of origin and also for evaluating adaptive success in pluralistic societies that encompass multiple cultures that may well have different views on how to judge child success or development (Motti-Stefanidi, 2018).

Third, relationships play a major role in development across the lifespan, including bonds with caregivers and family, friends and colleagues, spiritual figures, mentors, and others. Resilience will depend on the social and emotional capital embedded in these relationships, reflected in attachment security, social support, and material resources available through relationships to meet challenges in life. War, famine, and other disasters frequently lead to separations and losses that undermine fundamental relationships protecting human development.

Fourth, human adaptive capabilities depend in multiple ways on healthy brain development and associated learning. A human brain in good working order is a formidable and flexible tool for adapting to changing circumstances, particularly when individual know-how is augmented by the problem-solving skills of other people and "smart" devices. Conflict, trauma, and poverty can undermine brain development as well as opportunities for learning in many distinct ways, described further below.

From a developmental systems perspective, *resilience refers to the capacity of a system to adapt successfully to challenges that threaten adaptive function, survival, or future development of the system* (Masten, 2014a, 2018). In developmental models, risk refers broadly to predictors of undesirable outcomes, typically judged against expectations for child development in a given context of culture, society, and historical time. Risk includes many forms of adverse experiences and challenges that could threaten adaptation or development. Resilience is often inferred from manifestations of adaptation judged to be desirable or "OK" in the context of risk or adversity, although resilience itself reflects many adaptive processes.

Models of adaptation focused on immigrant youth have integrated concepts from development, acculturation, and social psychology with concepts from developmental research on resilience (Motti-Stefanidi, 2018). Investigators studying migrant children, youth, and families have elucidated both the common and unique processes reflected in adaptation by immigrant children and their families (Bornstein, 2017; Masten, Liebkind, & Hernandez, 2012; Motti-Stefanidi, 2018; Phinney, Horenczyk, Liebkind, & Vedder, 2001; Suárez-Orozco, Motti-Stefanidi, Marks, & Katsiaficas, 2018). Commonalities and differences are examined further below.

Research on resilience centers on the following three fundamental questions (Masten & Barnes, 2018):

• What are the risks or adversities that threaten adaptation or development?
• What are the criteria for evaluating adaptive success?
• What are the promotive or protective factors and processes that support positive responses, recovery, and/or future development in the context of the risks or adversities under study?

In the following sections, we examine these questions based on resilience research in the context of catastrophic adversity and migration.

Challenges for Adaptation and Development in the Context of Catastrophic Adversity and Migration

Large scale calamities underscore the dependence of every individual on the function of multiple systems, some of which are internal, such as the immune system and other biological self-regulation systems, and most of which are external to the individual (Masten & Narayan, 2012). Human individuals of all ages depend in many ways on other people and multiple socioecological systems for survival and development (Bronfenbrenner & Morris, 2006). When disaster strikes, wars rage on, or poverty endures, basic needs for survival (e.g., clean water, food, shelter, care for young children, medical care) are threatened and many systems that support or protect healthy development are compromised, including family, education, healthcare, public safety, cultural traditions, communication, and transportation. In addition, these situations generate levels of acute or chronic fear, pain, and trauma that can overwhelm human capacity for adapting biologically and psychologically to stress (Fazel et al., 2012; Garbarino, Governale, Henry, & Nesi, 2015; Masten, Narayan, Silverman, & Osofsky, 2015; Miller & Jordans, 2016; Shonkoff et al., 2012; Thommessen & Todd, 2018).

War and long-term political conflicts can lead to malnutrition and starvation due to dangers of growing or transporting food, contamination, or in situations when food and water supplies are deliberately cut off from populations. Famine may result from wars or political actions that destroy crops, interfere with planting, cut off supplies, or deliberately attempt to starve groups of people (de Waal, 2015, 2017). The long-term impact of temporary starvation perpetrated by the Nazis during World War II has been studied in victims of the "Dutch Hunger Winter" (Painter, Roseboom, & Bleker, 2005; Schulz, 2010). Life-long health was affected, with evidence that developmental timing mattered. Results of this work suggest that there were programming effects on metabolic systems, depending on when a fetus or child experienced malnutrition, that contributed to later health issues in a context of post-war nutritional abundance.

Developmental timing effects also have been observed in studies of extreme trauma induced by war, terror, or natural disasters (Masten, 2014a; Masten et al., 2015). Studies of radiation effects on children in Japan after World War II and also after the nuclear accident at Chernobyl showed biological timing effects depending on the age of exposure (Fushiki, 2013). Developmental timing effects also have been observed years later for children in relation to *fears* of pregnant mothers about radiation exposure following Chernobyl (independent of actual exposure). These effects could be mediated by biological stress in the mother (Huizink et al., 2008).

Many studies have documented age-related differences in exposure to trauma in the context of war and disaster (Masten & Osofsky, 2010; Masten et al., 2015). Young children often experience less direct exposure to the horrors of war or disaster, in part because they are actively sheltered by adults and also because they lack a full understanding of the situation. Adolescents, in contrast, often are enlisted to help or fight, have greater understanding of the situation and future consequences, and are more connected to other people who may be harmed. On the other hand, young children are more dependent on caregivers and thus more vulnerable than older children to the loss of caregiving in hazardous times. Young children also are more susceptible to anxiety and fear induced by separation from their attachment figures.

Witnessing or experiencing violence is one of the most traumatic consequences of armed conflicts for children and youth, and a key motivator for flight and migration (Fazel et al., 2012; Masten et al., 2015; Menjívara & Perreirab, 2017). Unfortunately, forced migration itself also poses dangers to children for experiencing violence (Fazel et al., 2012; Menjívara & Perreirab, 2017). Violence in these situations would be expected to have complex effects on development, depending on timing, gender, culture, situation, and how the violence is interpreted. As noted above, older children and youth are more likely to become engaged in dangerous conflicts as combatants, have greater awareness of what is happening, and greater risk of sexual violence or exploitation. Young children are less cognizant of the meaning and long-term consequences of both community disintegration and migration; at the same time, however, young children are more vulnerable to separation and loss of care and protection from adult caregivers.

Older children and adolescents also are more likely to migrate on their own without the protection of adult family members. Unaccompanied children who migrate to the US from Central America may experience beatings, robbery, rape, extortion, loss of limb, or death along the journey to the US-Mexico border, and they are also vulnerable to trafficking (Chavez & Menjivar, 2010; Linton, Kennedy, Shapiro, & Griffin, 2018; Menjívara & Perreirab, 2017).

One of the most horrific stressors of wars and violent political conflicts is the forced enlisting of children into armed conflict. Young people recruited into war, by choice or by force, often experience life-threatening violence, both witnessing and perpetrating atrocities. Research has shown that effects vary by length of time as a child soldier and gender-related experiences, with risk for sexual trauma higher for girls and dangers of armed combat higher for boys (American Psychological Association, 2010; Betancourt et al., 2010; Masten et al., 2015). Over time, child soldiers may begin to identify with the captors (Barber, 2009; Boothby, Crawford, & Mamade, 2009). Based on their intensive study of former child soldiers from Mozambique, Boothby and colleagues (2009) reported that boys with the armed group RENAMO for less than six months described themselves as *victims*, whereas boys with the armed group for a year or longer more viewed themselves as *members* of RENAMO.

The complex journey of a young adolescent into extreme violence, drug-facilitated brainwashing, rehabilitation, recovery, and eventual self-forgiveness, was vividly described by Ishmael Beah in his brutally honest and horrifying autobiography, *A Long Way Gone: Memoirs of a Boy Soldier*, published in 2007. Beah was forced into the Revolutionary United Front as a child soldier during the civil war in Sierra Leone. After he migrated to the US, Beah graduated from Oberlin College and subsequently became a goodwill ambassador for UNICEF, advocating for children affected by war.

A review of the evidence on exposure to war, violence, and terrorism suggests that child soldiers suffer from guilt and that strong guilt is a critical predictor of mental health (Drury & Williams, 2012). Thus, it is not surprising that culturally-based ceremonies of purification and forgiveness have been implicated as protective processes in the rehabilitation of child soldiers (Masten et al., 2015).

Trauma levels are so high among children coerced to become child soldiers that variation in adaptation observed after rescue or release can be more related to the qualities of the recovery environment (e.g., ongoing support or violence) than the severity of trauma during captivity (Klasen et al., 2010). However, research also has shown that some youth exposed to violent political conflict over time, particularly youth in oppressed groups, become politically active, and engage in voluntary violence to support the cause (Quota et al., 2008). Similarly, in the current "age of terror" there are concerns that disadvantaged youth who experience discrimination, racism, and exclusion are at risk for radicalization (Motti-Stefanidi & Salmela-Aro, 2018; Verkuyten, 2018).

Many children, youth, and families also flee "structural violence" in countries where there is chronic socioeconomic disparity and oppression with little hope of improvement (Dawes & van der Merwe, 2014; Menjívara & Perreirab, 2017). Physical, political, and structural violence often co-occur in low-income countries, leading to high rates of traumatic displacement and migration.

Children who experience natural or technological disasters also are exposed to life-threatening trauma, injuries, separations, and loss, as well as temporary or permanent relocation. Moreover, these disasters often have an abrupt onset. Tornadoes, earthquakes, tsunami, floods, pipeline explosions, or wildfires can destroy a community with little warning. Research has shown striking dose effects of exposure in such disasters, with more severe symptoms of trauma associated with greater exposure to danger, destruction, death, and loss (Masten et al., 2015).

Nonetheless, despite the abrupt onset of many natural and technological disasters, there often are chronic causes that lead up to acute events. Evidence is growing, for example, that the most ominous long-term threat to human life on the planet is gradual climate change related to human activities (van Lange, Jorireman, & Milinski, 2018). Climate change is strongly associated with more extreme weather events resulting in rising frequencies of damaging storms and floods as well as increasing threats from global warming on drought, wildfires, and rising sea levels (Stott, 2016). These global threats, in turn, contribute to conditions for violent conflict or a "push" for migration as populations seek safe homes or land, food, and clean water (Marks, Woolverton, & Garcia Coll, this volume).

In wars and disasters alike, multiple systems that support human life and well-being can be affected simultaneously, making it difficult or impossible to remain in the same place. After multiple community systems collapse, whether by bombs or a tsunami, people are displaced. When natural and built environments are destroyed or contaminated, or extreme danger persists, families migrate in search of safety, survival necessities, and future opportunities for their children.

Flight and migration carry their own challenges and risks. Families may be forced to leave everything behind or move to places where they have no relational or cultural ties. Social support in the host country, including perceptions of acceptance and social connectedness, is important for children's psychological functioning (Fazel, Reed, Panter-Brick & Stein, 2012). There may well be dangers along the way to a new home and it can be very challenging to find a welcoming destination of asylum. Host nations and communities vary enormously in the resources and opportunities they provide (Masten et al., 2012; Motti-Stefanidi, 2017; see Marks et al., this volume). Unaccompanied child migrants detained at the border often encounter barriers to receiving services, and these services may not address trauma they have experienced fleeing their home country or on their journey to their new home (Roth & Grace, 2015).

Children migrating in the context of danger confront complex developmental tasks. In addition to typical developmental challenges that all young people face in any context, immigrant children and youth often confront challenges of acculturation, learning a new language, and discrimination against migrants or ethnic minorities (Motti-Stefanidi, 2018; Motti-Stefanidi & Masten, 2017). Traumatized immigrant children face normative and acculturative challenges with the residual neurobiological and psychological effects of experiencing terror and extreme adversity, often lacking basic social and socioeconomic supports. Evidence suggests that exposure to war may alter the capability of adolescents to cope with acculturative stressors, such that adolescent immigrants exposed to war have higher levels of anxiety and more conduct problems, as well as academic problems, than adolescent immigrants not previously exposed to war (Patel et al., 2017).

Defining Adaptive Success in the Context of Catastrophe and Migration

Research on resilience in the context of adversity, including adversities that may trigger or accompany migration, also requires investigators to define and assess adaptive success. Criteria are needed in any study of resilience to evaluate how people are doing. Positive adaptation or adjustment in children and youth can be defined in different ways, varying from psychological well-being to school success. Researchers also have defined resilience in terms of low or absent symptoms of distress or trauma, particularly in situations where such symptoms are very common, including exposure to life-threatening violence or devastating losses of war, terror attacks, and disasters (Masten et al., 2015; Motti-Stefanidi, 2017).

Developmental models of resilience often define positive adaptation in relation to age-salient developmental tasks expected for children of a given age, culture, and historical time (Masten, 2014b; Masten & Coatsworth, 1998; Motti-Stefanidi, 2018; Sroufe, 1979; Sroufe, Egeland, Carlson, & Collins, 2005). These tasks reflect the expected behavior and accomplishments for children over the course of development in the eyes of parents, teachers, other community members, society, and eventually, the child himself or herself. Some developmental tasks, such as learning to walk or speak the language of the family, are universal, while others are more unique to a context or historical period, such as learning to weave or hunt for food. Expectations to attend school and succeed in learning have spread rapidly over the past century across many societies as they developed economically.

Why does success in these tasks matter to parents or societies? One likely reason is because competence in these tasks forecasts future success in highly valued adult developmental achievements, such as work, contributing to the community, and raising a family. In other words, "competence begets competence" and there is a considerable body of developmental evidence supporting this thesis (Masten, 2014b; McCormick, Kuo, & Masten, 2011). In addition, success or failure in one area of adaptive functioning can spread to affect other domains or levels of adaptive function, often described as a cascade effect (Masten & Cicchetti, 2010). In development, cascades of this kind reflect the interplay of interdependent dynamic systems over time. As a result, successes (or problems) can multiply or spread over time among interconnected systems, within a single person across levels, from one domain of behavior to another in an individual, in relationships or among family members, among peers or classmates at school, between individuals and other social systems, and even across generations.

In the context of migration, developmental tasks can be complicated by additional challenges that accompany adaptation and acculturation in a new country, including learning a new language and contending with discrimination (Motti-Stefanidi & Masten, 2017). Acculturation generally refers to the changes that arise from interactions of one culture with one or more other cultures at the individual or group level (Bornstein, 2017; Sam & Berry, 2016). In the context of migration, individuals and families often must adapt to differences between their cultures of origin and destination country or community in values, practices, and social structures, as well as expectations for parenting and developmental tasks (Motti-Stefanidi, 2018; Weine, 2008). The nature of the challenges involved in navigating these differences and acculturating will depend on many variations in the cultures and situations involved (Bornstein, 2017).

For immigrant youth, Motti-Stefanidi and her colleagues have argued that positive adaptation includes developmental tasks faced by all youth, acculturative tasks faced specifically in contexts of immigration, and also psychological well-being (Motti-Stefanidi, 2017, 2018; Suárez-Orozco et al., 2018). Moreover, in contexts where immigrants are mingling with non-immigrant youth in significant numbers or the population is diverse due to historical migration, all young people have the challenge of living alongside and respecting people from other cultures (Motti-Stefanidi, 2018; Sam & Berry, 2016). The Council of Europe (2016) called for all young people to develop intercultural competence. In diverse, pluralistic societies such as the United States, Canada, and the European Union, intercultural competence can be viewed as an indicator of competence and an essential skill for adaptation (Motti-Stefanidi, 2017).

The interplay of acculturation and developmental tasks has been examined both empirically and conceptually (Motti-Stefanidi, 2018; Motti-Stefanidi & Masten, 2017). Academic achievements that reflect success in the developmental tasks related to learning and school require skills in the language of the receiving nation and its schools. For immigrant children and youth, acquiring the necessary level of language skills is a key acculturative task that influences success in developmental tasks related to academic achievement (e.g., Suárez-Orozco, Suárez-Orozco & Todorova, 2009). A study of Cambodian immigrants to the US who survived the Khmer Rouge regime found that English language skills, which varied among these immigrant youth, predicted greater success in school (Hubbard, 1997). A longitudinal study of immigrant youth in Greece found that the orientation of the youth toward the host culture, viewed as a core acculturative task for immigrant youth, prospectively predicted positive change in self-efficacy, a key developmental task domain in this investigation (Reitz, Motti-Stefanidi, & Asendorpf, 2013).

What happens when life is profoundly disrupted by large-scale conflicts or disasters? In the immediate aftermath of trauma, survival and recovery are paramount considerations (Masten et al., 2015). Multiple patterns of response have been observed and assessed in the context of extreme adversity, often described as adaptive pathways or trajectories.

Theoretically, multiple pathways reflecting resilience or vulnerability would be expected, shaped by the complex nature and interactions among individual and developmental differences, timing and severity of challenges, and resilience capacity and resources available (Masten & Cicchetti, 2016). In recent years, empirical support for theoretical adaptive pathways has been accumulating as a result of improved data, with repeated measures over time, and more advanced analytic strategies (Masten & Cicchetti, 2016). Trajectories have been empirically studied among children and youth who have survived severe trauma related to war or conflict (e.g., Betancourt, McBain, Newnham, & Brennan, 2013; Punamäki, Palosaari, Diab, Peltonen, & Qouta, 2015) and natural or technological disasters (e.g., La Greca, Lai, Joormann, Auslander, & Short, 2013; Osofsky, Osofsky, Weemes, King, & Hansel, 2015).

After severe, traumatic experiences, it is common to observe a drop in adaptive function followed by recovery as threats diminish, help is provided, and capacity for resilience is mobilized at many levels. Success in developmental tasks may wane in salience as individuals, families, and communities focus on survival and recovery. However, over the long-term, the importance of these tasks re-emerges, sometimes in new forms, reflecting either a "new normal" in a recovering community or a new context altogether. Migration adds complexity to the processes of recovery, particularly when people must move quickly to safety or struggle to find temporary shelter or a new home.

Immigrant families and youth settling into new cultures may seek to succeed in old ways, new ways, and in mixed ways that reflect the blending of past and present circumstances and cultures. Conflicts can arise as parents and youth work out their goals and expectations in new contexts (Motti-Stefanidi, 2018). Parents and their children, particularly their adolescents, are likely to navigate acculturation issues in different ways and also at different rates (Bornstein, 2017). Role reversal or conflicts can arise between parents and children as a result of these differences (Thommessen & Todd, 2018).

One of the most basic questions in the study of children and youth who have migrated is whether immigrant status represents a risk factor for success in developmental tasks, either in the short-term or the long-term, as defined by either the culture of origin or the culture of destination. The literature on this basic question is complex, with mixed findings.

Evidence of better than expected adaptation in developmental task domains among first generation immigrant youth compared with later generations and native youth, particularly in the US, led to the concept of the "immigrant paradox" (Garcia Coll & Marks, 2012). Despite many challenges and often low socioeconomic status, first generation immigrant youth may show greater success and fewer problem behaviors. Evidence from studies in the US and Canada support this phenomenon (Garcia Coll & Marks, 2012). Explanations include selection factors, motivation of parents seeking a better life for their children, and also cultural protective factors, such as the support of extended family and community among immigrants from more collectivistic cultures. However, results vary by age or grade and gender and also by culture or country of origin and of destination. Research in Europe shows less support for the immigrant paradox and a more mixed picture of adaptation across generations (Motti-Stefanidi, 2014, 2017). A meta-analysis of 51 European studies found that immigrant status was a risk factor for academic and behavioral problems (Dimitrova, Chasiotis, & van de Vijver, 2016). In addition, a study of data from 20 countries indicated that immigrant students have lower average reading performance in most countries, and also that second generation immigrant students have higher reading scores than first generation immigrant students (Organization for Economic Cooperation and Development, 2010). Studies also indicate that refugee children have higher risk for psychological problems than native or non-refugee migrant children (Thommessen & Todd, 2018).

Promotive and Protective Influences for Adaptation in the Context of Catastrophe and Migration

What makes a difference for children and youth in the aftermath of catastrophic adversity, particularly when they are displaced? It is crucial to understand promotive and protective influences that facilitate positive adaptation and development for young people whose lives are turned upside down by the chaos and dangers of warfare, disaster, or disintegrating societies. Knowledge can guide humanitarian efforts as well as policies and practices by governments to address the welfare of children and youth whose lives are threatened by traumatic migration.

Resilience of refugees can be viewed as a special case in the context of the larger literature on adaptation to extreme adversity during and following war, disaster, and other catastrophes at the community or country level. Although there is limited research on promotive and protective processes specifically in refugee children (discussed further below), there is considerable evidence that can be drawn from a larger literature that is relevant to the special situation of refugees.

The literature on promotive and protective factors associated with better adaptation or recovery in life-threatening situations related to large-scale trauma exposure underscores the key roles of relationships and context in resilience, as well as individual child capabilities (Fazel et al., 2012; Masten et al., 2015; Tol et al., 2013). Relational and contextual influences include effective families and schools, access to resources, opportunities in the recovery context, and supports for immigrant families and children. As noted above, large scale violence and disasters are so harmful in part because they destroy or diminish, at least temporarily, the capacity of key systems that support and protect healthy child development, including parenting, education, healthcare, and a sense of community or cultural coherence.

Children with good learning skills, including self-regulation skills, are generally more successful in new environments (Masten, 2014b). Cognitive flexibility may be especially helpful for children navigating acculturation challenges, particularly when cultural "code switching" is required to meet diverse expectations at school and at home. It is interesting to note in this regard that bilingualism appears to promote the development of executive function skills (Bialystok, 2015). For immigrant children who must learn a new language, individual language-learning aptitude and age of migration matter (Motti-Stefanidi & Masten, 2017; Titzmann & Lee, 2018). Studies by Corak (2012) of immigrant children in Canada indicated that younger children who more readily acquire fluent language skills have an advantage for academic achievement.

Children who are motivated to succeed with positive views of their capabilities generally have an advantage for school success (Masten & Coatsworth, 1998). Research among immigrant children supports this finding as well (Motti-Stefanidi, 2018). Positive views of the self, including positive ethnic identity, are also associated with success among immigrant and refugee youth. Positive ethnic identity appears to be particularly protective for immigrant youth and may serve to counter risks stemming from discrimination (Doty, 2016; Motti-Stefanidi, 2018).

Parenting and family resilience more broadly are crucial protective influences for children experiencing severe and disruptive trauma (Masten et al., 2015; Masten & Palmer, 2019). Parenting is an important protective process in the context of war and disaster, and evidence suggests that parental care acts as a mediator and moderator of the relationship between, on the one hand, traumatic exposure, and, on the other, distress and psychopathology (Dekel & Solomon, 2016; Miller & Jordans, 2016; Sriskandarajah, Neuner, & Catani, 2015). Parenting and family function can be disrupted by trauma and injury to parents, while access to effective caregiving protects children against the adverse effects of exposure to war, violence, and terrorism. Parental care can predict post-traumatic stress disorder, and positive parenting practices may reduce post-traumatic stress disorder symptoms (Dubow et al., 2012; Feldman,

Vengrober, Eidelman-Rothman, & Zagoory-Sharon, 2013; Feldman, Vengrober, & Ebstein, 2014). In a study of Israeli and Palestinian youth exposed to political conflict, the quality of parenting showed protective effects on post-traumatic stress symptoms in the youth (Dubow et al., 2012). Moreover, in a rare experimental study of parenting and parent-child relationships, Dybdahl (2001) showed that an intervention for Bosnian families following the war was successful in boosting maternal warmth and support to their five- and six-year-old children. In addition to the medical care that all families received during the study, mothers in the treatment group also received a psychosocial intervention focused on parenting and the parent–child relationship in a weekly group that met for five months. The parenting intervention resulted in better maternal mental health as well as better children's weight gain and psychological functioning.

Parents and caregivers in parenting roles protect children in multiple ways. They provide emotional security as well as physical safety. Early observations from World War II continue to be corroborated in modern research showing the importance of keeping families together and supporting parents so that they can fulfill their roles as protectors for children (Masten et al., 2015). Humanitarian agencies and emergency responders recognize that maintaining or restoring proximity to primary caregivers is a top priority in crisis situations (Federal Emergency Management Agency, 2013; Masten, 2014a).

Parents also regulate the routines of family life, such as eating, sleeping, healthcare, spiritual practices, and home management that provide a sense of continuity and "normal life" to children, as well as cultural continuity (Fiese, 2006; Walsh, 2013, 2016). Maintaining and restoring family routines is widely recognized as important to child recovery in the aftermath of war and disaster (Masten et al., 2015).

Studies of refugee children and youth indicate similar protective influences of parenting and family resilience (Doty, 2016; Fazel et al., 2012; Weine, 2008). Children who migrate under traumatic conditions fare better when they are accompanied by parents and family, when the family as a system shows cohesion and support to family members, including children, when mothers have good mental health, and when parental education in the home country is higher. These protective influences all reflect familiar qualities of competence and resilience observed in parents and families of children manifesting resilience, as identified in the general literature on resilience (Masten, 2018).

Qualities of the community, including access and support for education, also have been implicated in the resilience of individual children and families, including refugees (Fazel et al., 2012; Masten & Cicchetti,

2016; Motti-Stefanidi, 2017, 2018). Effective schools, which generally play key roles in nurturing resilience and protecting child development, also are important for acculturation success (Barrett, 2018; Schachner, Juang, Moffitt, & van de Vijver, 2018; Vedder & Motti-Stefanidi, 2016). School can play a critical role in normalizing the lives of children in the aftermath of war or disaster. Resuming school is a powerful symbol of recovery and normalization to children, parents, and community members (American Psychological Association, 2010; Masten, 2014b; Masten et al., 2015; Motti-Stefanidi, 2018). Qualities of the school environment also matter, including relationships with teachers and peers, perceived safety, the prevalence of discrimination, and the level of conflict or bullying within the school (Fazel et al., 2012; Schachner et al., 2018).

School is also a central context for peer interactions, with the potential to support or undermine resilience (Masten & Cicchetti, 2016). As children grow older, peer relations become increasingly important as a source of influence and social-emotional support. Friendships with pro-social peers can promote competence (Masten & Coatsworth, 1998) and positive interactions at school with peers can reduce intergroup conflict and spur acculturation (Barrett, 2018; Beelmann & Heinemann, 2014; Motti-Stefanidi, 2014, 2017; Schachner et al., 2018).

Group interventions engaging peers have proven to be effective in interventions to support recovery of youth affected by war and migration (Betancourt, Meyers-Ohki, Charrow, & Tol, 2013; Betancourt et al., 2014; Panter-Brick, Dajani, Eggerman, Hermosilla, Sancilio, & Ager, 2018). These interventions often take place in school settings, although some are implemented in refugee camps.

Protective processes embedded in cultural practices, including religious practices and beliefs, were neglected in the early history of resilience science, but this research domain is now flourishing (Masten & Cicchetti, 2016). The Resilience Research Centre in Halifax, led by Ungar and colleagues, has played a leading role in advancing research on resilience from a cultural perspective (Theron, Liebenberg, & Ungar, 2015; Ungar, Ghazinour, & Richter, 2013; Wachs & Rahmann, 2013). This international group of investigators has contributed methods as well as findings from diverse cultures on rituals and traditions that support resilience of children and youth.

Cultural beliefs and practices support resilience in many ways, and often are passed down in families from generation to generation, affording a sense of continuity as well as practical knowledge. Cultural practices support individual and family resilience through meaning-making, rituals and routines, social support, and many other processes. Catastrophic adversities that lead to migration can disrupt longstanding cultural practices that support positive adaptation and development, particularly in the context of wars based on ethnic purging or genocide. Accounts of Cambodian youth who survived the efforts of the Khmer Rouge to destroy their ethnic culture have observed the salutary effects of recovering their traditional language, songs, dances, and spiritual practices (Wright, Masten, Northwood, & Hubbard, 1997). Destination communities vary in their attitudes and support of cultural practices brought to the host country by refugees, as well as in their socioeconomic and educational supports (Noble, 2012).

Resilience of children and families who migrate to a new context also depends on supports at a societal level for immigrants and refugees. Families and children fare better when societies welcome and support immigrants, both in practical and psychological ways (Marks, McKenna, & Garcia Coll, 2018; Motti-Stefanidi, 2018). Evidence indicates better adaptation of children and families in societies that support cultural pluralism, welcome and assist immigrants in resettlement and integration into society, and provide more economic supports (Marks et al., 2018; Motti-Stefanidi & Masten, 2017; Suarez-Orozco et al., 2018). Specific protections for unaccompanied minors are less studied, but also likely to play a substantial role in the resilience of these particularly vulnerable children (Menjivara & Perreirab, 2017).

Issues and Controversies

There are many challenges for investigators aiming to study effects of adversities on children during or following catastrophic adversities of war or disaster (Masten et al., 2015). The need for better evidence is compelling, but there are daunting challenges for implementing ethical and meaningful research on natural patterns of recovery or the effects of intervention in conditions marked by suffering, trauma, chaos, danger, and scarce resources.

There are profound ethical issues to consider when parents and children are suffering from the consequences of extreme violence, war, disaster, or traumatic migration (Masten et al., 2015; Thommessen & Todd, 2018). Extreme stress poses one kind of issue for obtaining voluntary consent (or assent by children), particularly when the level of psychological or even physical risk posed by research is unclear. Moreover, in some situations, research participation could make families a target of violence.

Another important issue concerns the understanding of research in cultures or communities less familiar with research (Panter-Brick et al., 2017). In addition, the methods for the research may not have been validated in the language, culture, or age group of the potential participants. Related ethical and methodological issues also arise when measures or concepts from one culture are applied to another.

Investigators must also be sensitive to the issue of *who* collects data. These issues include sensitivity to the culture of the participants, language issues, and ways that the presence of an interpreter alters the processes of consent and participation, and potential misperceptions about the nature and purpose of research (Masten et al., 2015; Panter-Brick et al., 2017; Thommessen & Todd, 2018).

For intervention studies, where randomized controlled trials (RCTs) may be the most convincing from a research point of view, there may be moral as well as practical issues that render the optimal design untenable (Masten & Narayan, 2012). The "no treatment" control group, for example, is not acceptable to most traumatized populations.

Numerous other methodological and design issues can be raised when research is undertaken in the wake of war or disaster (Masten & Narayan, 2012; Masten et al., 2015). Disaster and conflict often destroy infrastructure that supports research, ranging from supplies to internet access. Moreover, it can be hazardous to collect data in the aftermath of destruction, whether it is due to natural disaster or human violence. In addition, disasters and conflicts can come with little warning, resulting in a situation where it is not possible to determine baseline levels of functioning in a population.

Conclusions and Future Directions

There is growing global concern about the well-being and development of children and youth affected by extreme violence in political conflicts or war and by major disasters (Masten, 2014a). These concerns will undoubtedly grow as the global impacts of climate change become more evident. Millions of children affected by conflict, starvation, and natural disasters in the twenty-first century live in low and middle-income countries with limited resources. As a result, there are an unprecedented number of refugees worldwide seeking safety and basic needs for survival, with some migrating to more developed countries.

The adaptation of children displaced by war or disaster can be studied from a risk and resilience perspective (Drury & Williams, 2012; Garmezy, 1983; Masten et al., 2015; Motti-Stefanidi, 2017). These children face very high levels of cumulative adversity linked to mass trauma experiences, including exposure to violence, terror, harm to their families, separation and loss, starvation, rape, and physical injury. Migration brings additional challenges, ranging from ongoing violence to an array of challenges that immigrants to a new land or culture may face, including discrimination.

The adaptation of refugee children and youth can be evaluated in various ways, including their success in achieving normative developmental tasks (of their culture of origin or the receiving culture or community) or acculturation tasks and psychological well-being or mental health (Motti-Stefanidi, 2017). Resilience factors that support positive adaptation or development among refugee children and youth include two major kinds of influences. One set of factors are common adaptive systems associated with resilience in diverse populations of children who experience a variety of significant adversities, such as close relationships with caring adults, good cognitive skills, or hope and belief that life has meaning. Another set of factors that promote positive adaptation are more specific to the situation of immigrant children who also must adapt to life in a new context and culture, such as learning new codes of acceptable conduct, a new language, or meeting bicultural developmental task expectations (Motti-Stefanidi, 2018).

As a result of these diverse influences, understanding and intervening to promote positive adaptation in the context of war, disaster, and other complex trauma experiences requires thoughtful integration of concepts and knowledge from different levels of analysis and disciplines about developing systems in changing contexts. These include the ways multi-level interactions shape the course of development; how individual differences influence responses to traumatic experiences; how individual, family, community, and cultural resilience are intertwined; and how all of these processes change with development. As a research agenda, this integration task is formidable.

There are certainly gaps in research, particularly with respect to evidence based on longitudinal studies and randomized controlled trials (Masten et al., 2015; Motti-Stefanidi, 2017; Fazel et al., 2012). Evidence linking macro-level functioning (at the community, cultural, or societal level) to family or child adaptation or recovery is practically non-existent. Nonetheless, there are signs of progress in this literature.

There is better evidence for interventions to protect, prepare, and foster recovery in young people exposed or likely to be exposed to the severe challenges of ongoing conflict, disaster, or migration to flee life-threatening danger. Scholars are beginning to tackle the challenges of sorting out the interplay of recovery from trauma, migration, and acculturation in relation to development, both in theoretical and empirical articles. There are notable efforts to address research issues and improve measurement for research on risk and resilience in war, disaster, and refugee situations. More attention is given to culture as an influence on how research is conceptualized and implemented (Motti-Stefanidi, 2018). Measures are validated more often across cultures and in field studies. Researchers are collaborating with humanitarian agencies and local experts to implement high quality research that is sensitive to socio-cultural context and the specific needs of displaced children and families in a given situation (Masten, 2014a).

Consequently, evidence is accumulating on the adaptation of children and youth who have endured devastating adversities that led them or their families to flee for safety and survival. Although there are gaps and limitations in knowledge, some key issues and findings are coming into focus that can guide policy and practice aimed at mitigating risk and supporting resilience. Some themes in this emerging literature echo findings from the broader literature on risk and resilience in war, terror, and disaster. Dose gradients of adversity are observed during the period of initial adversity and also during recovery. Exposure to extreme violence and separation or loss of primary caregivers is associated with greater risks to children. Better adaptation and recovery are observed for children and youth with caring parents or family, social support, self-regulation skills, hope and belief that life has meaning, with restoration of normal routines in the context of family, school, peer, or cultural systems, and with community support. For refugee children and families, the quality of support of receiving communities also is important, including attitudes toward migrants, economic supports, educational opportunities, healthcare, and legal assistance for asylum.

Evidence suggests that the horrors of war and disaster can have lasting consequences for children. However, it also is clear that children recover and their resilience can be promoted before, during, and following life-threatening adversities. Many of the major protective systems for child development, the drivers of resilience across the lifespan, are malleable and renewable resources. As we gain knowledge about resilience processes and the best ways to nurture resilience in the lives of children, it will be possible to prepare and protect children and their future development through strategic, well-timed, and well-targeted interventions in communities, families, and individuals. The multi-system nature of complex adaptive systems in human development also suggests that it will be important to align intervention efforts across sectors (horizontally), across system levels (vertically), and across generations to optimize resilience.

References

American Psychological Association (2010). *Resilience and Recovery after War: Refugee children and families in the United States.* Washington, DC: American Psychological Association.

Barber, B. K. (2009). *Adolescents and War: How youth deal with political violence.* New York: Oxford University Press. doi:10.1093/acprof:oso/9780195343359.001.0001

Barrett, M. (2018). How school can promote the intercultural competence of young people. *European Psychologist, 23*(1), 93–104. doi:10.1027/1016-9040/a000308

Beah, I. (2007). *A Long Way Gone: Memoirs of a boy soldier.* New York: Crichton Books.

Beelmann, A. & Heinemann, K. S. (2014). Preventing prejudice and improving intergroup attitudes: A meta-analysis of child and adolescent training programs. *Journal of Applied Developmental Psychology, 35*(1), 10–24. doi:10.1016/j.appdev.2013.11.002

Betancourt, T. S., Borisova, I. I., Williams, T. P., Brennan, R. T., Whitfield, T. H., de la Soudiere, M., … Gilman, S. E. (2010). Sierra Leone's former child soldiers: A follow-up study of psychosocial adjustment and community reintegration. *Child Development, 81*(4), 1077–1095. doi:10.1111/j.1467-8624.2010.01455.x

Betancourt, T. S., McBain, R., Newnham, E. A., & Brennan, R. T. (2013). Trajectories of internalizing problems in war-affected Sierra Leonean youth: Examining conflict and postconflict factors. *Child Development, 84*, 455–470. doi:10.1111/j.1467-8624.2012.01861.x

Betancourt, T. S., Meyers-Ohki, S. E., Charrow, A. P., & Tol, W. A. (2013). Interventions for children affected by war: An ecological perspective on psychosocial support and mental health care. *Harvard Review of Psychiatry, 21*(2), 70–91. doi:10.1097/HRP.0b013e318283bf8f

Betancourt, T. S., Newnham, E. A., Hann, K., McBain, R. K., Akinsulure-Smith, A. M., Weisz, J., Lilienthal, G. M., & Hansen, N. (2014). Addressing the consequences of violence and adversity: The development of a group mental health intervention for war-affected youth in Sierra Leone. In G. Raynaud, S. Gau, & M. Hodes (Eds.), *From Research to Practice in Child and Adolescent Mental Health* (pp. 157–177). Lanham, MD: Rowman & Littlefield.

Bialystok, E. (2015). Bilingualism and the development of executive function: The role of attention. *Child Development Perspectives, 9*(2), 117–121. doi:10.1111/cdep.12116

Boothby, N., Crawford, J., & Mamade, A. (2009). Mozambican child soldier life outcome study. In B. K. Barber (Ed.), *Adolescents and War: How youth deal with political violence* (pp. 238–254). New York: Oxford University Press.

Bornstein, M. H. (2017). The specificity principle in acculturation science. *Perspectives on Psychological Science, 12*(1), 3–45. doi:10.1177/1745691616655997

Bronfenbrenner, U. & Morris, P. A. (2006). The bioecological model of human development. In W. Damon & R. M. Lerner (Eds.), *Handbook of Child*

Psychology,Vol. 1: Theoretical Models of Human Development (6th ed., pp. 793–828). New York: John Wiley. doi:10.1002/9780470147658.chpsy0114

Chavez, L. & Menjívar, C. (2010). Children without borders: A mapping of the literature on unaccompanied migrant children to the United States. *Migraciones Internacionales, 5*(3), 71–111. doi:10.17428/rmi.v5i18.1080

Corak, M. (2012). Age at immigration and the education outcomes of children. In A. S. Masten, K. Liebkind, & D. J. Hernandez (Eds.), *Realizing the Potential of Immigrant Youth* (pp. 90–111). Cambridge. Cambridge University Press. doi:10.1017/CBO9781139094696

Council of Europe (2016). Intercultural matters. Retrieved from: www.coe.int/en/web/Pestalozzi/intercultural

Dawes, A. & van der Merwe, A. (2014). Structural violence and early child development. In Leckman, J. F., Panter-Brick, C., & Salah, R. (Eds.) *Pathways to Peace: The transformative power of children and families* (pp. 233–250). Cambridge, MA: MIT Press.

de Waal, A. (2015). Ending mass atrocity and ending famine. *The Lancet, 386*, 1528–1529. doi:10.1016/S0140-6736(15)00480-8

———— (2017). The end of famine? Prospects for the elimination of mass starvation by political action. *Political Geography, 62*, 184–195. doi:10.1016/j.polgeo.2017.09.004

Dekel, R. & Solomon, D. (2016). The contribution of maternal care and control to adolescents' adjustment following war. *Journal of Early Adolescence, 36*(2), 198–221. doi:10.1177/0272431614561263

Dimitrova, R., Chasiotis, A., & van de Vijver, F. (2016). Adjustment outcomes of immigrant children and youth in Europe. *European Psychologist, 21*(2), 150–162. doi:10.1027/1016–9040/a000246

Doty, J. (2016). Resilience in immigrant and refugee families. In J. Ballard, E. Wieling, & C. Solheim (Eds.), *Immigrant and Refugee Families* (pp. 165–179). Minneapolis, MN: University of Minnesota Libraries Publishing.

Drury, J. & Williams, R. (2012). Children and young people who are refugees, internally displaced persons or survivors or perpetrators of war, mass violence and terrorism. *Current Opinion in Psychiatry, 25*(4), 277–284. doi:10.1097/YCO.0b013e328353eea6

Dubow, E. F., Huesmann, L. R., Boxer, P., Landau, S., Dvir, S., Shikaki, K., & Ginges, J. (2012). Exposure to political conflict and violence and post-traumatic stress in Middle East youth: Protective factors. *Journal of Clinical Child & Adolescent Psychology, 41*(4), 402–416. doi:10.1080/15374416.2012.684274

Dybdahl, R. (2001). Children and mothers in war: An outcome study of a psychosocial intervention program. *Child Development, 72*(4), 1214–1230. doi:10.1111/1467–8624.00343

Elder, G. H., Jr. (1974/1999). *Children of the Great Depression: Social change in life experience.* Boulder, CO: Westview Press.

Fazel, M., Reed, R. V., Panter-Brick, C., & Stein, A. (2012). Mental health of displaced and refugee children resettled in high-income countries: Risk and protective factors. *The Lancet, 379*, 266–282. doi:10.1016/S0140-6736(11)60051-2

Federal Emergency Management Agency. (2013). *National Preparedness Report*. Washington, DC: Homeland Security. Retrieved from www.fema.gov/media-library-data/20130726-1916-25045-3721/npr2013_final.pdf

Feldman, R., Vengrober, A., & Ebstein, R. P. (2014). Affiliation buffers stress: Cumulative genetic risk in oxytocin–vasopressin genes combines with early caregiving to predict PTSD in war-exposed young children. *Translational Psychiatry*, 4(3), e370. doi:10.1038/tp.2014.6

Feldman, R., Vengrober, A., Eidelman-Rothman, M., & Zagoory-Sharon, O. (2013). Stress reactivity in war-exposed young children with and without posttraumatic stress disorder: Relations to maternal stress hormones, parenting, and child emotionality and regulation. *Development and Psychopathology*, 25(4pt1), 943–955. doi:10.1017/S0954579413000291

Fiese, B. H. (2006). *Family Routines and Rituals*. New Haven, CT: Yale University Press.

Freud, A. & Burlingham, D. T. (1943). *War and Children*. Oxford: Medical War Books.

Fushiki, S. (2013). Radiation hazards in children: Lessons from Chernobyl, Three Mile Island and Fukushima. *Brain and Development*, 35(3), 220–227. doi:10.1016/j.braindev.2012.09.004

Garbarino, J., Governale, A., Henry, P., & Nesi, D. (2015). Children and terrorism. Social Policy Report. *Society for Research in Child Development*, 29(2), 1–38.

Garcia Coll, C. & Marks, A. K. (Eds.) (2012). *The Immigrant Paradox in Children and Adolescents: Is becoming American a developmental risk?* Washington, DC: American Psychological Association. doi:10.1037/13094-000

Garmezy, N. & Rutter, M. (Eds.). (1983). *Stress, Coping, and Development in Children*. Baltimore, MD: Johns Hopkins University Press.

Hubbard, J. J. (1997). *Adaptive Functioning and Posttrauma Symptoms in Adolescent Survivors of Massive Childhood Trauma* (Doctoral dissertation). Retrieved from ProQuest.

Huizink, A. C., Dick, D. M., Sihvola, E., Pulkkinen, L., Rose, R. J., & Kaprio, J. (2008). Chernobyl exposure as stressor during pregnancy and behaviour in adolescent offspring. *Acta Psychiatrica Scandinavica*, 116(6), 438–446. doi:10.1111/j.1600-0447.2007.01050.x

Klasen, F., Oettingen, G., Daniels, J., Post, M., Hoyer, C., & Adam, H. (2010). Posttraumatic resilience in former Ugandan child soldiers. *Child Development*, 81(4), 1096–1113. doi:10.1111/j.1467-8624.2010.01456.x

La Greca, A. M., Lai, B. S., Joormann, J., Auslander, B. B., & Short, M. A. (2013). Children's risk and resilience following a natural disaster: Genetic vulnerability, posttraumatic stress, and depression. *Journal of Affective Disorders*, 151(3), 860–867. doi:10.1016/j.jad.2013.07.024

Linton, J. M., Kennedy, E., Shapiro, A., & Griffin, M. (2018). Unaccompanied children seeking safe haven: Providing care and supporting well-being of a vulnerable population. *Children and Youth Services Review*, 1–11. doi:10.1016/j.childyouth.2018.03.043

Luthar, S. S. (2006). Resilience in development: A synthesis of research across five decades. In D. Cicchetti, & D. J. Cohen (Eds.), *Developmental*

Psychopathology, Vol. 3: Risk, Disorder, and Adaptation (2nd ed., pp. 739–795). Hoboken, NJ: Wiley and Sons. doi: 10.1002/9780470939406.ch20

Marks, A. K., McKenna, J. L., & Garcia Coll, C. (2018). National immigration receiving contexts: A critical aspect of native-born, immigrant, and refugee youth well-being. *European Psychologist, 23,* 6–20. doi:10.1027/1016–9040/a000311

Masten, A. S. (2014a). Global perspectives on resilience in children and youth. *Child Development, 85,* 6–20. doi: 10.1111/cdev.12205

(2014b). *Ordinary Magic: Resilience in development.* New York: Routledge.

(2018). Resilience theory and research on children and families: Past, present, and promise. *Journal of Family Theory and Review, 10*(1), 12–31. doi:10.1111/jftr.12255

Masten, A. S. & Barnes, A. J. (2018). Resilience in children: Developmental perspectives. *Children, 5,* 98. doi.org/10.3390/children5070098

Masten, A. S., Best, K. M., & Garmezy, N. (1990). Resilience and development: Contributions from the study of children who overcome adversity. *Development and Psychopathology, 2*(4), 425–444. doi:10.1017/S0954579400005812

Masten, A. S. & Cicchetti, D. (2010). Developmental cascades. *Development and Psychopathology.* doi:10.1017/S0954579410000222

(2016). Resilience in development: Progress and transformation. In D. Cicchetti (Ed.), *Developmental Psychopathology* (3rd ed., Vol. 4, pp. 271–333). New York: Wiley. doi:10.1002/9781119125556.devpsy406

Masten, A. S. & Coatsworth, J. D. (1998). The development of competence in favorable and unfavorable environments: Lessons from research on successful children. *American Psychologist, 53*(2), 205. doi:10.1037/0003-066X.53.2.205

Masten, A. S., Liebkind, K., & Hernandez, D. J. (Eds.). (2012). *Realizing the Potential of Immigrant Youth.* Cambridge: Cambridge University Press.

Masten, A. S. & Narayan, A. J. (2012). Child development in the context of disaster, war, and terrorism: Pathways of risk and resilience. *Annual Review of Psychology, 63*(1), 227–257. doi:10.1146/annurev-psych-120710-100356

Masten, A. S., Narayan, A. J., Silverman, W. K., & Osofsky, J. D. (2015). Children in war and disaster. In R. M. Lerner (Ed.), M. H. Bornstein and T. Leventhal (Eds.), *Handbook of Child Psychology and Developmental Science, Vol. 4: Ecological Settings and Processes in Developmental Systems* (7th ed., pp. 704–745). New York: Routledge. doi: 10.1002/9781118963418.childpsy418

Masten, A. S. & Osofsky, J. D. (2010). Disasters and their impact on child development: Introduction to the special section. *Child Development, 81*(4), 1029–1039. doi:10.1111/j.1467-8624.2010.01452.x

Masten, A. S. & Palmer, A. (2019). Parenting to promote resilience in children. In M. H. Bornstein (Ed.), *Handbook of Parenting* (3rd ed., pp. 156–188). New York: Routledge.

McCormick, C. M., Kuo, S. I-C., & Masten, A. S. (2011). Developmental tasks across the lifespan. In K. L. Fingerman, C. A. Berg, J. Smith, &

T. C. Antonucci (Eds.), *Handbook of Lifespan Development* (pp. 117–139). New York: Springer.

Menjívar, C. & Perreira, K. M. (2017). Undocumented and unaccompanied: Children of migration in the European Union and the United States. *Journal of Ethnic and Migration Studies*, 1–21. doi:10.1080/1369183X.2017.1404255

Miller, K. E. & Jordans, M. J. D. (2016). Determinants of children's mental health in war-torn settings: Translating research into action. *Current Psychiatry Reports*, *18*(6), 58. doi:10.1007/s11920-016-0692-3

Motti-Stefanidi, F. (2014). Immigrant youth adaptation in the Greek school context: A risk and resilience developmental perspective. *Child Development Perspectives*, *8*(3), 180–185. doi:10.1111/cdep.12081

(2017). Immigrant and refugee youth positive adaptation and development. In J. E. Lansford & P. Banati (2017). *Handbook of Adolescent Development Research and Its Impact on Global Policy*. Oxford: Oxford University Press.

(2018). Resilience among immigrant youth: The role of culture, development and acculturation. *Developmental Review*. doi:10.1016/j.dr.2018.04.002

Motti-Stefanidi, F. & Masten, A. S. (2017). A resilience perspective on immigrant youth adaptation and development. In *Handbook on Positive Development of Minority Children and Youth* (pp. 19–34). Springer, Cham. doi:10.1007/978-3-319-43645-6_2

Motti-Stefanidi, F. & Salmela-Aro, K. (2018). Editorial challenges and resources for immigrant youth positive adaptation: What does scientific evidence show us? *European Psychologist*, *23*(1), 1–5. doi.org/10.1027/10169040/a000315.

Noble, B. (2012). Promoting the well-being of immigrant youth: A framework for comparing outcomes and policies. In A. S. Masten, K. Liebkind, D. J. Hernandez (Eds.), *Realizing the Potential of Immigrant Youth* (pp. 413–437). Cambridge: Cambridge University Press. doi:10.1017/CBO9781139094696

Obradovic, J., Shaffer, A., & Masten, A. S. (2012). Risk and adversity in developmental psychopatholgy: Progress and future directions. In *The Environment of Human Development: A handbook of theory and measurement* (pp. 35–57). Cambridge: Cambridge University Press.

OECD (2010). *Closing the Gap for Immigrant Students: Policies, practice, and performance*. Paris: OECD.

Osofsky, J. D., Osofsky, H. J., Weems, C. F., King, L. S., & Hansel, T. C. (2015). Trajectories of post-traumatic stress disorder symptoms among youth exposed to both natural and technological disasters. *Journal of Child Psychology and Psychiatry*, *56*(12), 1347–1355. doi:10.1111/jcpp.12420

Painter, R. C., Roseboom, T. J., & Bleker, O. P. (2005). Prenatal exposure to the Dutch famine and disease in later life: An overview. *Reproductive Toxicology*, *20*(3), 345–352. doi:10.1016/j.reprotox.2005.04.005

Panter-Brick, C., Dajani, R., Eggerman, M., Hermosilla, S., Sancilio, A., & Ager, A. (2018). Insecurity, distress and mental health: Experimental and randomized controlled trials of a psychosocial intervention for youth affected by the Syrian crisis. *Journal of Child Psychology and Psychiatry*, *59*(5), 523–541. doi:10.1111/jcpp.12832

Panter-Brick, C., Hadfield, K., Dajani, R., Eggerman, M., Ager, A., & Ungar, M. (2017). Resilience in context: A brief and culturally grounded measure for Syrian refugee and Jordanian host-community adolescents. *Child Development*, *89*(5), 1803–1820. doi:10.1111/cdev.12868

Patel, S. G., Staudenmeyer, A. H., Wickham, R., Firmender, W. M., Fields, L., & Miller, A. B. (2017). War-exposed newcomer adolescent immigrants facing daily life stressors in the United States. *International Journal of Intercultural Relations*, *60*, 120–131. doi:10.1016/j.ijintrel.2017.03.002

Phinney, J. S., Horenczyk, G., Liebkind, K., & Vedder, P. (2001). Ethnic identity, immigration, and well being. An interactional perspective. *Journal of Social Issues*, *57*(3), 493–510. doi:10.1111/0022-4537.00225

Punamäki, R.-L., Palosaari, E., Diab, M., Peltonen, K., & Qouta, S. R. (2015). Trajectories of posttraumatic stress symptoms (PTSS) after major war among Palestinian children: Trauma, family- and child-related predictors. *Journal of Affective Disorders*, *172*, 133–140. doi:10.1016/j.jad.2014.09.021

Qouta, S., Punamäki, R.-L., & El Sarraj, E. (2008). Child development and family mental health in war and military violence: The Palestinian experience. *International Journal of Behavioral Development*, *32*, 310–321. doi:10.1177/0165025408090973

Reitz, A. K., Motti-Stefanidi, F., & Asendorpf, J. B. (2013). Mastering developmental transitions in immigrant adolescents: The longitudinal interplay of family functioning, developmental and acculturative tasks. *Developmental Psychology*, *50*(3), 754–765. doi:10.1037/a0033889

Roth, B. J. & nGrace, B. L. (2015). Falling through the cracks: The paradox of post-release services for unaccompanied child migrants. *Children and Youth Services Review*, *58*, 244–252. doi:10.1016/j.childyouth.2015.10.007

Sam, D. L. & Berry, J. W. (Eds.) (2016). *Cambridge Handbook of Acculturation Psychology* (2nd ed.). Cambridge: Cambridge University Press.

Schachner, M. K., Juang, L., Moffitt, U., & van de Vijver, F. J. R. (2018). Schools as acculturative and developmental contexts for youth of immigrant and refugee background. *European Psychologist*, *23*(1), 44–56. doi:10.1027/1016-9040/a000312

Schulz, L. C. (2010). The Dutch Hunger Winter and the developmental origins of health and disease. *Proceedings of the National Academy of Sciences*, *107*(39), 16757–16758. doi:10.1073/pnas.1012911107

Shonkoff, J. P., Garner, A. S., Siegel, B. S., Dobbins, M. I., Earls, M. F., Garner, A. S., ... Wood, D. L. (2012). The lifelong effects of early childhood adversity and toxic stress. *Pediatrics*, *129*(1), e232–e246. doi:10.1542/peds.2011-2663

Sriskandarajah, V., Neuner, F., & Catani, C. (2015). Predictors of violence against children in Tamil families in northern Sri Lanka. *Social Science & Medicine*, *146*, 257–265. doi:10.1016/j.socscimed.2015.10.010

Sroufe, L. A. (1979). The coherence of individual development: Early care, attachment, and subsequent developmental issues. *American Psychologist*, *34*, 834–841. doi:10.1177/016502549201500103

Sroufe, L. A., Egeland, B., Carlson, E. A., & Collins, W. A. (2005). *The Development of the Person: The Minnesota study of risk and adaptation from birth to adulthood*. New York: Guildford Press.

Stott, P. (2016). How climate change affects extreme weather events. *Science*, *352*(6293), 1517–1518.

Suárez-Orozco, C., Motti-Stefanidi, F., Marks, A., & Katsiaficas, D. (2018). An integrative risk and resilience model for understanding the adaptation of immigrant origin children and youth. *American Psychologist, 73*(6), 781–796.

Suárez-Orozco, C., Suárez-Orozco, M. M., & Todorova, I. (2009). *Learning a New Land: Immigrant students in American society*. Cambridge, MA: Harvard University Press.

Theron, L. C., Liebenberg, L., & Ungar, M. (Eds.) (2015). *Youth Resilience and Culture: Commonalities and complexities*. New York: Springer.

Thommessen, S. A., & Todd, B. K. (2018). How do refugee children experience their new situation in England and Denmark? Implications for educational policy and practice. *Children and Youth Services Review, 85*, 228–238. doi:10.1016/j.childyouth.2017.12.025

Titzmann, P. F. & Lee, R. M. (2018). Adaptation of young immigrants. *European Psychologist, 23*(1), 72–82. doi:10.1027/1016–9040/a000313

Tol, W. A., Song, S., & Jordans, M. J. D. (2013). Annual research review: Resilience and mental health in children and adolescents living in areas of armed conflict: A systematic review of findings in low- and middle-income countries. *Journal of Child Psychology and Psychiatry, 54*(4), 445–460. doi:10.1111/jcpp.12053

Ungar, M., Ghazinour, M., & Richter, J. (2013). Annual research review: What is resilience within the social ecology of human development? *Journal of Child Psychology and Psychiatry, 54*(4), 348–366. doi:10.1111/jcpp.12025

United Nations High Commission on Refugees (2018). *Global Trends: Forced displacement in 2017*. Retrieved from: www.unhcr.org/5b27be547

Van Lange, P. A. M., Joireman, J., & Milinski, M. (2018). Climate change: What psychology can offer in terms of insights and solutions. *Current Directions in Psychological Science*. doi.org/10.1177%2F0963721417753945

Vedder, P. H., & Motti-Stefanidi, F. (2016). Children, families, and schools. In D. L. Sam & J. Berry (Eds.), *Cambridge Handbook of Acculturation Psychology* (2nd ed.). Cambridge: Cambridge University Press.

Verkuyten, M. (2018). The benefits of studying immigration for social psychology. *European Journal of Social Psychology, 48*(3), 225–239. doi:10.1002/ejsp.2354

Vindevogel, S. (2017). Resilience in the context of war: A critical analysis of contemporary conceptions and interventions to promote resilience among war-affected children and their surroundings. *Peace and Conflict: Journal of Peace Psychology, 23*(1), 76–84. doi:10.1037/pac0000214

Wachs, T. D., & Rahman, A. (2013). The nature and impact of risk and protective influences on children's development in low-income countries. In *Handbook of Early Childhood Development Research and its Impact on Global Policy*. doi:10.1093/acprof:oso/9780199922994.003.0005

Walsh, F. (2013). Community-based practice applications of a family resilience framework. In D. Becvar (Ed.), *Handbook of Family Resilience* (pp. 65–82). New York: Springer.

(2016). *Strengthening Family Resilience* (3rd ed.). New York: Guilford Press.

Watt, N. F., Anthony, J. E., Wynne, L. C., & Rolf, J. E. (1984). *Children at Risk for Schizophrenia: A longitudinal perspective.* New York: Cambridge University Press.

Weine, S. (2008). Family roles in refugee youth resettlement from a prevention perspective. *Child and Adolescent Psychiatric Clinics of North America, 17*(3), 515-viii. doi:10.1016/j.chc.2008.02.006

Werner, E. E. & Smith, R. S. (1982). *Vulnerable, but Invincible: A longitudinal study of resilient children and youth.* New York: McGraw-Hill.

Wright, M. O., Masten, A. S., Northwood, A., & Hubbard, J. J. (1997). Long-term effects of massive trauma: Developmental and psychobiological perspectives. In D. Cicchetti & S. L. Toth (Eds.), *Rochester Symposium on Developmental Psychopathology: The effects of trauma on the developmental process* (Vol. 8, pp. 181–225). Rochester, NY: University of Rochester Press.

5 Children's Migratory Paths Between Cultures: The Effects of Migration Experiences on the Adjustment of Children and Families

Amy K. Marks, G. Alice Woolverton,
and Cynthia García Coll

Introduction

Migration – the movement of groups and individuals to new borders, lands, cultural contexts, or nation states – has driven the evolution of our species and continues to drive the development of our children. The types of values, experiences, daily activities, and developmental possibilities shared by groups of children are shaped by the cultural, environmental, and historical contexts in which they migrate and reside (Yoshikawa & Way, 2008). Many notable moments in history, from wars to natural disasters, have served as precipitants to the movement of people and the shaping of their traditions. In our current historical context, the movement of children and their families is increasingly prevalent. A full 25 percent of the childhood population in the US are either born abroad or are born in the US to immigrant parents (Child Trends, 2013). Collectively, we refer to these children as *immigrant origin children and youth*, terminology that acknowledges the shared experiences of US children living in diverse immigrant origin families (Suarez-Orozco, Motti-Stefanidi, Marks & Katsiaficas, 2018).

In considering the developmental possibilities of immigrant origin children and youth, the ways in which children migrate and the sociopolitical circumstances surrounding migration clearly matter. Many immigrant origin children and youth come to the US with families whose educational, social, and economic resources are plentiful. Others arrive with little financial resources, educational opportunity, or social supports. Refugees and asylum seekers – two groups typically holding few socioeconomic resources to aid in their own family's resettlement – have reached their highest global rate since World War II, with approximately 1.65 million people displaced in one year alone (OECD, 2016).

Children make up a very large portion of world-wide refugees, fleeing war and ethnic persecution in record numbers – all contexts that matter greatly for their development both in terms of risk and resilience (Pieloch, McCullough, & Marks, 2016). This chapter considers how these important characteristics of migration and the psychological tasks involved with adapting to a new cultural context shape children's development. A contemporary perspective of migration, acculturation, and their theoretical linkages to child development are presented first. These sections are followed by a historical context analysis of acculturation typologies. We focus on Mexico-US migration as a case study for illustrating the importance of understanding the impacts of national receiving contexts and acculturation types on children's psychological adaptation and well-being.

Contemporary Perspectives: Types of Migration and Linkages to Children's Well-being

Children have taken on unique roles in family migration processes throughout history. There are myriad pathways of migration for children and youth, each with unique pre-migration and post-migration contexts and considerations. Among Mexican and Central American families, for example, children are often the last link in what has been termed *chain migration*, a practice in which members of a family migrate in gradual stages (Orellana, Thorne, Chee, & Lam, 2001). In the 1990s, families from Asia with economic resources sent their children to the US to attend schools (often referred to as "parachute children") and ultimately build social networks and pathways that would later help their parents immigrate to the US (Orellana et al., 2001). Whether children arrive with, before, or after their caregivers, family separations and reunions are commonplace during migration (Dreby, 2010). Such separations and reunions can be very stressful for caregivers and children alike, particularly when long periods of time pass without co-residing (Suarez-Orozco, 2015).

To gain a deeper understanding of migration's potential impact on child development, understanding migration contexts in pre-migration, migration/settlement, and post-migration stages provides a helpful framework. Although not all children and families will migrate in a singular fashion, sometimes resettling multiple times during the childhood period, considering these phases of migration separately sheds light on some of the unique aspects of psychological adaptation and adjustment children undergo as they immigrate. Each stage consists of its own challenges and potential, with pre-migration factors ranging from new economic opportunity to acute violence and danger among refugee and asylum-seeking immigrants.

Contemporary migration and settlement in the US is often a protracted and legally complex process, contributing to uncertainty and a lack of access to appropriate resources to ease entry into the receiving country (e.g., Suarez-Orozco, Yoshikawa, Teranishi, & Suarez-Orozco, 2011). As such, immigrant origin children and youth's psychological experiences during migration are directly shaped by the local and national policies of the receiving country (Marks, McKenna, & Garcia Coll, 2018). Children's post-migration experiences also are influenced by the political climate of the receiving society, and are uniquely shaped by psychological acculturation processes. Thus, pre-migration, settlement, and post-migration contexts and experiences are vitally and uniquely important to shaping immigrant origin children's developmental trajectories.

Pre-migration influences on child well-being. Regardless of the ways by which children migrate, the decision to migrate is almost never a child's choice. Instead, the choice is made for them: a parent seeking better employment, a sibling following academic opportunities, a family member waiting to reunite with them abroad. During pre-migration, global economic, geopolitical, environmental, and complex social forces (APA, 2012) often contribute to children and their families experiencing mounting stress or pressure to move to countries with greater opportunities and wealth. Thus, "push" factors (e.g., absence of jobs in the home country) and "pull" factors (e.g., plentiful jobs in the destination country) dynamically propel large-scale migration (Castles & Miller, 2009). For families contemplating migration, pull factors, such as tempting opportunities for educational advancement or plentiful job prospects, a loved one ready to receive them abroad, or increased likelihood of personal safety, encourage a family to migrate and make a decision about a migration destination (Castles & Miller, 2009).

Push factors include economic hardship, unsafe living environments, an absence of jobs or other opportunities, and daily stressors that might cause families to seek a better life elsewhere. For refugee and asylum seeking children and families, push factors may include war, fear of persecution, and other extreme hardships that can expose children to trauma, serious threats to safety and well-being, and death. Historically, wars (e.g., in the US: World War II, the Vietnam War) and political upheavals in local contexts (e.g., Haitians to the US) have long been behind the displacement of people (Wood, 1994). Most recently, geopolitical unrest in Syria led to the largest refugee crisis since World War II (OECD, 2016). Importantly, such push factors have strong implications for children's development. Experiencing pre-migration trauma is associated with negative mental health outcomes; children from refugee backgrounds who immigrate to Western countries are approximately ten times more likely than same age peers to report symptoms consistent with post-traumatic stress disorder (PTSD; Fazel, Wheeler, & Danesh, 2005).

Another source of refugee and asylum-seeker push factors are human-induced climate changes, which have led to increases in extreme temperatures and precipitation events (Stott, 2016), and environmental disasters (e.g., rising sea levels and floods, droughts, cyclones, monsoons, hurricanes). Such environmental events have increased human morbidity, decreased agricultural yield and livestock, and are pushing people out of their home countries in unprecedented numbers (McLeman, 2014). In the past eight years, environmental events have accounted for over 25 million such displacements (Internal Displacement Monitoring Centre, 2016). Taken together, understanding the many forms of pre-migration experiences a family may endure is of particular importance when considering the historical, political, economic, and health implications of migration among children.

Migration and settlement influences on child well-being. During migration, the journey to a new home may be brief or quite prolonged with many stops on the way to permanent resettlement. In some cases, resettlement seems never to come for families caught in temporary legal statuses or without legal documentation that provides a clear pathway to citizenship (Brabeck & Xu, 2010; Menjivar, 2006). In such cases, migration does not lead to a fully legal permanent home for the child with benefits associated with US citizenship. Instead, resettlement itself becomes a way of life, growing up "in the shadows" without clear protections and rights within the new homeland and with added challenges associated with documentation status. Undocumented legal status in the US prevents immigrant children access to benefits such as healthcare, and public programs such as food stamps (Yoshikawa, Godfrey, & Rivera, 2008). Undocumented legal status is also associated with increased psychological distress and economic hardship among Latino immigrant parents, which is in turn predictive of lower cognitive abilities among their preschool-aged children (Yoshikawa, Godfrey, & Rivera, 2008).

While the public perception of US immigration is often a clear demarcation between "legal" and "illegal," many variants of ambiguous documentation statuses plague our complex and deeply broken immigration system without clear paths to citizenship for families with ambiguous legal statuses (Motomura, 2008). In fact, nearly one million immigrant youth live in such ambiguous documentation status families (sometimes referred to as liminal legality; Menjivar, 2006). Similar to undocumented immigrants, those with liminal legal statuses are also excluded from many benefits associated with US citizenship, and liminal legality may be associated with unique psychological challenges of legal uncertainty. A growing body of research about liminal and mixed legal status families demonstrates that children living in mixed legal status homes have fewer positive educational, economic, and mental health outcomes, even after controlling for indicators of ethnicity and socioeconomic status (Yoshikawa, Suárez-Orozco & Gonzales, 2016). Living in a mixed-status home as a child born in the US with an unauthorized parent is associated with risks to a child's cognitive and psychological well-being. Specifically, such children show lower levels of cognitive development and academic achievement and progress during early and middle childhood (Yoshikawa, 2011), and higher rates of internalizing mental disorders (i.e., depression, anxiety, and withdrawal) and externalizing behavioral problems (i.e., aggressive acting out; Landale, Hardie, Oropesa, & Hillemeier, 2015). These outcomes may stem from indirect exosystem level factors such as poor parental working conditions and from direct individual level factors such as lack of access to higher education and public programs that benefit child development, chronic fear of parental deportation, stigma associated with one's family's legal status, and social isolation (Yoshikawa et al., 2016).

Post-migration influences on child well-being. In post-migration, many contextual complexities arise that may either hinder or facilitate child development. Services available for parents to find suitable work, availability of healthcare and shelter, and language-learning supports in school are just a few of the many resources shown to matter significantly to children's well-being as they resettle (Yoshikawa, 2011). After migration, psychological acculturation processes unfold within families in complex ways that shape child and family functioning. *Acculturation* refers to the psychological processes of acquiring new cultural skills, values, beliefs, and languages as an individual resides in or encounters a new cultural context (Berry, 1997).

A large international study of immigrant youth by Phinney et al. (2006) demonstrated that those who had minimal involvement in their country of origin's culture (low enculturation) and strong involvement in their host country's culture (strong acculturation) reported low support for family obligations, poor psychological adaptation (including lower self-esteem and higher psychological distress), and negative sociocultural adaptation (including school adjustment and behavioral problems). Immigrant youth who favored their country of origin's culture over their host country's demonstrated lower rates of psychological distress but had trouble with sociocultural adaptation. Finally, those who reported strong involvement in both their country of origin and host countries' cultures (integration profile) had the best psychological and sociocultural outcomes, suggesting that the balance of enculturation and acculturation developmental processes are vital to an immigrant child's well-being in multiple domains. This *biculturalism* is therefore an essential developmental competency that promotes optimal adaptation and well-being among immigrant origin children and youth (Marks, Godoy, & García Coll, 2013).

It is vitally important to acknowledge, however, that not all receiving contexts for migrant families are supportive in providing opportunities to practice and develop biculturalism. In a recent cross-national immigration policy and child well-being analysis, countries with policies that promote positive integration of immigrants into the host society and provide clear pathways to citizenship tended to have healthier child populations among native and immigrant children alike (Marks, McKenna, & Garcia Coll, 2018). In other research, family trauma and historical oppression are now well understood to have multi-generational negative effects within families (Shabad, 1993; Prager, 2003), increasing anxiety and related disorders among those who experience safety issues and extreme poverty prior to immigration and preventing successful bicultural adaptation within families (Paat & Green, 2017). Such adjustment challenges can then lead to parent–child conflict and lack of successful communication patterns within families after immigration (Paat & Green, 2017). Among those who experience trauma and systematic oppression in their host country, post-immigration connection to one's cultural identity is associated with better coping post-immigration (Johnson, Thompson, & Downs, 2009).

Additionally, post-migration living conditions and cultural contexts are particularly important to shaping developmental trajectories of children born in the host country (Yoshikawa & Way, 2008). Specifically, the ways in which the new context is concordant or discordant with the parents' culture of origin – in terms of values, language, and parenting strategies – and to what degree these youth are exposed to and identify with their parents' cultural heritage, will shape how US-born children relate to their parents (see empirical research in Canada on this subject; Beiser, Puente-Duran, & Hou, 2015). Discordance between parents' typically strong alignment with their culture of origin's beliefs and their US born children's more acculturated beliefs is common and is associated with parent–child conflict (Ansary, Scorpio, & Catanzarity, 2013). Additionally, a recent study demonstrated that an often unintended consequence of migration is a loss of parenting effectiveness when immigrant parents and their children do not speak the same language (Schofield et al., 2017). It is therefore vital for receiving communities to support immigrant families in their post-migration acculturation experiences in order to enable biculturalism among children.

Contemporary Theoretical Approaches Linking Migration to Child Development

Just as there are many migratory pathways a child might take on their journey to a new homeland, there are equally diverse developmental experiences and responses children make to the changes and stressors they encounter during their pre-migration, migration, and post-migration experiences. As is true with all children, immigrant origin children and youth experience hardship, risk, and serious challenges to their growth and development, while also showing tremendous resilience and many successes. To capture the varied and complex processes of how migration impacts children's development, scholars have long noted the importance of understanding shifting ecological and cultural contexts and their changes over time (e.g., Bronfenbrenner & Morris, 2006).

The experiences of acculturation involve many aspects of social and psychological development. Consequently, children must often learn new languages, form new ethnic/racial, religious, and cultural identities, and gain a host of new social skills to effectively interact with peers, teachers, and community members in their new contexts. Once thought to be distal influences on children's development, these cultural adaptations are now understood as essential every-day experiences that shape and support children's growth and development (Vélez-Agosto, Soto-Crespo, Vizcarrondo-Oppenheimer, Vega-Molina, & García Coll, 2017). The social and linguistic skills required for children to acculturate are therefore linked to their general well-being, potential for academic success, and opportunities for civic engagement. In short, how a child acculturates to their new environment greatly shapes the later developmental and life trajectories (see Suarez-Orozco, Motti-Stefanidi, Marks, & Katsiaficas, 2018).

To organize the many forces shaping the development of immigrant origin children and youth, Suarez-Orozco and colleagues recently put forth a new integrative and ecological model of immigrant youth development (Suarez-Orozco et al., 2018). This model situates the migration experience from the most distal global forces that push and pull on a family, through the various policies that shape resettlement, to the local school and neighborhood contexts that shape children's day-to-day lives. In the model, linkages extend from the environment of reception – how openly newcomers are received, the policies and programs available during resettlement, and the popular attitudes towards migrants – to children's psychological adaptation and well-being.

Thus, as presented in the above conceptual model, immigrant origin children and youth's developmental tasks (such as self-regulation and academic progress), psychological adjustment to migration (including mental health, self-esteem, and life satisfaction), and acculturative tasks (including learning languages, acquiring cultural social competencies, and forming new social, ethnic, and national identities) are shaped by all of the migratory experiences, political reception of immigrants, and global forces preceding their journeys. All of these cultural, social, and political contexts are, of course, both created and defined by their historical settings.

A Historical Context Case Study: Shifts in Mexico-US Immigration Characteristics and Acculturation

This nuanced and increasingly contextualized theoretical framing of migration's impacts on child development is quite novel, as is the field's consensus that biculturalism provides the greatest opportunity for children's positive adaptation and well-being. Not a full century ago, scholars of immigration took a largely *assimilationist* perspective on immigrant origin child and youth development. According to assimilationist perspectives, the goal of adaptation to a new cultural environment is to entirely conform to and fit within the surrounding host culture (Stonequist, 1935). In this framework, the process of assimilation is unidirectional, such that the newest members of society are expected to adopt the cultural values, language, and customs of the receiving community quickly, while abandoning their culture-of-origin traditions. A successful assimilation therefore occurs when immigrants become full participants in their host country's society without changing any elements of the receiving community (Eisenstadt, 1985).

Psychologically, we now understand that countries or communities that emphasize assimilation create environments in which immigrants feel pressure to assimilate into mainstream culture and suppress their ethnic origin identities, thereby disrupting positive adaptation (Dimitrova, Aydinli, Chasiotis, Bender, & van de Vijver, 2015). Adolescents living in such climates experience increased psychological challenges (Schneider, Crul, & Van Praag, 2014). A study comparing acculturation and assimilation adaptation profiles among adolescents found that, compared to integrated Latino immigrant youth who maintained a bicultural identity, youth who were highly assimilated to US culture reported higher rates of aggression (Sullivan et al., 2007). Assimilationist views stand in contrast to multicultural perspectives, which value acculturative bidirectional exchange and mutual influence between two cultures – not adopting one for the other, but making room for both and inspiring new cultural traditions to take root as well (Berry, 1997). Though now it is well-documented that biculturalism, both at the individual (Marks, Godoy, & Garcia Coll, 2013) and societal levels (Marks, McKenna, & Garcia Coll, 2018), has many benefits for children and their families, assimilationist perspectives were dominant in the early twentieth century.

To highlight this contrast between assimilationist and bicultural orientations among children's acculturation strategies, we use the historical case of Mexican-US migration as an illustration. Evaluating immigration from Mexico to the US from the early twentieth century to present day reveals a complex and unique history of migratory patterns, assimilation, acculturation, and children's psychological adjustment. Mexico currently represents the largest country of origin among immigrants in the US. Approximately 29 percent of the foreign-born US population in 2010 was of Mexican origin, and the majority of residents leaving Mexico come to the US (Passel, D'Vera Cohn & Gonzalez, Barrera, 2012). Historically, large scale migration from Mexico to the US began in 1918, when a US law encouraged Mexican nationals to migrate on a temporary contract basis to the US for agricultural work that offered better pay than local job opportunities (Cardenas, 1975). Due to the seasonal nature of agricultural work and the proximity of Mexico to the US that allowed for temporary migration, Mexico was exempt from exclusionary laws enacted in the 1920s that limited large scale permanent immigration from Europe to the US

Nearly 500,000 Mexican nationals immigrated to the US for labor jobs between 1918 and the onset of the Great Depression in 1929 (Cardenas, 1975). This was accompanied by pervasive racism towards Mexican immigrants due to their darker skin tone and stereotypes that portrayed them as naturally migratory and preferable as laborers than permanent citizens. While scholarly writing about the experiences of Mexican immigrants during this time is scarce, research suggests that working conditions for Mexican laborers in the US were poor, and labor practices were discriminatory; Mexican immigrants who settled permanently in Southern California, for example, experienced more significant community and housing segregation than immigrants settling in California from European countries (Spalding, 1993).

During the Great Depression, mass unemployment in the US caused immigration from Mexico to the US to subside. After the Depression, widespread demand for labor in the US resulted in legal agreements that again allowed temporary but not permanent migration of Mexican nationals to the US. However, during the post-World War II (1944–54) decade of economic prosperity, restrictions on permanent immigration were largely unenforced, and over one million Mexican immigrants settled in the US in 1954 alone. Mexican immigrants were often referred to as "illegal aliens" during this decade, because permanent immigration from Mexico to the US remained illegal but was increasingly common and unenforced.

As economic prosperity slowed in the mid-1950s, attempts to control unauthorized immigration began, both by apprehending migrant individuals and enforcing border control and by enacting laws that made it challenging for Mexican immigrants in the US to obtain social security cards and permanent job opportunities (Cardenas, 1975). The Mexican-born permanent resident population in the US grew rapidly in the 1970s alongside increased risks associated with crossing the US-Mexico border regularly for temporary employment opportunities in the US, in addition to increasing year-round job opportunities in the late 1950s and the expiration of temporary work program laws in the 1960s (Passel, D'Vera Cohn & Gonzalez, Barrera, 2012). By 1980, the Mexican-born population living in the US was 2.2 million, approximately half of whom were unauthorized (Warren & Passel, 1987).

Understanding immigration from Mexico to the US from a historical perspective sheds light on significant patterns of attitudes toward Mexican-origin immigrants. During periods of economic hardship, the pressure to prevent immigration, both permanent and temporary, from Mexico and secure jobs for US nationals increased. During such periods, national policies that limited immigration and made it challenging for Mexican immigrants in the US to obtain legal status and job opportunities (Cardenas, 1975) fostered social climates that increased discrimination and negative attitudes toward immigrants (Viruell-Fuentes, Miranda, & Abdulrahim, 2012). According to the Integrative Risk and Resilience Model (Figure 5.1), such receptivity at the national level presented significant risks to children's adjustment (e.g., lowering children's self-esteem and threatening their well-being) and acculturation (e.g., threatening biculturalism through assimiliationist models). Noting that many "pull" factors were in place at various points in the Mexican-US migratory history, it makes sense that in periods of economic growth, a greater need for laborers in the US meant that legal restrictions were relaxed and permanent immigration from Mexico to the US increased. The resulting historical attitudes towards Mexican immigrants as temporary migrant laborers, alongside resistance towards bicultural approaches to their incorporation into US society, produced inconsistent policies and their enforcement (Cardenas, 1975).

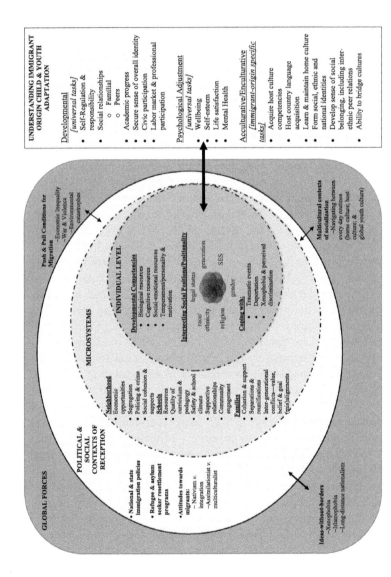

Figure 5.1 Integrative risk and resilience model for the adaptation of immigrant origin children and youth to the host country. SES – socioeconomic status

Source: Suarez-Orozco et al., 2018

In the wake of increased permanent migration from Mexico to the US in the 1970s, research about the post-migration experiences of these immigrants also increased. During this time, the assimilationist perspective continued to be predominant, and research interest focused on factors that fostered successful assimilation to US society. In a sample of Mexican immigrants entering the US legally between 1973–74, the two most common push factors for migration to the US were work, wages, or living conditions (49.6%) and reuniting with family (28.1%), the latter of which highlights the shift towards permanent networks of Mexican-origin families in the US (Tienda, 1980). Though some believed that close family ties prevented assimilation to US society, a more common view portrayed immigrants with strong family networks as advantaged in successful assimilation. This study revealed that proximity of kinship after settlement in the US predicted increased social support and successful assimilation into US society three years after immigration. Although theories of biculturalism and acculturation post-dated this study, its results suggest the social importance of ties to ethnic origin family members and perhaps culturally relevant Mexican practices among immigrants who settled in the US in the 1970s. Despite this, research about the experiences of Mexican immigrants of the 1970s is greatly limited in coverage of child adaptation or acculturation, and the experiences of unauthorized immigrants during this time.

Tying History to the Present: Contemporary Research and Perspectives on Mexican-Origin Children and Youth

In the 1990s and 2000s, research about the adaptive experiences of children from Mexican immigrant families living in the US increased, with specific interest in understanding cultural identity and acculturative processes in this population (e.g., Portes & Rumbaut, 2001). Bernal and colleagues were among the first to explore ethnic identity among Mexican-American children, studying children between the ages of 6 and 10 years whose parents ranged from first to third generation immigrants (Bernal et al., 1990). Findings revealed that older children were more likely to correctly identify their ethnicity and understand ethnicity as constant compared to younger children. Although most children in the study spoke primarily English at home, speaking Spanish at home was associated with stronger preferences towards Mexican identity. While this study aligned with prior findings about ethnic identity from a developmental stage perspective, it lacked a nuanced exploration of acculturation and biculturalism that may be unique to Mexican-American children.

Addressing these gaps, a later study sought to understand how first, second, and third generation Mexican-American children aged 7–9 years differed from each other and from a group of Anglo-American children in nuanced domains of cultural identity (Buriel, 1993). The study found that all groups of Mexican-American children identified strongly with American identity, highlighting the rapidity of adopting American ethnic identities among even first generation Mexican-American children in the sample. Although identification with Mexican culture decreased from first to second generation children, both groups identified more strongly with Mexican than with American ethnicity, highlighting that acculturation in this group was not accompanied with loss of native cultural identification and instead resulted in bicultural identity formation. Interestingly, although third generation Mexican-American children resembled Anglo-American children in their ethnic identities, likely due to lack of exposure to Mexican culture at home compared to their first and second-generation peers, all groups demonstrated high respect for cultural differences, suggesting a foundation for the development of cultural competency (Buriel, 1993).

Research has also explored the familial dynamics of Mexican immigrant families, and how family context affects children's adaptation. The importance of family dynamics on child adjustment was first established in the literature among non-immigrant families. Poverty and familial conflict are associated with adjustment problems in children. Maternal parenting practices – specifically supportive parenting and consistent discipline – attenuate the effects of family poverty and conflict on these outcomes (Fauber et al., 1990; Lempers, Clark-Lempers, & Simons, 1989). In exploring whether and how these results are replicable in Mexican-American families, and how parental level of acculturation affects these patterns, Dumka et al. (1997) found that supportive parenting and consistent discipline partially mediated and weakened the influence of family conflict on child depression and conduct disorder. Interestingly, higher maternal acculturation was also associated with less inconsistent discipline, which in turn predicted lower depression and conduct disorder in children.

Subsequent research found that in Mexican-American families, higher levels of maternal acculturation was associated with less hostile parenting practices and greater marital conflict, which were associated with parent-rated child adjustment problems (Parke et al., 2004), thereby highlighting the complexity of acculturation effects on family systems and child adjustment levels. Recent findings exploring the relationship between consistent discipline and substance use in Mexican-American adolescents also found that consistent discipline was associated with decreased adolescent substance use, but only in parent–child dyads with shared language preference (either English or Spanish; Schofield et al., 2017). These results suggest that parent–child concordance in acculturation processes may significantly impact parenting effectiveness and child adjustment. The long-term implications of child adjustment among Mexican-American immigrants were explored by Santos and colleagues. Their findings revealed that among Mexican-American adults, those who retrospectively reported dysfunctional familial experiences were more likely to experience conflict at home and work as adults (Santos, Bohon, & Sanches-Sosa, 1988).

Research from the past two decades has also found that school context also plays a vital role in shaping the positive and negative experiences of Mexican-American youth in domains of school belonging, acculturation, academic performance, and discrimination. Among first and second generation Mexican-American middle and high school students, those who perceived their school environments as unwelcoming were more likely to report discrimination by teachers at school and receive lower grades (Stone & Han, 2005). Later research in younger (8–11 years) first and second generation Mexican-American children also found that peer discrimination was negatively associated with a sense of school belonging (Brown & Chu, 2012).

This study extended the knowledge base by finding that in classrooms with teachers who actively valued ethnic diversity, Mexican-American students were more likely to have positive feelings about their ethnic identity, less likely to perceive discrimination, and more apt to feel positive feelings of school belonging (Brown & Chu, 2012). Positive feelings of belonging and connectedness to one's school and positive feelings of pride towards one's ethnicity were also found to be associated with elevated standardized test scores among Mexican-American youth (Santos & Collins, 2016). Interestingly, interaction effects in this study revealed that among those with high ethnic pride, positive school connectedness did not further increase test scores, but among those with low ethnic pride, positive school connectedness protected against low test scores, highlighting the significance of one's school in providing a supportive environment to Mexican-American youth who may be feeling negatively about their ethnicity (Santos & Collins, 2016).

Contemporary research emphasizing biculturalism at the individual, family, and school contextual levels supports an acculturative approach that balances enculturation and acculturation as essential for children's optimal growth and development. Further, examined within the complex and inconsistent historical policies that have surrounded immigration from Mexico to the US, today's continued efforts to prevent unauthorized migration from Mexico to the US highlights how we have arrived in a current state of mixed legal status family migration patterns and deeply rooted negative national attitudes toward Mexican-US immigrants (Marks, McKenna, & Garcia Coll, 2018).

These unpredictable and punishing approaches to migration have created a developmental landscape of discrimination, fear of deportation, and many other types of social, educational, and health-related insecurities among Mexican immigrant origin children and youth in the US (Androff et al., 2011). While many immigrant origin children and youth continue to thrive with resilience to these hardships across the lifespan, it is no wonder that many immigrant youth also experience mental health challenges and limited socioeconomic mobility as well. With new research showing direct linkages between the well-being of immigrant and native-born youth populations (Marks et al., 2018), the healthy, bicultural integration of immigrant origin children and youth in the US should be a top political priority to secure its optimal future.

In summary, the last few decades of research on Mexican-origin children and youth point to the deep connections among migration experiences on the one hand, and children's development on the other. This research base is now very robust, with many scholars, disciplines, and theoretical orientations newly developed and working hard to understand the intricacies of Latino migration experiences (not just youth of Mexican origin) and their developmental consequences for children and youth (see Suarez-Orozco, Abo-Zena, & Marks, 2015). From this broad research base, we now know that the post-migration qualities of acculturation, ethnic/racial identity development experiences, and the support or harm from institutions such as schools are meaningful for shaping children's educational prospects and health (Marks & Garcia Coll, in press). Policies aimed at supporting the integration of families into the host society are therefore essential. Research evidence would support immigration practices that promote family reunification, limit family members' deportations, and provide a welcoming, multicultural approach to immigration. In addition, positive and multicultural sociocultural values and attitudes in the receiving country are important for both immigrant communities and native-born child populations (Marks, McKenna, & Garcia Coll, 2018).

References

Androff, D., Ayon, C., Becerra, D., Gurrola, M., Salas, L., Krysik, J., et al. (2011). US immigration policy and immigrant children's well-being: The impact of policy shifts. *Journal of Sociology and Social Welfare*, 38(1), 77–98. doi: 10.1177/14733325011418871

Ansary, N. S., Scorpio, E., & Catanzariti, D. (2013). Parent-adolescent ethnic identity discrepancies and adolescent psychosocial maladjustment: A study of gender differences. *Child & Adolescent Social Work Journal, 30*(4), 275–291.

Beiser, M., Puente-Duran, S., & Hou, F. (2015). Cultural distance and emotional problems among immigrant and refugee youth in Canada: Findings from the New Canadian Child and Youth Study. *International Journal of Intercultural Relations, 49*, 33–45. doi: 10.1016/j.ijintrel.2015.06.005

Bernal, M. E., Knight, G. P., Garza, C. A., Ocampo, K. A., & Cota, M. K. (1990). The development of ethnic identity in Mexican-American children. *Hispanic Journal of Behavioral Sciences, 12*(1), 3–24.

Berry, J. W. (1997). Immigration, acculturation, and adaptation. *Applied Psychology: An International Review, 46*, 62–68.

Brabeck, K. & Xu, Q. (2010). The impact of detention and deportation on Latino immigrant children and families: A quantitative exploration. *Hispanic Journal of Behavioral Sciences, 32*(3), 341–361.

Bronfenbrenner, U. & Morris, P. A. (2006). The bioecological model of human development. In R. M. Lerner & W. Damon (Eds.), *Handbook of Child Psychology* (6th ed., Vol. 1, pp. 793–828). Hoboken, NJ: Wiley.

Brown, C. S. & Chu, H. (2012). Discrimination, ethnic identity, and academic outcomes of Mexican immigrant children: The importance of school context. *Child Development, 83*(5), 1477–1485.

Buriel, R. (1993). Acculturation, respect for cultural differences, and biculturalism among three generations of Mexican American and Euro American school children. *Journal of Genetic Psychology, 154*(4), 531–543.

Cardenas, G. (1975). United States immigration policy toward Mexico: An historical perspective. *Chicano Latin Review, 2*, 66.

Child Trends. (2013). *Immigrant Children: Indicators on children and youth.* Washington, DC: author. Retrieved from www.childtrends.org/?indicators=immigrant-children.

Dimitrova, R., Aydinli, A., Chasiotis, A., Bender, M., & Van de Vijver, F. J. (2015). Heritage identity and maintenance enhance well-being of Turkish-Bulgarian and Turkish-German adolescents. *Social Psychology, 46*(2), 93–103.

Dumka, L. E., Roosa, M. W., & Jackson, K. M. (1997). Risk, conflict, mothers' parenting, and children's adjustment in low-income, Mexican immigrant, and Mexican American families. *Journal of Marriage and the Family, 59*, 309–323.

Eiscnstadt, S. N. (1985). Assimilation sociale. *Encyclopaedia universalis, 2*, 942–930.

Fauber, R., Forehand, R., Thomas, A. M., & Wierson, M. (1990). A mediational model of the impact of marital conflict on adolescent adjustment in intact and divorced families: The role of disrupted parenting. *Child Development, 61*(4), 1112–1123.

Fazel, M., Wheeler, J., & Danesh, J. (2005). Prevalence of serious mental disorder in 7000 refugees resettled in western countries: A systematic review. *Lancet. 365*: 1309–1314.

Internal Displacement Monitoring Centre. (2016). Global report on internal displacement.

Johnson, H., Thompson, A., & Downs, M. (2009). Non-Western interpreters' experiences of trauma: The protective role of culture following exposure to oppression. *Ethnicity & Health, 14*(4), 407–418.

Landale, N. S., Hardie, J. H., Oropesa, R. S., & Hillemeier, M. M. (2015). Behavioral functioning among Mexican-origin children: Does parental legal status matter? *Journal of Health and Social Behavior, 56*(1), 2–18.

Lempers, J. D., Clark-Lempers, D., & Simons, R. L. (1989). Economic hardship, parenting, and distress in adolescence. *Child Development, 60*(1), 25–39.

Marks, A. K. & Garcia Coll, C. (in press). Education and developmental competencies of ethnic minority children: Recent theoretical and methodological advances. *Developmental Review.*

Marks, A. K., Godoy, C. M., & Garcia Coll, C. (2013). An ecological approach to understanding immigrant child and adolescent developmental competencies. In L. Gershoff, R. Mistry, & D. Crosby (Eds.), *The Contexts of Child Development* (pp. 75–89). New York: Oxford University Press.

Marks, A. K., McKenna, J., & Garcia Coll, C. (2018). National receiving contexts: A critical aspect of immigrant and refugee youth adaptation. *European Psychologist, 23*(1), 6–20. doi: 10.1027/1016–9040/a000311

McLeman, R. A. (2014). *Climate and Human Migration: Past experiences, future challenges.* Cambridge: Cambridge University Press.

Menjivar, C. (2006). Liminal legality: Salvadoran and Guatemalan immigrants' lives in the United States. *American Journal of Sociology, 111*(4), 999–1037.

Motomura, H. (2008). Immigration outside the law. *Columbia Law Review, 108*(8), 01–09.

OECD. (2016). *International Migration Outlook 2016.* Paris: OECD Publishing. Retrieved from http://dx.doi.org/10.1787/migr_outlook-2016-en

Orellana, M. F., Thorne, B., Chee, A., & Lam, W. S. E. (2001). Transnational childhoods: The participation of children in processes of family migration. *Social Problems, 48*(4), 572–591.

Paat, Y. F. & Green, R. (2017). Mental health of immigrants and refugees seeking legal services on the US-Mexico border. *Transcultural Psychiatry, 54*(5–6), 783–805.

Parke, R. D., Coltrane, S., Duffy, S., Buriel, R., Dennis, J., Powers, J., & Widaman, K. F. (2004). Economic stress, parenting, and child adjustment in Mexican American and European American families. *Child Development, 75*(6), 1632–1656.

Passel, J. S., D'Vera Cohn, G. B. A., & Gonzalez-Barrera, A. (2012). *Net Migration from Mexico Falls to Zero – and Perhaps Less.* Washington, DC: Pew Hispanic Center.

Phinney, J. S., Berry, J. W., Vedder, P., & Liebkind, K. (2006). The acculturation experience: Attitudes, identities and behaviors of immigrant youth. In J. W. Berry, J. S. Phinney, D. L. Sam, & P. Vedder (Eds.), *Immigrant Youth in Cultural Transition: Acculturation, identity and adaptation across national contexts* (pp. 71–115). Mahwah, NJ: Lawrence Erlbaum Associates.

Pieloch, K. A., McCullough, M. B., & Marks, A. K. (2016). Resilience of children with refugee statuses: A research review. *Canadian Psychology, 57*(4), 330–339. doi: 10.1037/cap0000073

Portes, A. & Rumbaut, R. G. (2001). *Legacies: The story of immigrant second generation.* Berkeley, CA: University of California Press.

Prager, J. (2003). Lost childhood, lost generations: The intergenerational transmission of trauma. *Journal of Human Rights, 2*(2), 173–181.

Santos, C. E. & Collins, M. A. (2016). Ethnic identity, school connectedness, and achievement in standardized tests among Mexican-origin youth. *Cultural Diversity and Ethnic Minority Psychology, 22*(3), 447–452.

Santos, S. J., Bohon, L. M., & Sánchez-Sosa, J. J. (1998). Childhood family relationships, marital and work conflict, and mental health distress in Mexican immigrants. *Journal of Community Psychology, 26*(5), 491–508.

Schneider, J., Crul, M., & Van Praag, L. (2014). Upward mobility and questions of belonging in migrant families. *New Diversities, 16*(1), 1–6.

Schofield, T. J., Toro, R. I., Parke, R. D., Cookston, J. T., Fabricius, W. V., & Coltrane, S. (2017). Parenting and later substance use among Mexican-origin youth: Moderation by preference for a common language. *Developmental Psychology, 53*(4), 778.

Shabad, P. (1993). Repetition and incomplete mourning: The intergenerational transmission of traumatic themes. *Psychoanalytic Psychology, 10*(1), 61–75.

Stone, S. & Han, M. (2005). Perceived school environments, perceived discrimination, and school performance among children of Mexican immigrants. *Children and Youth Services Review, 27*(1), 51–66.

Stonequist, E. V. (1935). The problem of marginal man. *American Journal of Sociology, 7,* 1–12.

Stott, P. (2016). How climate change affects extreme weather events. *Science, 352*(6293), 1517–1518.

Suarez-Orozco, C. (2015). Family separations and reunions. In C. Suarez-Orozco, M. Abo-Zena, & A. K. Marks (Eds.), *Transitions: The development of children of immigrants* (pp. 27–31). New York: New York University Press.

Suarez-Orozco, C., Abo-Zena, M., & Marks, A. K. (2015). *Transitions: The development of immigrant children.* New York: New York University Press.

Suarez-Orozco, C., Motti-Stefanidi, F., Marks, A. K., & Katsiaficas, D. (2018). An integrative risk and resilience model for understanding the development and adaptation of immigrant origin children and youth. *American Psychologist, 73*(6), 781–796.

Suarez-Orozco, C., Yoshikawa, H., Teranishi, R. T., & Suarez-Orozco, M. M. (2011). Growing up in the shadows: The developmental implications of unauthorized status. *Harvard Educational Review, 81*(3), 438–472.

Sullivan, S., Schwartz, S., Prado, G., Huang, S., Pantin, H., & Szapocznik, J. (2007). A bidimensional model of acculturation for examining differences in family functioning and behavior problems in Hispanic immigrant adolescents. *Journal of Early Adolescence, 27,* 405–430.

Tienda, M. (1980). Familism and structural assimilation of Mexican immigrants in the United States. *International Migration Review, 14,* 383–408.

Velez-Agosto, N. M., Soto-Crespo, J. G., Vizcarrondo-Oppenheimer, M., Vega-Molina, S., & Garcia Coll, C. (2017). Bronfenbrenner's Bioecological Theory revision: Moving culture from the macro to the micro. *Perspectives on Psychological Science, 12*(5), 900–910. doi: 10.1177/1745691617704397

Viruell-Fuentes, E. A., Miranda, P. Y., & Abdulrahim, S. (2012). More than culture: Structural racism, intersectionality theory, and immigrant health. *Social Science & Medicine, 75*(12), 2099–2106.

Warren, R. & Passel, J. S. (1987). A count of the uncountable: Estimates of undocumented aliens counted in the 1980 United States Census. *Demography,*
24(3), 375–393.

Wood, W. B. (1994). Forced migration: Local conflicts and international
dilemmas. *Annals of the Association of American Geographers, 84*(4), 607–634.

Yoshikawa, H. (2011). *Immigrants Raising Citizens: Undocumented parents and*
their young children. New York: Russell Sage Foundation.

Yoshikawa, H., Godfrey, E. B., & Rivera, A. C. (2008). Access to institutional
resources as a measure of social exclusion: Relations with family process
and cognitive development in the context of immigration. *New Directions for*
Child and Adolescent Development, 15(121), 63–86.

Yoshikawa, H., Suárez-Orozco, C., & Gonzales, R. (2016). Unauthorized status
and youth development in the United States: Consensus statement of the
Society for Research on Adolescence. *Journal of Research on Adolescence,*
27(1), 1–16.

Yoshikawa, H. & Way, N. (2008). From peers to policy: How broader social
contexts influence the adaptation of children and youth in immigrant families. *New Directions in Child and Adolescent Development, 121,* 1–8.

6 Education in Historical and Cultural Perspective

Robert Crosnoe

Introduction

The educational system is part of the vast institutional machinery of developed societies, fulfilling major social and economic functions that are crucial to the stability, productivity, and health of the population. This system profoundly influences the lives of individual children, whose educational experiences both reflect their family backgrounds and community contexts and forecast their future trajectories of socio-economic attainment, family formation, and health. As such, the educational system links the various stages of life over developmental time and connects generations over historical time. Yet, it is also more than an institutional system, as schools represent proximate contexts in which developing young people live their daily lives, connect with others, and figure out who they are. Thus, education is both a macro-level and micro-level context for understanding the early life course (Arum, 2000; Bryk & Schneider, 2004; Crosnoe, 2011).

Given this multi-level role of the educational system for individuals and society, historical evolution in the system can create important new demands on young people while also opening up new opportunities for them. Certainly, education in the developed world has changed a great deal over the last several decades, and so have the students – and student populations – that schools are serving. Digging into such changes can shed light on the role of education in young people's lives and the responsivity of educational systems to young people, including successes and failures in both. This chapter explores this evolution – and what it means through the connection between the rising value of educational attainment and the increasing diversification of the child population in the new globalized world.

Specifically, I will begin by discussing how global economic restructuring has raised the lifelong economic returns to higher education and, in the process, changed the organization of earlier levels of schooling in important ways. Next, the discussion will turn to issues of diversity and inequality and how racial, socioeconomic, and other advantages and disadvantages can affect the current academic experiences and future prospects of young people as they try to navigate the educational system. This discussion will also describe how recognition of the cumulative effects of inequality has focused attention on early intervention, including efforts to provide more opportunity for early childhood education. I will close with a spotlight on strategic policy and programmatic efforts to address inequalities in contemporary education, selecting one strategy apiece for multiple levels of educational intervention – targeting schools a whole, curricular structures within schools, ecological transactions between schools and other contexts, and the psychological processes of young people themselves. Throughout, I will focus most closely on the educational system I know the best – the US system – but will also draw parallels and contrasts with education in other developed countries to give a fuller picture of what kind of change is happening and how it is similar and different across countries.

Two Historical Trends in the United States and Other Developed Countries

Of course, education has changed in many fundamental ways over my lifetime in the United States and across the world. Because all of those changes cannot possibly be covered in this chapter, I am going to focus on two here. They are important to discuss because they are inter-related, they reflect how education is intricately connected to other global systems, they can both be discussed in terms of educational and developmental implications, and they demonstrate how experiences early in life can have lifelong consequences.

There is a macro-level background to both of these changes that needs to be discussed to set the stage. That background concerns global economic restructuring and its effects on the labor markets of the United States and other developed countries.

Basically, since the early 1970s, globalization, technological innovation, and other social forces have converged to reshape the economies of affluent societies, which are now structured less by the manufacturing sector and more by information and service sectors. As a result of this restructuring, the shape of labor markets has been transformed from a pyramid shape to an hourglass shape. The former is characterized by a broad layer of low-paying insecure jobs requiring little education at the bottom, a narrower but still broad layer of good stable jobs requiring basic educational credentials (e.g., high school diploma) in the middle, and a small layer of professional jobs requiring advanced educational credentials (e.g., college degree) at the top. In this labor market, people from a wide variety of backgrounds who persist through the public education system can secure stable employment with enough pay and benefits to maintain a middle class lifestyle and then use that security to sponsor the social mobility of their children. The unionized jobs of the early- to mid-twenty-first-century US auto industry – often viewed as a foundation of the middle class and its intergenerational mobility – are a good example of that middle layer. In the hourglass-shaped labor market, that bottom layer of insecure jobs remains, the top layer of professional jobs has greatly expanded to a similar size, and the middle has been completely hollowed out. As a result, there are clear "winners" and clear "losers" in the labor market, with little in between. The closing of US auto plants in the late twenty-first century symbolizes this restructuring and what it means for the middle class and social mobility. Although globalization and associated restructuring have affected the labor markets of most developed countries, these effects are perhaps more acutely felt by contemporary Americans, given the lack of state support for and investment in families in this country relative to other affluent societies (Bernhardt et al., 2001; Fischer & Hout, 2006; Goldin & Katz, 2009).

With this background laid out, we can turn to the implications of economic restructuring for higher education and how lower levels of schooling have responded in turn.

Rising Returns to Education

One of the clearest effects of global economic restructuring has been on the value of educational attainment, especially higher education. In the hourglass-shaped economy, the most effective means of pushing through the bottleneck is to accrue advanced educational credentials, including bachelor's degrees and higher-level degrees in the United States. Consequently, the lifelong "returns" of persisting into and through higher education – in other words, how much people benefit from investing time and money in higher education – have reached truly historic levels, greatly affecting the lives of young people traversing the educational system in the process (Goldin & Katz, 2009).

The most common illustration of such rising returns to investments in higher education is the earnings premium, which refers to the increase in income that one earns over time after receiving a college degree (or higher) rather than completing education with secondary schooling (e.g., at high school graduation in the United States). Figure 6.1 tracks the earnings premium for a bachelor's degree for Americans into their mid-30s. It shows that the premium has risen dramatically since the

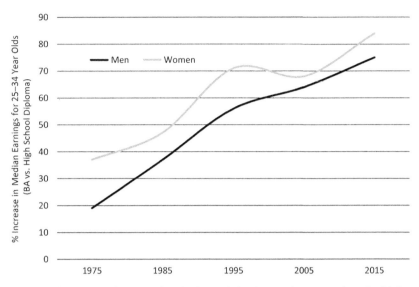

Figure 6.1 Recent historical trends in the earnings premium for higher education in the United States, by gender
Source: Baum & Ma, 2007; Ma et al., 2016

early-1970s, the period often discussed as the real start of economic restructuring. This increase has been greater – albeit more uneven – for women than men over these four-plus decades, which were also a period of rapid increase in the labor force participation of women in the United States and in many other countries (Buchman, Diprete, & McDaniel, 2008; Hout, 2012; Ma et al., 2016; Taylor et al., 2014). Such returns can also be found in the other life course domains, including marriage, fertility, health, and even life expectancy (Lynch, 2003; McLanahan, 2004; Schwarz & Mare, 2005).

Clearly, educational attainment makes a major difference in the lives of contemporary Americans as well as their counterparts in other developed countries. Not surprisingly, then, demand for higher education – in terms of the number of people who want to attend college and who actually do enrol – has also increased in recent decades. Figure 6.2 illustrates this trend, demonstrating the steady increase of enrollment in two-year and four-year colleges in the United States that is contemporaneous with the more dramatic increase in the earnings premium. Just as in other countries, more people are at least attempting to extend their educational careers beyond secondary school. Again, this phenomenon has been more pronounced for women, who overtook men in college enrollment

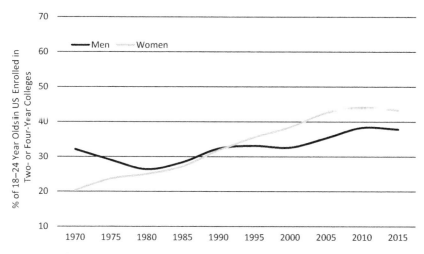

Figure 6.2 Recent historical trends in higher education enrollment in the United States, by gender
Source: National Center for Education Statistics, 2017

in the early 1990s (and even earlier for four-year college enrollment) and subsequently reached parity with or exceeded men in many different kinds of graduate education (Buchmann et al., 2008; National Center for Education Statistics, 2017).

The interplay of rising returns to investments in higher education and increasing enrollment in higher education have helped to create a "college for all" mentality in the United States and other developed countries. This mentality emphasizes higher education as the natural outcome of the educational career at the expense of other dimensions of socioeconomic attainment, such as going directly into trades or through vocational training. Despite its clear value in the aggregate, however, higher education is not for everyone, with many young people having skills, interests, and proclivities that might be better suited to direct labor market entry after high school than continuing into higher education. What's more, higher education is not accessible by everyone, as the rising costs of enrolling in postsecondary institutions – especially elite institutions – have outstripped the real or perceived means of many young people and their families. This issue of access is even more pronounced in the United States than in other countries that invest more in supporting young people's educational pursuits, as the costs of enrollment – and supporting oneself while enrolled – are borne solely by the individual (Grodsky & Jones, 2007; Kane, 2004; Rosenbaum, 2001). Interestingly, evidence suggests that the returns to college-going are greatest for young people who are the least likely to go to college (e.g., lower-ability, more disadvantaged backgrounds; see Hout, 2012), but how realistic college-going is for many is definitely an issue.

This educational change has significant developmental implications, especially given the extensive research on the ways that young people see their futures and how they structure their lives with those imagined or desired futures in mind. Consider the theoretical work in developmental psychology (e.g., Eccles, 2011) on young people's educational expectations and how they factor into their current academic behavior. The new college for all climate and the increasingly normative image of college-going in the life course surely provide a new context for those expectations for the future and what they mean for behavior far earlier in life.

Curricular Differentiation

The rising returns to investments in higher education and the associated college for all mentality have created downward pressure on lower levels of the educational system across countries (e.g., K-12 schools in the United States). This pressure involves preparing students for higher education, in terms of academic skill development but also planning, goal orientation, and the development of "non-cognitive" skills, such as persistence and community engagement. Today's youth need the kinds of academic credentials that colleges desire (e.g., credits in advanced subjects, honors credits, high test scores) and the academic preparation to succeed in college curricula (e.g., well-developed math and writing skills, effective study habits). Moreover, there is an increasing emphasis on academic paths that are well aligned with the new global economy, such as science, technology, engineering, and math (or STEM) (Adelman, 2006; National Research Council, 2011; Schneider, 2007).

In this context, the curricula of contemporary high schools in the United States have become increasingly differentiated in ways that contrast differentiated curricula in many European countries. There are many different subjects being taught in US high schools in addition to the core coursework in math, social studies, science, and English, and each subject can be internally broken down into specific areas (e.g., chemistry vs. biology), levels (regular vs. honors), and sections (morning vs. afternoon), with many other possible points of differentiation (e.g., Advanced Placement, dual college-credit). This differentiation has created an explosion of choice, where students are confronted with a plethora of pathways to take to some desired endpoint, especially attending some level of higher education (Morgan, 2005). This trend is a long-term one. The phrase "Shopping Mall High School" was coined back in the 1980s to refer to such differentiation and the many choices that contemporary students must shop through to construct their educational pathways (Powell, Cohen, & Farrar, 1985).

The contrast to this curricular differentiation within schools in the United States is the across school differentiation of curricula in other developed countries, especially those in Europe. Their systems tend to be marked by very clear "branch points" that send students into very different types of secondary schools with their own unique curricula designed to lead to a specific endpoint, such as attending college or entering the labor market. Germany is a good example. In the German system, children attend the same type of school, where they are exposed to a general academic curriculum, for several years until age 10 or so. At that branch point, their perceived aptitudes divert them into the academic secondary school preparing students for entry into higher education and especially elite institutions (i.e., gymnasium) or into vocational-focused schools or schools that mix academic and vocational training. Thus, German youth are differentiated by the type of school they attend, while US students are differentiated by the track they are following through the same type of school (Buchmann & Park, 2009). In the former system, students appear to have less choice, with more set and inflexible pathways and little movement in between pathways. In the latter system, however, the paradox is that each move that students take (e.g., enrolling in course A vs. course B in the first year of high school) locks them more and more into a pathway because the system is so cumulative, with each course building on the one before it and leading directly into the next. Even amidst seemingly abundant choice, therefore, different students effectively follow self-reinforcing pathways that diverge from each other over time as their realistic (vs. possible) choices narrow from year to year (Crosnoe & Muller, 2014; Morgan, 2005).

Such curricular differentiation – in both its within-school form and across-school form – also has significant developmental implications, much like the rising returns to investments in higher education. In a cumulative system where early behaviors and choices greatly affect end-of-school outcomes and the importance of end-of-school outcomes for the transition into adulthood is high, even short-term developmental problems can have long-term consequences. For example, a young person who experiences some of the social ups and downs of adolescence (e.g., some isolated instance of peer victimization, temporary bouts of emotional distress) may be distracted from schoolwork for one semester of high school and then recover and leave that problem behind. Yet, that point-in-time distraction could alter their academic pathways towards higher education – e.g., because of an uncharacteristic poor grade in a core course that requires a repeat or denies entry into some special program – in a way that is hard to correct after the fact. Consequently, even a temporary developmental disruption continues to have educational consequences long after recovery (Crosnoe, 2011).

Convergence of Historical Trends

In the restructured global economy of the twenty-first century, young people in many different societies are in greater need of higher education to maximize their odds of social and economic success, which increases the importance of their journeys through lower levels of education to the point of gaining access to higher education. The stakes have risen, and the educational system has become seemingly more open in theory, but also more cumulative and deterministic in practice. In this context, how young people think about the future takes on added significance, and the potential lingering consequences of the "normal" turbulence of adolescence have grown. There is, of course, another layer of complexity to consider, which concerns the ways in which such implications of these trends intersect with racial/ethnic, socioeconomic, and other kinds of stratification to create and reinforce inequality in a society over time – societal inequality that is felt in the lives of individual children and adolescents. I turn to that issue next.

Spotlight on Inequality in Increasingly Diverse Societies

The composition and size of the US population has changed considerably over the last several decades, and many of the major population changes of this kind are intricately connected with the rising economic inequality of the country over the last half century. Although more extreme in the United States than in many other developed societies, this pace of diversification and its links with economic inequality are not confined to this country. Together, these two trends affect the health of the population and the functioning of societal institutions, including the educational system, and, in the process, reshape the developmental contexts of young people navigating those systems or affected by them.

Racial/Ethnic Diversification

As shown in Figure 6.3, the population of young people in the United States was at least two-thirds White (i.e., of European ancestry) towards

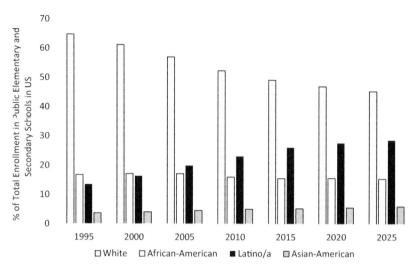

Figure 6.3 Reported and projected racial/ethnic breakdown of the United States public school population
Source: National Center for Education Statistics, 2015

the end of the twentieth century. After just over a decade of the twenty-first century, however, it could be classified as a majority–minority population – in other words, Whites no longer make up a majority of US youth. That trend will continue into the future, with a growing representation of Latino/a and Asian-American youth and, although not shown in the figure, multi-racial youth. This racial/ethnic diversification reflects the increase in migration from Latin America and Asia into the United States in the wake of the reform of federal immigration laws in the mid-1960s and then the differential fertility rates across various racial/ethnic groups (e.g., declining fertility among Whites matched with higher fertility in non-White groups) in subsequent years (Kao & Thompson, 2003; National Center for Education Statistics, 2015).

The racial/ethnic diversification of the child and adolescent population means that schools must serve much more heterogeneous student bodies filled with young people with different needs, talents, and interests. For example, the rise of migration to the United States from across the world has increased the number of English language learners in schools and the number of different languages being spoken in their homes and communities. This change has been both a challenge and opportunity, as many schools have been overwhelmed by the academic needs of students from diverse linguistic backgrounds while others have figured out new ways to scaffold their learning. The result has been a reconceptualization of the instruction and learning process, centering on the need to maintain students' exposure to academic curricula and instruction in their home languages until they are capable of learning in English so that they do not fall behind academically (see Takanishi & Le Menestrel, 2017). As another example, more diverse student bodies have led schools and districts to consider the ethnocentrism of their curricula and open up new fields of teaching and learning for students in order to reflect a broader worldview and to be more culturally responsive (Dee & Penner, 2017). As a final example, more diverse schools mean that young people have more experience interacting with peers and teachers of different backgrounds, but evidence also suggests that such schools can sometimes house more discord and competition among different racial/ethnic groups that make them less healthy developmental contexts for young people. The take-home message from such research is that schools must make more concerted efforts to socially integrate students from diverse backgrounds beyond just bringing them together inside a school (Johnson, Crosnoe, & Elder, 2001).

Socioeconomic Stratification

Figure 6.4 tracks the Gini ratio over the course of economic restructuring in the United States. This statistic measures the level of economic inequality in a population, ranging from 0 (where everyone receives an equal share of income) to 1 (where income is concentrated in a single group). It has risen almost a full point since 1970, which is a substantial increase that puts the United States near the top among developed countries (US Census Bureau, 2017). In other words, the United States is a relatively unequal society, and this inequality is on the rise.

This inequality needs to be considered in the context of the rising returns to investments in higher education and the rising costs of higher education. On one hand, enrolling in and completing higher education can have a substantial impact on the future life trajectories of young people, especially those from more disadvantaged and/or disenfranchised backgrounds. On the other hand, the expense of initially enrolling in and then persisting through higher education has risen considerably to reduce access by young people from these more disadvantaged and/or disenfranchised backgrounds, particularly access to selective four-year colleges. This expense has also led to a dramatic increase in student loan debt. As a result, the young people who most need to attend college are the least likely to be able to do so, contributing to the intergenerational transmission of socioeconomic inequality. Notably from a developmental

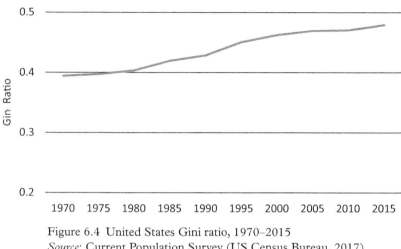

Figure 6.4 United States Gini ratio, 1970–2015
Source: Current Population Survey (US Census Bureau, 2017)

standpoint, this inequality is not just a reflection of the actual costs of higher education but also how young people perceive the costs of higher education and the barriers that such costs represent, both overall and vis-à-vis its potential benefits (Goldrick-Rab, 2016; Grodsky & Jones, 2007; Hoxby, 2004). How young people foresee their future educational trajectories in this new economic landscape, how much they (and those around them) understand what is required of them earlier in the educational career, whether they and their parents are able to plan accordingly, and how well societal institutions are serving them in this process all become important considerations in a cumulative and differentiated educational system leading up to the point of college entry.

Primary and Secondary Effects

The interdisciplinary literature on educational stratification features many different conceptual approaches to understanding how family-based markers of inequality – such as family socioeconomic status (SES), race/ethnicity, or immigrant status – and individual markers of inequality (e.g., LGBTQ status) can create and exacerbate the gradual divergence in the trajectories of young people from different backgrounds through the complex curricular landscape of modern educational systems. Here, I focus on one particular conceptual approach out of many, chosen because it reflects the cumulative consequences of inequality over time that are rooted in processes that are both academic and non-academic, systemic and individualistic. This approach – which I label primary/secondary effects – captures the journey that students take through their educational careers and the ways that their family backgrounds and other traits and characteristics can direct and redirect this journey at different points along the way.

Originally formulated by Boudon (1974), the primary/secondary effects framework contrasts two ways that family socioeconomic circumstances influence academic transitions, but this framework is useful for thinking about a variety of stratification systems (including race/ethnicity and immigration) as well as understanding academic progress and educational attainment more broadly (Jackson, 2013). Basically, *primary effects* concern disparities in aptitude and performance at some point in the educational career that are rooted in the heritability of academically-relevant traits and the cumulative nature of social and academic experiences up to that point (Erikson et al., 2005; Jackson et al., 2007).

In other words, a student from some privileged position in society (e.g., family with high socioeconomic status, membership in a powerful racial/ethnic group) is more like to attain some valued academic credential (e.g., accruing an Advanced Placement credit in the United States or equivalent in other educational systems, enrolling in an elite college) than someone from a less privileged position in society because the former is or appears to be more academically prepared and have better developed academic skills at that point. He or she might have gained that advantage in preparation and skill at that point in the educational career because, for many years, that privileged position kept opening up new and better academic opportunities (e.g., high-quality preschool, a more academically rigorous elementary school, supplemental tutoring in core subjects or test-taking, extracurricular enrichment) that facilitated a greater pace and level of learning and skill development over time. What matters at that single point in time is not how this advantage came to be – or whether it emerged from an unfair and unequal social system or more meritocratically – but simply the fact that this advantage exists at all (Alexander, Entwisle, & Olson, 2014; Duncan & Murnane, 2011; Goldthorpe, 2000).

Such primary effects can be differentiated from *secondary effects*, which shine more light on inequality in the system and how it builds over time. Secondary effects involve the disparities in some academic outcomes that emerge at some point in the educational career, even among young people from different positions in society who have the same level of aptitude and preparedness at that point. They arise because even similar ability students can make different academic moves and transitions within a range of choices, options, and opportunities presented to them by that shared ability level (Breen & Goldthorpe, 2000; Morgan, Spiller, & Todd 2013).

Let's go back to that comparison between a young person from a privileged strata or group in society and one from a less privileged background, but this time they both have the same level of prior achievement, test scores, and other criteria that gives them an equal chance to accrue that Advanced Placement credit (or its equivalent in other educational systems) or to gain entry to that elite college. Yet, despite being in a seemingly equal position, the former student gets that credit or enrolls in that college, and the latter does not. Perhaps that is because the more privileged student was more likely to have parents who understood how important Advanced Placement experience is as preparation for future college studies or teachers who pushed him or her towards sending in an application, or perhaps the gatekeepers (e.g., counselors controlling enrollment in Advanced Placement courses or college admissions officers) conflated that student's privilege with her or his suitability for that academic opportunity. What matters at that point in the educational career is how non-academic advantages can create inequalities even when there are no academic differences influencing those inequalities (Crosnoe & Muller, 2014; Goldthorpe, 2000; Morgan, 2005).

Of course, primary and secondary effects can and do intersect. Consider the case of two students, one from a socioeconomically and racially/ethnically advantaged background and one in a more disadvantaged position, who reach the start of some level of schooling with the same amount of academic preparation and skill. Despite this important similarity, the former student is placed in a more rigorous and rewarded curricula than the latter because of the strategizing of parents, the advocacy of teachers, and/or discrimination that works in her or his favor. These secondary effects mean that this student then has more opportunities to learn, achieve, and develop skills over the next several years. When the two students reach the next level of schooling, they no longer have the same amount of academic preparation and skill. The more privileged one has more than the less privileged one and, as a result of these newly emergent primary effects, gets selected for a new curriculum that is more advanced. In this interplay, primary and secondary effects feed off each other, and the two students' academic trajectories diverge the longer that they remain in the system. By the end of secondary schooling, this divergence is wide enough to have a large impact on whether and where they enroll in higher education, which, in turn, affects how they transition into and through adulthood.

The convergence of primary and secondary effects can have a lasting impact on educational and subsequent life course trajectories. This impact can arise in the branched educational systems (e.g., where curricular differentiation occurs across schools) found in many European countries as well as in the more open system (e.g., where curricular differentiation occurs across schools) found in the United States. Yet, how this impact arises can differ across these two types of systems. In the branched system, primary and secondary effects can most clearly be seen at the formal branch points. For example, the branch that sends some students into advanced academic training and higher education and other students towards vocational training and the labor market occurs later in the United Kingdom than in Germany, at around age 16. At this point, there is a very clear difference between socioeconomically advantaged students and socioeconomically disadvantaged students, with the former more likely to go the academic route than the latter. This difference can be explained partly by the primary effects of socioeconomic status on this transition (i.e., the more advantaged students have accrued more academic credentials over time than more disadvantaged students, so they "look" like better candidates) and partly by the secondary effects of socioeconomic status on this transition (i.e., the more advantaged students are more likely to go this route than more disadvantaged students with the same grades and skill levels because they have greater resources on which they can draw to understand the system and meet its perceived challenges). Because branch points are less formal in the US system, primary and secondary effects are more diffuse across many years, build gradually over time, and do not clearly present a critical point of intervention (Breen & Goldthorpe, 2001; Buchmann & Park, 2009; Erikson et al., 2005; Jackson et al., 2007; Morgan et al., 2013).

Diversity, Inequality, and the Nature of Modern Systems

Primary and secondary effects provide a useful lens through which to consider the implications of an increasingly diverse and unequal population on the individual experiences of students in schools, regardless of culture or system. In such populations, social, economic, and demographic markers can become points of difference that create competition and raise the odds of such stratifying processes and their links with differential treatment, stereotyping, and bias (implicit and explicit). Given how cumulative differentiated educational systems can be, these processes can shape the trajectories of young people gradually, so that seemingly small differences in opportunity at any one point of schooling can be compounded over time into large end-of-school outcomes. Those end-of-school outcomes, in turn, have an outsized impact on the transition into higher education in an era in which that transition has become profoundly consequential to the life course (Alexander et al., 2014; Morgan, 2005).

This process of cumulative advantage in primary and secondary effects fostered by educational systems – and the meaning of this cumulative advantage for the rest of life – has increased attention to the potential value of early intervention, including and especially in the United States. Ample evidence suggests that young children enter formal schooling with small but noticeable socioeconomic, racial/ethnic, and immigration-related disparities in academic skills, such as literacy and numeracy. These disparities reflect both primary and secondary effects and then lead to differences in subsequent treatment and opportunities in a self-propagating sequence. Rather than target academic disparities when and where they are largest, an alternate strategy is to target the small early disparities that eventually grow into larger ones. In other words, eliminate or reduce primary effects early in children's lives so that they cannot then repeat over time or be exacerbated by secondary effects (Alexander et al., 2014). Econometric evidence does suggest that such a strategy is feasible, with investments in early childhood interventions (e.g., investing in high-quality early childhood education programs prior to the start of formal schooling) bringing greater long-term returns in the form of adult outcomes (e.g., more education, higher earnings, lower odds of criminal justice contact) than human capital interventions targeting older youth (Heckman, 2006). The idea is to enrich the educational experiences of children from disadvantaged backgrounds when they are still young, before those backgrounds have had a large effect on their learning and on their opportunities to learn. This early intervention approach has become popular across the United States and in a wide variety of countries with different kinds of educational systems, including the creation of state-sponsored universal pre-K programs (Washbrook et al., 2012; Britto, Yoshikawa, & Boller, 2011; Zigler, Gilliam, & Jones, 2006).

Notably, many of the early childhood education programs designed to block primary effects on early skill development often incorporate more holistic approaches to education that go beyond academic skills and a strict focus on the child. Instead, they target development more broadly to include the acquisition of social and emotional skills, they include programs for parents to help them better manage children's lives, and they seek to build bridges between educational programs and the larger communities in which they are situated. Many of these holistically oriented programs following developmentally appropriate and culturally responsive practices are specially tailored for parents of color and/or for immigrant parents, aiming to break down barriers between them and the schools serving their children, demystify the educational system for those with less familiarity with its often unwritten rules and cultural assumptions, and enabling educators to see the strengths that such parents bring to the mission of educating their children (Genishi & Dyson, 2009; Tobin, Adair, & Arzubiaga, 2013; Zigler et al., 2006). These added features of early childhood education are important because they target the secondary effects that can make a difference to children's educational opportunities even when their academic skill development is being attended to adequately.

This early childhood intervention approach to social, economic, and demographic inequality in a cumulative, differentiated, and consequential educational system serving an increasingly diverse population has grabbed the focus of educational policy and practice in recent years and the scientific research aiming to inform both. Yet, it is far from the only approach. Its importance – and it *is* important – cannot crowd out other perspectives and strategies, including those related to primary and secondary effects at later stages of schooling. In the next section, therefore, I discuss a selection of approaches to reducing educational inequality in the modern era, each one targeting a different level of the ecology of education in the United States and other countries.

Strategies for Serving Students in the New Educational Order

In the United States and other developed countries, education has become highly differentiated and cumulative with great consequences for the future, with these various features exacerbating the intergenerational transmission of inequality as diversity among students has increased. On the individual level, young people are developing – not just academically but also socially, psychologically, and emotionally – within this system, enjoying the opportunities it affords some, bumping up against constraints it places on others, and learning lessons about themselves and the world. Across levels, primary and secondary effects differentiate the experiences and prospects of diverse groups of young people and differentiate the trajectories of individual youth.

Early childhood intervention is one potential strategy to counter these primary and secondary effects and break the often strong link between family background and social position on one hand and learning and achievement on the other. If we move past that early intervention focus, what other strategies might work? Because an exhaustive description of potential strategies is not possible here, I instead pick four that highlight different points of entry in educational inequality in contemporary systems, starting with the most contextual level and then working down to individual students. For each, I will discuss the philosophy behind the strategy and also point out the many challenges of realizing the potential of that strategy that have been experienced in the "real world."

Changing School Through Integration

Can the composition and organization of schools be changed to reduce the divergence of educational and developmental trajectories of young people from different backgrounds and social positions?

The common school ideal is relevant to answering this question. It refers to a major foundational principle of the US educational system that also had wide influence on the construction of public systems in other countries. This ideal contends that, in democratic societies, state-sponsored schools should educate children from diverse socioeconomic strata under one roof, both out of principle but also to promote more social cohesion among socioeconomically diverse segments of the population. The common school ideal was also considered to be crucial to the goal of creating a more meritocratic educational system and, more broadly, a more equitable society. To ensure that success in life was predicated on skills, ability, and effort and not a function of background and circumstances, young people from more advantaged and more disadvantaged strata of society had to have the same opportunities, and attending the same school was thought to be one key step towards equality of educational opportunity (Coleman & Hoffer, 1987; Cremin, 1980). As such, this ideal has long made school integration/desegregation efforts a central component of the educational policy agenda aiming to reduce educational inequality, but the nature of these efforts has evolved over time.

One important aspect of the evolution of school integration/desegregation efforts has involved the shift in focus from race/ethnicity to socioeconomic status. Of course, for much of US history, the common school ideal was undermined in theory and practice by the long (and widely accepted) exclusion of African-American youth from school and then their segregation from other students in separate schools. The landmark *Brown vs. Board of Education* decision by the US Supreme Court in 1954 ended the legal segregation of public schools by race/ethnicity, at least symbolically if not in immediate practice. Eventually, large-scale school desegregation did occur, with substantial increases in within-school racial/ethnic diversity and gradual reductions in the racial achievement gap (Cottrol, Diamond, & Ware, 2003; Tyson, 2011). Nevertheless, the persistent conflict over racial/ethnic desegregation – and other racial/ethnic-focused policies and programs like affirmative action – in the United States led to increasingly successful challenges to desegregation plans in federal and state courts in the late twentieth century and early twenty-first century as well as legislative actions to roll back these plans. As a result, many racial/ethnic desegregation plans were abandoned, and racial/ethnic segregation began to increase again (Clotfelter, Ladd, & Vigdor 2005; Mickelson, 2001; Reardon & Owens, 2014; Reardon, Yun, & Eitle, 2001; Tyson, 2011). In 2007, the US Supreme Court weighed in to validate this trend, handing down the *Parents Involved* decision to effectively end the recognition of racial balance in schools as a compelling state interest.

As support for racial/ethnic desegregation plans as a means of reducing educational disparities waned, support for socioeconomic desegregation plans – which use indicators of socioeconomic status (typically family income) as a factor in student assignments to create more heterogeneous public schools (Kahlenberg, 2001) – increased considerably. Indeed, the *Parents Involved* decision actually held up socioeconomic desegregation as an acceptable alternative to racial/ethnic desegregation. This return to the socioeconomic focus of the common school ideal reflects the clear evidence that low socioeconomic status clearly undermines the academic progress of young people. At all stages of schooling, from early childhood education up through higher education, students from low-income families and/or who have parents with low levels of education have lower levels of achievement (e.g., grades, test scores) and attainment (e.g., diplomas, degrees) than the general population. These academic disparities – which reflect a variety of processes from the institutional to the interpersonal – then help to explain why growing up in economically disadvantaged circumstances is associated with being economically disadvantaged as an adult, particularly as the long-term returns to investments in higher education increase (Arum 2000; Duncan et al., 1998; Mayer, 1997; Raver, Gershoff, & Aber, 2007; Reardon, 2011).

Moving students from socioeconomically disadvantaged backgrounds into more middle class and affluent schools could be a way to improve their educational opportunities and future prospects in the cumulative, differentiated, and consequential curricula of contemporary US education for reasons that are both academic and developmental. In such schools, young people who have grown up in socioeconomically disadvantaged circumstances *should*: 1) be exposed to more socioeconomically advantaged peers with more advanced vocabularies, more developed skills, and stronger engagement; 2) enter better-organized classrooms with low student/teacher turnover and a greater proportion of instructional time for activities aiming to build higher-order cognitive and academic skills; and 3) interact with socioeconomically advantaged parents, who tend to be more involved in schooling matters, have power to advocate for students, and provide access to networks of social and financial capital (Kahlenberg, 2001). These reasons are empirically supported by evidence of significant associations between the aggregate socioeconomic status of the student body of a school (e.g., average family income) and higher average academic achievement among students from disadvantaged backgrounds in that school (Rothstein, 2004; Rumberger & Palardy, 2005; Sui-Chu & Willms, 1996).

The push for socioeconomic desegregation has another underlying motivation, which is that desegregating schools in relation to socioeconomic status could theoretically desegregate them by race/ethnicity without explicitly targeting race/ethnicity. That is because socioeconomic status is so closely correlated with race/ethnicity (and immigration status) in the United States. Consequently, socioeconomically segregated schools also are often racially/ethnically segregated schools, and associated socioeconomic disparities in academic progress and educational attainment also are often racial/ethnic disparities. Doing something about one, therefore, could do something about the other (Kahlenberg, 2001; Plank, 2000; Rothstein, 2004).

Reflecting these motivations, socioeconomic desegregation plans have been enacted in a number of locales across the United States. The expected gains in academic achievement from these new kinds of desegregation plans have not been consistent, and some of these plans have been scaled back (Bazelon, 2008; Flinspach & Banks, 2005; Kahlenberg, 2001; Mercer, 2003; Plank, 2000). Perhaps the dissatisfaction with these plans – and associated conflicts with schools and districts – among affluent families blocked their success, or perhaps their implementation was faulty. Another possibility is that socioeconomic disparities in academic achievement is too intransigent to reduce with just a single type of school reform.

Research with a broader focus has also suggested that the developmental experience of being a socioeconomically disadvantaged young person attending a socioeconomically advantaged school may chip away at the benefits of such attendance. Compared to attending a school with socioeconomically similar students, that student may be more likely to struggle fitting in, be stigmatized, or be at a competitive disadvantage for access to valued opportunities (e.g., entry into an honors program, a seat in an advanced course). Those problems might not eliminate the academic benefits of being in a more middle class or affluent school but could dilute them. If so, then socioeconomic desegregation plans need to also include strategies for socially integrating new students into their schools (Crosnoe, 2009).

Changing Curricula Within Schools Through Intensification

Can the dilution of choice in the modern academic curriculum reduce the divergence of educational and developmental trajectories of young people from different backgrounds and social positions?

The policy push for curricular intensification is relevant to answering this question. Intensification refers to policies and practices that attempt to increase the level of academic rigor to which young people from diverse backgrounds and different abilities are exposed by constraining the range of options available to them. Basically, in any one school grade, some young people might be taking higher-level and more challenging coursework while others take lower-level and less challenging coursework. One perspective is that young people need to be in curricula that are aligned with their ability levels, so that the challenges of a course above one's level of ability and preparation depresses learning over time. Another more theoretically informed perspective is that young people will "rise" to the level of challenges that they face, so that challenging coursework will actually boost learning over time (Domina & Saldana, 2011; Oakes, 2005; Weinstein, 2002).

In this sense, the uneven distribution of young people from advantaged and disadvantaged backgrounds across highly differentiated curricula – especially the concentration of the former in more rigorous curricula and the latter in less challenging curricula – will likely widen disparities in academic progress and educational attainment. That uneven distribution reflects discriminatory practices and perceptions that steer young people from different backgrounds into different curricula but also from the seemingly logical actions of young people themselves and their parents (e.g., thinking that young people might be better off in less challenging coursework). Catholic schools tend to have less differentiated curricula with little difference across ability levels in the courses that young people take, which constrains the degree to which school practices or student/parent actions can lead to systematic differences in the courses in which young people from advantaged and disadvantaged backgrounds enroll. This "no bad choices" tradition is often given as a reason for the empirical evidence suggesting that there is higher overall achievement and less pronounced achievement disparities in Catholic schools than in other kinds of private schools and in public schools (Coleman & Hoffer, 1987; Lee, Smerdon, Alfeld-Liro, & Brown, 2000; Morgan, 2001). It also motivated more recent curricular intensification efforts. Make young people take the same courses, so these subtle but pernicious influences – especially in the form or secondary effects – cannot create or exacerbate disparities.

Consider the case of recent curricula reforms in California middle schools, which have aimed to increase persistence in the STEM pipeline by using algebra as the accountability benchmark for 8th graders in the state. Some districts responded by all but requiring all 8th graders to take algebra. The thought was that this requirement would eliminate student and school choice of which math course to take and theoretically reduce opportunities for primary and secondary effects, not just in enrollment at that point but in subsequent enrollments at later points that are predicated on experience with algebra. The results were more complicated. Evaluation of this curricular intensification policy in a large and diverse school district revealed that it did greatly increase the proportion of 8th graders who enrolled in algebra – enabling them to take higher-level math coursework in high school and also reduced racial/ethnic and socioeconomic disparities in algebra enrollment. Yet, the expected gains in math test scores among 8th graders in the district over the next two years did not materialize, presumably because the greater inclusiveness brought on by curricula intensification diluted the selectivity of the population of math students and perhaps the rigor of the curriculum that they were receiving (Domina et al., 2015, 2014).

This research on curricular intensification in California reflects national patterns aligned with the concept of maximally maintained inequality, which contends that educational inequalities will only decline once demand for some valued credential among the most powerful groups in society has been satisfied (see Hout, 2006). Basically, evening out disparities in enrollments at early steps of the STEM sequence (e.g., Algebra) tends to push back disparities into later steps in the sequence (e.g., Calculus) (Domina & Saldana, 2011). These unintended consequences do not mean that curricula intensification should be abandoned but rather that implementing curricular intensification plans in the absence of other kinds of supports and without awareness of how inequality works could backfire. The cumulative, differentiated, and consequential nature of contemporary education is too complex for single – and simplistically implemented – strategies aiming at the reduction of inequality to work.

Changing Connections between Schools and Communities Through Partnership

Can strengthening ecological transactions reduce the divergence of educational and developmental trajectories of young people from different backgrounds and social positions?

The concept of family–school–community partnerships is relevant to answering this question. Such partnerships involve the active, ongoing, and bidirectional transactions among the parents, educators, and other community members focused on serving a child's or adolescent's educational pursuits and general well-being (Epstein, 2011). It grew out of the closely related concept of parental involvement in education, which, as the term suggests, was focused on parental behavior often in the absence of other considerations and actors. For example, parents can support and facilitate the academic progress and educational attainment of their children through a variety of means, including home-based behaviors such as shared reading, school-based behaviors such as volunteering at school, and community-based behaviors such as enrolling children in extracurricular activities (with more developmentally appropriate variants on these three kinds of behaviors as children grow into adolescents). Across developmental time and stages of schooling, these behaviors are associated with a broad array of positive academic outcomes, including indicators of academic achievement but also school behaviors (Pomerantz, Moorman, & Litwack, 2007).

Consequently, there has been significant federal, state, and local policy investment in efforts to increase parental involvement in education. The goal of such efforts is not just that parental involvement is good for young people overall but also that it might be especially important to the success of young people from more disadvantaged or disenfranchised backgrounds and communities. If so, then increasing parental involvement in these segments of the population might reduce associated disparities in academic progress and educational attainment (Christenson & Sheridan, 2001; Domina, 2005; Epstein, 2011). In the context of the cumulative, differentiated, and consequential educational system characteristic of many developed countries today, increased parental involvement could be especially helpful for reducing secondary effects at major transition points in the educational career that build on past primary effects and create new ones moving forward (Crosnoe & Muller, 2014).

This attention to parental involvement in education as a policy tool for promoting educational equity among children in the modern educational system has been contested. In part, these tensions concern perceived racial/ethnic biases in research, practice, and policy that have set up the parenting behaviors and values of more affluent, European American, and US-born parents as an ideal and devalued or dismissed other ways that parents may support their children's academic pursuits. Specifically, the former tend to equate active, vocal, managerial, and especially school-based involvement behaviors with "good" parenting. Parents who do not engage in those behaviors, then, might be looked down upon by school personnel, who view them as not caring about education, even if they engage in a wide variety of less visible but still important behaviors outside of the school domain (e.g., encouragement, instilling values, guiding behavior). At the same time, such a contested perspective on parental involvement tends to place too much responsibility for schools' successes and failures on the shoulders of parents, as if any parental behavior occurs in a vacuum. The truth is that the effectiveness of parental efforts to facilitate children's learning and achievement depends on what schools are doing and, in particular, how school actions and perspectives align with what parents are doing, support parents' intentions, and elicit and respect parents' engagement. Those bidirectional exchanges are also nested in communities, which have value systems, norms, and opportunity structures that make it easier or harder for families and schools to work with each other. The fact that racial/ethnic minority parents, immigrant parents, and low-income parents are especially unlikely to have their needs and wishes met and answered by schools or to be welcomed into a true bidirectional relationship with schools links the one-sidedness of the parental involvement model in practice to the inequality it is supposed to address (Crosnoe, 2015; Domina, 2005; Lareau, 2003; Robinson & Harris, 2014; Tobin et al., 2013).

The response to this criticism of parental involvement in education as a central component of policy and programmatic efforts to reduce inequality and improve equity in the educational system has been the emphasis on building family–school–community partnerships. Such partnerships still revolve around the educational involvement of parents, but this involvement is conceptualized as a process that is both interactive and parallel with what is occurring in schools and situated in a larger community. Children and adolescents approach their education going back and forth between school-like families and family-like schools, creating a more seamless educational environment with synced norms and values, consistency in learning activities and supports, and mutual awareness of the unique inputs of each actor and how those inputs complement each other. Although labor-intensive to construct, such partnerships can better promote the learning and development of a more diverse spectrum of students (Epstein, 2011; Rimm-Kaufman & Pianta, 2000).

Changing Students through Mindset Interventions

Can empowering the motivation and engagement of individual youth in the modern academic curriculum reduce the divergence of educational and developmental trajectories of young people from different backgrounds and social positions?

The scientific literature on learning mindsets – and associated intervention strategies – is relevant to answering this question. Learning mindsets refer to how young people think about their own abilities and the translation of abilities into achievement-oriented behavior. Specifically, some young people develop a fixed mindset and are then more likely to view academic failures (e.g., poor test score, low grade, trouble with homework) as a sign that they lack some inherent ability necessary to do well in that domain of schooling. As a result, they come to expect that they cannot succeed in that domain no matter how hard they try, and their motivation and effort then decline as they avoid future academic challenges. Other students have a growth mindset, which encourages them to think of ability as a talent that they have to build through effort and hard work and skills as something that they develop rather than something that they just have. As a result, an academic failure is a sign that they need to exert more effort to develop skills in that domain, evidence that there is more work to do. Subsequently, their engagement increases, and they take on more academic challenges. Young people develop fixed or growth mindsets through a variety of mechanisms, including parental reactions to their academic accomplishments (or lack thereof), both overt and covert cues from teachers, and media (Dweck, 2006).

Notably, mindsets can also be changed. Indeed, mindset theory informed the construction of classroom-based (and then web-based) interventions that attempt to teach young people that their brains are like muscles, growing and gaining strength through exercise (i.e., rigorous learning activities). Early experimental evaluations of such interventions suggested that they did indeed increase learning mindsets in children and adolescents, who then subsequently had better academic outcomes than young people without such mindsets, even those with the same level of academic opportunities. Such observed effects of mindset interventions were especially pronounced for young people with lower levels of prior academic progress, levels that are more common in historically disadvantaged and disenfranchised segments of the population. These US results were also replicated in other developed countries (Paunesku et al., 2015; Yeager & Dweck, 2012; Yeager & Walton, 2011).

One problem with these interventions is that evaluations were typically conducted with small and specialized samples, reducing generalizability and inviting criticisms about replicability. In 2014, the National Study of Learning Mindsets conducted an experiment testing the effects of a mindset intervention with a national probability sample of young people in their first year at public high schools in the US Among over 12,000 young people from across the socioeconomic and demographic spectrum, the brief online intervention did slightly increase achievement and higher-level coursework. This effect, however, varied across schools – defined by the composition of the student body and the overall achievement norms of the school – in complex ways. As one example, young people in schools in the middle of the overall achievement distribution tended to benefit more from the intervention than those in schools with achievement histories at the lowest of highest ends of the distribution (Yeager et al., 2016; Yeager et al., forthcoming).

The point here is that achievement in school – and disparities in achievement – is not just about the academic opportunities presented to young people by their schools and communities. How young people think about school and perceive themselves also matters. That is a developmental phenomenon that requires developmentally informed approaches. At the same time, the causes of low achievement and achievement disparities are not solely about individual young people. Where they live and attend school also affects the degree to which developmental considerations factor into achievement outcomes within and across groups. This person x context interplay is often absent from the philosophical underpinnings and design of educational policy and practice, which is why primary and secondary effects are difficult to reduce, let alone completely eradicate.

Integrating Lessons

These four policy and programmatic approaches to reducing inequality and increasing equity in the context of a cumulative, differentiated, and consequential educational system are certainly not the only strategies available, but they are prominent examples of evidenced-based approaches that cross disciplinary lines and levels of educational intervention. Research related to each on its own typically tells a similar story, which is that the problem of inequality – as symbolized by the concept of primary and secondary effects – is too complex for single strategies. There is no simple fix but instead pieces of a larger multifaceted approach that recognizes the interplay of academic progress and development more generally, of the school as an educational institution and a context of social relations. Common schools are a start, but, in those schools, there needs to be attention to social integration and efforts to incorporate families and communities in ways that help young people see and take advantage of opportunities available to them.

Conclusion

Modern education is just that – modern. It has evolved considerably in response to (and anticipation of) dramatic changes in the world, including the restructuring of the economy and the diversification of the population, to become: a) more cumulative, with each step on a path through curricula and schools doing more to lock young people into a future educational fate; b) differentiated, with a range of perceived choices that belie how constrained young people's paths are; and c) consequential, with future implications that create pressures on young people early in life and crowd out other potential paths to adulthood. In describing this evolution, I have focused on the United States, but I want to reiterate that these issues are observed in and relevant to a host of developed countries around the world.

Many aspects of this evolution have increased threats to equality of opportunity and educational equity in an educational system struggling to meet the needs of a diverse array of students from many different kinds of backgrounds, with apparent markers of aptitude and skill among young people interacting with the processes of institutional, family, and individual decision-making to send young people in different directions towards the future. These problems are well known and have been subjected to a large amount of interdisciplinary research, and the evidence resulting from this research has informed ample action in policy and practice. Some strategies try to change schools, some try to change what is going on inside schools, some strategies change the ways that schools interact with the families and communities they serve, and some strategies eschew the context to change students themselves. Each of these solutions also comes with problems.

The theories and concepts of developmental science offer a way of addressing these problems, including the problems with the solutions targeting the original problems. Educational policy and practice should be developmentally informed, recognizing what young people need at each stage of schooling and how these needs change over time, situating young people and schools in the overlapping contexts of the larger ecology, emphasizing that sometimes academic issues require attention to non-academic processes, and matching the goal of being developmentally responsive to young people with the goal of being culturally responsive to their families and communities (Genishi & Dyson, 2009; Yeager, Dahl, & Dweck, 2018).

References

Adelman, C. (2006). *The Toolbox Revisited: Paths to degree completion from high school through college.* Washington, DC: US Department of Education.

Alexander, K. L., Entwisle, D. R., & Olson, L. S. (2014). *The Long Shadow: Family background, disadvantaged urban youth, and the transition to adulthood.* New York: Russell Sage Foundation.

Arum, R. (2000). Schools and communities: Ecological and institutional dimensions. *Annual Review of Sociology, 26,* 395–418.

Baum, S. & Ma, J. (2007). *Education Pays: The benefits of higher education for individuals and society.* Washington, DC: College Board.

Bazelon, E. (2008). The next kind of integration. *New York Times Magazine.* July 20.

Bernhardt, A., Morris, M., Handcock, M. S., & Scott, M. A. (2001). *Divergent Paths: Economic mobility in the new American labor market.* New York: Russell Sage.

Boudon, R. (1974). *Education, Opportunity, and Social Inequality.* New York: Wiley.

Breen, R. & Goldthorpe, J. H. (2001). Class mobility and merit: The experience of two British birth cohorts. *European Sociological Review, 17,* 81–101.

Britto, P. R., Yoshikawa, H., & Boller, K. (2011). Quality of early childhood development programs in global contexts: Rationale for investment, conceptual framework and implications for equity. *Social Policy Report, 25*(2), 3–23.

Bryk, A. & Schneider, B. (2003). *Trust in Schools: A core resource for improvement.* New York: Russell Sage.

Buchmann, B., DiPrete, T. A., & McDaniel, A. (2008). Gender inequalities in education. *Annual Review of Sociology, 34,* 319–337.

Buchmann, C. & Park, H. (2009). Stratification and the formation of expectations in highly-differentiated educational systems. *Research in Social Stratification and Mobility, 27,* 245–267.

Christenson, S. L. & Sheridan, S. M. (2001). *School and Families: Creating essential connections for learning.* New York: Guilford.

Clotfelter, C. T., Ladd, H. F., & Vigdor, J. L. (2005). Federal oversight, local control, and the specter of "resegregation" in southern schools. *National Bureau of Economic Research Working Paper Series* 11086.

Coleman, J. S. & Hoffer, T. (1987). *Public and Private High Schools: The impact of communities,* New York: Basic Books.

Cottrol, R. J., Diamond, R., & Ware, L. B. (2003). *Brown v. Board of Education: Caste, culture, and the Constitution.* Lawrence, KS: University Press of Kansas.

Cremin, L. A. (1957). *The Republic and the School: Horace Mann on the education of free men.* New York: Teachers College Press.

Crosnoe, R. & Muller, C. (2009). Low-income students and the socioeconomic composition of public high schools. *American Sociological Review, 74,* 709–730.

(2011). *Fitting in, Standing Out: Navigating the social challenges of high School to get an education.* New York: Cambridge University Press.

(2014). Family socioeconomic status, peers, and adolescents' path to college. *Social Problems, 61,* 1–23.

(2015). Continuities and consistencies across home and school systems. In Sheridan, S. M. & Moorman, E. (Eds.), *Research on Family-School Partnerships: An interdisciplinary examination of state of the science and critical needs* (pp. 61–80). New York: Springer.

Dee, T. S. & Penner, E. K. (2017). The causal effects of cultural relevance: Evidence from an ethnic studies curriculum. *American Educational Research Journal, 54*(1), 127–166.

Domina, T. (2005). Leveling the home advantage: Assessing the effectiveness of parental involvement. *Sociology of Education, 78*, 233–249.

Domina, T., McEachin, A., Penner, A., & Penner, E. (2015). Aiming high and falling short: California's eighth-grade algebra-for-all effort. *Educational Evaluation and Policy Analysis, 37*, 275–295.

Domina, T., Penner, A. M., Penner, E. K., & Conley, A. (2014). Algebra for All: California's eighth-grade Algebra initiative as constrained curricula. *Teachers College Record, 116*, 1–32.

Domina, T. & Saldana, J. (2012). Does raising the bar level the playing field? Mathematics curricular intensification and inequality in American high schools, 1982–2004. *American Educational Research Journal, 49*, 685–708.

Duncan, G. J., Brooks-Gunn, J., Yeung, W. J., & Smith, J. R. (1998). How much does childhood poverty affect the life chances of children? *American Sociological Review, 63*, 406–423.

Duncan, G. J. & Murnane, R. J. (Eds.). (2011). *Whither Opportunity? Rising inequality, schools, and children's life chances.* New York: Russell Sage Foundation.

Dweck, C. S. (2006). *Mindset: The new psychology of success.* New York: Random House.

Eccles, J. (2011). Gendered educational and occupational choices: Applying the Eccles et al. model of achievement-related choices. *International Journal of Behavioral Development, 35*(3), 195–201.

Epstein, J. L. (2011) *School, Family, and Community Partnerships: Preparing educators and improving schools.* Boulder, CO: Westview Press.

Erikson, R., Goldthorpe, J. H., Jackson, M., Yaish, M., & Cox, D. R. (2005). On class differentials in educational attainment. *Proceedings of the National Academy of Sciences of the United States of America, 102*, 9730–9733.

Fischer, C. S. & Hout, M. (2006). *Century of Difference: How America changed in the last one hundred years.* New York: Russell Sage.

Flinspach, S. E. & Banks, K. E. (2005). Moving beyond race: Socioeconomic diversity as a race-neutral approach to desegregation in the Wake County schools. In Borger, J. C. & Orfield, G. (Eds.), *School Segregation: Must the south turn back?* (pp. 261–280). Chapel Hill, NC: University of North Carolina Press.

Genishi, C. & Dyson, A. H. (2009). *Children, Language, and Literacy: Diverse learners in diverse times.* New York: Teachers College Press.

Goldin. C. & Katz, L. (2009). *The Race between Technology and Education.* Cambridge, MA: Harvard University Press.

Goldrick-Rab, S. (2016). *Paying the Price: College costs, financial aid, and the betrayal of the American dream.* Chicago, IL: University of Chicago Press.

Goldthorpe, J. H. (2000). *On Sociology: Numbers, narratives, and the integration of research and theory.* Oxford: Oxford University Press.

Grodsky, E. & Jones, M. T. (2007). Real and imagined barriers to college entry: Perceptions of cost. *Social Science Research, 36*, 745–766.

Heckman, J. (2006). Skill formation and the economics of investing in disadvantaged children. *Science, 312*, 1900–1902.

Hout, M. (2006). Maximally maintained inequality and essentially maintained inequality. *Sociological Theory and Methods, 21*, 237–252.

(2012). Social and economic returns to college education in the United States. *Annual Review of Sociology, 38,* 379–400.

Hoxby, C. (2004). *College Choices: The economics of where to go, when to go, and how to pay for it.* Chicago, IL: University of Chicago Press.

Jackson, M. (Ed.). (2013). *Determined to Succeed? Performance, choice and education.* Palo Alto, CA: Stanford University Press.

Jackson, M., Erikson, R., Goldthorpe, J. H., & Yaish, M. (2007). Primary and oooondary effects in class differentials in educational attainment: The transition to A-level courses in England and Wales. *Acta Sociologica, 50,* 211–229.

Johnson, M. K., Crosnoe, R., & Elder, G. H. (2001). Students' attachment and academic engagement: The role of race and ethnicity. *Sociology of Education, 74,* 318–340.

Kahlenberg, R. (2001). *All Together Now: Creating middle class schools through public choice.* Washington, DC: Brookings Institution.

Kane, T. (2004). College-going and inequality. In K. Neckerman (Ed.) *Social Inequality* (pp. 319–354). New York: Russell Sage.

Kao, G. & Thompson, J. (2003). Race and ethnic stratification in educational achievement and attainment. *Annual Review of Sociology, 29,* 417–442.

Lareau, A. (2003). *Unequal Childhoods: Class, race, and family life.* Berkeley, CA: University of California Press.

Lee, V. E., Smerdon, B. A., Alfeld-Liro, C., & Brown, S. L. (2000). Inside large and small high schools: Curriculum and social relations. *Educational Evaluation and Policy Analysis, 22,* 147–171.

Lynch, S. (2003). Cohort and life course patterns in the relationship between education and health: A hierarchical perspective. *Demography, 40,* 309–332.

Ma, J., Pender, M., & Welch, M. (2016). *Education Pays 2016: The benefits of higher education for individuals and society.* Washington, DC: College Board.

Mayer, S. E. (1997). *What Money Can't Buy.* Cambridge, MA: Harvard University Press.

McLanahan, S. (2004). Children and the second demographic transition. *Demography, 41,* 607–628.

Mercer, A. (2003). Socioeconomic balance: School board to consider the issue that divided community a decade ago. *LaCrosse Tribune.* January 19, 2003.

Mickelson, R. A. (2001). Subverting Swann: First- and second-generation segregation in teh Charlotte-Mecklenburg schools. *American Education Research Journal, 38,* 215–252.

Morgan, S. L. (2001). Counterfactuals, causal effect heterogeneity, and the Catholic school effect on learning. *Sociology of Education, 74,* 341–374.

(2005). *On the Edge of Commitment: Educational attainment and race in the United States.* Stanford, CA: Stanford University Press.

Morgan, S. L., Spiller, M. W., & Todd, J. J. (2013). Class origins, high school graduation, and college entry in the United States. In Jackson, M. (Eds.), *Determined to Succeed? Performance versus choice in educational attainment* (pp. 279–305). Palo Alto, CA: Stanford University Press.

National Center for Education Statistics. (2015). Digest of Education Statistics: Enrollment and percentage distribution of enrollment in public elementary and secondary schools, by race/ethnicity and region: Selected years, fall 1995 through fall 2026. https://nces.ed.gov/programs/digest/d16/tables/dt16_203.50.asp

(2017). Digest of Education Statistics: Percentage of 18- to 24-year-olds enrolled in degree-granting postsecondary institutions, by level of institution and sex and race/ethnicity of student: 1970 through 2015. https://nces.ed.gov/programs/digest/d16/tables/dt16_302.60.asp

National Research Council. (2011). *Successful K-12 STEM Education: Identifying effective approaches in science, technology, engineering, and mathematics.* Washington, DC: National Academies Press.

Oakes, J. (2005). *Keeping Track: How schools structure inequality* (2nd ed.). New Haven, CT: Yale University Press.

Paunesku, D., Walton, G. M., Romero, C., Smith, E. N., Yeager, D. S., & Dweck, C. S. (2015). Mind-set interventions are a scalable treatment for academic underachievement. *Psychological Science, 26,* 784–793.

Plank, S. (2000). *Finding One's Place: Teaching styles and peer relations in diverse classrooms.* New York: Teachers College Press.

Pomerantz, E. M., Moorman, E. A., & Litwack, S. D. (2007). The how, whom, and why of parents' involvement in children's academic lives: More is not always better. *Review of Educational Research, 77*(3), 373.

Powell, A. G., Farrar, E., & Cohen, D. K. (1985). *The Shopping Mall High School: Winners and losers in the educational marketplace.* Boston, MA: Houghton-Mifflin.

Raver, C. C., Gershoff, E., & Aber, L. (2007). Testing equivalence of mediating models of income, parenting, and school readiness for White, Black, and Hispanic children in a national sample. *Child Development, 78,* 96–115.

Reardon, S. F. (2011). The widening academic achievement gap between the rich and the poor: New evidence and possible explanations. In Duncan, G. J. & Murnane, R. (Eds.), *Whither Opportunity? Rising inequality, schools, and children's life chances* (pp. 91–116). New York: Russell Sage Foundation.

Reardon, S. F. & Owens, A. (2014). 60 years after Brown: Trends and consequences of school segregation. *Annual Review of Sociology, 40,* 199–218.

Reardon, S. F., Yun, J. T., & Eitle, T. M. (2001). The changing structure of school segregation: Measurement and evidence of multiracial metropolitan-area school segregation, 1989–1995. *Demography, 37,* 351–364.

Rimm-Kaufman, S. E. & Pianta, R. C. (2000). An ecological perspective on the transition to kindergarten: A theoretical framework to guide empirical research. *Journal of Applied Developmental Psychology, 21,* 491–511.

Robinson, K. & Harris, A. L. (2014). *The Broken Compass: Parental involvement with children's education.* New York: Harvard University Press.

Rosenbaum, J. (2001). *Beyond College for All: Career paths for the forgotten half.* New York: Russell Sage.

Rothstein, R. (2004). *Class and Schools: Using social, economic, and educational reform to close the Black-White achievement gap.* Washington, DC: Economic Policy Institute.

Rumberger, R. W. & Palardy, G. J. (2005). Does segregation still matter? The impact of social composition on academic achievement in high school. *Teachers College Record, 107,* 1999–2045.

Schneider, B. (2007). *Forming a College-Going Community in US Schools*. Seattle, WA: Bill and Melinda Gates Foundation.

Schwartz, C. R. & Mare, R. D. (2005). Trends in educational assortative marriage from 1940 to 2003. *Demography, 42*, 621–646.

Sui-Chu, E. H. & Willms, J. D. (1996). Effects of parental involvement on eighth-grade achievement. *Sociology of Education, 69*, 126–141.

Takanishi, R. & Le Menestrel, S. (2017). *Promoting the Educational Success of Children and Youth Learning English: Promising futures*. Washington, DC: National Academies Press.

Taylor, P., Parker, K., Fry, R., Cohn, D., Wang, W., Velasco, G., & Dockterman, D. (2011). *Is College Worth It?* Washington, DC: Pew Research Center.

Tobin, J., Adair, J. K., & Arzubiaga, A. (2013). *Children Crossing Borders: Immigrant parent and teacher perspectives on preschool for children of immigrants*. New York: Russell Sage Foundation.

Tyson, K. (2011). *Integration Interrupted: Tracking, Black students, and acting White after Brown*. Oxford: Oxford University Press.

US Census Bureau. (2017). *Gini Indexes for Households, by Race and Hispanic Origin of Householder: 1967 to 2016*. Washington, DC: Author.

Washbrook, E., Waldfogel, J., Bradbury, B., Corak, M., & Ghanghro, A. A. (2012). The development of young children of immigrants in Australia, Canada, the United Kingdom, and the United States. *Child Development, 83*, 1591–1607.

Weinstein, R. (2002). *Reaching Higher: The power of expectations in schooling*. Cambridge, MA: Harvard University Press.

Yeager, D. S., Dahl, R. E., & Dweck, C. S. (2018). Why interventions to influence adolescent behavior often fail but could succeed. *Perspectives on Psychological Science, 13*, 101–122.

Yeager, D. S. & Dweck, C. S. (2012). Mindsets that promote resilience: When students believe that personal characteristics can be developed. *Educational Psychologist, 47*, 302–314.

Yeager, D. S., Hanselman, P., Walton, G., Crosnoe, R., Muller, C., ... Dweck, C. (forthcoming). A focus on heterogeneity reveals where a brief, scalable psychological intervention improves adolescents' educational trajectories and where it does not.

Yeager, D. S., Romero, C., Paunesku, D., Hulleman, C. S., Schneider, B., Hinojosa, C., Yeon, H., O'Brien, J., Flint, K., Roberts, A., Trott, J., Greene, D., Walton, G., & Dweck, C. (2016). Using design thinking to improve psychological interventions: The case of the growth mindset during the transition to high school. *Journal of Educational Psychology, 108*, 374–391.

Yeager, D. S. & Walton, G. M. (2011). Social-psychological interventions in education: They're not magic. *Review of Educational Research, 81*, 267–301.

Zigler, E., Gilliam, W. S., & Jones, S. M. (2006). *A Vision for Universal Preschool Education*. New York: Cambridge University Press.

Part III

Social, Legal, and Technological
Change: Impact on Children

7 The Urban World of Minority and Majority Children

Tama Leventhal, Julius Anastasio, and Veronique Dupéré

The United States has a long and well-documented history of economic and racial segregation (Massey, 1996, 2016). As a result, large US cities are characterized by an extreme concentration of both poverty and affluence, more so than cities in other Western countries (e.g., Galster, 2012; Oreopoulos, 2008; Sampson, 2011). This unequal distribution of resources across space means that advantages or disadvantages tend to converge both in children's families and neighborhood contexts. To illustrate, in recent years, about 15 percent of the poor in the United States were doubly disadvantaged because in addition to being poor, they lived in high-poverty neighborhoods (Kneebone & Holmes, 2016). Combined with other global trends, the concentration of poverty and affluence in large metropolitan areas has had important consequences not only for children's health and development, but also for their social mobility (Chetty & Hendren, 2018; Leventhal, Dupéré, & Shuey, 2015).

The goal of this chapter is to address how urban dynamics at the neighborhood level are linked to children's development. To do so, we first review trends in the spatial concentration of poverty and inequality in the United States in recent decades. Then, we turn to theoretical models describing how local communities, with a focus on urban settings, influence children's development. We then cover methodological issues, followed by an overview of empirical studies linking neighborhood socioeconomic conditions and children's development, notably their educational, behavioral, and socioemotional outcomes. In conclusion, we discuss implications for policy and practice and future directions.

The Rise and Proliferation of Concentrated Poverty and Inequality

Persistent and increasing geographic concentration of neighborhood poverty has occurred within large American cities since the 1970s, despite a brief but sharp reduction in concentrated high-poverty neighborhoods (census tracts with poverty rates of at least 40 percent) during the 1990s

(Jargowsky, 1997, 2003; Kneebone, Nadeau, & Berube, 2011; Massey, 1996; Wilson, 1987). It should be noted that rural areas can be vulnerable to economic downturns as is well illustrated by the effects of the farm crisis in the United States during the 1980s (Conger & Elder, 1994). Urban concentrated poverty was amplified after the Great Recession, to the point that the number of high-poverty neighborhoods in the United States doubled between 2000 and 2010 (Bishaw, 2014; Jargowsky, 2015; see also Schoon and Bynner, this volume, for a comparison of the effects of the Great Recession in the United States, the United Kingdom, and Germany). The proliferation and concentration of high-poverty urban neighborhoods has had the most profound consequences for poor minorities, who accounted for nearly four out of five residents of high-poverty neighborhoods between 1970 and 1990 (Jargowsky, 1997; Massey, 1996). Over the past 50 years, the spatial concentration of poverty was outpaced by that of affluence (percentage of college-educated residents, high-income residents, and professionals/managers) and its concomitant benefits and privileges (Massey, Fischer, Dickens, & Levy, 2003). Thus, the stratification and concentration of both poverty and affluence have contributed to rising inequality.

As concentrated poverty spread across the country, it has done so unevenly, and increasingly has grown beyond urban and rural centers into suburban areas. Although the total number of suburban poor surpassed that in cities, they were more dispersed than in urban areas. As a result, the overwhelming majority of high-poverty neighborhoods are located in US cities, with the nation's 100 largest metropolitan areas accounting for 70 percent of all high-poverty neighborhoods (Kneebone, 2014). US cities have an average concentrated poverty rate of 25.5 percent, compared with 13.7 percent in small metro areas, and 7.1 percent in both suburbs and rural communities (Kneebone, 2017). However, growth in concentrated poverty since 2000 has been most pronounced in smaller metropolitan (cities of <1 million) and micropolitan (cities of 10,000–50,000) areas (Jargowsky, 2013).

Increasing Racial Inequality and Segregation

Rising socioeconomic inequality has not been evenly distributed across the entire US population as well. Urban neighborhoods historically have been characterized by residential inequality along race and socioeconomic lines, and the spatial processes of neighborhood inequality that unfolded over the past four decades are magnified by racial and ethnic segregation (Sampson, 2011). Despite the doubling of poor European Americans over the past several decades, poor minorities remain more likely to live in high-poverty areas. Extensive research going back decades documents the overrepresentation and increased concentration of minorities in poor urban neighborhoods in America, particularly African-Americans and Latinos (Jargowsky, 1997, 2015; Massey & Denton, 1993; Reardon, Fox, & Townsend, 2015).

For a variety of reasons, such as discrimination in the real estate and banking industries, biased public policies, and more general structural racism, African-Americans continue to be the most residentially segregated group in the United States (Massey & Denton, 1993; Wilson, 1987). A quarter of African-Americans live in high-poverty neighborhoods (Kneebone, 2014). The fastest growth in the African-American concentration of poverty since 2000 was not in the largest cities, but in less resourced, smaller metropolitan areas with populations of 500,000 to 1 million (Jargowsky, 2015).

Although African-American segregation is declining, Latinos and Asians remain at least as segregated in 2010 as they were in 1980. However, African-Americans and Latinos live in poorer and more racial/ethnically concentrated neighborhoods than European Americans or Asians, regardless of income (Bischoff & Reardon, 2014). Since the Great Recession, residential segregation of low-income Hispanics grew significantly in urban areas (Bischoff & Reardon, 2014), as well as within the suburban and rural areas in which they are increasingly settling (Burton, Lichter, Baker, & Eason, 2013; Lichter et al., 2010).

For the better part of the twentieth century, US immigration policy led to most immigrants settling within ethnic enclaves in a few major cities. In 2000, two-thirds of immigrants lived in the country's six largest states – California, New York, Texas, Florida, Illinois, and New Jersey (Capps & Fortuny, 2006). Immigrant families, a majority of whom are racial/ethnic minorities, are over-represented in neighborhoods of concentrated poverty (Hook, Brown, & Kwenda, 2004). Changes to immigration policy and the economy have resulted in immigrants becoming less concentrated, with settlement patterns shifting to newer, smaller metropolitan and suburban areas (Sampson, 2011).

Spatial Inequality and System Level Effects

As described, neighborhoods in urban areas are often marked by high levels of spatial inequality (i.e., the unequal geographic distribution of poor and non-poor people), largely driven by increased segregation of poverty and affluence. This situation has profound implications for the social, economic, and political contexts of urban neighborhoods and by extension their often minority residents. Specifically, poorer neighborhoods have fewer fiscal resources and lower-quality public services despite their greater needs, with lower human and social capital undermining the political efficacy of citizens within these communities (Cortright & Mahmoudi, 2014). These urban spatial and economic inequalities often stem from political disenfranchisement and policies that favor wealthy rather than low-income or minority communities (Bonnie, Johnson, Chemers, & Schuck, 2013). The resulting policies have led to severe disinvestment in minority neighborhoods, persistent segregation, declining economic opportunities for residents of poor neighborhoods, as well as growing links between minority neighborhoods and the criminal justice system, notably the differential and biased treatment of residents in these areas by the police and other justice authorities (Sampson & Loeffler, 2010; Sharkey, 2013).

Urban neighborhood inequality can have particularly adverse consequences for location-based social institutions such as schools, especially within poor minority and immigrant communities. High-poverty schools are often ineffective, have disproportionately high dropout rates, and low levels of overall academic achievement (Lleras, 2008; Orfield & Lee, 2005). To this point, the largest cities in the United States are home to the majority of high school dropouts among minorities, and are the source of significant and increasing numbers of minority adolescent incarcerations (DePaoli, Balfanz, & Bridgeland, 2016; Kim, Losen, & Hewitt, 2010). Disproportionally high racial and ethnic disparities also exist in school's use of harsh disciplinary practices such as suspension, expulsion, and arrest (Cauffman, Shulman, Bechtold, & Steinberg, 2015; Kim et al., 2010; Wadhwa, 2017). The increased national formalization and expansion of schools' Zero-Tolerance and mandatory expulsion policies over the past several decades have further exacerbated this issue (Cauffman et al., 2015), with mandatory expulsion policies being most common in urban school districts with high minority student populations (Curran, 2017; Verdugo, 2002).

While crime has significantly declined over the past two decades, it remains highly concentrated in cities' most violent and disadvantaged neighborhoods (Friedson & Sharkey, 2015). Mirroring the geographically concentrated nature of crime, a small and enduring proportion of urban neighborhoods bear the disproportionate brunt of US mass incarceration. Beginning in the 1970s, the loss of economic opportunities in urban African-American communities led to subsequent increases in crime, delinquency, and incarceration rates that remain high to this day (Wilson, 1996).

Theoretical Perspectives

Spatial inequalities and their system level impacts on schools, employment opportunities, criminal and juvenile justice systems and the like have major consequences for children and families. In this section, we turn to theoretical perspectives that inform our understanding of the neighborhood context and children's development, with attention to urban settings.

This chapter is guided by both broad theoretical conceptualizations of human development, stressing the importance of situating developing children in context, and by specific models focusing on the role of the urban neighborhood context. These two theoretical lenses are reviewed in turn.

General ecological models of human development pioneered by Bronfenbrenner highlighted how children's development is influenced by larger contexts in which children and their families are embedded (Bronfenbrenner & Morris, 2007; see also Elder, Shanahan, & Jennings, 2015). In these models, the multiple contexts to which children are directly exposed in their everyday life are thought to shape development, with neighborhoods representing only one context among others like schools or peer groups. In addition, these contexts channel more distal ecological influences, brought about for instance by macrolevel forces such as segregation and economic downturns. Ecological models also emphasize the variable impact of contextual influences depending on cross-context and individual by context interactions. More recently, Relational Developmental Systems (RDS) approaches have pushed these models further towards holistic considerations of individuals and contexts, underscoring webs of relations, mutual influences, and processes operating as integrated systems (Lerner & Overton, 2008; Overton, 2015).

Given this chapter's focus on urban neighborhoods, notably their socioeconomic conditions, and links to children's development, we ground this chapter generally in RDS theories. Broad theoretical perspectives on child development are meant to be complemented by more specific theories and hypotheses directly relevant to a particular field of inquiry (Overton, 2015). In studying urban neighborhood contexts and child development, these theories help to understand not only how neighborhoods, particularly their socioeconomic status (SES), is associated with children's development, but also how neighborhood SES is affected by other contexts, such as family and peers. These theories also explicate how neighborhood SES and associated conditions (e.g., access to services, exposure to violence) might interact with individual characteristics such as child age or personality in shaping development. Finally, these theories highlight developmental and historical timing, underscoring the need to explore how neighborhood SES may be differentially associated with developmental pathways in different historical periods (Elder et al., 2015). In light of this broad ecological and systems conceptual approach, urban neighborhood contexts are considered in this chapter alongside, and in relation with, other key contextual and individual characteristics (e.g., families, culture, gender). In the literature linking urban neighborhood environments and child development, specific theoretical models and conceptual frameworks have been proposed, focusing on neighborhood structure, processes, and their interrelations.

Neighborhood Structure

Neighborhood structure refers to compositional attributes of residents, generally measured via census indicators as described earlier. A key structural characteristic thought to be relevant for child development is neighborhood poverty/low SES or concentrated disadvantage (Duncan & Brooks-Gunn, 1997; Sampson, Sharkey, & Raudenbush, 2008). Poor, disadvantaged urban neighborhoods are generally defined as circumscribed areas within a city with high rates of poverty, or of other markers of disadvantage, like unemployment, receipt of public assistance or segregation (see Sampson, Morenoff, & Earls, 1999; Sampson, Raudenbush, & Earls, 1997). Beyond poverty and disadvantage, other structural aspects are thought to influence the social fabric of neighborhoods in ways that are relevant for children. They include residential instability, indexed by high levels of resident turnover and low levels of homeownership, and immigrant concentration, captured by measures like the proportion of foreign-born residents. At the other end of the spectrum, neighborhood affluence is generally defined by a concentration of residents with high incomes, college degrees, and professional/managerial jobs (Jencks & Mayer, 1990). Affluent or high SES neighborhoods also tend to have high levels of homeownership and residential stability, and high concentrations of White residents (Sampson, 2011). Neighborhood poverty, instability, and immigrant concentration are traditionally viewed as potential threats to children's development, whereas neighborhood affluence is thought to provide advantages. However, both disadvantaged and affluent neighborhoods are heterogeneous, and one neighborhood can confer both benefits and risks simultaneously (Luthar & Barkin, 2012; Sharkey & Faber, 2014; Small & Feldman, 2012). For instance, some research suggests that children in affluent, suburban neighborhoods demonstrate more problem behaviors, notably substance use, than their peers from poor, urban neighborhoods

(Luthar & Barkin, 2012; Luthar & Latendresse, 2005), but such research is quite limited, mixed in nature (e.g., Lund & Dearing, 2013), and strictly non-experimental. Positive or negative, the potential impacts of neighborhood structural characteristics are thought to be channeled via various social and institutional processes, described next (Leventhal & Brooks-Gunn, 2000; Leventhal, Dupéré, & Brooks-Gunn, 2009; Leventhal, Dupere, et al., 2015).

Neighborhood Processes

Two broad types of neighborhood processes delineating residents' lived experiences in their neighborhood have been described in the literature, referring to informal interactions between residents or to more formal ones within institutions. Data about these processes are typically obtained directly from residents via surveys for instance, or from local administrative data like police records.

Neighborhood resident interactions. A first class of neighborhood processes often invoked to explain potential links between neighborhood poverty and children's development revolves around social norms and values shared by *local residents*. In that regard, a particularly prominent concept is that of collective efficacy, defined as residents' social cohesion and beliefs that they can intervene on behalf of the common good (Bandura, 2000; Elliott et al., 1996; Sampson et al., 1999, 1997). In highly disadvantaged neighborhoods, aspects such as insufficient collective resources, social isolation and fear and mistrust of strangers erode collective efficacy, thus reducing residents' capacity to contain unwanted behaviors like violence and child maltreatment and, in turn, local children's exposure to crime and violence and other threats to their well-being (Molnar, Buka, Brennan, Holton, & Earls, 2003). Residential instability and ethnic heterogeneity are also described as factors disrupting the creation of strong and enduring social ties between neighbors, leading to social networks too tenuous to effectively support collective actions (see Boggess & Hipp, 2010; Stolle, Soroka, & Johnston, 2008). Specifically, residential turnover, population loss, and linguistic and cultural barriers may weaken local networks and hinder cohesion. However, when immigrants sharing a common ethnic background are concentrated in a given neighborhood, linguistic and cultural cohesion may be enhanced, creating an environment facilitating collective efficacy and supportive of children's development (e.g., Jackson, Browning, Krivo, Kwan, & Washington, 2016).

Neighborhoods are thought to influence children's daily social environment not only via the general strength or weakness of relatively loose local networks between residents, but also via close personal relationships with parents and peers. Research suggests that neighborhoods matter to *parents* (Franco, Pottick, & Huang, 2010; Guterman, Lee, Taylor, & Rathouz, 2009), as living in a structurally disadvantaged neighborhood may impose numerous sources of stress on parents and family relationships. For instance, parents in disadvantaged neighborhoods may be more likely to be chronically exposed to crime and incivilities, and in turn develop negative emotions impinging on their parental capacities due to fear of crime, a sense of powerlessness and mistrust, and even poor mental and physical health (Blair, Ross, Gariepy, & Schmitz, 2014; Conger & Donnellan, 2007; Coulton, Crampton, Irwin, Spilsbury, & Korbin, 2007; Ludwig et al., 2011, 2012; Paschall & Hubbard, 1998). The associations between neighborhood context and parental well-being and parenting behaviors are likely to matter for children's development (see Shuey & Leventhal, in press, for review). Longitudinal studies with diverse samples reveal that diverse parenting behaviors (i.e., parental warmth and monitoring, consistent discipline, and provision of home-based learning opportunities) help explain links between neighborhood SES and children's achievement and behavioral outcomes (Dupere, Leventhal, Crosnoe, & Dion, 2010; Kohen, Leventhal, Dahinten, & McIntosh, 2008; Shuey & Leventhal, 2017). Another important stressful event associated with neighborhood disadvantage is incarceration of a family member (Sampson & Loeffler, 2010). This major stressor is likely to significantly disrupt family relationships, and in turn, children development, thus representing another potential pathway through which neighborhoods may affect children (Kirk & Sampson, 2013; Murray, Farrington, & Sekol, 2012; Wakefield & Apel, 2016).

Aside from parents, *peer* relationships may channel potential neighborhood influences on children's outcomes. Developing positive and meaningful peer relationships is a vital part of healthy child development, especially during adolescence, when relationships beyond the family are increasingly important to meet changing developmental needs (Rubin, Bukowski, & Bowker, 2015). Neighborhoods are the source of a large portion of children's friends (Dolcini, Harper, Watson, Catania, & Ellen, 2005), and as such can shape intimate peer relationships, via friendships or romantic relationships for instance, as well as the larger normative peer context to which children are exposed. Disadvantaged neighborhoods are characterized not only by a concentration of economic problems like poverty and joblessness, but also of other associated social problems like juvenile delinquency (Sampson, 2011). The higher prevalence of these problems means that children in poor neighborhoods are more likely to form friendships and eventually romantic relationships with peers burdened by such issues (Wilson, 2015). In turn, peer characteristics influence children's behavior through interpersonal interactions, for instance having delinquent friends heightens the risk of their own deviant behaviors via deviancy training (Dishion, Andrews, & Crosby, 1995; Dodge, Dishion, & Lansford, 2006; Shortt, Capaldi, Dishion, Bank, & Owen, 2003).

Beyond such direct interactional processes, neighborhood peers influence behavior by more diffuse means like norms and representations. For instance, Harding's (2011) cultural heterogeneity model posits that children living in disadvantaged neighborhoods are exposed to a wider set of cultural scripts and role models than their peers from more advantaged neighborhoods, with this diversity in both mainstream and variant pathways creating confusion and opening the way for suboptimal or deviant choices. Another process, generally referred to as "relative deprivation," "big fish little pond," or the "frog pond" effect (Crosnoe, 2009; Jencks & Mayer, 1990), proposes that peer influences also depend on comparative processes in which children define their relative standing based on their immediate social context (e.g., neighborhood). For instance, children who excel academically may have a higher academic self-concept if they live in a neighborhood where academic outcomes are suboptimal than if they live in a neighborhood comprised largely of other high-achieving children (Clampet-Lundquist, Edin, Kling, & Duncan, 2011; Fauth, Leventhal, & Brooks-Gunn, 2007; Luthar & Barkin, 2012). These two models lead to contrasting hypotheses regarding the connection between the presence of disadvantaged peers in children's neighborhoods and their developmental outcomes: The first normative model leads to the prediction of worse outcomes, whereas relative deprivation models anticipate better outcomes, particularly for struggling or disadvantaged children. In fact, both could operate in parallel and somewhat cancel out each other's effect (Crosnoe, 2009; this volume; Crosnoe & Benner, 2015). For this reason, considering both simultaneously may be necessary to fully understand how the influence of the neighborhood context plays out.

Neighborhood institutional resources. Neighborhood institutional resources – opportunities or services that foster economic, educational, physical, and socioemotional well-being – may also contribute to the association between neighborhood SES and children's development. Institutional resources that are especially relevant to children include child care, schools, after school programs, recreational centers/ youth programming, health and social services, libraries, and employment opportunities (e.g., Leventhal & Brooks-Gunn, 2000; Vandell, Larson, Mahoney, & Watts, 2015). As children spend a large portion of their waking hours within these local institutions, they may represent a powerful mechanism relaying potential neighborhood influences to developmental outcomes (Burchinal, Magnuson, Powell, & Hong, 2015; Crosnoe & Benner, 2015). Given increasing neighborhood inequality in the United States as described earlier, many local institutions are likely to be uniformly composed of either disadvantaged or advantaged participants from surrounding neighborhoods (Raikes, Torquati, Wang, & Shjegstad, 2012; Ryan, 2010), with consequences regarding the variety and quality of neighborhood institutions available to families (Reardon & Bischoff, 2011).

A first aspect influencing the quality of local institutions is financial resources. Local institutions' budgets are often tied to local tax revenues based on property values and business activities, meaning that more disadvantaged neighborhoods may lack the financial capital necessary to create and sustain needed services (Granger, 2008; Leventhal, Dupéré, & Shuey, 2015). When financial capital is lacking, it is difficult to hire and retain competent staff (Leventhal, Dupéré et al., 2015). For institutions located in disadvantaged neighborhoods, the problems associated with less competent staff and high staff turnover are compounded because children from poor families present higher rates of social, behavioral, and learning difficulties. In other words, staff members with less training and experience must manage children with more problems, a situation likely to lead many to feel overwhelmed and to quit, in a cycle further reducing staff stability and quality. In turn, children suffer developmentally as a result of high staff turnover and instability (Burchinal et al., 2015).

In addition to reduced financial capital and its consequences, institutions in disadvantaged neighborhoods also have less access to social capital than those located in affluent communities. In institutions serving children, parents are a primary source of social capital. Affluent, highly educated parents can and do invest more resources in their children's development than more disadvantaged parents, and typically expect and advocate for their local institutions to provide high quality services for their children (Conger, Conger, & Martin, 2010; Lareau, 2003). For example, parent participation in school-related activities is higher in more affluent communities than in those that are more disadvantaged, have high minority populations, or have large immigrant populations (Greenman, Bodovski, & Reed, 2011; Grigorenko & Takanishi, 2010). Beyond increased connectivity, social efficacy, social capital, and parental involvement have other ramifications, such as supporting the flow of information exchange, which in turn likely supports the growth and preservation of well-functioning services that benefit all neighborhood children (Small, 2009). Through such processes, the quality of local institutions may explain potential links between neighborhood SES and children's development (Leventhal & Brooks-Gunn, 2000; Leventhal et al., 2009; Sampson, Morenoff, & Gannon-Rowley, 2002).

Methodological Issues

The theoretical perspectives informing the study of children's development in urban neighborhood context should be understood in light of methodological considerations. Because a comprehensive review of this topic is beyond the scope of this chapter, we focus here on one critical issue, selection bias, and then briefly review study designs as related to this challenge.

Selection bias, also referred to as omitted variable bias, is perhaps the primary methodological challenge for researchers trying to isolate the effects of neighborhood contexts, urban or otherwise, on children's development (Leventhal, Dupéré et al., 2015). This bias exists because the association between neighborhood conditions, such as poverty, and children's development may be driven by other factors that affect families' choice of residence and may underlie differences in children's development (e.g., parental motivation).

A variety of research designs and methodologies are used to address this challenge. Randomized experiments remain the "gold standard" for isolating neighborhood effects on children's development because random assignment of participants to control and intervention groups should balance groups on measured and unmeasured background differences (e.g., genetic predispositions, Shadish, Cook, & Campbell, 2002). The most recent and well-known experiment in the neighborhood literature is the Moving to Opportunity for Fair Housing Demonstration (MTO) study funded by the US Department of Housing and Urban Development (Goering & Feins, 2003). In MTO, families living in public housing in high-poverty neighborhoods (i.e., poverty rates of 40% or higher) were randomly assigned to an intervention group who received assistance to move to private housing in low-poverty neighborhoods (i.e., poverty rates of 10% or lower), a comparison group who received assistance to move to private housing in neighborhoods of their choice, or a control group who remained in place (the findings from MTO are discussed in the next section).

Although experimental studies are useful for minimizing threats related to selection bias, they are also limited in key ways. Because experiments are expensive and extremely complicated, they are rarely conducted, and when they are, they tend to focus on very specific populations, raising potential generalizability problems. For instance, experimental studies typically evaluate social programs aimed at improving the lives of extremely poor families (Leventhal, Dupéré et al., 2015). Thus, it is unclear if findings generated from these programs apply to other families, poor or non-poor, who were not included. As a result, additional research designs are needed to complement randomized experiments.

Quasi-experiments are one such alternative that is also quite effective at minimizing selection bias, at least in instances where "treatment" exposure approximates random assignment (Shadish et al., 2002). Such studies take advantage of the fact that some families' neighborhoods of residence change because of conditions over which they have little or no control and not because of their characteristics, choices, and/or preferences, whereas other families (i.e., "comparison" group) are not exposed to the same changes. For example, the oldest quasi-experimental neighborhood study and the inspiration for MTO is the Gautreaux Program, which was the result of a 1976 court order to desegregate Chicago's public housing. During its operation from 1976 to 1998, over 7,000 families were given housing vouchers (or rent subsidies) that were to be used in low-poverty, racially integrated neighborhoods, with a majority of families to be placed outside of the city limits (Rubinowitz & Rosenbaum, 2000). Because of limited housing availability at times, families were placed inside and outside of the city, in more or less poor and segregated neighborhoods respectively, based on housing availability that was presumably random.

Unlike experimental and quasi-experimental studies, non-experimental or correlational designs are common in the neighborhood literature. A large majority of research on neighborhood socioeconomic conditions uses longitudinal, nationally representative studies (e.g., the Panel Study of Income Dynamics; Hill, 1991). Other research, particularly relevant to the urban context, uses city-based samples, often linked to administrative sources (e.g., Sharkey, Tirado-Strayer, Papachristos, & Raver, 2012). The most significant of these city-based studies employ neighborhood-based designs in which children and families are sampled from different types of neighborhoods (e.g., Project on Human Development in Chicago Neighborhoods (PHDCN); Sampson et al., 2002).

Studies using correlational designs typically use a variety of statistical techniques to minimize potential selection bias. These approaches range from regression analyses that control for individual and family background characteristics related to neighborhood selection (e.g., family income, parent education, race/ethnicity) to more rigorous analytic strategies such as propensity score matching, instrumental variable analysis, or fixed effects (Leventhal & Brooks-Gunn, 2011). Propensity score methods use various strategies to match children who are otherwise similar on a wide range of observed background characteristics except for the types of neighborhoods in which they live (e.g., Wodtke, Harding, & Elwert, 2011). Instrumental variable analyses minimize unmeasured correlations between neighborhood characteristics and children's outcomes by means of a two-stage regression approach (e.g., Foster & McLanahan, 1996). Finally, fixed effects analyses take advantage of variation in individuals' own exposure to different neighborhood conditions over time, holding unmeasured family characteristics constant (e.g., Timberlake, 2007).

Review of Neighborhood Socioeconomic Status and Children's Development

This section takes a comprehensive, but not exhaustive, approach to reviewing the research on neighborhood socioeconomic conditions – poverty or disadvantage and affluence or advantage – and children's development. This literature is extensive and reviewed in detail elsewhere (e.g., Leventhal, Dupéré et al., 2015; Sampson et al., 2002), thus this section forefronts studies that meet certain standards of quality and rigor. Our goal is to rely on the strongest evidence possible for making some general conclusions about what is currently known about neighborhood SES and children's development.

As such, we highlight longitudinal studies and ones using experimental designs to address selection or omitted variable bias as described in the previous section. It is important to note that not all the work reviewed here is limited to urban neighborhoods, but most of the key studies that will be featured, as described in the previous section, are based in urban settings and have diverse samples. Furthermore, poverty and disadvantage are overrepresented in urban areas as described earlier, so findings on this aspect of neighborhood SES based on national data sets are likely applicable to urban contexts. Finally, because results regarding differences by important individual characteristics such as children's age or developmental status (children vs. adolescents), gender, and race/ethnicity are rather mixed, we focus on broad patterns, while noting such differences when consistent patterns exist.

A large majority of the studies on neighborhood SES and children's development are non-experimental. Much of this research is longitudinal, but neighborhood SES is typically measured at a single point in time. Some of the most compelling evidence from this body of work comes from meta-analyses synthesizing results from studies that meet certain quality standards (Chang, Wang, & Tsai, 2016; e.g., Johnson, 2013). The findings confirm general patterns documented across numerous individual studies. Specifically, living in a neighborhood marked by greater socioeconomic disadvantage is associated with children's worse emotional, social, and behavior functioning such as conduct problems and delinquency. On the contrary, greater neighborhood advantage or affluence is favorably associated with children's achievement-related outcomes, such as test scores, and educational attainment. Across this research, neighborhood SES "effects" tend to be small or modest.

Another line of non-experimental, longitudinal research considers children's temporal and cumulative exposure to neighborhood socio-economic conditions and links with their developmental outcomes. This work reveals that although the association between neighborhood SES and children's development may take several years to arise (Sampson et al., 2008; Turley, 2003), the timing, duration, and nature of these experiences appear to matter. For example, in the Panel Study of Income Dynamics, cumulative exposure to neighborhood poverty since birth was more strongly associated with high school dropout and early child-bearing than a single point in time estimate at 14 years of age (Crowder & South, 2011; South & Crowder, 2010). Other work with this same sample suggests this risk may be enhanced among African-American children growing up in the most disadvantaged neighborhoods (Wodtke et al., 2011).

Additional studies also reveal the importance of cumulative exposure to neighborhood SES for long-term outcomes, notably in urban samples (Alexander, Entwisle, & Olson, 2014) and for the neighbor-hood advantage-achievement link (see Leventhal, 2018, for review). For instance, recent economic analysis of administrative data indicated that cumulative exposure to "better" neighborhoods across late childhood and adolescence (ages 9–23) was associated with greater young adult earnings (Chetty & Hendren, 2018). Some studies have even incorporated longitudinal measures of children's outcomes in add-ition to neighborhood SES. For instance, an investigation with a diverse US sample found that greater neighborhood affluence in early childhood was associated with children's superior achievement at that time, and the association endured through 15 years of age by working indirectly via middle childhood achievement (Anderson, Leventhal, & Dupéré, 2014). As noted earlier, however, greater neighborhood affluence is sometimes linked with more risky behavior, at least in adolescence (e.g., drug use; Luthar & Barkin, 2012). Likewise, other research supports the salience of exposure to neighborhood SES in early childhood (e.g., Wheaton & Clarke, 2003). This sensitivity may exist because early childhood is a period of rapid developmental changes, and early environmental inputs may have trajectory-setting effects that carry forward into adolescence and beyond (Shonkoff, Boyce, & McEwen, 2009).

Despite rather consistent patterns across the non-experimental research, it is often criticized on the grounds of selection bias. In an effort to address this concern, researchers have used more robust analytic techniques as described earlier. Across this work the general conclusions do not change appreciably, but in many cases, effect sizes are reduced (Leventhal, Dupéré et al., 2015). For example, one such study using propensity score methods that drew on data from PHDCN, also suggests the prominence of early childhood. Among African-American children, living in a severely disadvantaged neighborhood at an early age was associated with sustained deficits in African-American children's later verbal ability, equivalent to missing a year or more of school (Sampson et al., 2008).

Another study using data from PHDCN and employing propensity score methods, points to possible non-linear effects related to neighborhood poverty. The study followed several cohorts of school-age children and adolescents and found that only boys' trajectories of violent behavior were worse if they lived in neighborhoods that either decreased or increased in poverty compared with their peers in stable neighborhoods (Leventhal & Brooks-Gunn, 2011). Youth in high- and moderate-poverty neighborhoods were more susceptible to these neighborhood poverty dynamics than youth in low-poverty neighborhoods. The findings were interpreted as possibly related to rises in social disorganization when neighborhood socioeconomic and related conditions are in flux.

Perhaps the strongest evidence to date for a connection between socioeconomic conditions and children's development comes from experimental and quasi-experimental studies because of their ability to minimize selection bias. Moving to Opportunity (MTO), described earlier, is most well-known in this regard. A 10-year evaluation found that adolescent girls, but not boys, whose families were given the opportunity to move to low-poverty neighborhoods reported better mental health than their peers in the control group, who stayed in high-poverty neighborhoods (Gennetian et al., 2012). In general, no program effects were evident for youth education, crime, or physical health. However, a longer term young adulthood follow-up based on administrative data from the Social Security Administration found that children who were 13 years or younger when their families moved to low-poverty neighborhoods, and who presumably were exposed to more advantaged neighborhoods earlier and longer than their older counterparts, were more likely to attend college and have higher earnings and less likely to be single parents in young adulthood than those in the control group (Chetty, Hendren, & Katz, 2015). No such benefits were seen among

MTO children who were older than 13 years of age when they moved to low poverty areas.

Beyond MTO, some quasi-experiments also provide evidence of a link between neighborhood socioeconomic conditions and children's development. For instance, a 10-year follow-up study of about 100 poor, minority youth whose families participated in the Gautreaux Program, described earlier, revealed that youth who moved to private housing in affluent suburban neighborhoods were less likely to drop out of high school and more likely to enroll in college preparatory classes and attend college than youth who moved to private housing in poor urban neighborhoods (Rubinowitz & Rosenbaum, 2000). Whereas a seven-year follow-up of another housing desegregation effort in Yonkers, NY found that low-income, minority youth who moved to low-rise publicly funded townhouses in primarily White middle-class areas of the city generally had unfavorable schooling and behavior outcomes compared with their peers from the old, high-poverty neighborhood, about half of whose families were on the waitlist for the new public housing (Fauth et al., 2007). These findings may be due to negative social comparison processes such as relative deprivation described earlier (see *Theoretical Perspectives*). Other more recent research of this sort also shows mixed or modest results (e.g., Massey, Albright, Casciano, Derickson, & Kinsey, 2013), but with one study of families in Denver public housing aligning with the MTO young adulthood findings (Galster & Santiago, 2017).

In sum, the highlighted research is consistent with the more general non-experimental work on neighborhood socioeconomic status and children's development, but is somewhat more complex. This complexity arises because studies trying to capture changes in neighborhood socioeconomic conditions as a means to limit selection bias often are confounded with other factors such as mobility or shifts in neighborhood conditions beyond poverty as well as other social contexts such as schools and peers. At the same time, income and/or racial/ethnic differences between mover children and families and their new neighbors may have been another challenge that hinders the formation of close ties and may subject movers to experiences of racism and discrimination. Finally, it is important to acknowledge that in almost all studies, families remained poor despite their potentially improved neighborhood conditions.

Implications and Future Directions

The urban world of minority and majority children is typically circumscribed by their neighborhood contexts. As reviewed earlier, US cities – both large and small – have shouldered the burden of rising concentrated poverty and not reaped the benefits of the corresponding growth in concentrated affluence. Rising spatial inequality places many children, especially those who are poor and minority, at risk for suboptimal development given the general disadvantages associated with exposure to neighborhood poverty and advantages associated with neighborhood affluence as described in this chapter. Of course, the causal nature of these associations is a source of continued debate, but the nature of the challenges confronting children's development in impoverished urban neighborhoods is not. In the remainder of this section we discuss implications for policy and practice and future directions.

It is unclear from empirical and theoretical work if targeting neighborhood socioeconomic conditions directly or indirectly (e.g., resident interactions and institutional resources) might be most effective at promoting children's development in urban contexts. Two primary types of policy initiatives strive to improve the socioeconomic conditions of neighborhoods in which families with children reside, typically with a focus on urban settings. The first approach entails mobility programs such as MTO, which increase low-income families' residential options and provide them with opportunities to relocate from disadvantaged neighborhoods to more advantaged ones. Although findings from these programs are mixed, as reviewed, public housing authorities across the United States are using a number of strategies to achieve this goal (e.g., pegging the amount of rent covered by housing subsidies to the local market, which permits low-income families to live in more socioeconomically advantaged neighborhoods).

The second policy effort is comprehensive community initiatives (CCIs), which invest in poor neighborhoods to improve current residents' living conditions (e.g., Zaff, Donlan, Pufall Jones, Lin, & Anderson, 2016). Unlike mobility programs, which target families, CCIs target neighborhoods. Perhaps the most well-known CCI is the Harlem Children's Zone (HCZ; Harlem Children's Zone, 2009). The initiative has a "pipeline" approach, covering the life course from before birth to college, and provides coordinated community-based services in the educational, health, and social domains. To date, evaluations of the program document benefits for children's achievement, especially for older children (Dobbie & Fryer Jr., 2011). What is less clear is whether the entire bundle of HCZ services is necessary, over and above the charter schools, to obtain achievement benefits. Because of the HCZ's success, President Obama launched the Promise Neighborhoods Initiative, a federal effort, to try to replicate its success across diverse communities, urban and otherwise. Although no systematic evaluations of these initiatives have been completed, initial findings indicate some progress towards improving children's academic outcomes (Hulsey, Esposito, Boller, & Osborn, 2015).

An alternative strategy is to tap the indirect pathways through which neighborhood socioeconomic conditions are thought to be associated with children's development in urban settings. We did not systematically cover this research because it was beyond the scope of this chapter (for a review see; Leventhal, Dupéré et al., 2015), but draw upon the theoretical models described earlier to consider this topic with a focus on neighborhood-level processes. In the case of neighborhood poverty and disadvantage, the link to children's social, emotional, and behavior outcomes is strongest, particularly externalizing behaviors (e.g., aggression), delinquency, and crime (e.g., Friedson & Sharkey, 2015). Neighborhood disorganization, disorder, and low collective efficacy are implicated as primary vehicles of transmission of neighborhood poverty to these outcomes (Leventhal, Dupéré, et al., 2015; Sampson et al., 2002).

Altering neighborhood social dynamics, however, is challenging, but efforts such as community policing, which typically involve collaboration between residents and police officers to combat crime, are promising (Corder, 2014). Another fruitful strategy is the use of restorative justice in schools, or the attempt to repair harm done to one youth by another through communication and engagement of all involved parties (students, teachers and administrators, parents). Restorative justice approaches attempt to foster trust and strengthen ties within a community by encouraging social control (e.g., more authority figures responding sensitively to children's antisocial behavior) and social cohesion (e.g., members of families whose children were in conflict connecting with one another; e.g., Bazemore & Schiff, 2015).

In the case of neighborhood affluence, the connection to children's achievement-outcomes is strongest (e.g., Dupere et al., 2010). Here, neighborhood institutional resources play a prominent role in conferring the advantages of neighborhood affluence to children's achievement (Leventhal, Dupéré et al., 2015). Therefore, ensuring that all children, especially in poor, urban neighborhoods, have access to institutional resources, notably quality childcare, schools, and youth programs, is a promising strategy as demonstrated by the Harlem Children's Zone (Dobbie & Fryer Jr., 2011). Others point to military service as another potential pathway out of poverty and extreme disadvantage for some urban youth, which may provide access to resources otherwise unavailable within disadvantaged communities (Elder, Wang, Spence, Adkins, & Brown, 2010; Wilmoth & London, 2013). In addition, enhancing the institutional resources available in these communities may serve to improve children's outcomes by strengthening social organization.

In conclusion, this chapter provides an overview of the dynamics within US urban neighborhoods and highlights the link between neighborhood socioeconomic conditions and children development with a conceptual and empirical lens. Although the focus was on the United States, similar demographic trends are evident in Europe and Canada, though less extreme, and the marked coincidence of structural disadvantage with racial segregation sets the United States apart (Oreopoulos, 2008; Wacquant, 2008). Thus, cross-national comparison would provide a useful counterpart to much of the work presented here. Likewise, much progress has been made in documenting the connection between neighborhood socioeconomic conditions and children's development and exploring the potential pathways through which they emerge. More high-quality work, however, is needed to understand the best ways to intervene – namely research using experimental design or rigorous statistical approaches such as propensity score matching or instrumental variable analysis. The challenges facing many children in urban neighborhoods demand additional resources at all programmatic levels.

References

Alexander, K., Entwisle, D., & Olson, L. (2014). *The Long Shadow: Family background, disadvantaged urban youth, and the transition to adulthood.* New York: Russell Sage.

Anderson, S., Leventhal, T., & Dupéré, V. (2014). Exposure to neighborhood affluence and poverty in childhood and adolescence and academic achievement and behavior. *Applied Developmental Science, 18*(3), 123–138.

Bandura, A. (2000). Exercise of human agency through collective efficacy. *Current Directions in Psychological Science, 9*, 75–78.

Bazemore, G. & Schiff, M. (2015). *Restorative Community Justice: Repairing harm and transforming communities.* Abingdon: Routledge.

Bischoff, K. & Reardon, S. F. (2014). Residential segregation by income, 1970–2009. In J. R. Logan (Ed.), *Diversity and Disparities: America enters a new century* (pp. 208–233). New York: Russell Sage Foundation.

Bishaw, A. (2014). *Changes in Areas with Concentrated Poverty: 2000 to 2010.* Washington, DC: United State Census Bureau, American Community Survey Reports.

Blair, A., Ross, N. A., Gariepy, G., & Schmitz, N. (2014). How do neighborhoods affect depression outcomes? A realist review and a call for the examination of causal pathways. *Social Psychiatry and Psychiatric Epidemiology, 49*(6), 873–887.

Boggess, L. N. & Hipp, J. R. (2010). Violent crime, residential instability and mobility: Does the relationship differ in minority neighborhoods? *Journal of Quantitative Criminology, 26*(3), 351–370.

Bonnie, R. J., Johnson, R. L., Chemers, B. M., & Schuck, J. (Eds.). (2013). *Reforming Juvenile Justice: A developmental approach.* Washington, DC: National Academies Press.

Bronfenbrenner, U. & Morris, P. A. (2007). The bioecological model of human development. In R. M. Lerner & W. Damon (Eds.), *Handbook of Child Psychology* (6th ed., Vol. 1, pp. 793–828). Hoboken, NJ: Wiley.

Burchinal, M., Magnuson, K., Powell, D., & Hong, S. S. (2015). Early childcare and education. In M. H. Bornstein & T. Leventhal (Eds.) & R. M. Lerner (Editor-in-Chief), *Handbook of Child Psychology and Developmental Science, Vol. 4: Ecological Settings and Processes in Developmental Systems* (7th ed., pp. 223–267). Hoboken, NJ: Wiley.

Burton, L. M., Lichter, D. T., Baker, R. S., & Eason, J. M. (2013). Inequality, family processes, and health in the "new" rural America. *American Behavioral Scientist, 57*(May), 1128–1151.

Capps, R. & Fortuny, K. (2006). *Immigration and Child and Family Policy.* Washington, DC: Urban Institute.

Cauffman, E., Shulman, E., Bechtold, J., & Steinberg, L. (2015). Children and the law. In M. H. Bornstein & T. Leventhal (Eds.) & R. M. Lerner (Editor-in-Chief), *Handbook of Child Psychology and Developmental Science, Vol. 4: Ecological Settings and Processes in Developmental Systems* (7th ed., pp. 616–653). Hoboken, NJ: Wiley.

Chang, L.-Y., Wang, M.-Y., & Tsai, P.-S. (2016). Neighborhood disadvantage and physical aggression in children and adolescents: A systematic review and meta-analysis of multilevel studies. *Aggressive Behavior, 42*(5), 441–454. http://doi.org/10.1002/ab.21641

Charis, E. K. & Scott, A. D. (2014). The power of place revisited: Why immigrant communities have lower levels of adolescent violence. *Youth Violence and Juvenile Justice, 13*(4), 345–366. doi:10.1177/1541204014547590

Chetty, R. & Hendren, N. (2018). The effects of neighborhoods on intergenerational mobility I: Childhood exposure effects. *Quarterly Journal of Economics, 133*(3), 1107–1162.

Chetty, R., Hendren, N., & Katz, L. F. (2016). The effects of exposure to better neighborhoods on children: New evidence from the Moving to Opportunity Experiment. *American Economic Review, 106*(4), 90, 855–902. doi.org/10.3386/w21156

Clampet-Lundquist, S., Edin, K., Kling, J. R., & Duncan, G. J. (2011). Moving at-risk teenagers out of high-risk neighborhoods: How girls fare better than boys. *American Journal of Sociology, 116*, 1154–1189.

Conger, R., Conger, K. J., & Martin, M. J. (2010). Socioeconomic status, family processes, and individual development. *Journal of Marriage and Family, 72*(3), 685–704.

Conger, R. & Donnellan, M. B. (2007). An interactionist perspective on the socioeconomic context of human development. *Annual Review of Psychology, 58*, 175–199.

Conger, R. & Elder, G. H. (1994). *Families in Troubled Times.* New York: Aldine de Gruyter.

Corder, G. (2014). Community policing. In M. D. Reisig & R. J. Kane (Eds.), *The Oxford Handbook of Police and Policing* (pp. 148–171). New York: Oxford University Press.

Cortright, J. & Mahmoudi, D. (2014). Lost in Place: Why the persistence and spread of concentrated poverty – not gentrification – is our biggest urban challenge. *City Observatory* (December). Retrieved from http://cityobservatory.org/lost-in-place/

Coulton, C. J., Crampton, D. S., Irwin, M., Spilsbury, J. C., & Korbin, J. E. (2007). How neighborhoods influence child maltreatment: A review of the literature and alternative pathways. *Child Abuse & Neglect, 31*, 1117–1142.

Crosnoe, R. (2009). Low-income students and the socioeconomic composition of public high schools. *American Sociological Review, 74*, 709–730.

Crosnoe, R. & Benner, A. D. (2015). Children at school. In M. H. Bornstein & T. Leventhal (Eds.) & R. M. Lerner (Editor-in-Chief), *Handbook of Child Psychology and Developmental Science, Vol. 4: Ecological Settings and Processes in Developmental Systems* (7th ed., pp. 268–304). Hoboken, NJ: Wiley. http://doi.org/10.1002/9781118963418.childpsy407

Crowder, K., & South, S. J. (2011). Spatial and temporal dimensions of neighborhood effects on high school graduation. *Social Science Research, 40*(1), 87–106.

Curran, F. C. (2017). The law, policy, and portrayal of zero tolerance school discipline: Examining prevalence and characteristics across levels of governance and school districts. *Educational Policy, online first*, 1–39. doi:10.1177/0895904817691840

DePaoli, J. L., Balfanz, R., & Bridgeland, J. (2016). *Building a Grad Nation: Progress and challenge in raising high school graduation rates.* Washington, DC: America's Promise.

Dishion, T. J., Andrews, D. W., & Crosby, L. (1995). Antisocial boys and their friends in early adolescence: Relationship characteristics, quality, and interactional process. *Child Development, 66*, 139–151.

Dobbie, W. & Fryer Jr., R. G. (2011). Are high-quality schools enough to increase achievement among the poor? Evidence from the Harlem Children's Zone. *American Economic Journal: Applied Economics, 3*, 158–187.

Dodge, K. A., Dishion, T. J., & Lansford, J. E. (2006). *Deviant Peer Influences in Programs for Youth: Problems and solutions.* New York: Guilford Press.

Dolcini, M. M., Harper, G. W., Watson, S. E., Catania, J. A., & Ellen, J. M. (2005). Friends in the 'hood: Should peer-based health promotion programs target nonschool friendship networks? *Journal of Adolescent Health, 36*, 267. e6–267.e15.

Duncan, G. J. & Brooks-Gunn, J. (Eds.). (1997). *Consequences of Growing Up Poor.* New York: Russell Sage Foundation Press.

Dupere, V., Leventhal, T., Crosnoe, R., & Dion, E. (2010). Understanding the positive role of neighborhood socioeconomic advantage in achievement: The contribution of the home, child care, and school environments. *Developmental Psychology, 46*(5), 1227–1244.

Elder, G. H., Jr., Shanahan, M. J., & Jennings, J. A. (2015). Human development in time and place. In M. H. Bornstein & T. Leventhal (Eds.) & R. M. Lerner (Editor-in-Chief), *Handbook of Child Psychology and Developmental Science, Vol. 4: Ecological Settings and Processes in Developmental Systems* (7th ed., pp. 6–54). Hoboken, NJ: Wiley. http://doi.org/10.1002/9781118963418.childpsy402

Elder, G. H., Jr., Wang, V., Spence, N. J., Adkins, D. E., & Brown, T. H. (2010). Pathways to the All-Volunteer Military. *Social Science Quarterly, 91*(2), 455–75. PMCID: PMC3181144

Elliott, D. S., Wilson, W. J., Huizinga, D., Sampson, R. J., Elliott, A., & Rankin, B. (1996). The effects of neighborhood disadvantage on adolescent development. *Journal of Research in Crime and Delinquency*, *33*(4), 389–426.

Fauth, R. C., Leventhal, T., & Brooks-Gunn, J. (2007). Welcome to the neighborhood? Long-term impacts of moving to low-poverty neighborhoods on poor children's and adolescents' outcomes. *Journal of Research on Adolescence*, *17*(2), 249–284.

Foster, E. M. & McLanahan, S. (1996). An illustration of the use of instrumental variables: Do neighborhood conditions affect a young person's chance of finishing high school? *Psychological Methods*, *1*(3), 249–260.

Franco, L. M., Pottick, K. J., & Huang, C.-C. (2010). Early parenthood in a community context: Neighborhood conditions, race-ethnicity, and parenting stress. *Journal of Community Psychology*, *38*(5), 574–590.

Friedson, M. & Sharkey, P. T. (2015). Violence and neighborhood disadvantage after the crime decline. *The Annals of the American Academy of Political and Social Science*, *660*, 341–358.

Galster, G. C. (2012). The mechanism(s) of neighbourhood effects: Theory, evidence, and policy implications. In M. van Ham, D. Manley, N. Bailey, L. Simpson, & D. Maclennan (Eds.), *Neighbourhood Effects Research: New perspectives* (pp. 23–56). Dordrecht: Springer Netherlands.

Galster, G. C. & Santiago, A. (2017). Neighbourhood ethnic composition and outcomes for low-income Latino and African American children, *Urban Studies*, *54*(2), 482–500.

Gennetian, L. A., Sanbonmatsu, L., Katz, L. F., Kling, J. R., Sciandra, M., Ludwig, J., … Kessler, R. (2012). The long-term effects of Moving to Opportunity on youth outcomes. *Cityscape*, *14*(2), 137–168.

Goering, J. & Feins, J. D. (Eds.). (2003). *Choosing a Better Life? Evaluating the Moving to Opportunity social experiment*. Washington, DC: Urban Institute Press.

Granger, R. C. (2008). After-school programs and academics: Implications for policy, practice, and research. *Social Policy Report*, *22*, 1–19.

Greenman, E., Bodovski, K., & Reed, K. (2011). Neighborhood characteristics, parental practices and children's math achievement in elementary school. *Social Science Research*, *40*(5), 1434–1444.

Grigorenko, E. L. & Takanishi, R. (Eds.). (2010). *Immigration, Diversity, and Education*. Abingdon: Routledge.

Guterman, N. B., Lee, S. J., Taylor, C. A., & Rathouz, P. J. (2009). Parental perceptions of neighborhood processes, stress, personal control, and risk for physical child abuse and neglect. *Child Abuse Neglect*, *33*(12), 897–906. http://doi.org/10.1016/j.chiabu.2009.09.008

Harding, D. J. (2011). Rethinking the cultural context of schooling decisions in disadvantaged neighborhoods: From deviant subculture to cultural heterogeneity. *Sociology of Education*, *84*(4), 322–339.

Harlem Children's Zone. (2009). *The HCZ Project*. Retrieved from www.hcz.org/index.php/about-us/the-hcz-project

Hill, M. (1991). *The Panel Study of Income Dynamics: The Sage series guides to major social science data bases* (Vol. 2). Newbury Park, CA: Sage.

Hook, J. Van, Brown, S. L., & Kwenda, M. N. (2004). Decomposition of trends in poverty among children of immigrants. *Demography*, *41*(4), 649–670.

Hulsey, L., Esposito, A. M., Boller, K., & Osborn, S. (2015). *Promise Neighborhoods Case Studies*. Cambridge, MA: Mathematica Policy Research.

Jackson, A. L., Browning, C. R., Krivo, L. J., Kwan, M.-P., & Washington, H. M. (2016). The role of immigrant concentration within and beyond residential neighborhoods in adolescent alcohol use. *Journal of Youth and Adolescence*, *15*(1), 17–34.

Jargowsky, P. A. (1997). *Poverty and Place: Ghettos, barrios, and the American city*. New York: Russel Sage Foundation.

(2003). *Stunning Progress, Hidden Problems: The dramatic decline of concentrated poverty in the 1990s*. Washington, DC: Brookings Institution.

(2013). *Concentration of Poverty in the New Millennium: Changes in the prevalence, composition, and location of high-poverty neighborhoods*, 1–29. New York: Century Foundation and Rutgers Center for Urban Research and Education.

(2015). *The Architecture of Segregation: Civil unrest, the concentration of poverty, and public policy*. New York: Century Foundation and Rutgers Center for Urban Research and Education.

Jencks, C. & Mayer, S. (1990). The social consequences of growing up in a poor neighborhood. In L. E. Lynn & M. F. H. McGeary (Eds.), *Inner-city Poverty in the United States* (pp. 111–186). Washington, DC: National Academy Press.

Johnson, O. (2013). Is concentrated advantage the cause? The relative contributions of neighborhood advantage and disadvantage to educational inequality. *Urban Review*, *45*(5), 561–585.

Kim, C. Y., Losen, D. J., & Hewitt, D. (2010). *The School-to-Prison Pipeline: Structuring legal reform*. New York: New York University.

Kirk, D. S. & Sampson, R. J. (2013). Juvenile arrest and collateral educational damage in the transition to adulthood. *Sociology of Education*, *86*(1), 36–62.

Kneebone, E. (2014). *The Growth and Spread of Concentrated Poverty, 2000 to 2008–2012*. Washington, DC: Brookings Institute.

(2017). *The Changing Geography of US Poverty*. Washington, DC: Brookings Institute.

Kneebone, E. & Holmes, N. (2016). *US Concentrated Poverty in the Wake of the Great Recession*. Washington, DC: Brookings Institute.

Kneebone, E., Nadeau, C., & Berube, A. (2011). *The Re-emergence of Concentrated Poverty: Metropolitan trends in the 2000s*. Washington, DC: Brookings Institute.

Kohen, D. E., Leventhal, T., Dahinten, V. S., & McIntosh, C. N. (2008). Neighborhood disadvantage: Pathways of effects for young children. *Child Development*, *79*(1), 156–169.

Lareau, A. (2003). *Unequal Childhoods: Class, race, and family life*. Berkeley, CA: University of California Press.

Lerner, R. M. & Overton, W. F. (2008). Exemplifying the integrations of the relational developmental system. *Journal of Adolescent Research*, *23*(3), 245–255.

Leventhal, T. (2018). Neighborhood context and children's development: When do neighborhoods matter most. *Child Development Perspectives*, *12*(40), 258–263.

Leventhal, T. & Brooks-Gunn, J. (2000). The neighborhoods they live in: The effects of neighborhood residence on child and adolescent outcomes. *Psychological Bulletin, 126*(2), 309–337.

(2011). Changes in neighborhood poverty from 1990 to 2000 and youth's problem behaviors. *Developmental Psychology, 47*(6), 1680–1698.

Leventhal, T., Dupéré, V., & Brooks-Gunn, J. (2009). Neighborhood influences on adolescent development. In R. M. Lerner & L. Steinberg (Eds.), *Handbook of Adolescent Psychology* (3rd ed., Vol. 2, pp. 411–443). Hoboken, NJ: Wiley.

Leventhal, T., Dupéré, V., & Shuey, E. (2015). Children in neighborhoods. In M. H. Bornstein & T. Leventhal (Eds.) & R. M. Lerner (Editor-in-Chief), *Handbook of Child Psychology and Developmental Science, Vol. 4: Ecological Settings and Processes in Developmental Systems* (7th ed., pp. 493–533). Hoboken, NJ: Wiley.

Lichter, D. T., Parisi, D., Taquino, M. C., & Grice, S. M. (2010). Residential segregation in new Hispanic destinations: Cities, suburbs, and rural communities compared. *Social Science Research, 39*(2), 215–230.

Lleras, C. (2008). Race, racial concentration, and the dynamics of educational inequality across urban and suburban schools. *American Educational Research Journal, 45*(4), 886–912.

Ludwig, J., Duncan, G. J., Genettian, L. A., Katz, L. F., Kessler, R. C., Kling, J. R., & Sanbonmatsu, L. (2012). Neighborhood effects on the long-term well-being of low-income adults. *Science, 337*, 1505–1510.

Ludwig, J., Sanbonmatsu, L., Genettian, L. A., Adam, E., Duncan, G. J., Katz, L. F., … McDade, T. W. (2011). Neighborhoods, obesity, and diabetes: A randomized social experiment. *New England Journal of Medicine, 365*(16), 1509–1519.

Lund, T. J. & Dearing, E. (2013). Is growing up affluent risky for adolescents or is the problem growing up in an affluent neighborhood? *Journal of Research on Adolescence, 23*(2), 274–282.

Luthar, S. S. & Barkin, S. H. (2012). Are affluent youth truly "at risk"? Vulnerability and resilience across three diverse samples. *Development and Psychopathology, 24*, 429–449.

Luthar, S. S. & Latendresse, S. J. (2005). Comparable "risks" at the SES extremes: Pre-adolescents' perceptions of parenting. *Development and Psychopathology, 17*, 207–230.

Marks, A. K., Ejesi, K., & García Coll, C. (2014). Understanding the US immigrant paradox in childhood and adolescence. *Child Development Perspectives, 8*(2), 59–64.

Massey, D. S. (1996). The age of extremes: Concentrated affluence and poverty in the twenty-first century. *Demography, 33*(4), 395–412.

(2016). Residential segregation is the linchpin of racial stratification. *City and Community, 15*(1), 4–7.

Massey, D. S., Albright, L., Casciano, R., Derickson, E., & Kinsey, D. (2013). *Climbing Mount Laurel: The struggle for affordable housing and social mobility in an American suburb.* Princeton, NJ: Princeton University Press.

Massey, D. S. & Denton, N. (1993). *American Apartheid: Segregation and the making of the underclass.* Cambridge, MA: Harvard University Press.

Massey, D. S., Fischer, M. J., Dickens, W. T., & Levy, F. (2003). The geography of inequality in the United States, 1950–2000. *Brookings-Wharton Papers on Urban Affairs*, 1–40.

Molnar, B. E., Buka, S. L., Brennan, R. T., Holton, J. K., & Earls, F. (2003). A multilevel study of neighborhoods and parent-to-child physical aggression: Results from the Project on Human Development in Chicago Neighborhoods. *Child Maltreatment, 8*(2), 84–97.

Murray, J., Farrington, D. P., & Sekol, I. (2012). Children's antisocial behavior, mental health, drug use, and educational performance after parental incarceration: A systematic review and meta-analysis. *Psychological Bulletin, 138*(2), 175–210. http://doi.org/10.1037/a0026407

Oreopoulos, P. (2008). Neighbourhood effects in Canada: A critique. *Canadian Public Policy, 34*(2), 237–258.

Orfield, G. & Lee, C. (2005). *Why Segregation Matters: Poverty and educational inequality. Race, Class, and Gender: An anthology* (pp. 416–426). Cambridge, MA: Harvard University: Civil Rights Project.

Overton, W. F. (2015). Processes, relations, and relational-developmental-systems. In F. Overton & P. C. M. Molenaar (Eds.) & R. M. Lerner (Editor-in-Chief), *Handbook of Child Psychology and Developmental Science, Vol. 1: Theory and Method* (7th ed., pp. 1–54). Hoboken, NJ: Wiley.

Paschall, M. J. & Hubbard, M. L. (1998). Effects of neighborhood and family stressors on African American male adolescents' self-worth and propensity for violent behavior. *Journal of Consulting and Clinical Psychology, 66*(5), 825–831.

Raikes, H., Torquati, J., Wang, C., & Shjegstad, B. (2012). Parent experiences with state child care subsidy systems and their perceptions of choice and quality in care selected. *Early Education & Development, 23*(4), 558–582.

Reardon, S. F. & Bischoff, K. (2011). *Growth in the Residential Segregation of Families by Income, 1970–2009.* US 2010 Project. Palo Alto, CA: Stanford University.

Reardon, S. F., Fox, L., & Townsend, J. (2015). Neighborhood income composition by household race and income, 1990–2009. *The Annals of the American Academy of Political and Social Science, 660*(1), 78–97.

Rubin, K. H., Bukowski, W. M., & Bowker, J. C. (2015). Children in peer groups. In M. H. Bornstein & T. Leventhal (Eds.) & R. M. Lerner (Editor-in-Chief), *Handbook of Child Psychology and Developmental Science, Vol. 4: Ecological Settings and Processes in Developmental Systems* (7th ed., pp. 175–222). Hoboken, NJ: Wiley.

Rubinowitz, L. S. & Rosenbaum, J. E. (2000). *Crossing the Class and Color Lines: From public housing to White suburbia.* Chicago: University of Chicago Press.

Ryan, J. E. (2010). *Five Miles Away, a World Apart: One city, two schools, and the story of educational opportunity in modern America.* New York: Oxford University Press.

Sampson, R. J. (2011). *Great American City: Chicago and the enduring neighborhood effect.* Chicago, IL: University of Chicago Press.

Sampson, R. J. & Loeffler, C. (2010). Punishment's place: The local concentration of mass incarceration. *Daedalus, 139*, 20–31.

Sampson, R. J., Morenoff, J. D., & Earls, F. (1999). Beyond social capital: Spatial dynamics of collective efficacy for children. *American Sociological Review, 64,* 633–660.

Sampson, R. J., Morenoff, J. D., & Gannon-Rowley, T. (2002). Assessing "neighborhood effects": Social processes and new directions in research. *Annual Review of Sociology, 28*(1), 443–478.

Sampson, R. J., Raudenbush, S. W., & Earls, F. (1997). Neighborhoods and violent crime: A multilevel study of collective efficacy. *Science, 277*(5328), 918–924.

Sampson, R. J., Sharkey, P. T., & Raudenbush, S. W. (2008). Durable effects of concentrated disadvantage on verbal ability among African-American children. *Proceedings of the National Academy of Sciences, 105,* 845–852.

Shadish, W. R., Cook, T. D., & Campbell, D. T. (2002). *Experimental and Quasi-Experimental Designs for Generalized Causal Inference.* Boston, MA: Houghton Mifflin.

Sharkey, P. T. (2013). *Stuck in Place: Urban neighborhoods and the end of progress toward racial equality.* Chicago, IL: University of Chicago Press.

Sharkey, P. T. & Faber, J. W. (2014). Where, when, why, and for whom do residential contexts matter? Moving away from the dichotomous understanding of neighborhood effects. *Annual Review of Sociology, 40*(1), 559–579.

Sharkey, P. T., Tirado-Strayer, N., Papachristos, A. V., & Raver, C. C. (2012). The effect of local violence on children's attention and impulse control. *American Journal of Public Health, 102*(12), 2287–2293.

Shonkoff, J. P., Boyce, W. T., & McEwen, B. S. (2009). Neuroscience, molecular biology, and the childhood roots of health disparities. *JAMA, 301*(21), 2252.

Shortt, J. W., Capaldi, D. M., Dishion, T. J., Bank, L., & Owen, L. D. (2003). The role of adolescent friends, romantic partners, and siblings in the emergence of the adult antisocial lifestyle. *Journal of Family Psychology, 17,* 521–533.

Shuey, E. A. & Leventhal, T. (2017). Pathways of risk and resilience between neighborhood socioeconomic conditions and parenting. *Children and Youth Services Review, 72,* 52–59. http://doi.org/10.1016/j.childyouth.2016.09.031

Shuey, E. A. & Leventhal, T. (in press). Neighborhoods and parenting. In M. H. Bornstein (Ed.), *Handbook of Parenting* (3rd ed.). New York: Taylor & Francis/Psychology Press.

Small, M. L. (2009). *Unanticipated Gains: Origins of network inequality in everyday life.* New York: Oxford University Press.

Small, M. L. & Feldman, J. (2012). Ethnographic evidence, heterogeneity, and neighborhood effects after Moving to Opportunity. In M. van Ham, D. Manley, N. Bailey, L. Simpson, & D. Maclennan (Eds.), *Neighborhood Effect Research: New perspectives* (pp. 57–77). Springer: Dordrecht.

South, S. J. & Crowder, K. (2010). Neighborhood poverty and nonmarital fertility: Spatial and temporal dimensions. *Journal of Marriage and Family, 72*(1), 89–104.

Stolle, D., Soroka, S., & Johnston, R. (2008). When does diversity erode trust? Neighborhood diversity, interpersonal trust and the mediating effect of social interactions. *Political Studies, 56*(1), 57–75.

Timberlake, J. M. (2007). Racial and ethnic inequality in the duration of children's exposure to neighborhood poverty and affluence. *Social Problems, 54*(3), 319–342.

Turley, R. N. L. (2003). When do neighborhoods matter? The role of race and neighborhood peers. *Social Science Research, 32,* 61–79.

Vandell, D. L., Larson, R. W., Mahoney, J. L., & Watts, T. W. (2015). Children's organized activities. In M. H. Bornstein & T. Leventhal (Eds.) & R. M. Lerner (Editor-in-Chief), *Handbook of Child Psychology and Developmental Science, Vol. 4: Ecological Settings and Processes in Developmental Systems* (7th ed., pp. 305–344). Hoboken, NJ: Wiley.

Verdugo, R. R. (2002). Race-ethnicity, social class, and zero-tolerance policies: The cultural and structural wars. *Education and Urban Society, 35*(1), 50–75.

Wacquant, L. (2008). *Urban Outcasts: A comparative sociology of advanced marginality*. Cambridge: Polity.

Wadhwa, A. (2017). *Restorative Justice in Urban Schools*. New York: Routledge.

Wakefield, S. & Apel, R. (2016). Criminal justice and the life course. In M. J. Shanahan, J. T. Mortimer, & M. K. Johnson (Eds.), *Handbook of the Life Course* (Vol. 2, pp. 301–319). Cham: Springer International Publishing.

Wheaton, B. & Clarke, P. (2003). Space meets time: Integrating temporal and contextual influences on mental health in early adulthood. *American Sociological Review, 68*(5), 680–706.

White, R. M. B., Knight, G. P., Jensen, M., & Gonzales, N. A. (2017). Ethnic socialization in neighborhood contexts: Implications for ethnic attitude and identity development among Mexican-Origin adolescents. *Child Development, 89*(3), 1004–1021. doi:10.1111/cdev.12772

Wilmoth, J. M. & London, A. S. (Eds.) (2013). *Life-Course Perspectives on Military Service*. New York: Routledge Press.

Wilson, W. J. (1987). *The Truly Disadvantaged: The inner city, the underclass, and public policy*. Chicago, IL: University of Chicago Press.

   (1996). *When Work Disappears: The world of the new urban poor*. New York: Alfred A Knopf.

   (2015). Understanding the emergence and persistence of concentrated urban poverty. In M. Chowkwanyun & R. Serhan (Eds.), *American Democracy and the Pursuit of Equality* (pp. 127–141). Abingdon: Routledge.

Wodtke, G. T., Harding, D. J., & Elwert, F. (2011). Neighborhood effects in temporal perspective. *American Sociological Review, 76*(5), 713–736.

Zaff, J. F., Donlan, A. E., Pufall Jones, E., Lin, E. S., & Anderson, S. (2016). Comprehensive community initiatives creating supportive youth systems: A theoretical rationale for creating youth-focused CCIs. In J. F. Zaff, E. Pufall Jones, A. E. Donlan, & S. Anderson (Eds.), *Community Initiatives for Positive Youth Development* (pp. 1–16). New York: Routledge.

8 Changing Family Forms: The Implications for Children's Development

Ross D. Parke

> Family is not a static institution but one that is constantly changing, being reworked, reshaped and re-imagined in complex and dynamic ways. (Goldberg, 2010)

As this quote suggests families are always in flux and in many ways serve as an ideal barometer of how society-wide changes across time shape this institution, which is centrally involved in the care and nurturance of our children. The goal of this chapter is to outline the shifts in how families are defined, constituted, and organized and, in turn, to examine the implications of these changes in family forms for children's development. Perhaps the most significant change has been toward an increasingly diverse set of family forms rather than a single or modal model of family. It is recognized that variability in terms of both the stability and forms of families has always been evident across historical epochs in response to social, economic political, and natural upheavals such as depressions, social revolutions, war, and famine.

The proliferation of a wide variety of family forms has challenged the centrality and necessity of the traditional nuclear family form as a context for successful socialization. New family forms challenge our views about the importance of gender of parents, sexual orientation of parents, biological relatedness of family members, and new routes to parenthood in defining family. Increases in divorce, the rise of stepfamilies, cohabitating couples, single parents, and adoption raise further questions about the links between both the number of parents and the biological ties among family members. The increasing fluidity and interchangeability of maternal and paternal roles as a result of the increase of women in the workforce raise further challenges to traditional family forms. To account for the relative success of these new family forms, it is suggested that process is more important than family forms or the identity of the players within the family who deliver these processes. It is proposed that the gender, sexual orientation or biological relatedness of the agent of delivery of the critical process ingredients for socialization (i.e., stimulation, nurturance, guidance, limit setting) or the family form in which these processes are enacted are less important than the processes itself. Second, an interdependent model of family functioning is proposed in recognition of the embeddedness of families in a variety of extended family as well as non-family community kin networks and institutions. This model reflects the increasing degree of outsourcing of tasks and responsibilities that were traditionally within the purview of the nuclear family. In part, this sharing of family responsibilities across a variety of family and non family support agents is a second reason for the success of new family forms. Finally, to maximize assistance available to a full range of family forms, it is critical that policy makers recognize the diversity of family forms and develop policies that more equitably tailor policies to support these new family forms beyond the nuclear family form.

Families in Historical Perspective

Beginning in the eighteenth century the first or "classic" demographic transition occurred in which there were historical declines in mortality and fertility in western countries and an ultimate balance between deaths and births (Lesthaeghe, 2014). In turn, households assumed nuclear and conjugal forms, composed of married couples and their children. Since the 1970s some have argued that a second demographic transition has taken place (Lesthaeghe, 2014; Lesthaeghe & van de Kaa, 1986) in which the stability envisioned by the earlier transition is challenged due to a variety of factors such as lower fertility due to more effective birth control which, in turn, led to more time for both education and employment opportunities for women. In combination with the women's liberation movement of the 1960s and 1970s as well as shifting attitudes toward marriage as a necessary context for the rearing of children and the sentiment /affectionate basis for marriage (Coontz, 2005), a variety of alternative family forms have emerged in the past 40 years (Brown, 2017; Parke, 2013). These demographic transitions should be viewed as descriptive guides rather than explanatory (Zaidi & Morgan, 2017) especially since there is considerable variability in the extent to which this framework applies across all cultures and countries or even within some countries.

A major casualty of these shifts has been the decline in the centrality of the nuclear family as the prototypic family form. In spite of our continuing cultural embrace of the nuclear family as the ideal family form, the reality is, in fact, quite different. An increasingly small percentage of families conform to the traditional version of the nuclear family. The outdated but still endorsed cultural definition of the ideal family form of two married parents of heterosexual orientation who have naturally conceived biological children and mothers and fathers who have clearly demarcated roles is less prevalent than in past decades. As

Table 8.1 *Overview of demographic, societal, and family characteristics, respectively, related to the first demographic transition (FDT) and second demographic transition (SDT) in Western countries*

First demographic transition	Second demographic transition
Marriage and child care	
Rise in proportions marrying, declining ages at first marriage	Fall in proportions married, rising ages at first marriage; more single parent households
Low or declining incidence of cohabitation	Increasing cohabitation, both pre- and post-marital
Low divorce rates	Rise in divorce, earlier divorce
Two biological parents	One or more social parent(s) through artificial insemination, surrogacy, adoption, foster care, or kinship (relative headed household)
Heterosexual couple	Homosexual, lesbian, bisexual, asexual
One major breadwinner (male)	Dual earner couple; job cycling in/out; reverse role families (mother as primary earner, father as caregiver)
Co-resident, part-time resident, shared custody, visitation access to children	Child care primarily by parents or extended family Childcare by parents and/or relatives, siblings, staff in child care homes and centers, neighbors, members of childcare co-operatives, members of a collective community
Fertility	
Declining marital fertility via reductions at older ages, lowering mean ages at first childbearing	Fertility postponement, increasing mean ages at parenthood, structural subreplacement fertility
Deficient contraception, parity and timing failures	Efficient contraception
Declining illegitimate fertility	Rising non-marital fertility, parenthood outside marriage (among cohabiting couples, single mothers)
Low final childlessness among married couples	Rising definitive childlessness among women ever in a union
Few alternative routes to fertility and parenthood except adoption by relatives or community members after death of a parent	Alternative routes to fertility and parenthood via adoption and the new reproductive technologies
Societal background	
Preoccupation with basic material needs: income, work conditions, housing, children and adult health, schooling, social security; solidarity a prime value	Rise of "higher order" needs: individual autonomy, expressive work and socialization values, self-actualization, grass-roots democracy, recognition; tolerance a prime value

Table 8.1 (*cont.*)

First demographic transition	Second demographic transition
Rising membership of political, civic, and community-oriented networks	Disengagement from civic and community-oriented networks
Strong normative regulation by churches and state, first secularization wave, political and social "pillarization"	Retreat of the state, second secularization wave, sexual revolution, refusal of authority, political "depillarization"
Segregated sex roles, familistic policies, "embourgeoisement" of the family with the breadwinner model at its core	Rising symmetry in sex roles, rising female education levels, greater female economic autonomy
Ordered life course transitions and dominance of one single nuclear family model	Flexible life course organization, multiple lifestyles, open future

Sources: Based on Lesthaeghe (2014) and Parke (2013)

Table 8.1 illustrates there are a variety of alterations in family forms, societal changes, and fertility shifts associated with these two demographic transitions that are linked with alternative versions of family beyond the ideal nuclear family form. In reality only about 30 percent of contemporary families fit this narrow traditional definition of family form (US Census Bureau, 2012). The decline in the centrality of the nuclear family form as the guiding template for the organization of family life is a major trend that forms the foundation of this chapter.

A second theme is that these shifts have not affected all levels of western societies in equal ways in part to the growing social, economic, and educational inequalities that have emerged (Osberg, 2015; Piketty, 2014). The impact of the growth of inequality has shaped family forms and functioning so that there is no longer a single story line that captures the changes in families but in broad terms several narratives as well as several sub plots as well. Sociologist Susan Brown (2017) has described this two-track system as "*two Americas*' in which family life is increasingly bifurcated by social class" (Brown, 2017, pp. 32–33). Similarly, Sociologist and demographer Frank Furstenberg (2014) has characterized this shift as the "two tier family system."

Well-educated and economically viable families follow a traditional pattern of stable marriage, low divorce rates, and a small number of children. Within these families fathers are increasing their involvement and moving slowly toward more equal participation with their wives in the care and rearing of children. On the other hand, due to lack of education and limited employment opportunities many individuals forgo marriage and in many cases co-residency and as a result live as single parent families. They often have children with different partners. In turn, patterns of father involvement in children's lives is more erratic and fathers with limited resources may focus their attention on a single child rather than across all of their biological prodigy (Edin & Nelson, 2013; McLanahan, 2004). Still others who are disadvantaged or members of minority groups often suffer serious disruptions in their family lives as a result of military deployment or high rates of incarceration. And still other families live separately due to patterns of incomplete migration, which results in new family forms created by these transnational fathers (or/and mothers). The aim is to capture both these dual or perhaps more accurately multiple tracks as well as some overall trends that affect the society more broadly.

Factors Promoting Shifts in Family Organization and Form: Society and Social Science as Contributors

Several factors have been suggested to account for these changes from a nuclear family form to a wider range of family forms. As is the case with broad social changes, multiple sets of societal level and individual level influences merit mention including economic shifts, demographic changes, fluctuations in attitudes about marriage and family, social policies, and cultural diversity. In addition social science theories and new empirical work have contributed to the changing ways in which we conceptualize both the possible forms that families can assume the effects of these shifting forms on children families.

Economic Influences Promoting Family Change

Perhaps the major catalyst for change in maternal and paternal family roles as well as the rise of new family forms is the increased participation of mothers in the paid labor force. As Figure 8.1 shows, in 1975 only 34 percent of mothers with preschool children were in the labor force; in 2013, this number was nearly 61 percent (Pew Research Center, 2015). For mothers with school age children (6 to 17) only 47 percent were in the work force in 1975 but the rate nearly doubled to 70 percent by 2014 (Pew Research Center, 2015). In 2012, 75 percent of employed mothers worked full time (35 hours per week or more) with 71 percent of mothers with preschoolers and 76 percent of mothers with school age children working full time (US Dept. of Labor, 2013).

Among mothers with children younger than 18, 75 percent of Blacks are in the labor force in comparison, to 70 percent among White

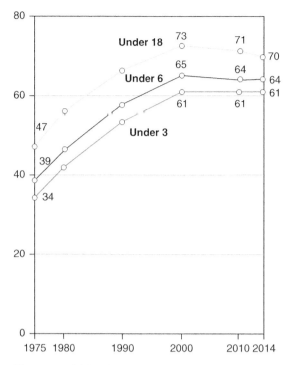

Figure 8.1 Rising labor force participation among mothers
Note: Mothers working full time or part time are included as being in
the labor force
Source: Bureau of Labor Statistics, Current Population Survey Data
2015, Pew Research Center

mothers in part due to the fact that more Black women are single and
the sole breadwinner. Some 64 percent of Asian mothers and 62 percent of Hispanic mothers are in the workforce. The relatively high
proportions of immigrants in these groups likely contribute to their
lower labor force involvement – foreign-born moms are much less likely
to be working than their US-born counterparts. These shifts toward
maternal employment outside the home are linked with several other
trends. First, economic pressures on lower class and even middle class
families in an era of increasing cost of living has required many two-
parent households to have both partners seek employment to make ends
meet (Brown, 2017). However, this is an incomplete picture since education is an even stronger predictor than economic need of the shifts
in maternal employment. According to a recent survey (Pew Research

Center, 2015), educated mothers are more likely to be in the labor force than less educated mothers. Only half (49%) of mothers who have not completed high school are in the workforce in part due to the lack of skills/education necessary for jobs in a technology-oriented economy. In contrast nearly 65 percent of high school graduates, 75 percent of those who have completed some college and 79 percent of those with at least a college degree are in the workforce. Recent trends in the educational attainment of males and females, namely that females are gaining more education than males has resulted in women often attaining higher levels of education than their male partner, a contrast with earlier eras. In turn, this has, in part led to this rise in mothers as the main breadwinner while some fathers are stay at home parents; in turn this has led to shifts toward greater female power within the family. In nearly 15 percent of married two-parent households women earn more of the family income than men (Pew Research Center, 2015), a further reminder of the gradual blurring of the boundaries between family/work roles for men and women.

Changing Societal Attitudes Concerning Family Roles and Family Forms

Moreover, social change is often driven not by only economic factors but by non-economic secular changes such as the women's movement and the men's movement (Parke, 2013; Parke & Brott, 1999), which both challenged the prevailing notion that childcare was only women's work and that non-domestic employment is the domain of men. This awareness on the part of women about the fulfilling possibilities of outside employment was fueled in part by the women's movement of the 1970s and beyond. Moreover, this early call to action was an important catalyst for a renewed dialogue about the role of both fathers and mothers in family life. Similarly, the men's movement helped focus attention on men's possible roles not only at work but as caregivers in the family as well (Parke & Brott, 1999). The recognition of new possible roles for men and women suggested that parents need not be restricted by the past ideologies associated with traditional family forms.

Another major catalyst for re-visiting the traditional concept of family was the increasing social acceptance of same-sex relationships as equivalent and deserving equal legal recognition as heterosexual relationships. In turn, there was an accompanying shift in attitudes concerning the acceptability and viability of same gender couples as parents. Accompanying this recognition was the assumption that same-sex partners could be parents and provide equivalent and satisfactory child rearing environments for children (Golombok, 2015; Patterson, 2016). These societal shifts in attitudes concerning the rights of same-sex couples to form family units presented a major challenge to our earlier privileging of heterosexual couple families as the major context for family formation and the socialization of children. Finally, the recent Supreme Court decision (Obergefell vs. Hodges, June 2015) that legalized same-sex marriage across the United States represented a further challenge to the historical view of marriage and family as anchored within a heterosexual union.

Medical Advances and the Rise of New Family Forms

The medical advances in reproductive technologies that provided new avenues for both infertile couples as well as single or same-sex partners to achieve parenthood was a further assault on our traditional views of both family formation and possible family forms (Goldberg, 2010; Golombok, 2015). These medical achievements offered new routes to parenthood beyond the historically limited avenue of two heterosexual biological parents. Through these techniques, single parents as well as same gender couples were offered new routes to achieve parenthood. In turn, these medical advances expanded the variety of family forms and the range of participants (egg and sperm donors, surrogates) who collectively were part of the reproductive process. These changes in the paths to parenthood raise complex questions about the definition of family and the roles played by various contributors to family formation (Parke, Gailey, Dimatteo, & Coltrane, 2012).

The Role of Social Science Theory in the Move Toward Diverse Family Forms

Shifts in how social scientists think about families have set the stage for the changes in the roles played by men and women in modern families and the ways in which the socialization of children is an enterprise shared with extended kin and non-family members. Theories that were historically aligned with the traditional view of the family have been challenged and replaced by more flexible contemporary views of family roles. Our decreased reliance on Freudian theory and its focus on the central role of mothers and feeding as the critical context for the adequate development of the infant's social and emotional development was a first step. Bowlby (1969) suggested that the early development of social relationships and, in particular, the development of an attachment bond between infants and their caregivers was based not on the feeding situation but a result of social interchanges (vocalizing, rocking, and touching) between the caregiver and the infant whether mother or father. A second blow to the primacy of the feeding context and therefore to the primacy of mothers in children's development came from Harlow (1958) who showed that rhesus monkeys spent more time clinging to a terry cloth surrogate mother who provided warmth and "contact comfort" over a wire-mesh surrogate who offered only food. Finally, Schaffer and Emerson (1964) found that human infants' attachment to their caregivers, including fathers and grandparents, was independent of the degree of their involvement in feeding. This set of empirical and theoretical advances led to a re-evaluation of the potential role that socialization agents beyond mothers such as fathers and other kin and non-kin could play in development. This early work paved the way to greater acceptance of child care by non-family members by the awareness that infants and children can develop and maintain social ties with several individuals beyond their immediate family members, including their child care providers (Howes & Spieker, 2016).

Another theoretical shift occurred in the 1970s that gave new impetus to the re-thinking of men's and women's roles in the family was the introduction of androgyny, which challenged viewing males and females in dichotomous terms, in which there is little overlap in the typical traits possessed by males and females (Bem, 1973). According to an androgynous view of gender men could be nurturant, and emotional, while women could be assertive and independent. This revised view of gender opened up the options available to both men and women and reduced the dichotomization of "the social world into the masculine domain of paid employment and the feminine domain of home and childcare" (Bem, 1973, p. 194).

A life span view of development (Elder, 2008; Elder & Cox, this volume; Elder, Shanahan & Jennings, 2015) suggested that certain behaviors and attitudes emerged in response to changing demands of life course events such as the transition to parenthood. Men who had become fathers were more sensitive to infant signals than non-fathers (Feldman et al., 2010). Parental behavior, in short, can be elicited under different circumstances rather than being viewed as a fixed set of traits. The increased acceptance of a family systems perspective (Cox & Paley, 2003) in which the interdependence of parenting partners is recognized stimulated a re-evaluation of family roles. Moreover, as we note below changing social attitudes concerning the roles of mothers and fathers, the recognition of men as caregivers and the greater acceptance of a same-sex couple as parents has changed the social landscape of potential parents.

Together these economic influences, especially work patterns for men and women, changing societal attitudes about families, medical advances in new reproductive technologies, social movements, and social science theory, together laid the foundation for both changes in gender-based family roles as well as the emergence of new family forms.

The Fluidity of Family Roles and Responsibilities

In this section we focus on the changing roles and responsibilities of mothers and fathers in families, especially the increased recognition of the dual roles of both mothers and fathers as caregivers and financial contributors. One major consequence is the challenge to the "ideal" family form in which men are breadwinners and women are child caregivers. In spite of shifts in cultural attitudes concerning the appropriateness and desirability of shared roles and equal levels of participation in routine caregiving and interaction for mothers and fathers, the shifts toward parity are small, but nonetheless real (Pleck, 2010). As noted above, more mothers are entering the work force, but current occupational arrangements still mean that the vast majority of fathers have less opportunity for interaction with their children than mothers. However, the gap is closing. Compared to mothers, fathers' total time in 2000 was 64.7 percent of time as mothers compared to 44.7 percent in 1965 (Bianchi et al., 2006). Others report similar trends. Yeung et al. (2001) found that the relative time fathers in intact families were directly engaged with children was 67 percent of the time that mothers were involved on weekdays and 87 percent of mothers' engagement on weekends. "Husbands and wives have never before had such similar workloads. For those who had children under the age of 18, women employed full time did just 20 min. more of combined paid and unpaid work than men did, the smallest difference ever reported"(Konisberg, 2011, p. 46). However, we are clearly not at 50/50 yet. Mothers still do more of the child caregiving such as feeding and diapering in infancy and in providing meals, school lunches, and clothing as the child develops than fathers (Pleck, 2010). And mothers continue to assume more managerial responsibility than fathers such as arranging social contacts, organizing schedules and medical checkups, and monitoring homework and school related tasks (Yueng et al., 2001). Nevertheless, this pattern of change underscores the plasticity and modifiability of maternal and paternal roles.

These family role changes are driven not only by maternal employment patterns, but by the new recognition of the competence of fathers as caregivers (Parke & Cookston, 2019) as well as new evidence that men as well as women are biologically prepared to parent their offspring. Hormonal levels are important determinants of paternal behavior (Storey et al., 2000) and males experience hormonal changes, prior to the onset of parental behavior and during infant contact (Feldman, 2019). In contrast to the myth of the biologically unfit father, this work suggests that men may be more prepared – even biologically – for parenting than previously thought. Men, just like women, are biologically evolved to be parents.

Our traditional focus on the gender of the parent may be too narrow a conceptualization of the issue of the necessary adult input for adequate child development. Instead, it may be helpful to recast the issue by asking whether exposure to male and female parents is the key, or whether it is exposure to the interactive style typically associated with either mothers or fathers that matters. In an examination of this issue, Ross and Taylor (1989) found that boys prefer the physical play style, whether it is mothers or fathers who engage in it. Their work suggests that boys may not necessarily prefer their fathers but rather their physical style of play. Further evidence is consistent with this gender of parent interchangeability argument. To illustrate gender of parent substitutability, Main & Weston (1981) examined the effects of a secure or insecure attachment relationship with mother or father on an infant's sociability with a stranger. The gender of the parent with whom the infant developed a secure attachment did not matter for the infant's sociability; the parents were substitutable for one another. Mothers and fathers were equally effective as support figures for their toddlers' cognitive progress, which suggests that parents of either gender are interchangeable (Ryan et al., 2006). Together, this evidence indicates that the style of parenting and the gender of the parent who delivers it can be viewed as at least partially independent. Moreover, they provide clarity on the important issue of how essential fathers (Silverstein & Auerbach, 1999) and mothers (Parke, 2013) are for the successful socialization of their children, an issue that we address below in our exploration of same gender parent families.

Diversity of Maternal and Paternal Roles

It is increasingly clear that the previous descriptions of the albeit slow emergence of fathers who are more actively involved in the care of their children, and shared the responsibilities of both caregiver and breadwinner with their partners, do not apply to all families (Doucet, 2013; Edin and Nelson, 2013). There is increasing recognition that there is a two-tier family system based to a large extent on social class (Furstenberg, 2014). The cultural trends described by the Second Demographic Transition involving new and involved fathers apply most clearly to economically and educationally advantaged families, but they apply less readily to less economically well off and less educated fathers and families. Especially as economic inequality has increased, it is important to recognize that economic disparities have yielded more variability across social class in the patterns of mother and father roles than is usually recognized. These patterns of differing levels of involvement underscore the variability across social class, education, and immigration status and illustrate that the overall trends as part of the SDT need to be qualified. To illustrate we consider poor disadvantaged fathers. However, incarcerated parents (Dellaire, 2019), transnational parents (Dreby, 2010), and military deployed parents (MacDermid Wadsworth, 2013) represent other examples of groups that are outside the broader social trends that characterize the changes in contemporary families. Parents in these families often engage in "parenting at a distance," which is often facilitated by recent advances in digital technologies (i.e., email, Skype, Facebook, cell phones) rather than in routine face to face contact characteristic of traditional family forms (see Greenfield, this volume for the effects of new communication technologies on children and families).

Disadvantaged Families and Patterns of Father-Child Contact

Recent work on fathers and families who are economically disadvantaged illustrates that the overall trends in increased father involvement and shared family roles are not applicable to all segments of society. In contrast to the profile of educated and economically well situated men, there is a group who have developed distinctive patterns of involvement and participation with their offspring and their partners.

According to the Fragile Families study, a major investigation of these disadvantaged families show that men in these families are often unmarried, of minority background (African-American or Latin American), and less educated and less likely to be employed (Carlson & McLanahan, 2010). A variety of other features characterize these families, such as early onset of parenthood and a decision not to marry. However, many parents are either cohabiting or in a partner relationship at the time that the baby is born (McLanahan et al., 2003). Middle-class men are more likely to marry, divorce, and re-marry, a pattern that has been termed the "Marriage-go-round" (Cherlin, 2009), but men in poverty are less likely to marry, but more likely than middle-class men to have multiple children with different partners. According to Edin and Nelson (2013), these disadvantaged men are on "the 'Family-go-round' where good fatherhood is accomplished by moving from one child to another" (2013, p. 189) as romantic relationships end and they move on to a new relationship and often a new bout of fathering. Fathering efforts are not evenly distributed across all offspring because few men are able to support or even maintain ties with several children. Instead, a pattern of selective fathering is more normative among poor unmarried men whereby a father selectively and serially invests his fathering capital in one or a few offspring. Instead of supporting the child's mother, many women are left to their own resources as many poor men are unable to play the traditional breadwinner role due to high unemployment or sporadic and low paying employment or intermittent incarceration. Again those most affected by incarceration are poor and minority individuals (see Dallaire, 2019 for a review of the effects of incarceration on families) and provide a further example of how the trends concerning more equal parental roles in contemporary families do not apply equally across racial and SES groups. Instead of a contemporary package deal in which a middle-class father is expected to be both a breadwinner and a nurturer, guide, and support for their child, many poor men elect to play only the nurturing role. This selective involvement choice represents a reversal of roles between the sexes because it is the mother who is the financial provider and the father the playmate to their child. While selective involvement allows men to perhaps father at least one child well, it leaves the women who have borne these other children to bear the major responsibility for not only the financial burden of rearing a child, but also leaves these "non-selected" children without support from their biological father. Clearly the patterns of contact between fathers and their offspring, the modes of support provided to either children or the biological mother, and the couple relationships among these poor families, in which fathers are often non-residential, are sufficiently unique from more typical married families to raise caution about any single profile of fathers in the current era. Instead there continues to be multiple faces of fatherhood and multiple forms of family arrangements.

Beyond Shifts within the Nuclear Family: The Delay and Decline of Marriage and the Rise of Cohabitation

Beyond the shifts in parental family roles and responsibilities, the routes to family formation itself have expanded. As Brown (2017) has observed "Historically, the path to family formation was relatively straightforward, if only because few socially accepted alternatives existed. A marker of adulthood, marriage was nearly universal through the 1960s. Many Americans viewed single men and women with derision and pity, affirming the popular belief that these individuals were mentally ill because they were not married" (p. 36). Fifty years later these views seem antiquated or even intolerant since less than half of all households

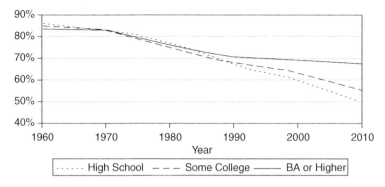

Figure 8.2 Percentage of population aged 30–44 who are married
Source: 1960–2000 Census; 2010 ACS

are headed by a married couple in contrast to 70 percent in the 1970s. In short, marriage is no longer a central and defining form upon which family life is organized (see Figure 8.2). Again note that marriage rates vary by educational level with less educated less likely to marry than the better educated. When marriage does occur, it is at a much later age than in the past: the median age when adults first marry continues to rise. In 2016, it was age 29.5 for men and 27.4 for women, up from ages 23.7 and 20.5, respectively, in 1947 (US Census Bureau, 2016). In the next sections several trends will be examined including the decline in marriage and the increase in cohabitation as an alternative to formal marriage, the rise of divorce and single parent households.

The Rise of Cohabitation as an Alternative Family Form

Since 1990, the number of cohabitating parents in which the couple lives together without being married has more than doubled. This increase is consistent with the characterization suggested by the Second DemographicTransition (Lesthaeghe, 2014). As one commentator noted, "The emergence of cohabitation as an alternative to marriage has been a key feature of the post-World War II transformation of the American family" (Lundberg, Pollak, & Stearns, 2016, p. 79). And in 2016, over 8 million US households were headed by cohabitating couples and about 38 percent of opposite-sex unmarried couples have a child under age 18 living with them (US Census Bureau, 2016). In 2013, 9 percent of households (1:20) in the USA were headed by a cohabitating couple, up from 3 percent in 1990. In comparison, the rate in Canada is 19 percent while in some European countries such as Sweden and France the rates of cohabitation are about 25 percent (Mitchell, 2014). At the same time in 1960, 73 percent of all children were living in a family with two married parents in their first marriage. By 1980, 61 percent of children were living in this type of family, and in 2014 less than half (46%) are in this traditional family form. For many contemporary families cohabitation is an alternative to marriage or for some a step or trial period before they take the plunge into marriage. In fact, nearly 30 percent of couples cohabitate before getting married while only 18 percent of men and 23 percent of women skip the cohabitation step and go directly to marriage (US Census Bureau, 2010). As Cherlin noted (2009): "We have witnessed over the past half century the unprecedented decline of marriage as the only acceptable arrangement for having sexual relations and for raising children. Marriage is still important but it is now optional: people can start relationships or have children without it" (p. 7). According to some estimates, almost 40 percent of children will spend time in a cohabiting household by age 12 (Kennedy & Bumpuss, 2011). Approximately half of these cohabiting families include a biological father and half involve a stepfather (Kreider, 2008). Most of the increase in the percentage of children being born to unmarried women since 1990 is due to births to women who are living with an unmarried partner (Cherlin, 2009). A recent report estimated that 58 percent of unmarried women who gave birth in 2010 were living with a partner in cohabitating households (Child Trends, 2015).

As in the case of all family forms, not all cohabitating families are alike. Educational level makes a major difference in timing, duration, and purpose of cohabitation (Lundberg et al., 2016). First, couple's attitudes toward this arrangement vary. In some cases, it is a prelude to marriage, in other cases it is an alternative to marriage, and in still others an arrangement without clear commitment (Smock, 2000). After a year of cohabitation, 24 percent of women with only a high school education become pregnant while 18 percent of those with some college education do, in contrast to only 5 percent of college educated women in a cohabitation family form. If college educated women do become pregnant in a cohabitating relationship, they are twice as likely to marry as those with only some college education (Copen, Daniels, & Mosher 2013). "For college graduates, increased cohabitation is part of a pattern of delayed marriage and childbearing to accommodate an extended period of education, facilitated by improved birth control and changes in social norms concerning premarital sex. For others, cohabitation appears to be a more direct substitute for marriage" (Lundberg et al., 2016, p. 82). Clearly, the decoupling of marriage and child bearing is more prevalent among the less rather the better educated. Second, the composition of cohabiting families varies too. Some consist of a couple with their biological children, while others involve a mother with biological children and a live-in stepfather. Still others are hybrid arrangements in which there are both biological and stepchildren in the household (Brown, 2017; Manning & Brown, 2012). In yet another type of unmarried-parent household, a mother and child maintain a "visiting" relationship with the child's father who is present periodically, but not on a regular basis. In a study of poor unmarried families, between 16 percent (White) and 43 percent (Black) of fathers were visiting dads (Carlson & McLanahan, 2010). In view of the prevalence of this type of arrangement, the effects on both mothers and children merits more attention. Moreover, they vary in duration from relatively brief periods to decades.

Overall cohabitation arrangements tend to be less stable and last for shorter periods of time than married relationships (Brown, 2017; McLanahan, 2011). However, stability varies with education. The median duration of cohabitations is somewhat longer for the less educated (22–24 months) than for college graduates (17 months), but is extremely short compared to marriage. The first premarital cohabitation arrangement is equally likely to dissolve within three years for all education groups, but college graduates are significantly more likely to transition into marriage and less likely to remain cohabiting for more than three years (Copen et al., 2013). A major barrier to understanding cohabitating families is the fact that there may be selection effects which determine who chooses to marry and who decides to cohabitate (Brown, 2017). Selection factors include socio-economic and educational resources, race, level of relationship commitment, and perhaps personal characteristics as well. Without taking these selection factors into account it is difficult to attribute differences in child outcomes between this family form and other forms such as married or single-parent households to family structure itself.

This shift is part of a larger pattern that is seen with divorce and remarriage, namely an increasingly high rate of family instability as parents and partners move in and out of various living arrangements. And this rate of social transitions is especially high in the United States compared to other western countries. By age 35, 10 percent of women in the United States have three or more husbands or live-in partners (married or cohabiting) while in Canada and France it is only 2 percent. Even in liberal Sweden only 4.5 percent of women have experienced three or more live-in partners by their mid-30s (Timberlake & Heuvline, 2008). Children born to cohabiting couples, for instance, are at least twice as likely to see their parents separate as are children whose parents are married at the time of their birth (Heuveline, Timberlake, & Furstenberg, 2003). In spite of the increasing prevalence of cohabitation as a family form, the preference for the "ideal" family form is still alive and well. Public sentiment lags behind social reality, with 43 percent saying that it is "bad for society for a cohabitating couple to be raising children" while another 41 percent indicated that it made no difference (Pew Research Center, 2011).

Children in Cohabitating Families

Cohabitating families face a variety of challenges. First, they tend to be less well off economically than two-parent married families, even though cohabitating families have more resources than single-parent families (Brown, 2017). College educated cohabitating families are equivalent or higher in terms of income while cohabiting non-college graduates are less well off than married families (Fry & Cohn, 2011). Second, they experience more transitions, which can be stressful for both parents and children alike and harmful to children's development (Cavanaugh & Huston, 2008). In general, children in cohabitating families are less well off in terms of a variety of cognitive, emotional, and social outcomes than children in married families (Brown, 2017) especially during adolescence. However, the size of the differences is relatively modest and not found in all studies (Clark & Nelson, 2000; Manning, 2002). Finally, race and ethnicity are important. Among White children, the differences in adjustment outcomes between married and cohabitating family forms is larger than the difference for Black and Hispanic children, in part, due to the greater acceptance of cohabitation among minority families. An example of how the normativeness of cohabitation modifies the effect on children is illustrated by a study of children born in cohabitating parent families in Puerto Rico, the Dominican Republic, and the United States. The non-mainland children suffered fewer externalizing problems than children born to parents residing in the United States (Fomby & Estacion, 2011). The presence of extended kin provides stability and a safety net to cushion the loss of a parent. In addition, the lessened stigma associated with cohabitation in their country of origin may contribute to the lessened effect of cohabitation on children's development. As cohabitation becomes increasingly prevalent and this form is increasingly accepted in the United States these ethnic differences may lessen. As the stigma associated with cohabitation decreases some of the benefits that are now the province of married families may flow to cohabitating families as well. Since cohabiting couples are generally poorer and less well educated, positive shifts in the economy will make a difference to the outlook for these families. In turn, with more economic resources the developmental outcomes for children may improve.

Finally, lessons can be learned from other countries such as Sweden and Norway where there are high rates of cohabitation, but fewer problems for either children or adults in these family forms (Cherlin, 2009). In these countries, this family form is already viewed as normative and the government programs that benefit married couple families are available to cohabitating families as well.

Divorce Trends and the Second Demographic Transition

One hundred years ago, the divorce rate in the United States was only about one divorce for every thousand people. By 1980, the rate had climbed to just over five divorces for every thousand people. This increase was associated with a reduction in the legal and moral restrictions against divorce and a shift in the focus of family life from economic dependence to emotional fulfillment. Since 1980, the tide has turned, and divorces have declined. Today, the rate is just under four divorces per thousand people – the lowest it has been in over 30 years. However, despite this decline, the divorce rate in the United States remains higher than that of any other country in the Western world (Amato, 2014), even though the divorce rate has increased in European countries over the past several decades and is rising in a variety of Asian countries as well (Amato & Boyd, 2015). According to Amato (2014) these trends can be viewed as consistent with the Second Demographic Transition (SDT) model (Lesthaeghe & Neidert, 2006). Changes such as shifts to low-replacement fertility, delays in timing of first marriages and the increase in cohabitation rates are all consistent with this model and may, in part, underlie the cross national increases in divorce rates. Together this suggests that the rise in divorce rates is not unique to a single country, but may have more general applicability across the developed and developing world according to the tenets of the SDT model.

However, recent evidence suggests a more complex portrait of divorce trends at least in the United States may be embedded in the overall demographic shifts associated with the SDT framework. Education, age, and race matter. More highly educated couples are less likely to divorce than less well educated couples and have lower rates of divorce than their peers in the preceding generation (Martin, 2006), while divorce rates for less educated women have continued to increase. According to Kennedy & Ruggles (2014) divorce varied by age with those couples under 40 less likely to divorce than an earlier generation while those over 40 were increasingly likely to divorce. For the younger age group this may be due to a selectivity effect by which only those who are committed formalize their relationship through marriage. The rise in divorce among older couples is part of the grey divorce revolution (Brown & Lin, 2012), which has seen a marked rise in divorce among older couples in part due to empty nests, retirement, or shifts in health (Brown, 2017). Finally, race is clearly linked to divorce rates with White, Hispanic and Asian couples less likely to divorce than Black couples (Bramlett & Mosher, 2002; Raley, Sweeney & Wondra, 2015). Again these patterns reflect the two-track system of change by which education, class, and race continue to be linked with different patterns of change over time.

A further shift is the change that has occurred in the nature of child custody arrangements following divorce. Since the 1980s there has been a change away from automatic maternal custody to an increase in joint custody arrangements in recognition that children need a continuing relationship with both parents. Still, the majority of custodial parents are mothers and more mothers than fathers have physical custody in joint custody arrangements (Kelly, Redenbach, & Rinaman, 2005). However, the number of fathers with sole custody has increased over the last several decades as a result of the growing national fatherhood movement, the growing recognition of fathers as significant parental figures and perhaps father-friendlier courts (Clarke-Stewart & Brentano, 2006). These general demographic trends in custody are evident not only in the United States but internationally as well. Nonetheless, mothers continue to have more opportunities for involvement in their children's lives after divorce than do fathers. This is further evidence of the cultural assumption, albeit a questionable one, that mothers are a more central socialization agent for children than fathers.

How are children affected by divorce? Overall, researchers have found that children from divorced families have more behavioral and emotional problems than children from two-parent families. They are more aggressive, non-compliant, and antisocial, less prosocial, have lower self-esteem, and experience more problems in their peer relationships (Amato 2001; 2014; Clarke-Stewart & Brentano, 2006; Hetherington, 2006). Cognitive aspects of development such as school progress and grades may suffer too (Kim, 2011). However, the differences between children in divorced and intact families are not large. A meta-analysis of studies comparing children in divorced and intact families showed that for psychological adjustment (depression and anxiety), the effect size was 0.31, and for conduct problems (aggression and misbehavior) it was 0.33 (Amato, 2001). Recently, Amato (2014) found that the patterns and effect sizes for the effects of divorce for European children is very similar to the American findings. In spite of the moderate effects, divorce has a stronger effect on children's problem behavior, and psychological stress than does race, illness, birth order, death or illness of a family member, or parents' low education. A variety of factors can either buffer or exacerbate the effects of divorce on children's adaptation including the child's gender, age, temperament, and the level of parental conflict or cooperation in the post-divorce period. As Amato (2014) notes, "Divorce is not a uniform experience for children, and the diversity of circumstances surrounding marital disruption means that children's reactions reveal a great deal of diversity" (p. 17).

Is remarriage harmful or helpful? High divorce rates create a large pool of experienced candidates for remarriage and about three quarters of divorced people remarry (Kreider & Fields, 2001). For divorced women, remarriage is a route out of poverty and in one study about one-third of women who remarried did it for economic reasons (Hetherington & Kelly, 2002). However, creating a stepfamily, especially when children are involved is not easy since there are no clear guidelines for the roles and responsibilities of each parent. It is most often the case that a man joins a mother and her children to create a "simple" stepfamily. Children in stepfamilies have more emotional problems than children in intact families or even divorced families (Clarke-Stewart and Brentano, 2006). Things are even more difficult for both the couple and the children if not just one parent but both parents bring their biological children into the new family to create a "complex" stepfamily. "Stepfamilies, like machines, are subject to the complexity principle: the more working parts, the greater the risk of breakdown. And in a complex stepfamily, breakdown often occurs in family cohesion. Alliances, scapegoating, and divisive loyalties appear. The children in the family clash; each parent sides with his biological child and; the unit divides into hostile, sometimes warring camps" (Hetherington & Kelly, 2002, pp. 196–197).

Not unexpectedly, dissolution rates are higher in complex than simple stepfamilies (Amato, 2005). Although the majority of stepchildren exhibit problems during the transition period immediately following remarriage, most show considerable resilience, and three quarters have no long-term problems (Hetherington & Kelly, 2002). Moreover, the differences between stepchildren and children in intact families are small. Most stepchildren do well in school and do not suffer from emotional or behavioral problems. The small differences suggest that there is a great deal of overlap between children in stepfamilies and those in intact nuclear families; in fact the overlap is greater than the difference. This suggests that children's adjustment is largely determined by the quality of the relationships in the stepfamily, just as it does in intact families, another indication that family process is more critical than form.

Not All Single-Parent Families Are a Result of Divorce: The Rise of Other Types of Single-Parent Families

One of the realities that many modern parents face is parenting alone. During the 1960–2016 period, the percentage of children living with only their mother nearly tripled from 8 to 23 percent and the percentage of children living with only their father increased from 1 to 4 percent (US Bureau of the Census, 2016). In the current era, among single parent families, most are mother-headed families (83%) while 17 percent lived in father-headed families (US Census Bureau, 2016). These rates vary by race of the family. In Asian families, the rates of single-parent households are low (10.2% of children living with only their mother; 4.0% living only with their father). In contrast, among Black households the rates are markedly higher: 49.7 percent of children live in mother only homes and another 3.6 percent in father only homes. For White children, 15.5 percent live in mother only families, while 3.8 percent are in father only households. Finally, 26 percent of Hispanic children live with only their mothers and 2.7 percent live with only their fathers (US Census Bureau, 2010).

Although parenting alone is a departure from the traditional family form, families arrive there by many different routes. While the largest group become single parents as a result of divorce, separation or death of a partner, others are young single mothers or fathers who often reach parenthood well before they planned to become a parent or simply did not want to wait until they were financially secure enough to marry. Others are single parents by choice who purposefully set out to become a parent even though they lack a partner, part of the larger trend in which child bearing and marriage are no longer as closely linked as in the past (Cherlin, 2009). There are many faces of single parenthood and there is a great deal of variability within each of these types of single-parent families. Again we see an overall increase in single parenthood across time, but beneath this overall profile lie distinctive patterns based on age, race/ethnicity, and education.

Although nearly half of women in the United States become single mothers after a divorce, this route to single parenthood is decreasing. In its place, there has been a steady increase in the percentage of single mothers who have never been married. Among White single mothers, two-thirds (66%) have been previously married, compared with nearly half (48%) of Latino single mothers, and a third (34%) of African-American single mothers (Mather, 2010). Forty percent of single mother families are poor, which is five times higher than married couple families (US Census Bureau, 2011). This impoverished group of single mothers has been of major concern to policy makers since poverty is linked with a variety of negative outcomes for both parents and children.

Poor Young Single Mothers

Young teen mothers represent an increasingly smaller portion of the single mother population. In fact, the US teen birth rate fell by more than one-third from 1991 through 2009, a long-term downward trend that has continued (Center for Disease Control and Prevention, 2011). In spite of this trend, teenage pregnancy remains a societal concern even though most single mothers are in their 20s and 30s and not teens. Most (75%) single mothers are employed, a rate that is even higher than for women in married families (Mather, 2010). However, their unemployment rate is higher and they hold poorly paying jobs in the service sector with limited benefits. Finally, their education is often limited to high school, which makes their chances of improving their career prospects limited.

Why do poor women have babies out of wedlock? The immediate causes include the fact that young people among all major cultural groups in the United States are initiating sexual behavior earlier and that people generally are marrying later (Brown, 2017). In addition, the cultural acceptance of single motherhood has increased dramatically over the last several decades (Cherlin et al., 2008). Moreover, for some young women, especially poor women, entry into motherhood is a valued and attainable goal. Motherhood for many young women is a higher priority than marriage and for many a fulfillment of a central life goal (Edin & Kefalas, 2005). While middle class women strive to establish a career and marriage before child bearing, many young poor women choose to have children first and address issues of career and marriage later, especially in view of their often bleak prospects for economic success or finding a viable partner (Edin & Kefalas, 2005).

Many single mothers face personal, economic, and social problems that make it very difficult for them to support and care for their children (Easterbrooks, Katz, & Menon, 2019). Stress, financial hardship, and lack of social support all contribute to poorer child outcomes in single-mother families, just as they do in two-parent families (Golombok, 2015). Many have argued that it is the poverty-related challenges that account for many of the difficulties that young mothers face rather than the lack of a second parent (McLanahan & Sanderfur, 1994).

The Fate of Children in Poor Single-Parent Families?

Children who grow up in poor single mother families are at risk for serious social emotional and academic problems (Brown, 2017; McLanahan, 2012). The negative effects on children are in part due to the less effective caregiving; poor single mothers are less warm and verbally stimulating than married mothers. Not all single mothers behave this way, nor are all children who grow up in poor single mother homes adversely affected. For example, when the effects of poverty and stress are taken into account the effects of single parenthood are lessened, which suggests that poverty-related stress rather than single mother status alone may be a factor in poor outcomes for children. Social support of either children or single parents themselves is related to improved functioning for parents as well as children (Easterbrooks et al., 2019). Race matters too. The more time that White children spend in single-parent families, the poorer their math outcomes and the greater their delinquency. For Black children, time in a single-parent family was unrelated to these outcomes (Dunifon & Kowaleski-Jones, 2002). Higher levels of social support in Black communities combined with the greater acceptance of single-parent family structure may contribute to these race-related patterns.

Not all young single mothers are destined for problems either in the short or even in the long term. Some young parents develop good lives for themselves and their children. When researchers followed African-American teen mothers into young adulthood and middle age (Furstenberg, Brooks-Gunn, & Morgan, 1987; Leadbeater, 2014) not all were destined to a life of poverty and welfare. In their early 30s, one-third had completed high school and nearly one-third had completed some post-high school education. About three quarters were working; only one quarter were on welfare (Furstenberg et al., 1987). By reducing stress through social support and by encouraging the development of a quality relationship with her children and an authoritative approach to control and discipline young mothers can be successful. Parenting process, not form, continues to be a better approach to understanding the effects of families on children.

Single Mothers by Choice

Another major change in families is that more women are deliberately choosing to become a single mother. There are many reasons for this trend including unlinking of marriage and motherhood, the decreased stigma associated with single motherhood and the growing economic independence of women (Cherlin, 2009). Many of these single mothers by choice are older (age 35–40), well-educated, upper middle class socioeconomically and employed in well-paying professional jobs (Golombok, Zadeh, Imrie, Smith, & Freeman, 2016; Hertz, 2006; Jadva, Badger, Morrisette & Golombok, 2009; Mather, 2010). They are less likely to be unemployed and more likely to have completed college and be in non-service sector jobs (17%) compared to younger and poorer single mothers (11%) (Mather, 2010). They can afford to have a child on their own, have not found a marriageable partner, and are motivated by "their biological clock." Therefore, they achieve motherhood by the use of new reproductive technologies or become pregnant with the assistance of a cooperative, but temporary male partner (Hertz, 2006). Others adopt a child either domestically or internationally as a route to achieving motherhood (Gailey, 2010). Again the economic/educational variability among single mothers is apparent since the opportunities for achieving parenthood either through adoption or through the new reproductive technologies are more available to better educated and higher income women than poorer or less educated ones.

What are the effects of growing up in these single-mother families where the effects of poverty are lessened? According to a recent study 4–9-year-old children conceived by donor insemination who were in either single mother or two-parent families, there were no differences in parenting quality between family types apart from lower mother–child conflict in solo mother families (Golombok et al., 2016). Neither were there differences in child adjustment. The findings suggest that solo motherhood, in itself, does not result in psychological problems for children. It was family processes, not family form that predicted child and maternal adjustment.

Beyond family processes (i.e., parenting style), the level of support matters in how well even economically viable single parents fare. In a study of Israeli older single mothers (average age of 43), their success as single mothers was due to support from others (Weissenberg, Landau, & Madgar, 2007). To access social support needed to raise a child alone some women moved back to their parent's home, closer to their extended families, or even to an apartment in the same building with their parents. Some even outsourced some of the household responsibilities by employing full time maids. Adaptation to the social circumstances of being a single parent by seeking and using social support from others is a key to being a well-functioning single parent. However, there are many forms that social support can assume and there are clearly many creative ways of managing single parenthood. Beyond the recognition that there are many types of single mothers, it is also clear that many single mother families are well functioning and their children are thriving in spite of the clear departure from the traditional family form. Next, we turn to another emerging family form – single fathers.

Single Fathers: A Growing Family Form

There are a variety of routes to becoming a single father. Some single men adopt a child, others become single fathers as a result of divorce, or the death or desertion of their spouse. In this era of Assisted Reproductive Technologies, single men can become fathers through the assistance of a surrogate and an egg donor. Just as in the case of single motherhood, variability is clearly evident and there is no single profile of single fathers, only multiple ones.

In 2016, there were 2 million single fathers. About 40 percent were divorced, 38 percent were never married, 16 percent were separated, and 6 percent were widowed (US Census Bureau, 2016). In other words, about one in six single parents is a man. One of the challenges faced by single fathers is the dichotomous cultural stereotypes as either superdads or needy and incompetent fathers. Neither view has much merit and serves only to perpetuate outdated myths about men's abilities to be competent parents.

Single fathers who have custody of their children experience the same stresses and challenges faced by single mothers including balancing work/family demands, financial issues, and finding adequate child care. As a group, they do differ not only from single mothers, but from men who do not gain custody. Fathers who gain post-divorce custody of their children are often older, better educated, more affluent, and enjoy better overall psychological well-being (Amato, 2000). In light of this selection bias, it is not surprising that many custodial fathers are quite competent homemakers and parents (Mendes, 1976). Since more contemporary parents share responsibility for a variety of household tasks, it is likely that the current cohort of divorced single dads are even better prepared for the responsibilities of single fatherhood (Deutsch, 1999).

How do the children develop with a single father? Early evidence suggested that children fared better when in the custody of the same gender parent: boys were better adjusted when with their dads and girls were better off when residing primarily with their mothers (Warshak & Santrock, 1983). Later studies have found that there is an advantage of father custody for children's self-esteem, anxiety, depression, and behavior problems, especially for boys (Clarke-Stewart & Hayward, 1996). While there continues to be a debate about whether children are better off with a same-sex parent, it is clear that father custody does offer children some advantages. Custodial fathers tend to have higher incomes than custodial mothers and are more likely to have emotional support from family and friends. Moreover, when children are in father custody, mothers are more likely to stay involved than are fathers of children in mother custody, so that children in father custody have the advantage of continued close ties with both parents. In a national study (Peterson & Zill, 1986) the nature of the custody arrangement may matter less than whether there is continued contact with both parents.

Single fathers are more effective parents when they are embedded in a network of social support so that the burden of caregiving is a shared responsibility. Single fathers tend to use additional caregivers (i.e., child's mother, babysitters, relatives, daycare centers, friends) more than single custodial mothers (Hetherington & Kelly, 2002). The total amount of contact with additional adult caregivers is directly linked to the child's warmth, sociability, and social conformity (Hetherington and Kelly, 2002). The viability of single father families is a further challenge to the traditional family form. Again it is important to underscore that there are class and race differences with poorer and less educated fathers being less likely to have the opportunity to be a single father family either through custody or other routes (Easterbrooks et al., 2019).

New Family Forms: Same Gender Parent Families and New Reproductive Technology Families

It is important to broaden our discussion about who is necessary for adequate socialization of children beyond mothers and fathers in nuclear families. Two bodies of evidence will illustrate that a wider range of family forms can provide adequate socialization contexts for children. First, the recent work on same-sex parental couples shows that the sexual orientation of the parents is secondary to their delivery of critical socialization experiences. Second, new work on individuals or couples who achieved parenthood through the use of the new reproductive technologies demonstrates that biological ties between the parent and the child are less critical than the quality of the socialization input provided by these caregivers for children's development.

Same Gender Parent Families

One of the noteworthy changes in the last 30 years has been the rise in the number of same gender parent families, which represents a marked departure from the traditional view of the family as a heterosexual couple as the child rearing partnership. In fact "parenthood was, until recently, considered to be an exclusive privilege of heterosexuality and this heteronormative view constitutes an important form of discrimination against sexual-minority individuals" (Gato, Santos & Fontaine, 2017, p. 310).

Although estimates vary, approximately 225, 000 children were being reared in same gender couple homes in the USA in 2013 (Gates, 2015; Payne & Manning, 2015). And the proportion of gay and lesbian couples that become parents has increased dramatically from 12 percent of couples in 1990 to nearly 19 percent of couples in 2009 (Gates, 2013). Lesbian couples are more than twice as likely to have children than gay couples (Gates, 2015), which is consistent with the culturally mandated bias that women are expected to become parents more than men. In fact, gay men often receive less support for their parental aspirations both from within the gay community and the wider society than either heterosexual men or women (Goldberg, Downing, & Moyer, 2012). In spite of recent legal and social advances that make same gender parenting more acceptable, significantly fewer same gender than heterosexual couples have children. Between 19 percent and 27 percent of same gender couples were parents in contrast to 43 percent of heterosexual couples have children (Gates, 2013). Race and ethnic variations are evident. About a quarter of individuals in same-sex couples are non-White and they are generally as racially and ethnically diverse as those in different-sex couples, though individuals in same-sex couples are less likely to be Asian, Native Hawaiian, or Pacific Islander (Gates, 2013). Fully a third of same-sex Hispanic couples and a quarter of African-American same-sex couples are raising children compared to 17 percent of White same-sex couples (Gates, 2012).

Even though most (90%) women have or intend to have children it is significantly less likely that lesbians will fulfill this aspiration (Chandra et al., 2005). The evidence suggests that substantial percentages of gay and lesbian adults want to become parents although the rates are lower than for heterosexual adults (Goldberg, 2010; Goldberg et al., 2012). In one national study, 52 percent of childless gay men and 41 percent of childless lesbians expressed a desire to have children (Riskind & Patterson, 2010). These rates are lower than heterosexuals where 53 percent of childless heterosexual women and 67 percent of childless men desired to become parents (Gates, Badgett, Chambers, & Mancomber, 2007). Thus, reduced desire for children may be responsible, in part, for lower parenthood rates among gay and lesbian adults. The social stigma surrounding gay and lesbian identity, the only recently removed legal barriers concerning same-sex marriage in the United States as well as the greater difficulties associated with adoption and perhaps accessing new reproductive technology services (Berkowitz & Marsiglio, 2007; Gato et al., 2017; Patterson & Riskind, 2010) all contribute to this lower rate of parenthood among non-heterosexual adults. As obstacles are removed and same gender parent families become socially acceptable, the differences between the desire to become a parent and the actual rates of parenting for heterosexuals and gay men and lesbians will diminish.

Recent work suggests that lesbian and gay couples who are also racial minorities experience heightened discrimination by health and fertility service providers due to their dual minority status (Wilson & Harper, 2013). For example, Blanchfield & Patterson (2015) found that minority women (non-White, sexual minority, or both) were nearly twice less likely to report receiving medical assistance to become pregnant than were heterosexual White women. Although the differences were mediated by either access to insurance or income discrepancies, the study does underscore the challenges facing dual minority couples.

Finally, and consistent with the argument that social shifts in family forms do not affect all groups in society equally, evidence suggests that same gender parent families have lower incomes and are more likely to be at the poverty level compared to heterosexual parent families. Nearly 24 percent of children in same gender parent households live in poverty compared to 14 percent of heterosexual households (Gates, 2015). The paradox is that the education level of gay couples is generally high but not necessarily among same-sex couples with children. While nearly half of those in same-sex couples have a college degree, only a third of those raising children have completed college. Moreover, same-sex couple parents also report higher rates of unemployment than their heterosexual counterparts. However, marriage matters. The socioeconomic discrepancy is especially evident among unmarried same gender parents (Gates, 2015). Together these differences in education and marriage rates may account for the socioeconomic disadvantages for same gender parents. However, as same-sex marriage has become more available in light of the US Supreme Court decision, these differences may decrease across time.

In contemporary Western societies, there are a variety of ways in which gay and lesbian couples can achieve parenthood. Many of the same-sex parents studied 20 or 30 years ago were previously married individuals in heterosexual relationships who later self-identified as gay or lesbian after a divorce. However, more recent studies have included gay and lesbian individuals or couples who have followed a diverse set of pathways to parenthood (Goldberg, 2010, 2012; Golombok, 2015). Instead of becoming a parent in a heterosexual relationship, common routes today are artificial insemination and adoption. Some suggest that there has been a generational shift in the routes to parenthood for both lesbians (Patterson & Riskind, 2010) and gay men (Goldberg, 2012).

Do child rearing and parenting practices differ between same sex and heterosexual families? There are no differences in parental knowledge of effective parenting skills or parenting stress levels between lesbian and heterosexual parents (Patterson, 2013). Moreover, there are few differences between the quality of parenting practices of lesbian couples and heterosexual couples (Golombok, 2015, 2019; Patterson, 2013). Lesbian and heterosexual mothers were similar in warmth and sensitive responsiveness in interacting with children, adolescents, and young adults (Golombok, 2015). Parenting by lesbian coparenting couples has been aptly described as "a double dose of a middle class 'feminine' approach to parenting" (Biblarz & Stacey, 2010, p.11) or an authoritative parenting style. In sum, there is little evidence that parenting quality differs across lesbian parent families and opposite sex parent families.

Although there has been less attention given to gay men as fathers compared to lesbians as mothers, current evidence suggests that gay men are competent parents (Golombok, 2015). Nor do two gay men "provide a double dose of masculine parenting" (Biblarz & Stacey, 2010, p. 12). Instead, their parenting approach more closely resembles lesbian than heterosexual coparents (Biblarz & Stacey, 2010) or mothers rather than heterosexual fathers. These observations suggest that it is overly simplistic to assume that gay and lesbian parenting is always based on a heterosexual couple model. Gay men, in some ways are least hindered by biological constraints and often develop what has been termed "degendered parenting" (Schacher et al., 2005), in which each father enacts and blends aspects of both mother and father roles into a creative, flexible, non-conventional but workable parenting role. Clearly, caregiving can be effectively provided not only by mothers (lesbian and heterosexual), but by a variety of partners, including both gay and heterosexual fathers.

Children reared by lesbian and gay parents are well adjusted and their gender role development is similar to children from heterosexual families (Goldberg, 2010; Patterson, 2013). A recent study using the National Survey of Children's Health data set found that children's general health, emotional difficulties, and coping behavior, did not differ in same gender and heterosexual families (Bos et al., 2017). Moreover, their self-identification as male or female was not affected by being reared in a same gender parent household (Golombok, 2015). Similarly, peer relationships do not differ as a function of being reared in a same gender parent. Nor do children in same gender families suffer academically. Rosenfeld (2010) found no differences in school retention and performance between children from gay/lesbian and heterosexual families.

"The similarity in school performance between children of same sex couples and children of heterosexual couples fails to support the gender essentialist theories of parenting, which argue that child development depends on having parental role models from both gender groups" (Rosenfeld, 2010, p. 773).

Is relationship stability different for heterosexual vs. same gender couples? Early work suggested that the relationship dissolution rate was higher for same gender than heterosexual couples (Blumstein & Schwartz, 1983). More recent studies suggest that stability of same gender partner relationships depends on the degree to which there is formalization of the union either through marriage, a civil union contract or other public forms of commitment. In a recent US study of a nationally representative sample, Rosenfeld (2014) found that rates of dissolution was higher for gay and lesbian couples than heterosexual couples, but after controlling for marriage and marriage-like commitments, the break-up rate was comparable for same-sex couples and heterosexual couples. Same-sex couples who had a marriage-like commitment had stable unions regardless of government recognition. Similarly, after Great Britain established civil partnerships for same-sex couples in 2005, Ross (2011) found that the break-up rate of same-sex civil partnerships in Britain was lower than the rate of heterosexual marriages. Finally, in a large-scale US study (14,000 individuals), same-sex couples reported *shorter* relationships than heterosexual couples (Joyner, Manning, & Bogle, 2017). However, the living arrangements and degree of commitment again matter. While cohabitation increases the longevity of same-sex relationships, same-sex couples are still more likely to break up more than heterosexual couples. Marriage, however, led to similar patterns of stability for both same-gender and heterosexual couples (Joyner et al., 2017). In sum, formalization of commitment appears to be a factor in closing the gap in stability of same and opposite sex couples.

Is sexual orientation of parent or family process more important? The quality of parenting in both same sex and heterosexual parent families is more important than the sexual orientation of the parents for children's development (Patterson, 2013). "Family structure, in itself, makes little difference to children's psychological development. Instead what really matters is the quality of family life" (Golombok, 2000, p. 99). A parenting pattern of warmth, sensitivity, and responsiveness in conjunction with appropriate limit setting and control (Baumrind's classic authoritative pattern) is associated with better outcomes in both same gender parent families and in heterosexual parent families (Golombok, 2015; Patterson, 2013). Clearly family process trumps sexual orientation in determining children's outcomes.

The Assisted Reproductive Technologies: Alternative
Routes to Parenthood

Another assault on the traditional family form comes from the new routes to parenthood allowed by the Assisted Reproductive Technologies (ART) (Parke et al., 2012). Since this route may involve surrogates or donated sperm or eggs, this clearly deviates from the traditional view of family formation as a biological process within the heterosexual family. As Cahn (2013) states, "Changes in the structure of the American family ... are causing a cultural rethinking of what constitutes a family. The [sperm/egg] donor world helps show that the meaning of family ... is changing and becoming more complex" (p. 31). In this century the routes to parenthood promise to be increasingly diverse. To date more than 50 million couples worldwide used assisted reproductive technologies to overcome infertility or the absence of a partner to achieve parenthood. Over 4.5 million children have been conceived as a result of these procedures (International Committee for Monitoring ARTs, 2012). This choice as a route to parenthood is especially welcome to individuals who have had medical challenges such as infertility, a condition that affects between 8 and 12 percent of adults worldwide (Spar, 2006).

Is access to ART another case of class, race, and age discrimination? Just as we have noted in other changes in family forms and formation, the progress toward making alternative paths to parenthood is not equally available across class and race and in this case even age. As a potential consumer of these ART services the country or even state or province in which you reside, education, income, and even age are factors in determining access to these alternative paths to parenthood. In the USA the cost accrued for successful delivery after in vitro fertilization (IVF) can be $41,000 after the first cycle and as much as $73,000 by the sixth cycle (Chambers, Sullivan, Ishihara, Chapman, & Adamson, 2009). In some, but not all parts of the globe, it is much less expensive ($24,500 in Japan and Scandinavia) or is covered by national health plans (e.g., Israel and Great Britain) (Chambers et al, 2009). Even in the USA, full insurance coverage is limited to 15 states and the coverage in other states varies widely. For most working class couples in the USA, the costs are too high and therefore available only to those with the ability to pay. According to health economists, "ability to pay for treatment ... plays a critical role in overall access to fertility treatment," and "choice to pursue expensive treatments, such as ART, [is] highly influenced by income" (Connolly et al., 2010, p. 607). The average user of IVF services in the United States is White, college educated with an above average income. Even in states where there is insurance coverage for these services, disparities in access to infertility services exist, with the majority of individuals accessing those services being White, highly educated, and wealthy. This exists in spite of the fact that rates of infertility are higher among minorities and less educated groups (Jain & Hornstein, 2005). Whether attitudes about acceptability of using these services or institutional barriers to access account for these differences is unclear. When surrogacy is involved, there is again an income discrepancy: the poor provide the womb and the rich pay for this service. In this case poor women can rent their wombs to richer women for $20,000 to $30,000 or much more if twins are involved and legal costs are taken into account (Twine, 2011). Other countries such as India with lower incomes offer these services for less than in the USA or Europe, but represents another way in which the rich are serviced by the poor. As Spar (2006) notes, "surrogacy is fundamentally a market relationship but one that almost always leaves poorer women serving their better-heeled sisters" (p. 93). In short, ART represents a middle class and generally White enterprise and by implication limits the reproductive rights of less wealthy and non-White individuals. This is a further example of the differential impact of changes in families on individuals who vary in their economic resources and educational attainment.

Are the children reared in family forms and who were conceived through NRT developing adequately? Studies of mothers and infants found no differences in the security of infant–mother attachment between IVF and natural conception families (McMahon & Gibson, 2002). With preschoolers and early school age, IVF mothers and fathers are more emotionally involved, showed greater warmth, interact more and report less parenting stress (Golombok, 2015) in comparison to natural conception parents. Longitudinal studies such as the European Study of Assisted Reproduction Families found that at early adolescence, a high level of warmth was found between IVF parents and their children, accompanied by an appropriate level of discipline and control (Golombok, 2015). At age 18, IVF adolescents continued to get along as well with their parents as children of natural parents; similar levels of closeness, warmth, and attachment were evident (Golombok et al., 2009). Even without genetic ties the parent–adolescent relationships were no different to naturally conceived children.

Another route to parenthood is surrogacy. Comparisons between egg donation families in which the mother experienced the pregnancy and surrogacy families, where the mother did not experience the pregnancy revealed no differences in the quality of parent–child relationships when the child was 3 or 7 years old (Golombok, 2015). In surrogacy families, one year after their child's birth, mothers and fathers were less stressed and reported better well-being compared to egg donor or natural conceiving families (Golombok, 2015). This suggests that the absence of a genetic or gestational link between the mother and the child does not appear to impact negatively on parent–child relationships. The rates of anxiety or depression among these "natural" parents were similar (Golombok, 2015).

Are children conceived through the use of ART at risk? IVF conceived children develop emotionally, socially, and cognitively as well as naturally conceived children (Golombok, 2015). Among school age children, both intellectual development and educational attainment were similar across the two groups (Golombok, 2015). Similarly, no differences in the cognitive development between surrogacy supported children and naturally conceived children have been found (Golombok, 2015). Nor are there any differences across IVF and naturally conceived mother–infant pairs in their security of attachment, nor any differences in children's psychological problems in the early school years or in adolescence based on work in either Europe or the United States (Golombok, 2015).

In the case of gamete donation families in which either a sperm or egg donor is involved, 5- to 12-year-old offspring are well adjusted socially (Golombok, 2015). Recently, an examination of the psychological adjustment of 7-year-olds in families created through surrogacy, egg donation, and natural conception found no differences among the groups in child adjustment (Golombok, 2015). ART conceived children regardless of whether they are genetically related or unrelated to their parents or born by gestational surrogacy do not differ in their levels of psychological adjustment.

Just as in the case of same gender parent families, in ART families family processes are more important for the successful development of children than the route to parenthood or the variations in genetic links between parents and children (Golombok, 2015; Parke, 2013). However, form cannot be ignored as some same gender parent families may confront discrimination and prejudice and their children may encounter negative reactions from their peers and classmates. By focusing on both form and process, we can better understand the circumstances under which a range of family forms can function effectively for both adults and children. Finally, the number of potential individuals who contribute to the reproductive process beyond the contracting parent or parents includes egg or sperm donors as well as a surrogate. The issue of social responsibilities or access to these various contributors in the new family raises difficult questions about the appropriate degree of porousness of the boundaries between the social family and these other contributors (Parke, 2013; Parke et al., 2012).

The Outsourcing-Interdependent Model of Contemporary Families

Another noteworthy trend is the fact that the modern family is increasingly an outsourcing unit in which child care responsibilities are distributed across both kin and non-kin outside the family (Hochchild, 2012). In light of these trends, such as the increase in maternal employment, the rise of non-standard work schedules, and the proliferation of single parent families, it is increasingly difficult to raise children without the co-operation of other individuals and institutions outside the family. By restricting our focus to the parent–child relationship, we fail to recognize that parents act as active managers of the children's social and intellectual opportunities outside the family such as schools, religious institutions, social clubs, and sports activities (Furstenburg et al., 1999; Parke, 2013). In all forms of families multiple players and social organizations are involved in children's lives even though the nature of the outsourcing varies across families. The key to better understanding how different family forms succeed in raising well-adjusted children lies in a fuller appreciation of the roles played by these outside agents in children's lives. The institutions and individuals who are part of the outsourcing network should not be viewed as competitive with families but rather as allies on behalf of children.

Extended Family as Socialization Agents

Both historical analyses and insights from other cultures remind us that the Western traditional and narrow definition of family is the exception rather than the rule. Instead, extended family arrangements and various degrees of non-family member involvement in the care and rearing of children is both historically and cross-culturally normative (Hrdy, 2009; Rogoff, 2003). In some cultures, cooperative caregiving by which care responsibilities are distributed among a wide number of individuals beyond the biological parents, including siblings and extended family members and non-kin, are common.

Relatives such as aunts, uncles or grandparents share caregiving responsibilities with members of the nuclear family, especially grandmothers who play a significant caregiving role either as a supplementary figure or as a provider of direct care or in cases where the mother is unavailable as the main custodial caregiver (Milardo, 2010; Smith & Wild, 2019). Even in our own society the number of custodial grandparents or at least co-parenting mother–grandparent dyads has increased in recent years (Pew Research Center, 2010).

Non-relatives as Caregivers

Most challenging to our western view of family forms is the fact that in many cultures non-relatives in the community either assume or share the tasks typically performed by parents in our culture. For example, among the Efe pygmies of Zaire, child care is shared between mothers and women in the community (Tronick et al., 1992). Children living in these child rearing contexts are more likely to survive and reach adulthood than children in less community based arrangements. In our own culture the lessons in co-operative forms of child care responsibility are available from other ethnic /racial groups such as African-American families as well as Latino and Asian immigrant families. African-Americans share a long tradition of collective responsibility for the care and rearing of children as illustrated by the continual endorsement of the tradition of extended family systems of kin and fictive kin (Stack, 1974). Both Asian and Latino immigrants and their children are more likely to live in either extended family living arrangements or have fictive kin in their social network, which may serve as a buffer against the adversities of life in a new country (Van Hook & Glick, 2007). These cross cultural and cross ethnicity and race examples present a major challenge to our narrow construal of family form and remind us that this view is neither universally endorsed nor necessarily in the best interests of western children and parents.

Institutional Partners as Other Forms of Outsourcing

In response to the decrease in time available to care for children, a wide variety of institutions have emerged to share in this responsibility. Child care centers, after school programs, and mentoring organizations are, in part, a response to the growing demand for assistance with the care, education, and protection of children. As McCartney noted, "in our contemporary society, child care is our form of shared child-rearing" (2015–2016, p. 37). At the same time it represents the continuation of a long history of outsourcing certain responsibilities by families to other institutions such as schools and religious organizations. Not only are socialization tasks outsourced, but biological ones are as well. Both gay and lesbian couples, as well as infertile couples, may use biological outsourcing such as ART in which donated eggs and/or sperm, as well as surrogates, can all play a role in achieving parenthood. The institutions and individuals who are part of the outsourcing network should not be viewed as competitive with families but rather as allies on behalf of children. These outsourcing arrangements do not undermine family relationships and in some cases may even compensate for poor ties between parents and their children (Howes & Spieker, 2016).

The Lag between Changes in Family Form and Family Policies

Policies in support of families have not kept pace with changing forms of families and are still based on a narrow definition of family as the nuclear family form. Instead, the diversity of alternative family forms which recognize the value of a wider network of caregivers who share in the responsibility of rearing children irrespective of caregiver age or gender, or kinship status needs to be given legitimacy by policy makers (Parke, 2013; Sugarman, 2008). Action on a variety of policy fronts is necessary including legal (i.e., custody laws), political (i.e., more equitable social security and tax provisions for non-traditional families), welfare reform (i.e., more support for single parent families), and even architectural domains (i.e., cohousing, multifamily housing). By casting a wider policy net, which recognizes the variety of contemporary family forms, greater acceptance and support for all forms of families can be achieved.

Conclusions

The traditional family form as the two-parent nuclear family is being supplemented by a variety of alternative family forms including single, cohabiting, same gender parent families and new reproductive technology assisted families. The cultural changes that are necessary to overcome the barriers and resistance to modifications in the traditional family model will be slow and require effort from many disciplines. By imagining and critically examining alternatives to the nuclear family form, greater acceptance as well as heightened interest in new family arrangements will ensue. By challenging researchers as well as policy makers to jointly embrace this agenda, better knowledge about family forms and their effects on children's outcomes will become available and provide a better basis for developing future social policies on behalf of families and children. Finally, the variability that underlies these broad shifts need to be fully acknowledged so that individuals at all socio-economic and educational levels can more fully benefit from these changes in routes to family formation and in family forms.

References

Amato, P. R. (2001). Children of divorce in the 1990s: An update of the Amato and Keith (1991) meta-analysis. *Journal of Family Psychology*, *15*, 355–370.
(2014). The consequences of divorce for adults and children: An update. *Drustvena Istrazivanja*, *23*, 5–24.

Amato, P. R. & Boyd, L. M. (2014). Children and divorce in world perspective. *Contemporary Issues in Family Studies: Global perspectives on partnerships, parenting and support in a changing world* (pp. 227–243). New York: Wiley-Blackwell.

Bem, S. L. (1993). *The Lenses of Gender: Transforming the debate on sexual inequality*. New Haven, CT: Yale University Press.

Berkowitz, D. & Marsiglio, W. (2007). Gay men negotiating procreative, father, and family identities. *Journal of Marriage & the Family, 69*, 366–381.

Bianchi, S. M., Robinson, J. P., & Milkie, M. (2006). *Changing Rhythms of American Family Life*. New York: Russell Sage Foundation.

Biblarz, T. J. & Stacey, J. (2010). How does the gender of parents matter? *Journal of Marriage and Family, 72*, 3–22.

Blanchfield, B. V. & Patterson, C. J. (2015). Racial and sexual minority women's receipt of medical assistance to become pregnant. *Health Psychology, 34*, 571–579.

Blumstein, P. & Schwartz, P. (1983). *American Couples: Money, work, sex*. New York: Morrow.

Bos, H. M. W., Kuyper, L., & Gartrell, N. K. (2018). A population-based comparison of female and male same-sex parent and different-sex parent households. *Family Process, 57*, 148–164.

Bowlby, J. (1969). *Attachment and Loss, Vol. 1: Attachment*. New York: Basic Books.

Bramlett, M. D. & Mosher, W. D. (2002). Cohabitation, marriage, divorce, and remarriage in the United States. *Vital Health Statistics, 23*, 1–93.

Brown, S. L. (2017). *Families in America*. Berkeley, CA: University of California Press.

Brown, S. L. & Lin, I-F. (2012). The gray divorce revolution: Rising divorce among middle-aged and older adults, 1990–2010. *Journals of Gerontology, Series B: Psychological Sciences and Social Sciences, 67*, 731–741.

Cahn, N. (2013). *The New Kinship: Constructing donor-conceived families*. New York: New York University Press.

Carlson, M. & McLanahan, S. (2010). Fathers in fragile families. In M. E. Lamb (Ed.), *The Role of the Father in Child Development* (5th ed., pp. 241–269). New York: Wiley.

Cavanaugh, S. E. & Huston, A. C. (2008). The timing of family instability and children's social development. *Journal of Marriage and the Family, 70*, 1258–1270.

Centers for Disease Control and Prevention (2011). *Multiple Births*. Atlanta, GA: Centers for Disease Control and Prevention.

(2016). *Teen Pregnancy in the United States*. Atlanta, GA: Centers for Disease Control and Prevention.

Chambers, G. M., Sullivan, E. A., Ishihara, O. et al. (2009). The economic impact of assisted reproductive technology: A review of selected developed countries. *Fertility and Sterility, 91*, 2281–2294.

Cherlin, A. J. (2009). *The Marriage-Go-Round: The state of marriage and the family today*. New York: Knopf.

Clarke-Stewart, A. & Brentano, C. (2006). *Divorce: Causes and consequences*. New Haven, CT: Yale University Press.

Clarke-Stewart, K. A. & Hayward, C. (1996). Advantages of father custody and contact for the psychological well-being of school-age children. *Journal of Applied Developmental Psychology, 17*, 239–270.

Connolly, M., Hoorens, S., & Chambers, G. M. (2010). The costs and consequences of ART: An economic perspective. *Human Reproduction, 16,* 603–613.

Copen, C. E., Daniels, K., & Mosher, W. D. (2013). First Premarital Cohabitation in the United States: 2006–2010 National Survey of Family Growth. National Health Statistics Reports, *64,* 1–15.

Child Trends Databank. (2015). *Births to Unmarried Women.* Bethesda, MD: Child Trends.

Coontz, S. (2005). *Marriage, a History: From obedience to intimacy or how love conquered marriage.* New York: Viking.

Cox, M. J. & Paley, B. (1997). Families as systems. *Annual Review of Psychology, 48,* 243–267.

Dallaire, D. (2019). Incarcerated parents. In M. Bornstein (Ed.) *Handbook of Parenting* (3rd ed., Vol. 4). New York: Routledge.

Deutsch, F. (1999). *Halving It All: How equally shared parenting works.* Cambridge, MA: Harvard University Press.

Doucet, A. (2013). Gender roles and fathering. In C. Tamis-LeMonda & N. Cabrera (Eds.) 2nd ed,. *Handbook of Father Involvement: Multidisciplinary perspectives* (pp. 297–319). New York: Routledge.

Dreby, J. (2010). *Divided by Borders: Mexican migrants and children.* Berkeley, CA: University of California Press.

Dunifon, R. E. & Kowaleski-Jones, L. (2002). Who's in the house? Race differences in cohabitation, single-parenthood and child development. *Child Development, 73,* 1249–1264.

Easterbrooks, M. A., Katz, R. C., & Menon, M. (2019). Adolescent parenting. In M. Bornstein (Ed.) *Handbook of Parenting* (3rd ed., Vol. 2). New York: Routledge.

Edin, K. & Kefalas, M. J. (2005). *Promises I Can Keep: Why poor women put motherhood before marriage.* Berkeley, CA: University of California Press.

Edin, K. & Nelson, T. (2013). *Doing the Best I Can: Fathering in the inner city.* Berkeley CA: University of California Press.

Elder, G. H., Jr. (1998). The life course as developmental theory. *Child Development, 69,* 1–12.

Elder, G. H., Jr, Shanahan, M. J., & Jennings, J. A. (2015). Human development in time and place. In R. M. Lerner (Ed. in chief), T. Leventhal, & M. Bornstein (Eds.). *Handbook of Child Psychology Developmental Science: Ecological settings developmental processes in systems.* New York: Wiley & Sons.

Feldman, R. (2019). The social neuroendocrinology of human parenting. In M. Bornstein (Ed.) *Handbook of Parenting* (3rd ed., Vol. 2). New York: Routledge.

Feldman, R., Gordon, I., Schneiderman, I., Weisman, O., & Zagoory-Sharon, O. (2010). Natural variations in maternal and paternal care are associated with systematic changes in oxytocin following parent-infant contact. *Psychoneuroendocrinology, 35,* 1133–1141.

Fry, R. & Cohn, D. (2011, June). *Living Together: The economics of cohabitation.* Washington, DC: Pew Research Center.

Furstenberg, F. F. (2014). Fifty years of family change: From consensus to complexity. In M. Carlson & D. R. Meyer (Eds.), *Family Complexity, Poverty, and Public Policy, Annals, 654,* 12–30.

Furstenberg, F. F, Brooks-Gunn, J., & Morgan, S. P. (1987). *Adolescent Mothers in Later Life.* New York: Cambridge University Press.

Furstenberg, F. F., Cook, T. D., Eccles, J., Elder, Jr., G. H., & Sameroff, A. (1999). *Managing to Make It: Urban families and adolescent success.* Chicago: University of Chicago Press.

Gates, G. J. (2012, April). *Same-Sex Couples in Census 2010: Race and ethnicity.* Los Angeles, CA: Williams Institute, UCLA School of Law.

(2015). *Demographics of Married and Unmarried Same Sex Couples: Analyses of the 2013 American community survey.* Los Angeles, CA: Williams Institute, UCLA School of Law.

(2015). Marriage and family: LGBT individuals and same sex couples. *Future of Children, 25*(2), 67–87.

Gates, G. J., Badgett, M. L., Macomber, J. E., & Chambers, K. (2007). *Adoption and Foster Care by Gay and Lesbian Parents in the United States.* Washington, DC: Urban Institute.

Gato, J., Santos, S., & Fontaine, A. M. (2017). To have or not to have children? That is the question: Factors influencing parental decisions among lesbians and gay men. *Sex Research and Social Policy, 14,* 310–323.

Goldberg, A. E. (2010). *Lesbian and Gay Parents and Their Children: Research on the family life cycle.* Washington, DC: American Psychological Association Press.

(2012). *Gay Dads: Transitions to adoptive fatherhood.* New York: New York University Press.

Goldberg, A. E., Downing, J. B., & Moyer, A. M. (2012). Why parenthood, and why now? Gay men's motivations for pursuing parenthood. *Family Relations, 61,* 157–174.

Goldin, C. & Katz, L. F. (2002). The power of the pill: Oral contraceptives and women's career and marriage decisions. *Journal of Political Economy 110,* 730–770.

Golombok, S. (2000). *Parenting: What really counts?* London: Routledge.

(2015). *Modern Families: Parents and children in new family forms.* Cambridge: Cambridge University Press.

Golombok, S., Mellish, L., Jennings, S., Casey, P., Tasker, F. et al. (2014). Adoptive gay father families: Parent-child relationships and children's psychological adjustment. *Child Development, 85,* 456–468.

Golombok, S., Owen, L., Blake, L. et al. (2009). Parent-child relationships and the psychological well-being of 18-year-old adolescents conceived by in vitro fertilisation. *Human Fertility, 12,* 63–72.

Golombok, S., Zadeh, S., Imrie, S., Smith, V., & Freeman, T. (2016). Single mothers by choice: Mother–child relationships and children's psychological adjustment. *Journal of Family Psychology, 30*(4), 409–418.

Harlow, H. F. (1958). The nature of love. *American Psychologist, 13,* 673–676.

Hertz, R. (2006). *Single by Chance, Mothers by Choice.* New York: Oxford University Press.

Hetherington, E. M. & Kelly, J. (2002). *For Better or Worse: Divorce reconsidered.* New York: Norton & Co.

Heuveline, P., Timberlake, J. M., & Furstenberg, Jr., F. F. (2003). Shifting childrearing to single mothers: Results from 17 western countries. *Population and Development Review, 29,* 47–71.

Hochschild, A. R. (2012). *The Outsourced Self: Intimate life in market times.* New York: Metropolitan Books.

Howes, C. & Spieker, S. (2016). Attachment relationships in the context of multiple caregivers. In J. Cassidy & P. Shaver (Eds.), *Handbook of Attachment: Theory, research, and clinical applications* (3rd ed). New York: Guilford Press.

Hrdy, S. B. (2009). *Mothers and Others: The evolutionary origins of mutual understanding.* Cambridge, MA: Harvard University Press.

International Committee for Monitoring Assisted Reproductive Technologies (July 2012). The world's number of IVF and ICSI babies has now reached a calculated total of 5 million. Paper presented at 28th annual meeting of ESHRE (European Society of Human Reproduction and Embryology), Istanbul, Turkey.

Jain, T. & Hornstein, M. D. (2005). Disparities in access to infertility services in a state with mandated insurance coverage *Fertility and Sterility, 84,* 221–223.

Jadva, V., Badger, S., Morrissette, M., & Golombok, S. (2009). "Mom by choice, single by life's circumstance": Findings from a large scale survey of the experiences of single mothers by choice. *Human Fertility, 12,* 175–184.

Joyner, K. A., Manning, W. D., & Bogle, R. H. (2017). Gender and the stability of same-sex and different-sex relationships among young adults. *Demography, 54,* 2351–2374.

Kelly, R. F., Redenbach, L., & Rinaman, W. (2005). Determinants of sole and joint physical custody arrangements in a national sample of divorces. *American Journal of Family Law, 19*(1), 25–43.

Kennedy, S. & Bumpass, L. (2011). Cohabitation and Trends in the Structure and Stability of Children's Family Lives. Paper presented at the Annual Meeting of the Population Association of America, Washington, DC.

Kennedy, S. & Ruggles, S. (2014). Breaking up is hard to count: The rise of divorce in the United States, 1980–2010. *Demography, 51*(2), 587–598.

Kimberly, C. & Moore, A. (2015). Attitudes to practice: National survey of adoption obstacles faced by gay and lesbian prospective parents. *Journal of Gay & Lesbian Social Services, 27,* 436–456.

Konigsberg, R. D. (2011, August 8). Chore wars. *Time,* 45–48.

Kreider, R. M. (2008). Improvements to demographic household data in the Current Population Survey: 2007. Housing and Household Economic Statistics Division Working Paper; Washington, DC.

Kreider, R. M. & Ellis, R. (2011). *Number, Timing, and Duration of Marriages and Divorces: 2009.* Current Population Reports. Washington, DC: US Census Bureau, pp. 70–125.

Leadbeater, B. (2014). *Growing Up Fast: Re-visioning adolescent mothers transitions to early adulthood.* New York: Psychology Press.

Lesthaeghe, R. (2014). The second demographic transition: A concise overview of its development. *Proceedings of the National Academy of Sciences, 111,* 18112–18115.

Lesthaeghe, R. & van de Kaa, D. (1986). Twee demografische transities? (Two demographic transitions?). In R. Lesthaeghe & D. van de Kaa (Eds.), *Bevolking–Groei en Krimp, Mens en Maatschappij.* The Netherlands: Van Loghum Slaterus, Deventer, Dutch, pp. 9–24.

Lipman, E. L., Boyle, M. H., Dooley, M. D. & Offord, D. R. (2002). Child well-being in single-mother families. *Journal of the American Academy of Child & Adolescent Psychiatry*, *41*, 75–82.

Lundberg, S., Pollak, R. A., & Stearns, J. (2016). Family inequality: diverging patterns in marriage, cohabitation, and childbearing. *Journal of Economic Perspectives: A Journal of the American Economic Association*, *30*(2), 79–102.

MacDermid Wadsworth, S. (2013). Understanding and supporting the resilience of a new generation of combat-exposed military families and their children. *Clinical Child and Family Psychology Review*, *16*, 415–420.

Main, M. & Weston, D. (1981). The quality of the toddler's relationship to mother and father: Related to conflict behavior and readiness to establish new relationships. *Child Development*, *52*, 932–940.

Manning, W. D. & Brown, S. L. (2012). Cohabitation and parenting. In N. J. Cabrera and C. S. LeMonda (Eds.), *Handbook of Father Involvement: Multi-disciplinary perspectives* (2nd ed., pp. 281–296). New York: Psychology Press.

Martin, S. P. (2006). Trends in marital dissolution by women's education in the United States. *Demographic Research*, *15*: 537–560.

Mather, M. (2010). *US Children in Single-Mother Families*. Washington, DC: Population Reference Bureau.

McCartney, K. (2015–16). Working moms deserve better. *Smith Alumnae Quarterly*, Winter, p. 37.

McLanahan, S. (2004). Diverging destinies: How children are faring under the second demographic transition. *Demography*, *41*(4), 607–627.

McLanahan, S. & Sandefur, G. (1994). *Growing Up with a Single Parent: What hurts, what helps*. Cambridge, MA: Harvard University Press.

Milardo, R. (2010). *The Forgotten Kin: Aunts and uncles*. New York: Cambridge University Press.

Mitchell, P. J. (2014, June). *Canadian Families in the Global Context: The world family map*. Ottawa: Institute of Marriage and Family.

Osberg, L. (2015). *Economic Inequality in the United States*. New York: Routledge.

Parke, R. D. (2013). *Future Families: Diverse forms, rich possibilities*. Malden, MA: Wiley-Blackwell.

Parke, R. D. & Brott, A. (1999). *Throwaway Dads*. Boston, MA: Houghton-Mifflin.

Parke, R. D. & Cookston, J. T. (2019). Fathers and families. In M. Bornstein (Ed.) *Handbook of Parenting* (3rd ed., Vol. 3). New York: Routledge.

Parke, R. D., Gailey, C., Coltrane, S., & DiMatteo, R. (2012). The pursuit of perfection: Transforming our construction of parenthood and family in the age of new reproductive technologies. In P. Essed & D. T. Goldberg (Eds.), *Clones, Fakes and Posthumans: Cultures of replication*. Amsterdam: Rodopi.

Patterson, C. J. (2013). Children of lesbian and gay parents: Psychology, law, and policy. *Psychology of Sexual Orientation and Gender Diversity*, *1*(S), 27–34.

Patterson, C. J. & Riskind, R. G. (2010). To be a parent: Issues in family formation among gay and lesbian adults. *Journal of GLBT Family Studies*, *6*, 326–340.

Payne, K. K. & Manning, W. D. (2015). Number of children living in same-sex couple households, 2013 NCFMR Family Profile FP-15-04. National Center for Family & Marriage Research, Bowling Green, OH: Bowling Green State University.

Pew Research Center Publications (2010). *Since the Start of the Great Recession, More Children Raised by Grandparents.* Washington, DC: Pew Research Center.

(2010). *The Return of the Multi-Generational Family Household.* Washington, DC: Pew Research Center.

(2015). Parenting in America: The American family today. Washington, DC: Pew Research Center, December 17.

Piketty, T. (2014). *Capital in the 21st Century.* Cambridge, MA: Belknap Press.

Pleck, J. H. (2010). A revised conceptualization of paternal involvement. In M. E. Lamb (ed.) *The Role of the Father in Child Development* (5th ed.). Hoboken, NJ: Wiley.

Raley, R. K., Sweeney, M. M., & Wondra, D. (2015). The growing racial and ethnic divide in US marriage patterns. *The Future of Children, 25,* 89–109.

Riskind, R. G. & Patterson, C. J. (2010). Parenting intentions and desires among lesbian, gay, and heterosexual individuals. *Journal of Family Psychology, 24,* 78–81.

Riskind, R. G., Patterson, C. J., & Nosek, B. A. (2013). Childless lesbian and gay adults self-efficacy about achieving parenthood. *Couple and Family Psychology: Research and practice, 2*(3), 222–235.

Rogoff, B. (2003). *The Cultural Nature of Human Development.* New York: Oxford University Press.

Rosenfeld, M. J. (2010). Nontraditional families and childhood progress through school. *Demography, 47,* 755–775.

(2014). Couple longevity in the era of same-sex marriage in the United States. *Journal of Marriage and Family, 76,* 905–918.

Ross, H., Gask, K. & Berrington, A. (2011). Civil partnerships five years on: 145 population trends. Office for National Statistics, Autumn.

Ross, H. & Taylor, H. (1989). Do boys prefer daddy or his physical style of play? *Sex Roles, 20,* 23–33.

Ryan, R. M., Martin, A., & Brooks-Gunn, J. (2006). Is one parent good enough? Patterns of mother and father parenting and child cognitive outcomes at 24 and 36 months. *Parenting: Science and Practice, 6,* 211–228.

Schacher, J. S., Auerbach, C. F., & Silverstein, L. B. (2005). Gay fathers expanding the possibilities for us all. *Journal of GLBT Family Studies, 1,* 31–52.

Schaffer, H. R. & Emerson, P. E. (1964). The development of social attachments in infancy. *Monographs of the Society for Research in Child Development, 29*(3, Serial No. 94).

Silverstein, L. B. & Auerbach, C. F. (1999). Deconstructing the essential father. *American Psychologist, 54,* 397–407.

Smith, P. K. & Wild, L. G. (2019). Grandparenting. In M. Bornstein (Ed.), *Handbook of Parenting* (2nd ed., Vol. 3). New York: Routledge.

Smock, P. J. (2000). Cohabitation in the United States: An appraisal of research themes, findings, and implications. *Annual Review of Sociology, 26,* 1–20.

Spar, D. L. (2006). *The Baby Business: How money, science, and politics drive the commerce of conception.* Cambridge, MA: Harvard University Press.

Stack, C. (1974). *All Our Kin: Strategies for survival in a black community.* New York: Harper and Row.

Storey, A. E., Walsh, C. J., Quinton, R. L., & Wynne-Edwards, D. E. (2000). Hormonal correlates of paternal responsiveness in new and expectant fathers. *Evolution and Human Behavior, 21,* 79–95.

Sugarman, S. D. (2008). What is a "Family"? Conflicting messages from our public programs. *Family Law Quarterly, 42,* 231–261.

Tronick, E. Z., Morelli, G. A., & Ivey, P. K. (1992). The Efe forager infant and toddler's pattern of social relationships: Multiple and simultaneous. *Developmental Psychology, 28,* 568–577.

Twine, F. W. (2011). *Outsourcing the Womb: Race, class and gestational surrogacy in a global market.* Routledge, New York.

US Census Bureau (2010). Current Population Survey (CPS). Washington, DC. (2011). Annual Social and Economic Supplement (Table PoV03). Washington, DC. (2012). Households and Families: 2010. Washington, DC. (2016). The Majority of Children Live With Two Parents, Census Bureau Reports. Washington, DC, November 17.

US Department of Labor (2013). *Working Mothers.* Washington, DC: Government Printing Office.

Van Hook, J. & Glick, J. E. (2007). Immigration and living arrangements: Moving beyond economic need versus acculturation. *Demography, 44,* 225–249.

Warshak, R. & Santrock, J. W. (1983). The impact of divorce in father-custody and mother-custody: The child's perspective. In L. A. Kurdek (Ed.) *Children and Divorce* (pp. 29–46). San Francisco, CA: Jossey-Bass.

Weissenberg, R., Landau, R., & Madgar, I. (2007). Older single mothers assisted by sperm donation and their children. *Human Reproduction, 22,* 2784–2791.

Wilson, B. D. M. & Harper, G. (2013). Race and ethnicity in lesbian, gay and bisexual communities. In C. J. Patterson & A. R. D'Augelli (Eds.). *Handbook of Psychology and Sexual Orientation* (pp. 281–296). New York: Oxford University Press.

Yeung, W. J., Sandberg, J. F., Davis-Kean, P. E., & Hofferth, S. L. (2001). Children's time with fathers in infant families. *Journal of Marriage and the Family, 63,* 136–154.

Zaidi, B. & Morgan, S. P. (2017). The second demographic transition theory: A review and appraisal. *Annual Review of Sociology, 43,* 473–492.

9 Communication Technologies and Social Transformation: Their Impact on Human Development

Patricia M. Greenfield

This chapter focuses on the developmental effects of communication technologies and their social transformations over human history – from print literacy to the Internet and smart phones. I use both diachronic (longitudinal) and synchronic (cross-sectional) comparison to shed light on historical shifts in both our own culture and across cultures. Because I have found no evidence that basic media effects are country or ethnicity specific, evidence from multiple countries provides a single unified portrait of how the historical march of media has affected values, learning environments, and individual development. Indeed, the cross-cultural evidence suggests that this is indeed a portrait of globalized social change and its implications for human development around the world. Nonetheless, I provide an example of how the global culture engendered by new communications technologies is expressed in a culture-specific way (Boz, Uhls, & Greenfield, 2016).

One major global trend is developmental: "Youth (ages 15–24) is the most connected age group. Worldwide, 71% are online compared with 48% of the total population. Children and adolescents under 18 account for an estimated one in three Internet users around the world. A growing body of evidence indicates that children are accessing the Internet at increasingly younger ages. In some countries, children under 15 are as likely to access the Internet as adults over 25" (UNICEF, 2017, p. 3). In the US in 2017, 42 percent of children between 0 and 8 had their own tablets, up from less than 1 percent in 2011 (Common Sense Media, 2017). While total screen time for US children zero to eight has not changed from 2011, there has been a major shift in the device used to access screens. In 2011, only 4 percent of screen time was used on mobile devices (tablets, smartphones); by 2017, the proportion of time had risen to 35 percent. Every other platform, including the TV, had lost time share.

Using a theory of social change, culture, and human development as a framework (Greenfield, 2009a, 2016), I explore developmental implications – social, cognitive, and neural – of the march of media through historical time and across geographical space. I draw on studies employing a variety of methods – content analysis, focus group, survey, field, lab, and fMRI experiments. While before–after comparisons are valuable but rare, there-are a number of other research designs that allow us to infer effects of the historical introduction and expansion of a particular communication technology.

Theory of Social Change, Culture, and Human Development

This theory of social change, culture, and human development is interdisciplinary, integrating concepts from sociology, anthropology, and psychology. It is also multilevel, positing causal relations among the levels (Greenfield, 2009a, 2015, 2018a). It incorporates sociodemographic variables at the top of the causal chain (with nineteenth-century roots in the German sociologist Tönnies, 1887/1957), cultural values at the next level down, and more traditional variables from developmental psychology at the next two levels – learning environment and individual development (Figure 9.1).

"Community" and "Society" summarize the features that anchor each end of the sociodemographic dimension (top level of Figure 9.1). "Community" denotes a small-scale social entity with social relations based on close personal and lifelong ties – e.g., a rural village, whereas "society" denotes a large-scale social entity with many relationships impersonal and transitory – e.g., an urban city. Each term, Community and Society, summarizes a complex of sociodemographic elements. These features of Community and Society provide anchors or endpoints for specific dimensions, listed on the sociodemographic level (top rectangle of Figure 9.1). All of the dimensions in the sociodemographic rectangle of Figure 9.1, including communication technologies, tend to covary and shift together (Greenfield, 2018a).

The top horizontal arrow in Figure 9.1 denotes the dominant direction of globalized social change – from Community to Society along multiple dimensions exemplified in the top rectangle. The focus in this chapter is on isolating effects of the shift from in-person communication to ever greater reliance on technologically mediated communication (top line of top rectangle, Figure 9.1, Communication Technologies). Relationships for which there is empirical evidence, described in the chapter, have been selected for inclusion. While the horizontal arrows represent the dominant direction of social change in the world, sociodemographic change can go in the opposite direction. In that case, all the horizontal arrows would be reversed.

We can think of Community features as being close to the environment in which human beings evolved. However, we have almost no "pure" communities left in the world. Most actual environments are somewhere in between the extreme endpoints on the various dimensions. The horizontal change arrows (Figure 9.1) therefore denote a direction of movement, not absolute locations on various scales.

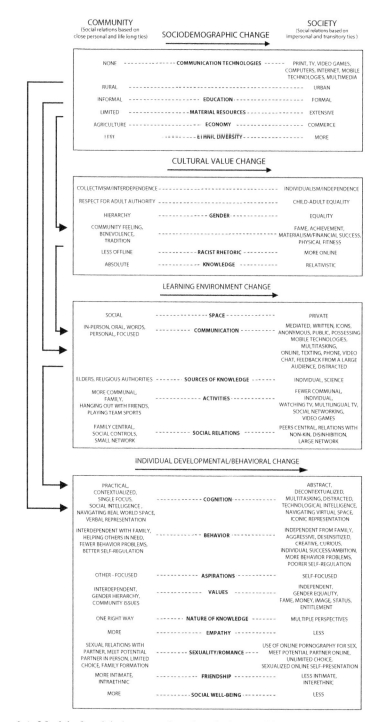

Figure 9.1 Model of social change, cultural evolution, and human development

Most important, the sociodemographic level (top rectangle, Figure 9.1) is at the top of the causal chain, influencing each lower level (vertical arrows from Sociodemographic level to Cultural Values, Learning Environment, and Behavioral Development (lower three rectangles, Figure 9.1). Each lower level is influenced by and adapted to the ones above it (see the vertical arrows from the Sociodemographic level to the Cultural Value level, from the Cultural Value level to the Learning Environment (which includes socialization), and from the Learning Environment to Individual Development and Behavior).

So when there is a shift on the top, Sociodemographic level from "Community" features in the direction of "Society" features, then there are correlated shifts on the lower levels of Cultural Values, Learning Environment, and Individual Development in the same direction; these shifts are denoted by the horizontal arrows in Figure 9.1. Each shift on a lower level is a theoretically driven prediction. Driven by sociodemographic change, these correlated changes on multiple levels constitute the heart of the theory of social change, culture, and human development. The remaining sections of this chapter provide empirical evidence for the predicted changes on the various levels triggered by changes in Communication Technologies (seen at the top of the Sociodemographic rectangle, Figure 9.1). Note that all the shifts that are diagrammed did not take place simultaneously. A sense of chronological order is given by the ordering in this chapter.

In summary, this chapter explores the cultural, socialization, and developmental implications of the long-term, globalized shift that has taken place from direct, in-person communication, the communication environment in which human beings evolved, to increasing amounts and complexity of technologically mediated communication. Figure 9.1 is a guide to the chapter that follows; it lists the particular shifts on the levels of Cultural Values, Learning Environment, and Individual Development (bottom three rectangles of Figure 9.1) brought about by the development of mediated communication in concert with the global rise of cities, commerce, formal education, wealth, and ethnic diversity (right side of top rectangle in Figure 9.1). On the level of cultural values, these global shifts have taken the world from greater collectivism to greater individualism (top line of Cultural Value Change rectangle in Figure 9.1) (Santos, Varnum, & Grossmann, 2017). Findings are placed on the Cultural level if they relate to cultural products or the group as a whole (rather than to specific individuals).

Both Sociodemographic shifts (top rectangle in Figure 9.1) and shifts in Cultural Values (second rectangle down, Figure 9.1) produce shifts in the Learning Environments of children and adolescents (third rectangle down, Figure 9.1). Socialization is taken to be part and parcel of the Learning Environment. Three important aspects of the Learning Environment are Social Relations, Activities, and modes of Communication.

Developmental change – the bottom of the causal chains depicted in Figure 9.1, is most directly influenced by sociodemographic shifts and shifts in the learning environment. Findings are placed on the Developmental level if they relate to understanding individual differences within a group or groups. The discussion of behavioral changes brought about by using mediated communication will, in most cases, focus on developmental populations – children, teens, and emerging adults. These changes are shown in the bottom rectangle of Figure 9.1. Although they are not included in the diagram, I will also discuss neural underpinnings of behavioral changes where known.

One tenet of the theory is that whatever sociodemographic factor or factors is/are changing most rapidly at a given time or place will be the major factor driving cultural and psychological change at that time or place. In the United States and many other parts of the world, digital communication technologies are currently changing more rapidly than any other aspect of the ecology, so my theory of social change and human development would predict that they would be the largest sociodemographic force shifting cultural values, learning environments, and human development. The shifts on all levels depicted in Figure 9.1 furnish a guide for this chapter, as I discuss each communication technology in historical order.

However, I begin with an overview of the sociodemographic level and the place of communication technologies in globalized social change. New technologies are part of a global sociodemographic cluster that has been moving over time away from social relations based on close personal and lifelong ties (Community) towards social relations based on more impersonal and transitory ties (Society). As the world has become wealthier, more urban, and more educated, advanced communication technologies have also become more widespread; they are a key part of the complex of variables at the top right side of Figure 9.1. At the same time, global disparities in wealth, education, and urbanization, both within and between countries, are associated with corresponding disparities in household Internet, mobile phone subscriptions, and broadband subscriptions (International Telecommunications Union, 2015, 2016, 2017; Pew Research Center; UNICEF 2017). While moving historically in a common direction, the sociodemographic factors defining Community (left side of top rectangle, Figure 9.1) cluster together and the sociodemographic factors defining Society (right side of top rectangle, Figure 9.1) cluster together, differentiating technology use both between and within countries. These patterns of intercorrelation and differentiation are all posited by the theory of social change, culture, and human development (Greenfield, 2009a, 2015, 2018a).

In the last 20 years, the major development in communication technologies lies in mobile cellular telephone subscriptions. In 1998, about 6 percent of the world's population had mobile cellular telephone subscriptions; by 2015, it was 96.8 percent (International Telecommunications Union, 2015). Accordingly, mobile technologies will receive extensive attention in this chapter.

Nonetheless, as each communication technology bursts upon the world stage, it functions (albeit more slowly) as a major social change, moving human development in the same direction as current technologies, which have then taken the trends much farther in the same direction. This is the rationale for creating one diagram (Figure 9.1) to summarize effects produced by communication technologies that developed at different chronological periods. Each major communication technology appears in this chapter in chronological order; I therefore begin with print and print literacy.

Print

Effect on Cultural Values and Learning Environment

Although the printing press was invented in the fifteenth century, we can still see the effects of print through various research designs carried out in the twentieth and twenty-first centuries. In Nigeria, Mallory Wober (1975/2014) discovered a social effect of introducing print literacy into a formerly oral environment. He found that acquiring literacy led to an increase in the individualistic value of privacy. In the 1960s, when literacy and schooling were just starting to expand in Nigeria, workers chose to live in a suburban housing development with yards in a quiet residential development (in preference to living in a crowded, noisy, sociable urban environment with lots of street life) in order to *be alone in peace and quiet* to read! So literacy not only increased the value of privacy, it was also the first (but not the last!) communication technology to modify the Learning Environment by reducing in-person interaction. These shifts in learning environment are diagrammed in Figure 9.1 as shifts from social space to private space and from in-person, oral communication to mediated, written communication (top of Learning Environment rectangle).

Effects on Cognitive Development: Decontextualized Thought

For the effects of literacy on cognitive development, I consider the case of Russia. As Russia developed formal education in rural areas after the Revolution of 1917, the learning environments of peasant farmers came to include literacy and schooling. The Russian Revolution ushered in social transformation – such as school-based literacy – in rural areas. Luria (1976) compared the cognitive strategies of farmers from remote villages without any school experience with participants having one to two years of school experience – and therefore basic literacy skills. Farmers with no schooling addressed his cognitive problems as concrete practical situations. After a few years of schooling with basic literacy skills, they took a more abstract cognitive approach, separating their thought processes from the practical situation. Again, this comparison was a cross-sectional model of what happened historically when print literacy and elementary schooling for children were introduced into an oral culture.

Here is a qualitative example of Luria's findings. Participants were shown drawings of a hammer, saw, log, and hatchet. They were asked, "Which ones are alike?" Rakmat was 39 years old and illiterate. He groups items by their use in a practical context (Luria, 1976, p. 56):

RAKMAT: "They're all alike. I think all of them have to be here ..."
LURIA: "But one fellow picked three things – the hammer, saw, and hatchet – and said they were alike ... Why do you think he picked these three things and not the log?"
RAKMAT:"Probably he's got a lot of firewood, but if we'll be left without firewood, we won't be able to do anything."

Thus, Rakmat constructs a practical situation in which all the items are necessary.

Contrast his response with that of Yadgar, who has had two years of school experience and has acquired basic literacy skills. He is shown drawings of a glass, saucepan, spectacles, bottle and is asked "Which ones are alike?" He answers: "The glass, spectacles, and bottle all fit together. They're made of glass, but the saucepan is metal." He immediately makes a category – material – that is removed from the practical context of use.

Quantitative analysis showed that Rakmat was typical of the group with no school or literacy experience, whereas Yadgar was typical of the group with one to two years of school and print literacy experience. In sum, learning environments that introduce literacy into a formerly illiterate environment (historical change) lead to a shift from practical, contextualized cognition to abstract, decontextualized cognition (diagrammed at the top of Developmental Change rectangle, Figure 9.1).

Literacy Development and the Brain

What neural changes underlie the development of print literacy? Comparing literate and illiterate adults in Brazil and Portugal, DeHaene and colleagues (2010) found that reading recruits speech areas of the brain – particularly for those who learned to read as children rather than as adults. Hence, we see a cost of learning to read to those neural circuits subserving oral communication. And potentially a cost to oral communication itself – in favor of print, a more abstract medium. Print is more abstract than oral communication because a spoken word refers to something in the real world; in contrast, a written word refers to a spoken word, which refers to something in the real world (Vygotsky, 1962). Hence, the written word is intrinsically more abstract than the spoken word – because it is farther removed from its referent in the real world. In essence, the brain is becoming more specialized for abstraction.

These findings on the neural differences between literate and illiterate individuals can serve as a proxy for what occurred historically when print literacy and schooling were introduced into cultures that had been exclusively oral in their communication. This cross-sectional research suggests a historical sequence: that the first medium, print, had neural costs in terms of the substrate used for oral communication; speaking and listening are key skills in a world in which all communication is in person and mediated communication does not exist (top left-hand line of Sociodemographic rectangle, Figure 9.1).

However, the place of print has been reduced in the total media landscape: reading for pleasure is currently in a decline. For example, from the mid 1970s to 2014, the number of twelfth graders and college freshmen in the US who did not read any books for pleasure in the prior year increased; and from 1991, the percentage of 8th and 10th graders who read magazines once a week or more plummeted from about 65 percent to about 10 percent in 2015 (Twenge, 2017). To a great extent, reading was initially replaced by our next medium, television.

Television

A unique field experiment compared what happened to children and to the community before and two years after television was introduced into a Canadian town that still did not have TV reception in 1973 (called Notel). Williams (1986) compared Notel with one town that had a single TV channel (Unitel) and a third town (Multitel) that had multiple channels. All three towns were assessed at both points in time.

Communal and Family Life

TV had the effect of reducing communal activities:

Both adolescents and adults in a town without television participated in more of their community's organized activities than did residents of towns with television;

however, their participation fell dramatically during the two years following TV's arrival. This was especially true of sports, but television also apparently affected attendance at community dances/suppers/parties, especially for youths, and attendance at meetings of clubs and other organizations, especially for adults. (Williams 1985, p. 272)

This reduction in communal activity as a result of a new communications technology is depicted on the first line of Activities in the Learning Environment rectangle, Figure 9.1.

Although television splintered the *community* of Notel, Livingstone (2009) sees television's initial stages as bringing a smaller collective unit, the *family*, together. However, this is a short-lived phenomenon that was very much at the mercy of larger sociodemographic and cultural trends:

For a time the arrival of television signaled a temporary but significant grouping of the family around the living room set ... However, historical evidence reveals that this only briefly bucks the longer-term trend toward the multiplication and diversification of media that has facilitated ... "living together separately" or, more abstractly, the processes of individualization, consumerism and globalization that characterize Western societies in late modernity. (Flichy, 2002; Livingstone, 2009, p. 153)

This second shift from family activity to individual activity is shown on the second line of Activities in the Learning Environment rectangle, Figure 9.1. Both changes are part of a trend toward individualization (top line of Cultural Value Change rectangle) as the social environment shifts away from the features of a community environment (Sociodemographic Change, top of Figure 9.1).

Children's Independence

In an examination of the relationship between children's independence and media exposure, Bailyn (1959) documented media in the life of fifth and sixth grade children in the United States in the 1950s. In support of the hypothesis that high exposure should be related to greater independence from family Bailyn, using visual media (television, movies, comic books) as an exposure index, found greater independence with more visual media exposure (top line of Behavior variables, Individual Developmental Change rectangle, Figure 9.1), but only for boys. Perhaps in the 1950s and at age 10 or 11, independence was not a possibility for girls (Ortner, 2003).

The cultural value of independence leads to the separation of self from the nuclear family and increased contacts with unknown others. Meyrowitz (1985) noted that this phenomenon of relating to strangers began with television where programming brought you into the homes and lives of people you would not otherwise know. Meyrowitz notes that television, by showing the adult lives of authority figures, such as parents, displaying behavior that is usually hidden from children in real life, has contributed to the decline of authority relations and rise of child–adult equality. Extended behind-the-scenes views of family life in reality television programming continue this trend. This cultural decline over time in respect for parental authority and rise in adult–child equality (diagrammed on the second line of the Cultural Value Change rectangle of Figure 9.1) is confirmed by the lived experience of today's grandparents in China and the United States (Huang, Greenfield, Zhou, & Wu, in preparation; Zhou, Yiu, Wu, & Greenfield, 2017).

Televised Violence, Aggression, and Desensitization

Returning to the study of Notel, we note that both verbal and physical aggression, as observed in the schoolyard, greatly increased in the community in the two years after television was introduced (Williams, 1986). Levels of aggression in Unitel and Multitel did not change over the same two-year period. However, rather inexplicably, Notel's overall level of physical and verbal aggression did not differ significantly from the other two towns at the time of the pretests, when Notel did not yet have television reception. Perhaps social controls were already in place in Unitel and Multitel in response to the communities' long-term experience with television. Another possible reason was that, in the longitudinal analysis, amount of time spent watching TV was not taken into account. Indeed, when self-reports of time spent watching TV were integrated into the data analysis, the role of TV was implicated: Aggregating data from all three towns two years after Notel had received television reception, the number of hours of TV watching was a significant predictor of physical aggression on the playground. In interpreting this result, we must keep in mind that violence was part of the TV offerings in all three towns.

The Notel experience reinforces the US Surgeon General's 1972 report that violent television stimulates aggressive behavior. Studies relating violent television to aggressive behavior have used short-term lab experiments, short-term field experiments, cross-sectional field studies, and longitudinal field studies. All research designs show the same findings: televised violence increases aggression (Bushman & Huesman, 2001).

One of the most alarming mechanisms in the TV-aggression connection is desensitization, whereby repeated exposure to televised or filmed violence "makes children more tolerant of aggression in other children and less emotionally responsive to violence themselves" (Drabman & Thomas, 1974; Greenfield, 1984, 2014, pp. 50–51). One eleven-year-old interviewed by *Newsweek* said, "You see so much violence that it is meaningless. If I saw someone really getting killed, it wouldn't be a big deal. I guess I am turning into a hard rock" (Greenfield, 1984/2014, p 51)

In a sense, society's acceptance of media violence indicates that desensitization has taken place across at least two generations since the 1970s. Because TV violence is often glamourized, sanitized, and trivialized (Bushman & Huesmann, 2001), it lacks the inhibiting qualities of in-person violence, which is terrifying, as bystander reactions to any of the recent mass shootings clearly indicate. Consequently, the transfer of social relations from the physical world to the virtual world opens the door to increased aggression in the real world. Technology's role in augmenting aggression and desensitizing viewers to violence is diagrammed on the second line, right-hand side of the Behavior cluster in the Individual Development rectangle, Figure 9.1.

Developing Prosocial Behavior and Reflection

But content and style can make a difference, even within the medium. For example, on public television in the United States, the Mr. Rogers program consistently modeled and talked about prosocial behavior. After watching Mr. Rogers once a day for ten days, preschool children improved in cooperating with adults more than with Sesame Street (which actually produced a decline) or a control group who watched nature and animal films (Tower, Singer, & Singer, 1979). However, cooperation with parents is probably not valued in society as much today as it was then: Our research indicates a significant decrease in cooperating with parents by obeying them (Huang, Greenfield, Wu, & Zhou, in preparation) from the generation who watched Mr. Rogers as young children (in our study, born between 1970 and 1990) to today's generation of children (in our study, born in the 2010s, a decade after the end of Mr. Rogers). Indeed, cooperation defined as a part of intelligence is found in small-scale agricultural communities in which social relations are based on personal ties (Serpell, 1984); it declines in importance as a society moves toward a more urban commercial ecology (Garcia, Rivera, & Greenfield, 2015).

Rates of diagnosed attention deficit/hyperactivity disorder (ADHD) quadrupled from 1989 to 2000 (Mandell, Thompson, Weintraub,

DeStefano, & Blank, 2005). At least some of this increase in impulsivity can be attributed to children's television viewing. Gadberry (1980) showed that restricting first grade children's TV for six weeks led to a more reflective cognitive style, while also leading to half as much viewing of commercial programs and one-sixth as much viewing of violent programs, compared with a matched group who had unrestricted viewing.

Indeed, on Public Television Mr. Rogers made young children more reflective: With his slow pace and reflective style, watching his program produced an increase in task persistence in play activities in kindergarten children (Friedrich & Stein, 1973). But Mr. Rogers' slow pace, his prosocial behavior, and teaching respect for adults were going against the grain of culture change even then. And this countercultural trend has not been maintained by any other children's show. Because slow-paced and prosocial television have been an exception to larger social and cultural trends, their influence has not been diagrammed in Figure 9.1.

So far, all of the media have been passively consumed by their users. But what happens when they become interactive? In general, we would expect effects to be stronger, and that is exactly what we find with video games.

Videogames

Links to Aggression and Prosocial Behavior

I begin in the 1990s with the connection between video game violence and aggressive behavior. Calvert and Tan's 1994 experiment showed that playing a violent electronic game enhanced physiological arousal and aggressive thoughts to a greater extent than simply watching the game. So, while myriad studies have linked TV violence and aggressive or violent behavior, we should not be surprised that enacting virtual violence in a game has stronger effects on motivation and behavior than simply watching it on a screen.

Anderson and Dill (2001) explored the connection between playing violent video games and aggressive or violent behaviors in both the lab and real life. First, real life: College students who reported frequently hitting (or threatening to hit) other students or attacking others with the idea of seriously hurting or killing them in the last year were often the same ones who enjoyed violent video games and played them most often. In the lab: Undergraduates pummeled their video game opponents with longer blasts of noise after playing a violent video game, compared with when they played a non-violent game. The effect was stronger for students who had been identified as having more aggressive personalities.

How generalizable are these effects? In 2010, Anderson and a group of international collaborators published a meta-analysis based on 136 studies around the world; they explored effects of violent video game play in the United States, Germany, Japan, and China. In all of the countries, playing violent video games increases the risk of aggressive behavior, aggressive thoughts, and aggressive feelings. Their meta-analysis also showed that violent video game play reduces the occurrence of both empathy and prosocial behavior, two reactions that could potentially curb violent behavior. This meta-analysis not only was the largest to date; it also was the first international comparison; and the researchers found no difference in video game effects on aggression, empathy, or prosocial behavior between Eastern and Western countries.

Obsessive video game playing (e.g., eight to 15 hours a day) has been linked to two mass shootings in the US, one in Columbine, Colorado and one in Parkland, Florida (Greenfield, 2018b; Greenfield & Juvonen, 1999). The question then arises: Why are violent video games popular all over the world, but mass shootings occur only in the US? The answer is that video games can provide an opportunity to practice and learn how to carry out mass murder (e.g., *Call of Duty*, the most popular game in the United States). But a potential shooter still needs the tools. The United States is unique in making those tools available: We are one of the very few countries in the world in which AR-15s and other semi-automatic and automatic assault weapons are readily available to consumers. So it is not violent video games alone, but the combination of video games with the availability in real life of the weapons used in the games that magnifies the risk (Greenfield, 2018b). Add in a lack of empathy, a trait that has been in decline over past decades in the United States (Konrath, O'Brien, & Hsing, 2011), and desensitization; and you have a recipe for occasional mass violence when these factors all come together.

On the other hand, prosocial video games promote prosocial behavior and prosocial behavior leads to playing prosocial games; these conclusions are solidly based on a correlational study of middle schoolers in Singapore, two longitudinal samples of Japanese children and adolescents, and an experimental study of US undergraduates (Gentile et al., 2009). However, around the globe, prosocial games are not nearly as popular as violent games: Although different games were at the top of the popularity list in different countries, ten of the 11 most popular video games around the world in 2017 were violent (Dilley, 2017). Clearly video games reflect and engender a global culture of violent behavior.

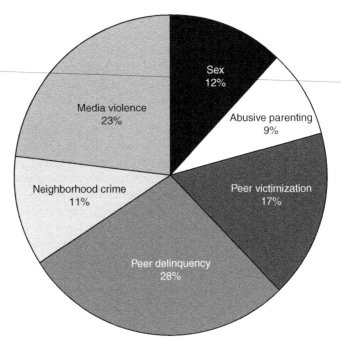

Figure 9.2 Percentage of variance in aggressive behavior accounted for by six predictors
Source: From Anderson et al. (2017). Reprinted with permission of author and Sage Publications

Multimedia Violence

But video game violence is just part of the contemporary picture. Video games simply add to the cumulative picture of media violence that includes television and film violence. Anderson and international colleagues (2017) included these three sources in a cross-cultural survey study of media violence, as well as other risk factors for aggression in seven nations: Australia, China, Croatia, Germany, Japan, Romania, and the United States. Figure 9.2 shows all risk factors and reveals the important role of media violence in the total causal picture. In the Developmental Change rectangle of Figure 9.1 (Behavior and Empathy lines), the influence of technology in reducing empathy and increasing desensitization and aggression are diagrammed.

Links to Cognitive Skills

In a community environment, not far removed from the environment in which human beings evolved, children learn about the physical world by observing, using, and creating real objects: helping adults to create clothing, shelter, and cultivating or hunting food. They learn about space by navigating in real outdoor space. In the shift to more urban, technological environments, more complex skills with the physical world, such as many types of engineering, are valued. Growing up in such environments, children are socialized to gain experience with many physical skills, from tying shoelaces to crafts to building with construction toys, a set of skills that has been termed "technological intelligence" (Mundy-Castle, 1974). What happens to technological intelligence when one learns about the physical world by observing, using, and creating virtual objects? What happens to spatial intelligence when one learns about space by mentally navigating and representing virtual space on a screen?

While television, with its necessity to coordinate different views of the same space, enhances children's ability to mentally construct space from a two-dimensional display (Salomon, 1994), more complex mental mapping is required and developed through video game play (Greenfield, 1993). And these skills in virtual space enhance technological intelligence applied to the real world. For example, video game players are well prepared for certain medical specialties such as laparoscopy (diagnosis or surgery performed in the abdomen or pelvis with the aid of a camera). Action video game skill and expertise predicted skill in laparoscopic tasks; in contrast, neither laparoscopic experience in the operating room nor years of surgical training predicted laparoscopic skill (Rosser et al., 2007). Hence, as shown on the Cognition line of the Developmental Change rectangle, Figure 9.1, the shift from navigating real space to navigating virtual space is enhanced by interaction with technology, particularly video games (right side of the Activities line, Learning Environment rectangle, Figure 9.1).

Another important visual skill in virtual space is reading icons. Icons and iconic representation are omnipresent throughout the virtual world, starting with the Macintosh interface (see the top, right side of the Communication line in the Learning Environment rectangle, Figure 9.1). A cross-cultural study (Los Angeles and Rome) of cognitive effects of video games demonstrated that college students' written representations of an electronic circuit simulation used more icons (and fewer words) after playing a computer-based version of the memory game, Concentration, compared with a more traditional physical version of Concentration (Greenfield, Camaioni, Ercolani, Weiss, Lauber, & Perucchini, 1994). The results linked iconic representation to technological intelligence: representing the circuits by drawing icons (rather than writing words) was positively correlated with better understanding of the simulated circuits.

At the time of that experiment, experience with computers was much less diffused in Italy than in the United States. In Rome, students used written words more frequently than they drew icons to represent their understanding of the electronic circuits. In contrast, students in Los Angeles drew icons more often than they wrote words to represent their understanding of the circuitry. The Roman sample also showed less understanding of the circuitry after watching the simulation than did the Los Angeles sample. Hence, iconic representation and the ability to process scientific/technological information on a screen can be seen as two components of advancing technological intelligence (shown on the right side of the Cognition line in the Developmental Change box). Video games are an important Communication Technology (right side, Sociodemographic Change rectangle), one that enhances the learning environment (right side of Activities line in Learning Environment rectangle) for technological intelligence (Cognition line in Developmental Change rectangle (Greenfield, 2009b). But because popular video games are overwhelmingly violent in content, this advance in technological intelligence comes at a cost to society.

Computers

Cognitive Effects

Computers continue the trend that began with print literacy towards abstract reasoning as technology advances. OLPC (One Laptop Per Child) is a US-based non-profit organization whose mission is to provide educational opportunities for the world's poorest children by giving them a laptop with software designed for self-empowered learning. A field experiment in Ethiopia explored the effect on abstract reasoning of computers distributed by OLPC to 10- to 15-year-olds (Hansen et al., 2012). Across seven schools, 202 children in Grades 6 and 7 were given laptops (all the children in three schools, half the children in a fourth); they were compared with 210 children who were not given laptops (all the children in three sociodemographically matched schools and the other half of the children in the fourth school). Laptops were mainly used at home and during breaks at school; they were rarely used for teaching purposes in class. The most frequent computer activities were writing, reading, and gaming. Hence, like the video game studies, this is a study of the cognitive effects of computers as informal learning environments.

Children with laptops significantly outperformed children without laptops on two abstract reasoning tests (analogies and categories).

Interestingly, the effects of laptops did not improve school performance. In line with the theory of social change and human development, the laptop effects were specific to cognitive abstraction. Hence the progression begun by print literacy, as shown in Luria's study of categorization and other cognitive skills, was continued by computer technology in the form of laptops (top right side of Cognition line, Developmental Change rectangle, Figure 9.1).

Social Effects

Another Ethiopian field experiment based on the OLPC program focused on the role of computers in group value change (Hansen, Postmes, Tovote, & Bos, 2014). Three control and three experimental schools were matched on several variables such as social status of the students. The organization had provided a laptop to all fifth and sixth graders in schools in the experimental condition. Two schools in each condition were located in the urban capital. One school in each condition was located in a rural area. The measurement of values took place at baseline and six months after laptop deployment in the experimental schools. A value measure adapted for children (Schwartz et al., 2001) and translated into two Ethiopian languages was used at both points in time. Laptops were set up so that the students could engage in a wide variety of activities including writing, taking photos, making videos, painting, and games.

All the results conformed to the theory of social change and human development that guides this chapter (Greenfield, 2009a, 2016). In both rural and urban schools, self-enhancement values (success and ambition), as well as the value of gender equality and multiple perspectives increased more over time for the children with laptops than without. (See Aspirations, Behavior, Values, and Nature of Knowledge lines of Developmental Change rectangle, Figure 9.1.) The same was true for self-direction (creativity, independence, and curiosity). (See Behavior line on right side of the Developmental Change rectangle of Figure 9.1.) In line with the guiding theory, all of these are values adapted to a highly educated, urban, wealthy, commercial, high tech society (right side of top rectangle, Figure 9.1). Also in line with the theory, laptop use often had a larger effect in rural schools than urban – because the technological and social change they brought about was much larger.

Contrary to theoretical expectations, benevolence and traditional values also increased as a function of laptop access and use. However, the enhancement of traditional values along with the augmentation of new values often occurs when a country is in the midst of rapid social transformation (e.g., China: Zhou, Yiu, Wu, & Greenfield, 2017). Or this may have happened because benevolence to outgroups (instead of family) becomes an adaptive trait in urban society.

Teen Chatrooms: Disinhibition, Anonymity, and Social Controls

The existence of public teen chatrooms in the 1990s provided a window into how adolescents communicate about two important social issues: ethnicity and sexuality. Because the chatrooms were anonymous and some chatrooms had adult monitors whereas others did not, we were also able to see interaction in an anonymous setting and how social monitoring moderated communications about these two topics.

Concerning ethnicity, we found that race and ethnicity were frequently mentioned in teen chat: 37 out of 38 half-hour transcripts had at least one racial or ethnic utterance (Tynes, Reynolds, & Greenfield, 2004); this frequency is patently greater than in offline interactions. While most references had a neutral or positive valence in both monitored and unmonitored chat rooms, chat participants, nonetheless, had a 19 percent chance of being exposed to racial or ethnic slurs (potentially about their own group) in monitored chat and a significantly higher (59%) chance in unmonitored chat. (See Racist Rhetoric line in Cultural Value Change rectangle.) Even in monitored chat, racist comments occur more often than one would expect offline. However, in the absence of social controls, such as a monitor, negative intergroup attitudes are disinhibited and surface even more frequently. The absence of social controls intrinsic to in-person communication produce disinhibited communication in this anonymous environment. This shift is diagrammed on the Social Relations line of the Learning Environment rectangle.

Disinhibition was also a feature of sexual communication in the same chatrooms (Subrahmanyam, Šmahel, & Greenfield, 2006). Sexual themes constituted 5 percent of all utterances (one sexual comment per minute); bad or obscene language constituted 3 percent of the sample (one obscenity every two minutes). The protected environment of monitored chat (hosts who enforce basic behavioral rules) contained an environment with less explicit sexuality and fewer obscenities than the freer environment of unmonitored chat. Our analysis again pointed to disinhibition in an anonymous environment, as it is unlikely that a teen would experience a sexual comment every minute in a group environment offline! Equally, our results again point to the inhibiting effect of an adult monitor, something that is absent from teen communication in today's virtual world.

Television in a Multimedia World

*Societal Values and the Preteen Media Environment Shift
in Synch Over Five Decades*

In the United States, content analysis of millions of books showed the rise of individualistic values, as well as materialism, from 1800 to 2000, these are values adaptive in an urbanized, commercial, technological ecology (Greenfield, 2013). These value trends in the overall cultural environment were mirrored in the learning environment provided by the most popular television shows watched by the preteen audience in the United States – at a time when television was still the most popular medium with this age group (Rideout, Foehr, & Roberts, 2010). At the Children's Digital Media Center of Los Angeles, we carried out a content analysis of changing values transmitted in the two most popular television shows with preteen audiences in each decade from 1967 to 2007 (Uhls & Greenfield, 2011). Each show was rated by participants for 17 values. Mirroring the rise of materialism in the general culture, desire for financial success became increasingly important in preteen shows from 1967 to 2007. Lagging behind in time, but nonetheless mirroring in a general way the rise of individualistic self-focus in the overall cultural environment, the value of fame, near the bottom of the value hierarchy for the first four decades of the TV study, rose in importance between 1997 and 2007, becoming the top-rated value in the fiction show *Hannah Montana* and the reality show, *American Idol*, the two most popular shows with preteen audiences in 2007. In this same ten-year period, the values of community feeling, benevolence, and tradition declined in importance in the top-rated shows and the more individualistic values of achievement and physical fitness rose significantly. These value shifts are all shown in the Cultural Value Change rectangle of Figure 9.1. During this period (1997–2007) the Internet expanded greatly as well. The hypothesis is that this expansion of a Communication Technology on the Sociodemographic level (Figure 9.1) was a causal factor in the Cultural Value shift shown at the next level down.

*Learning Environment and Individual Development: Preteen
Discourse Reveals Uptake of Fame and Wealth Values Portrayed
in the Shows in a New Multimedia Context*

Our subsequent qualitative research showed uptake of the portrayed values in preteen focus groups conducted in Los Angeles in 2010 (Uhls & Greenfield, 2012); the groups consisted of children between 10 and 12 years of age. Before the group conversation began, children wrote down individually their one or two most important values from a list of seven. The individualistic value of fame was the only value to appear significantly above chance as the children's top value; this result mirrored its importance in popular preteen television.

The focus group discussions made it clear that these preteen children were processing values from their favorite television shows. The following quote from a middle-school boy highlights awareness of fame as a value being transmitted by both *Hannah Montana,* a favorite show in 2007, and *iCarly*, the favorite show in 2010, when the focus groups were conducted: "both get famous from sponsors" (Uhls & Greenfield, 2012, p. 320).

Another middle-school boy was explicit about the importance of audience size, a key component of fame:

[BOY 1]: Um, my friends and I are making a YouTube Channel …
[M]: Why are you doing that? … For fun? Or do you have a goal?
[BOY 1]: Our goal is to try and get a million subscribers. (Group V, Middle-school boys) (Uhls & Greenfield, 2012, p. 321)

This dialogue also exemplifies the fact that children were enacting the value of fame by posting videos on YouTube, a video-sharing site, and trying to become famous themselves. They were going from being consumers to actors in an interactive, multimedia environment.

But adults were a socializing force in this transition: In several cases, children reported that an authority figure such as a teacher was posting their activities on YouTube. The implicit message from these authority figures was the value of seeking a broader audience than could be acquired face-to-face.

A last example illustrates the perceived connection between fame and wealth, two values adapted to a technological urban commercial ecology. An elementary school boy says, "Oh, so when I'm famous, I'll get more rich. And I'll become a millionaire" (Uhls & Greenfield, 2012, p. 319). Hence, he links two of the values that rose together in preteen television over the decades; this quote exemplifies the subjective reality of the link between fame and money. Thus values portrayed on the cultural level in TV shows are reflected on the individual level (see right side of Values line in the Developmental Change rectangle).

Learning Environment and Individual Development: The Same Pattern on a Larger Scale

Connections between new media and this set of values were generalized by our national survey of 315 US youth between 9 and 15 years of age (Uhls, Zgouru, & Greenfield, 2014). Watching television and using a social networking site (right side of Learning Environment rectangle) predicted self-focused aspirations – fame, image, money, and status (right side of Developmental rectangle). Non-technology activities, most of which had a significant social component (left side of Learning Environment rectangle), were associated with collectivistic other-focused aspirations – e.g., helping your family, helping others in need (left side of Developmental rectangle). The non technology activities – such as hanging out with friends and playing team sports – were all activities that existed historically before television and social networking sites. Hence, we can infer that the advent of television and social network sites led to an historical augmentation in self-focused aspirations and values, while reducing other-focused aspirations.

Mobile Technologies

Enter the Cell Phone: Expansion of Social Networks Beyond the Family

The decline of family as the center of one's social network and the inclusion of unrelated others are major features of the shift from small communities to large, urban societies. Manago (2019) has studied the effect of cell phone communication on the social networks of Maya adolescents in Zinacantan, Chiapas, Mexico, a place in which cellphones are a very recent introduction into their close-knit community. She found that both owning a mobile device and Facebook use predicted greater overall proportion of non-kin in the entire network. This was a predicted relationship between Activities and Social Relations in the Learning Environment (right side of Figure 9.1).

Intergenerational Value Shift: The Role of Mobile Technologies

Among Arab citizens of northern Israel, adolescent girls are the first generation to have mobile technologies during their teenage years; correlatively, they value female independence and egalitarian gender roles more than their mothers or grandmothers (Weinstock et al., 2015). In terms of individual differences, statistical modeling showed that possessing more mobile technologies (Learning Environment) predicts a higher value placed on gender equality and independence (Individual Development) (right side, bottom two levels, Figure 9.1).

Peer Relations Benefit at the Cost of Family Relations

Ling and Yttri (2005) expanded this theme of independence from family with their study of cellphone use by teens in Norway, a country in which smart phones became popular very early. Teens used their phones to establish boundaries, i.e., separation from their parents. Here is an example from their focus-group study:

NINA (18): "With some telephones, you can do it like [if a call comes] from some numbers it goes right into voicemail. Like if your parents call, it goes right into voicemail."

...

ARNE (17): "If I'm out on the weekend and things like [that], then I do that."
MODERATOR: "Whom do you exclude?"
ARNE (17): "The family"
Then three other kids in the group say they do it too.

Norwegian teens also used their phones to increase the privacy of their communications, expanding on the effect of print, as well as asserting their independence from family (Ling & Yttri, 2005, p. 227) (right side of Learning Environment and Developmental Change rectangles, Figure 9.1). Here is an example:

RITA (18): It's okay for somebody to leave a message in my voice mail, instead of the family's voice mail. I can call them back. It's more private.
ERICA (17): If I'm not home and if I didn't have a mobile telephone, then my parents would know about all the people I hang out with ... When you have a mobile telephone, you have a private voice mail and a private telephone.

Clearly the cell phone is being used to enhance peer relations at the expense of family relations. This change in the Learning Environment is diagrammed in the Social Relations line of Figure 9.1.

Yet parents often give phones to their emerging adolescents so that they can keep track of them. This practice can cause conflict between parents and their adolescent children (Turkle, 2011). At the same time, technology makes possible helicopter parenting whereby parents and children are in close touch – often by mutual agreement – while emerging adult children are in college or traveling. This practice has produced negative reactions from those who think that children should be developing more independence at this stage of life (Turkle, 2011) or have found associations with depression and lowered life satisfaction (Schiffrin, 2014).

Adults' Use of Mobile Technology: A New Component of the Child Learning Environment

Radesky and colleagues (2014) carried out observations in fast-food restaurants in 15 neighborhoods in Boston. They observed groups in which there was an adult with one or more children between 0 and 10 years of age. In 40 out of the 55 observations, the adult used a mobile device after sitting down. The researchers focused their observations on caregiver absorption with the device, which was defined as the extent to which the primary focus of caregiver's attention and engagement is with the device rather than the child. Of those 40, 16 of the adults engaged in almost continuous use, with typing. That is, the caregiver was multitasking between childcare and electronic communication. In response, the children they were with tested the limits or engaged in provocative behaviors. The adults, for their part, generally ignored child behavior, then scolded; repeated instructions in robotic manner, insensitive to child's expressed needs. Clearly, adult attention was elsewhere. Here we see the predicted relationship between mobile technologies (right side of Sociodemographic Change rectangle) and multitasking (right side of Learning Environment Change rectangle).

Older Children Use Mobile Technologies While with Their Parents

As Turkle in her book *Alone Together* (2011) notes, the same situation as in the fast food restaurants can occur not only to the child, but to the parent when a child is focused on a mobile device to the exclusion of a parent. Turkle recounts a trip to Paris with her college-age daughter. They are sitting in a café when her daughter receives a call from a friend in Boston and makes a lunch date with her for later in the week – without even telling her friend that she is out of town. The idea that her daughter's attention was distracted from the here and now of Paris by her mobile phone is disturbing to her mother. Turkle catalogues all the situations in which parents and children alike split their attention between the present social situation and a virtual one: parents check e-mail as they push strollers; children text their friends, and parents email and text coworkers during family dinners and during shared television viewing sessions. Again, communication technologies lead to distraction from the here and now.

Effects of Parental Technoference on Children and Adolescents

McDaniel and Radesky (2018) followed up the qualitative study in fast-food restaurants with a quantitative survey study of problematic technology use by parents and technoference. Technoference was defined as technology-based interruptions in parent–child interactions. Problematic technology use was diagnosed by questions such as "When my mobile phone alerts me to new messages, I cannot resist checking them" and "I often think about calls or messages I might receive on my mobile phone." Mothers and fathers, almost all European American, were surveyed in 170 families; focal children were between one and five years of age. Problematic mobile technology use by parents predicted their perceptions of greater technoference in their interactions with their child. Greater technoference in the mother–child relationship, in turn, predicted greater child externalizing and internalizing behaviors. More mediated communication in the learning environment predicted more behavior problems (right side, Figure 9.1: Communication line, Learning Environment rectangle; Behavior line, Developmental rectangle).

Turkle (2011) notes the same problem in adolescence: "Hannah, sixteen, is a solemn quiet high school junior. She tells me that for years she has tried to get her mother's attention when her mother comes to fetch her after school or after dance lessons. Hannah says 'the car will start; she'll be driving, still looking down, looking at her messages, but still no hello'" (Turkle, 2011, p. 164). Turkle reports hearing many such stories. Uhls (2015) notes how this type of parent behavior will then serve as a model for the children parents are raising.

Distracted Walking, Bicycling, and Driving

Indeed, parental absorption with their phones may be one cause of distracted walking, bicycling, and driving by adolescents. Texting while driving is a serious teen issue. Turkle (2011) tells of Roman, an 18-year-old high school senior, who "admits that he texts while driving and he is not going to stop" (p. 162). He, like his high school peers, needs to feel connected all the time. Many studies show that, contrary to some popular ideas, multitasking leads to doing no task well (Ophir, Nass, & Wagner, 2009; Turkle, 2011); so it should be no surprise that when youth walk, bicycle, or drive distracted by mobile technologies, accidents happen (Stavrinos, Pope, Shen, & Shwebel, 2018).

Social Networking

The Cost to Family Relations

Surveys of US teens and their parents showed that nearly one in three parents felt that the time their teen spent on social networking interfered with family life. The more time a teen spent in social networking, the less support they felt they were receiving from their parents. Teens generally were operating quite independently of parental knowledge online: 38 percent of parents had not seen their child's social network profile; 62 percent of parents had never talked to their teen about social networking; 50 percent of teens accessed social network profile from bedroom, out of sight of parents (Rosen, 2007; Rosen et al., 2008). That percentage would be much higher now with the proliferation of smart phones. Surveys around the world – United States, New Zealand,

Canada, Israel, Korea, and China – show correlations between time spent online and lower levels of perceived closeness to parents (Manago, Guan, & Greenfield, 2015). Teens have strategies for using social networking sites to expand their independence from their families: they often fabricate key identifying information like name, age, and location to protect themselves from the watchful eye of parents (boyd, 2007). Hence, as predicted by the theoretical model, social networking activities make families a less important part of the adolescent learning environment (Figure 9.1, Learning Environment Change).

The Explosion of "Friends"

With social networking, the number of contacts has exploded. But this trend began well before social media. In 1985, Meyrowitz wrote: "Through television, strangers are experienced as intimates" (p. 137). In social media, strangers can be "friends." Manago, Taylor, and Greenfield (2012) found that college students' Facebook averaged 440 "friends." In these networks, only 21 percent were close connections (best friend, very good friend, good friend, current boy- or girlfriend, family member, roommate). Nonetheless, the average size of this category of close connections was 80. We can surely question how close one can feel with such a large number of "close" connections. This study also uncovered the psychological importance of audience size. Larger estimates of the audience for one's status updates were correlated with greater self-esteem. Controlling for self-esteem, overall network size was the only variable to significantly predict life satisfaction. Given its importance for self-esteem and life satisfaction, one can imagine the psychological pressure that is created for young Facebook users to attract a large audience and a large network of "friends" (feedback from a large audience and large network, right side of Communication and Social Relations lines in Learning Environment Change rectangle, Figure 9.1).

The Power of the "Like"

This pressure is increased with the power of the "like." In a study simulating Instagram in an fMRI scanner, both giving and getting "likes" activated the reward centers of the teen and emerging adult brain – the same neural networks activated in classical addictions (Sherman, Greenfield, Hernandez, & Dapretto, 2017; Sherman, Hernandez, Greenfield, & Dapretto, in press; Sherman, Payton, Hernandez, Greenfield, & Dapretto, 2016). The neural evidence is backed up by young people's personal experience: James, a college student in Georgia, said: "When you go on social media you post a status or you post a picture and all of a sudden you get all those likes, you get all those affirmations from people, and it can be addictive because you have the constant pats on the back" (Twenge, 2017, pp. 56–57). Interviews across the USA by reporter Nancy Jo Sales indicated that this experience is common: girls are constantly in search of "likes" and positive comments. They also feel pressured to post sexy and revealing photos because they know that those get the most "likes" (Sales, 2016; Twenge, 2017). Their Learning Environment includes feedback from a large audience (right side of Communications line in the Learning Environment Change rectangle) and it impels them to create a sexualized self-presentation (right side of Sexuality/Romance line in the Developmental Change rectangle).

The Cost in Well-Being

"College students who had used Facebook for a longer time and those who spent more time each week on the site tended to agree more often that others were happier … Students who included more people whom they didn't personally know as their Facebook 'friends' agreed more often that others had better lives" (Gardner & Davis, pp. 101–102).

The activation of social comparison appears to be the culprit (Manago et al., 2008). Turkle (2011) describes the agonies of self-presentation that teenagers go through in constructing their Facebook profiles. Identity becomes self-presentation in one's social network profile. Photos including the poster receive consistently more "likes" than those that do not (Greenfield, Evers, & Dembo, 2017); thus the narcissism of constant self-presentation is audience driven.

While the importance of self-presentation is a universal attribute of the social networking culture, pre-existing differences in cultural values play a role in how individualistically the self is presented. For example, in a comparison of adolescent Facebook users in Turkey and the United States, self-promoting presentations were significantly more frequent in the United States than in Turkey (Boz, Uhls, & Greenfield, 2016). This difference reflects the more individualistic value system of the United States, compared with Turkey.

Social Media Augment a Suite of Values Adapted to an Urban, Educated, Commercial, and Ethnically Diverse World

Twenge's (2017) analysis of the national teen survey, Monitoring the Future, shows that teens who spend more time (ten or more hours) on social networks are more likely to value materialism and entitlement and are less likely to care about most social issues that involve the community than teens who spend less time. More time on social networks is also linked to gender equality and a positive attitude toward ethnic diversity in friendships. These findings indicate that social media further reinforce the materialistic value that we found on preteen television (Uhls & Greenfield, 2011). And they indicate that the effects of mobile technology in developing the value of gender equality in our Arab study (Weinstock, Ganayiem, Igbariya, Manago, & Greenfield, 2014) may generalize to an effect of social media in the United States. Given that one of the features of an urban ecology is ethnic diversity, it appears that social media help to make this characteristic valued positively in friendship. All of these changes in individual values (shown on the Values and Friendship lines of the Developmental Change rectangle) are linked to an increase in social networking in the Activities line on the right side of the Learning Environment Change rectangle (Figure 9.1).

A Multimedia World

Cognitive Effects: Epistemic Thinking Becomes More Relativistic

Weinstock (2015) explored intergenerational shifts in epistemology as a function of the role of technology in the same multigenerational sample of Arab citizens of Israel introduced earlier. In the domain of metacognition, Community-adapted epistemologies stress familial or religious authority as sources of knowledge and a single correct perspective. In contrast Society-adapted epistemologies emphasize science or personal experience as sources of knowledge, along with multiple viewpoints. As expected on theoretical grounds, science and personal experience as sources of knowledge, along with diverse perspectives, increased from grandmothers to mothers to teenage daughters. Relevant to the role of communications technologies, greater exposure to multilingual TV and possessing more mobile technologies were elements of the Learning Environment Change that predicted increase in acceptance of multiple perspectives on the level of Individual Development (Nature of Knowledge, right side of Figure 9.1).

The Cognitive Cost of Multitasking

Everyday multitasking with electronic devices, common among all age groups, is most frequent in the youngest generations (Carrier, Rosen, Cheever, & Lim, 2015). Summarizing multiple studies, the authors conclude that studying, doing homework, learning during lectures and from other sources, grades, and GPA are all negatively affected by con-current multitasking with technology (Carrier et al., 2015). We conclude that the shift to multitasking in the Learning Environment (third level, right side of Communication line, Figure 9.1), made possible by the development of Communications Technologies (top level, Figure 9.1), leads to Developmental Change in the direction of distracted cognition (bottom level, right side of Cognition line, Figure 9.1).

Mediated Communication: The Cost to Close Relations

Human beings evolved in a world of in-person communication. All forms of mediated communication are chronologically subsequent. We all know about the convenience of textual communication, but what about its costs? And what are the social implications of other types of mediated communication? Telephone was the first synchronous tech-nology for vocal communication. Audio-visual chat added a visual dimension, making it most similar to in-person communication. We explored the relationship of these diverse ways of communicating to social bonding and sense of closeness with a college friend (Sherman, Michikyan, & Greenfield, 2013). In a laboratory experiment, students felt closest to a friend and emitted more behavioral signs of closeness (e.g., smiling, gesturing) when they talked to the friend in person. They felt most distant and emitted fewest behavioral signs of closeness when they communicated by text. Audio communication (a simulation of telephone) was a little better for the sense of intimacy than text; and audio-visual chat, adding another feature of in-person communication, was better still. But no medium was associated with the same sense of closeness as in-person communication. Hence, we can conclude that one cost of the convenience of textual communication in the proximal Learning Environment is social intimacy, a Developmental Change (Figure 9.1). Because text is a chronologically recent addition to the communications armoire, whereas in-person communication is the oldest, this study models what happened historically in the shift toward textual (and other kinds of) mediated communication.

Perhaps the evolutionary history of human beings is such that they crave the closeness of in-person communication. Perhaps the sacrifice of social closeness found by Sherman and colleagues is one reason that Pea and colleagues (2012) found, in a 2010 online survey of 3,461 North American girls ages 8–12, that social well-being was associated with lower levels of uses of media for interpersonal interaction (e.g., phone, online communication). Video use and media multitasking were also associated with lower social well-being. Conversely and most important, face-to-face communication was associated with a positive sense of social well-being. The Developmental Change in Friendship associated with this Communication shift in Learning Environment (Figure 9.1) emphasizes the social cost of going against our evolutionary heritage. The findings also provide a developmental precursor to Sherman et al.'s study of bonding between college friends.

Family Relations at a Distance

Nevertheless, as young lives become more global – such as the lives of international students – new media can bridge distance. Among Chinese international students, students who had open phone and email communication with family members also had a greater sense of family cohesion, compared with students who did not have this communication (Kline & Liu, 2005; Manago, Guan, & Greenfield, 2015).

Cyberbullying

The question for a volume focused on social change is: What difference does it make to have cyberbullying transferred to the screen from the schoolyard? Swiss seventh and eighth graders identified two characteristics that make bullying the most severe: publicity (in their experiment, being available to one's whole class vs. communicated only to the victim) and anonymity (Sticca & Perren, 2013). Publicity and anonymity are two characteristics that cyberbullying (by text or social media) frequently has, but classical in-person bullying never has (see right side of Communication line of Learning Environment Change rectangle, Figure 9.1). These qualities make bullying feel the most severe. So, given the normative situation of having hundreds of "friends" on social media, large audience size of the perpetrator becomes a negative for the victim of cyberbullying. Besides anonymity and publicity, another factor that makes cyberbullying worse than schoolyard bullying is that there is no way to get away from the tormentors. For all these reasons, it is not surprising that the suicide risk for cyberbullying is higher than for offline school bullying (Twenge, 2017).

A cross-cultural study exploring cyberbullying and cybervictimization in Tanzania and Canada concluded that the phenomena are very similar in both locations, despite the slower uptake of the technology in Tanzania, a country with very limited material resources (Shapka, Onditi, Collie, & Lapidot-Lefler, 2018). This lack of cross-cultural difference in two very different ecologies raises the possibility that the basic phenomena of cyberbullying are universal, a function of the affordances provided by the technology.

Disinhibition in Cybercommunication

In line with findings in teen chat in the 1990s (Tynes, Reynolds, & Greenfield, 2004), a national poll in 2011 found that 71 percent of 14 to 24-year-olds said people are more likely to use racist and sexist language online or through texting (Gardner & Davis, 2013). A teen interviewed by Gardner and Davis said, "I think kids my age find it easier to make fun of someone through a veiled post on Facebook or Twitter. I think they forget who they are online and use [their online profile] as a separate identity almost that loses responsibilities and is invincible to consequences because it is just black ink on a screen" (pp. 112–113). Again we find disinhibited social relations online (right side, Social Relations line, Learning Environment Change, Figure 9.1).

At the same time, a national survey, Monitoring the Future, showed that psychological well-being of adolescents dropped noticeably starting in 2012, after rising for many years (Twenge, Martin, & Campbell, 2018). Why? The years 2012–2013 marked the market saturation of smartphones. Indeed, the psychological well-being of adolescents was lowest in years when adolescents spent more time online and on social media and when more Americans owned smartphones. Psychological well-being was highest in years when adolescents spent more time with their friends in non-mediated activities. Increases in new media screen activities preceded the decrease in psychological well-being, rather than the reverse. In terms of individual differences, adolescents who spent more time on electronic communication and screens (e.g., social media, texting, electronic games, Internet) were less happy, less satisfied with their lives, and had lower self-esteem. "In contrast, adolescents who spent more time on non-screen activities such as in-person social interaction, sports/exercise, print media, and homework had higher psychological well-being" (Twenge et al., 2018, p. 8). "The least happy adolescents were those low in in-person social interaction and high in electronic communication, and the happiest were those high in in-person social interaction and low in electronic communication" (Twenge et al., 2018, p. 10). In short, more in-person communication and less mediated communication in the Learning Environment predicts more social well-being in Development (Figure 9.1).

How Communication Technologies have Altered Expressions of Sexuality and Partner Choice

Sexuality. Watching a porn video was a minority experience in the 1970s for young adult men; it became a majority experience in the 2010s. The age of access also went down: "As early as 2005, 42% of 10- to 17-year-olds said they had seen some online pornography in the last year, two-thirds of them unwittingly" (Twenge, 2017, p. 212). Unwitting exposure to sexuality on a screen can have a lasting negative effect (Cantor, Mares, & Hyde, 2003).

In a sample of male college students, 89.1 percent were currently using pornography, and almost all used the Internet to access it. "Of the 413 participants who reported current pornography use, 99.5% used it at least occasionally for masturbation." (Sun, Bridges, Johnson, & Ezzell, 2016, p. 988). In addition, pornography users tended to integrate pornography into sex with a partner. Finally, more frequent use of pornography was related to lesser enjoyment of sexually intimate behaviors, such as cuddling and kissing.

Overlapping the chronological period in which the use of pornography has risen is a period in which there has been a decline in having sex with a partner. From 1989 to 2016 there was a steady increase between the ages of 20 and 24 in the percentage of men and women that had had no sexual partners since age 18 (Twenge, 2017). Hence there has been a decline in sex with a partner, a social form of sexuality, and a rise in masturbation to pornography, an individualistic form of sexuality made possible by Internet technology. The use of online pornography was also correlated with lesser enjoyment of sexual intimacy, as well as integrating pornography into sex with a partner. So we see a continuation of technology as promoting ever more depersonalized and less intimate human relations. Masturbation to pornography is at the opposite end of a spectrum anchored by sexual relations in a committed relationship. It is very far from the evolutionary meaning of sex as an expression of commitment to family formation (Manago, Greenfield, Kim, & Ward (2014) (diagrammed on the Sexuality line of the Developmental Change rectangle, Figure 9.1).

Partner choice. The importance of choice is a fundamental individualistic value. Dating websites offer choice of partners that can be overwhelming and even counterproductive (D'Angelo & Toma, 2017). In line with the hypothesis that communications technologies push values and behavior in an individualistic direction, an increasing number of people in almost every age group are expanding their choice of partners by using dating websites. Between 2013 and 2015, the largest increase was among emerging adults, the 18- to 24-year-old group (Pew Research Center, 2016). Focusing on this age group, D'Angelo & Toma (2017) created a lab simulation of online dating. They found that college students who had been given a larger set of potential partners were less satisfied with their choices a week later than those who had been given a smaller set. This relationship is diagrammed on the Sexuality line of the Developmental Change rectangle. So excessive choice in Internet dating (probably in the hundreds for the 18–24-year-olds) has its costs in relationship satisfaction.

Mental Health: ADHD and Conduct Disorder

In a large long-term survey using daily momentary assessments with a diverse group of high-risk teens, daily reports of time spent using digital technologies and number of text messages sent (right side, Communication line, Learning Environment level, Figure 9.1) were associated with increased symptoms of ADHD and conduct disorder that same day, plus poorer self-regulation and increases in symptoms of disordered conduct 18 months later (right side, Behavior line, Developmental level, Figure 9.1) (George, Russell, Piontak, & Odgers, 2018). However, digital technology use on a given day was also associated with lower same day anxiety levels. This may be because technology use was allaying FOMO – fear of missing out.

Another study confirms the ADHD findings. A large cohort of teens in Los Angeles was followed over two years (Ra et al., 2018). At the start of the study, none had symptoms of ADHD. At the end of two years, those who reported engaging in various digital media activities (such as texting or social networking, the most common activity) many times a day exhibited significantly more ADHD symptoms than others who were less active in various forms of digital communication. Turkle's (2015) experience with a group of emerging adults explains how and why this may occur: To demonstrate their preferred mode of communication, they included her in a group chat on WhatsApp, switching rapidly between talk in the room and chat on their phones, which often took the form of images, photos, or videos. Rapid behavior switches are a real-world example of ADHD style; but this behavior had become normative in this high tech communication environment.

Conclusion

The spread and development of ever more effective communication technologies is an important component of the global sociodemographic cluster that includes urbanization, formal education, and wealth. These elements are synergistic; but the focus here has been on technology, currently the most powerful motor of social change in the United States and, arguably, the world. Individualistic values and gender equality are promoted by the expansion of technologically mediated communication, while violent media, especially the interactive medium of video games, cause real-world aggression on a global scale.

In the world in which human beings evolved, all communication was in person; bonding and intimacy are promoted by this modality. In-person communication also exerted implicit social controls. As more and more communication has become technologically mediated, the opportunity to be with someone else who is not present has mushroomed; the in-person social setting has decreased in importance. Communication has also become more anonymous and depersonalized, leading to the disinhibition of racism, sexuality, and cyberbullying in cyberspace and to less intimate communication. In the realm of sexuality and partnering, sexuality has become more depersonalized, while the individualistic value of choice overwhelms and breeds dissatisfaction with romantic choices. At the same time, mediated communication is adaptive in a globalized, mobile world where friends and family may be far away. However, we have seen that the implications of departing from our evolutionary heritage of in-person social relations are broad and deep.

In the environment in which human beings evolved, cognition was focused on acting on the physical world to meet subsistence concerns – food, shelter, clothing. In an urban, commercial environment with a high level of educational opportunity, abstract thinking is valued; and communications technology – whether it be print literacy or computers – is a force that moves cognition towards ever greater abstraction. Over time the world has gone from in-person to mediated communication. Therefore, the values and cognitive processes induced by expanding communication technologies represent historical change, as this chapter has endeavored to show. Research is desperately needed to counteract the dehumanizing aspects of expanded communication technologies and reduce the costs to well-being and social closeness, without losing the benefits of efficiency and connection with those at a distance. Technological tools elicit common reactions around the world. Communications technologies provide the universal culture of a globalized world.

References

Anderson, C. A. & Dill, K. E. (2000). Video games and aggressive thoughts, feelings, and behavior in the laboratory and in life. *Journal of Personality and Social Psychology, 78*, 772–790.

Anderson, C. A., Ihori, N., Bushman, B. J., Rothstein, H. R., Shibuya, A., Swing, E. L., Sakamoto, A., & Saleem, M. (2010). Violent video game effects on aggression, empathy, and prosocial behaviour in Eastern and Western countries: A meta-analytic review. *Psychological Bulletin, 136*, 151–173.

Anderson, C. A., Suzuki, K., Swing, E. L., Groves, C. L., Gentile, D. A., Prot, S., ... Petrescu, P. (2017). Media violence and other aggression risk factors in seven nations. *Personality and Social Psychology Bulletin*, 43, 986–998.

Bailyn, L. (1959). Mass media and children: A study of exposure habits and cognitive effects. *Psychological Monographs: General and Applied*, 73, 1–48.

boyd, d. (2007). *Why Youth Heart Social Network Sites: The role of networked publics in teenage social life*. Cambridge, MA: Berkman Center for Internet and Society Research Publication Series.

Boz, N., Uhls, Y. T. & Greenfield, P. M. (2016). Cross-cultural comparison of adolescents' online self-presentation strategies: Turkey and the United States. *Cyber Behavior, Psychology and Learning*, 6, 1–16.

Bushman, B. & Huesman, L. R. (2001). Effects of televised violence on aggression. In D. G. Singer & J. L. Singer (Eds.), *Handbook of Children and the Media* (pp. 223–254). Thousand Oaks, CA: Sage.

Calvert, S. L. & Tan, S.-L. (1994). Impact of virtual reality on young adults' physiological arousal and aggressive thoughts: Interaction versus observation. *Journal of Applied Developmental Psychology*, 15, 125–139.

Cantor, J., Mares M.-L., & Hyde, J. S. (2003). Autobiographical memories of exposure to sexual media content, *Media Psychology*, 5, 1–31.

Chou, H. G. & Edge, N. (2012). "They are happier and having better lives than I am": The impact of Facebook on perception of others' lives. *Cyberpsychology, Behavior, and Social Networking*, 15, 117–121.

Common Sense Media (2017). *The Common Sense Census: Media use by kids age zero to eight*. Retrieved from www.commonsensemedia.org/research/the-common-sense-census-media-use-by-kids-age-zero-to-eight-2017, July 7, 2018.

D'Angelo, J. D. & Toma, C. L. (2017). There are plenty of fish in the sea: The effects of choice overload and reversibility on online daters' satisfaction with partner choice. *Media Psychology*, 20, 1–27.

Dehaene, S., Pegado, F., Braga, L. W., Ventura, P., Filho, G. N., Jobert, A., ... Cohen, L. (2010). How learning to read changes the cortical networks for vision and language. *Science*, 330, 1359–1364.

Dilley, J. (2017). The most popular video games in the world. Retrieved July 18, 2018 from www.cabletv.com/blog/popular-video-games-world-map/

Drabman, R. S. & Thomas, M. H. (1974). Does media violence increase children's toleration of real-life aggression? *Developmental Psychology*, 10, 418–421.

Flichy, P. (2002). New media history. In L. Lievrouw & S. Livingstone (Eds.), *Handbook of New Media: Social shaping and consequences of ICTs* (pp. 136–150). London: Sage.

Friedrich, L. K. & Stein, A. H. (1973). Aggressive and prosocial television programs and the natural behavior or preschool children. *Monographs of the Society for Research in Child Development*, 38, 1–63.

Gadberry, S. (1980). Effects of restricting first graders' TV-viewing on leisure time use, IQ change, and cognitive style. *Journal of Applied Developmental Psychology*, 1, 45–57.

Garcia, C., Rivera, N., & Greenfield, P. M. (2015). The decline of cooperation, the rise of competition: Developmental effects of long-term social change in Mexico. *International Journal of Psychology*, 50, 6–11.

Gardner, H. & Davis, K. (2013). *The App Generation: How today's youth navigate identity, intimacy, and imagination in a digital world.* New Haven, CT: Yale University Press.

Gentile, D. A., Anderson, C. A., Yukawa, S., Ihori, N., Saleem, M., Ming, L. K., Shibuya, A., Liau, A. K., Khoo, A., Bushman, B. J., Huesmann, L. R., & Sakamoto, A. (2009). The effects of prosocial video games on pro-social behaviors: International evidence from correlational, longitudinal, and experimental studies. *Personality and Social Psychology Bulletin, 35,* 752–763.

George, M. J., Russell, M. A., Piontak, J. R., & Odgers, C. J. (2018). Concurrent and subsequent associations between daily digital technology use and high-risk adolescents' mental health symptoms. *Child Development, 89,* 78–88.

Greenfield, P. M. (1984/2014). *Mind and Media: The effects of television, video games, and computers.* Cambridge, MA: Harvard University Press. Reprinted in 2014 as 30th Anniversary Classic Edition by Psychology Press, New York.

(1993). Representational competence in shared symbol systems: Electronic media from radio to video games. In R. R. Cocking & K. A. Renninger (Eds.), *The Development and Meaning of Psychological Distance* (pp. 161–183). Hillsdale, NJ: Erlbaum.

(2009a). Linking social change and developmental change: Shifting pathways of human development. *Developmental Psychology, 45,* 401–418.

(2009b). Technology and informal education: What is taught, what is learned. *Science, 323,* 69–71.

(2013). The changing psychology of culture from 1800 through 2000. *Psychological Science, 24,* 1722–1731.

(2016). Social change, cultural evolution, and human development. *Current Opinion in Psychology, 8,* 84–92.

(2018a). Studying social change, culture, and human development: A theoretical framework and methodological guidelines. *Developmental Review.*

(2018b, March). Violent video games and assault weapons can turn into a lethal combination. *Miami Herald. www.miamiherald.com/opinion/op-ed/article205433529.html*

Greenfield, P. M., Camaioni, L., Ercolani, P., Weiss, L., Lauber, B., & Perucchini, P. (1994). Cognitive socialization by computer games in two cultures: Inductive discovery or mastery of an iconic code? *Journal of Applied Developmental Psychology, 15,* 59–85.

Greenfield, P. M., Evers, N. F. G., & Dembo, J. (2017). What types of photographs do teenagers "like"? *International Journal of Cyber Behavior, Psychology and Learning, 7*(3).

Greenfield, P. M. & Juvonen, J. (1999). A developmental look at Columbine. *APA Monitor,* July/August.

Hansen, N., Koudenburg, N., Hiersemann, R., Tellegen, P. J., Kocsev, M., & Postmes, T. (2012). Laptop usage affects abstract reasoning of children in the developing world. *Computers in Education, 59,* 989–1000.

Hansen, N., Postmes, T., Tovote, K. A., & Bos, A. (2014). How modernization instigates social change: Laptop usage as a driver of cultural value change and gender equality in a developing country. *Journal of Cross-Cultural Psychology, 45,* 1229–1248.

Huang, V. B., Greenfield, P. M., Wu, M., & Zhou, C. (in prep). Intergenerational differences in child behaviors and parent socialization in the United States.

International Telecommunications Union (2015). *The World in 2015: ICT facts and figures.* Retrieved on 7/13/2018 from www.itu.int/en/ITU-D/Statistics/Documents/facts/ICTFactsFigures2015.pdf

(2016). *The World in 2016: ICT facts and figures.*

(2017). *The World in 2017: ICT facts and figures.*

Kağıtçıbaşı, C. (2007). *Family, Self, and Human Development across Cultures: Theory and application* (2nd ed.). Mahwah, NJ: Erlbaum.

Kline, S. L. & Liu, F. (2005). The influence of comparative media use on acculturation, acculturative stress, and family relationships of Chinese international students. *International Journal of Intercultural Relations, 29,* 367–390.

Konrath, S. H., O'Brien, E. H., & Hsing, C. (2011). Changes in dispositional empathy in American college students over time: A meta-analysis. *Personality and Social Psychology Review, 15,* 180–198.

Ling, R. & Yttri, B. (2005). Control, emancipation and status: The mobile telephone in the teen's parental and peer group control relationships. In R. Kraut (Ed.), *Information Technology at Home.* Oxford: Oxford University Press.

Livingstone, S. (2009). Half a century of television in the lives of our children. *The Annals of the American Academy of Political and Social Science, 625,* 151–163.

Luria, A. R. (1976). *Cognitive Development: Its cultural and social foundations.* Cambridge, MA: Harvard University Press.

Manago, A. M. (2014). Connecting societal change to value differences across generations: Adolescents, mothers and grandmothers in a Maya community in southern Mexico. *Journal of Cross-Cultural Psychology, 45,* 868–887.

Manago, A. M., Greenfield, P. M., Kim, J., & Ward, L. M. (2014). Changing cultural pathways through gender role and sexual development: A theoretical framework. *Ethos, 42,* 198–221.

Manago, A. M., Guan, A. S., & Greenfield, P. M. (2015). New media, social change, and human development from adolescence through the transition to adulthood. In L. A. Jensen (Ed.), *The Oxford Handbook of Human Development and Culture.* Oxford: Oxford University Press.

Manago, A. M. & Pacheco, P. (2019). Globalization and the transition to adulthood in a Maya community in Mexico: Communication technologies, social networks, and views on gender. In J. McKenzie (Ed.), Globalization as a Context for Youth Development. *New Directions for Child and Adolescent Development, 164,* 1–15.

Manago, A. M., Taylor, T., & Greenfield, P. M. (2012). Me and my 400 friends: The anatomy of college students' Facebook networks, their communication patterns, and well-being. *Developmental Psychology, 48,* 369–380.

Mandell, D. S., Thompson, W. W., Weintraub, E. S., Destefano, F., & Blank, M. B. (2005). Trends in diagnosis rates for autism and ADHD at hospital discharge in the context of other psychiatric diagnoses. *Psychiatric Services, 56,* 56–62.

McDaniel, B. T. & Radesky, J. S. (2018). Technoference: Parent distraction by technology and associations with child behavior problems. *Child Development, 89,* 100–109.

Meyrowitz, J. (1985). *No Sense of Place: The impact of electronic media on social behavior.* New York: Oxford University Press.

Mundy-Castle, A. C. (1974). Social and technological intelligence in Western and non-Western cultures. *Universitas, 4,* 46–52.

National Institute of Mental Health (1972). *Television and Growing Up: The impact of televised violence.* Report to the Surgeon General, United States Public Health Service.

Ophir, E., Nass, C., & Wagner, A. D. (2009). Cognitive control in media multitaskers. *Proceedings of the National Academy of Sciences, 106,* 15583–15587.

Ortner, S. B. (2003). *New Jersey Dreaming: Capital, culture, and the class of '58.* Durham, NC: Duke University Press.

Pea, R., Nass, C., Meheula, L., Rance, M., Kumar, A., Bamford, H., Nass, M., Simha, A., Stillerman, B., Yang, S., & Zhou, M. (2012). Media use, face-to-face communication, media multitasking, and social well-being among 8- to 12-year-old girls. *Developmental Psychology, 48,* 327–336.

Pew Research Center (2016). Five facts about online dating. Retrieved July 16, 2018 from www.pewresearch.org/fact-tank/2016/02/29/5-facts-about-online-dating/

Ra, C. K., Cho, J., Stone, M. D., De la Cerda, J., Goldenson, N. I., Moroney, E., ... Leventhal, A. M. (2018). Association of digital media use with subsequent symptoms of attention-deficit/hyperactivity disorder among adolescents. *JAMA, 320,* 255–263.

Radesky, J. S., Kistin, C. J., Zuckerman, B., Nitzberg, B. S., Gross, J., Kaplan-Sanoff, M., & Augustyn, M., & Silverstein, M. (2014). Patterns of mobile device use by caregivers and children during meals in fast food restaurants. *Pediatrics, 133,* e833–e849.

Rideout, V. J., Foehr, U. G., & Roberts, D. F. (2010). *Generation M2: Media in the lives of 8–18 year olds.* Menlo Park, CA: Kaiser Family Foundation.

Rosen, L.D. (2007). *Me, MySpace, and I: Parenting the net generation.* New York: St. Martin's Press.

Rosen, L. D., Cheever, N. A. & Carrier, L. M. (2008). The association of parenting style and child age with parental limit setting and adolescent MySpace behavior. *Journal of Applied Developmental Psychology, 29,* 459–471.

Rosser, J. C., Lynch, P. J., Cuddihy, L., Gentile, D. A., Klonsky, J., & Merrell, R. (2007). The impact of video games on training surgeons in the 21st century. *Archives of Surgery, 142,* 181–186.

Sales, N. J. (2016). *American Girls: Social media and the secret lives of teenagers.* New York: Knopf.

Salomon, G. (1994). *Interaction of Media, Cognition, and Learning: An exploration of how symbolic forms cultivate mental skills and affect knowledge.* New York: Routledge.

Santos, H. I., Varnum, M. E. W., & Grossmann I. (2017). Global increases in individualism. *Psychological Science, 28,* 1228–1239.

Schiffrin, H. H., Liss, M., Miles-McLean, H., Geary, K. A., Erchull, M. J., & Tahner, T. (2014). *Journal of Child and Family Studies, 23,* 548–557.

Schwartz, S. H., Melech, G., Lehmann, A., Burgess, S., Harris, M., & Owen, V. (2001). Extending the cross-cultural validity of the theory of basic human values with a different method of measurement. *Journal of Cross-Cultural Psychology, 32,* 519–542.

Serpell, R. (1984). Research on cognitive development in Sub-Saharan Africa. *International Journal of Behavioral Development, 7,* 11–127.

Shapka, J. D., Onditi, H. Z., Collie, R. J., & Lapidot-Lefler, N. (2018). Cyberbullying and cybervictimization within a cross-cultural context: A study of Canadian and Tanzanian adolescents. *Child Development, 89,* 89–99.

Sherman, L. E., Greenfield, P. M., Hernandez, L. M., & Dapretto, M. (2017). Peer influence via Instagram: Effects on brain and behavior in adolescence and young adulthood. *Child Development,* doi: 10.1111/cdev.12838

Sherman, L. E., Hernandez, L. M., Greenfield, P. M., & Dapretto, M. (2018). What the brain "likes": Neural correlates of providing feedback on social media. *Social Cognitive and Affective Neuroscience, 13,* 699–707.

Sherman, L. E., Michikyan, M., & Greenfield, P. M. (2013). The effects of text, audio, video, and in-person communication on bonding between friends. *CyberPsychology: Journal of Psychosocial Research on Cyberspace, 7*(2), Article 3. doi: 10.5817/CP2013-2-3

Sherman, L. E., Payton, A. A., Hernandez, L. M., Greenfield, P. M., & Dapretto, M. (2016). The power of the *like* in adolescence: Effects of peer influence on neural and behavioral responses to social media. *Psychological Science, 27,* 10027–10035.

Stavrinos, D., Pope, C. N., Shen, J., & Schwebel, D. C. (2018). Distracted walking, bicycling, and driving: Systematic review and meta-analysis of mobile technology and youth crash risk, *Child Development, 89,* 118–128.

Sticca, F. & Perren, S. (2013). Is cyberbullying worse than traditional bullying? Examining the differential role of medium, publicity, and anonymity for the perceived severity of bullying. *Journal of Youth and Adolescence, 42,* 739–750.

Subrahmanyam, K., Šmahel, D., & Greenfield, P. M. (2006). Connecting developmental processes to the internet: Identity presentation and sexual exploration in online teen chatrooms, *Developmental Psychology, 42,* 395–406.

Sun, C., Bridges, A., Johnson, J., & Ezzell, M. B (2016). Pornography and the male sexual script: An analysis of consumption and sexual relations. *Archives of Sexual Behavior, 45,* 983–994.

Tönnies, F. (1957). *Community and Society (Gemeinschaft und Gesellschaft),* trans. C. P. Loomis. East Lansing, MI: Michigan State University Press. (Original work published in German in 1887.)

Tower, R. B., Singer, D. G., & Singer, J. L. (1979). Differential effects of television programming on preschoolers' cognition, imagination, and social play. *American Journal of Orthopsychiatry, 49,* 265–281.

Turkle, S. (2011). *Alone Together: Why we expect more from technology and less from each other.* New York: Basic Books.

(2015). *Reclaiming Conversation: The power of talk in a digital age.* New York: Penguin Press.

Twenge, J. (2017). *iGen: Why today's super-connected kids are growing up less rebellious, more tolerant, less happy – and completely unprepared for adulthood – and what that means for the rest of us.* New York: Atria Books.

Twenge, J. M., Martin, G. N., & Campbell, W. K. (2018). Decreases in psychological well-being among adolescents after 2012 and links to screen time during the rise of smartphone technology. *Emotion, 18,* 765–780.

Tynes, B., Reynolds, L., & Greenfield, P. M. (2004). Adolescence, race and ethnicity on the Internet: A comparison of discourse in monitored vs. unmonitored chat rooms. *Journal of Applied Developmental Psychology, 25,* 685–698.

Uhls, Y. T. & Greenfield, P. M. (2011). The rise of fame: An historical content analysis. *Cyberpsychology: Journal of Psychosocial Research on Cyberspace*, 5(1), article 1.

(2012). The value of fame: Preadolescent perceptions of popular media and their relationship to future aspirations. *Developmental Psychology*, 48, 315–326.

Uhls, Y. T., Zgourou, E., & Greenfield, P. M. (2014). 21st century media, fame, and other future aspirations: A national survey of 9–15 year olds. *Cyberpsychology: Journal of Psychosocial Research on Cyberspace*. 8(4), article 5.

UNICEF (2017). *Children in a Digital World: The state of the world's children 2017*.

Vygotsky, L. S. (1962). *Thought and Language*. Cambridge, MA: MIT Press.

Weinstock, M. (2015). Changing epistemologies under conditions of social change in two Arab communities in Israel. *International Journal of Psychology*, 50, 29–36.

Weinstock, M., Ganayiem, M., Igbariya, R., Manago, A. M., & Greenfield, P. M. (2015). Societal change and values in Arab communities in Israel: Intergenerational and rural-urban comparisons. *Journal of Cross-Cultural Psychology*, 44, 19–38. doi: 10.1177/00220221/1455/792

Williams, T. B. (1985). Implications of a natural experiment in the developed world for research on television in the developing world. *Journal of Cross-Cultural Psychology*, 16, 263–287.

(1986). *The Impact of Television: A natural experiment in three communities*. Orlando, FL: Academic Press.

Wober, M. (1975/2014). *Psychology in Africa*. International African Institute. Republished as a Psychology Revival. New York: Routledge.

Zhou, C., Yiu, V., Wu, M., & Greenfield, P. M. (2017). Perception of cross-generational differences in child behavior and parent socialization. *Journal of Cross-Cultural Psychology*, 49(1), 62–81.

Part IV

Views of the Interdisciplinary Dialogue:
From Developmental Science
and Sociology

10   A Developmentalist's Viewpoint: "It's About Time!" Ecological Systems, Transaction, and Specificity as Key Developmental Principles in Children's Changing Worlds*

Marc H. Bornstein

Introduction

Philosophers through the ages – from Heraclitus "*No man ever steps in the same river twice,*" through Robert Allen Zimmerman (aka Bob Dylan) "*The times they are a changin …*'" – have stressed *time* as a critical variable in life. Certainly, *developmental science* sees time as central, and both of the science's principal empirical designs – cross-sectional and longitudinal – incorporate time as the independent variable. Paradoxically, however, many construals of time have been neglected. Historical time is a notable example. We inhabit an urbanizing, globalizing, and diversifying restless world that is ever changing in wealth and education, materialism and individualism (Greenfield, this volume), and institutions that are centrally concerned with the upbringing of children, like the family, are perpetually in flux (Parke, this volume).

There are many reasons for this relative inattention. One is that developmental science, dating from Darwin or Freud, is only about 100 years old and therefore encompasses only a small number of generations of scientists. A second reason is that, at any given moment in time, the developmentalist has access only to contemporary phenomena and they are constrained. Of the past, the present, and the future, common categorical demarcations of time, Leslie Poles Hartley observed: "The past is a foreign country; they do things differently there"; the present is ephemeral and evanescent; and no one has access to the future. Third, longitudinal study (of the two methods where the real developmental pay dirt is found) definitionally unfolds through time, takes time, and depends logistically on steady funding and continuing cooperation and availability of participants.

* Supported by an International Research Fellowship in collaboration with the Centre for the Evaluation of Development Policies at the Institute for Fiscal Studies, London, UK, funded by the European Research Council under the Horizon 2020 research and innovation programme (grant agreement No 695300-HKADeC-ERC-2015-AdG).

Developmentalists today pretend to a "life span" framework. How else to discover all-important social pathways, cumulative processes, trajectories, transitions, and turning points in life (Elder, Shanahan, & Jennings, 2015). Lives are lived in temporally changing contexts. Consider the following case study from Schoon and Bynner (this volume) who contrasted experiences of different cohorts of 16- to 25-year-olds coming of age between 2000 and 2012 and making the transition to adulthood before and after the advent of the Great Recession of 2007–2008. That economic shock rushed or put the brakes on youth transitions. Germane to our interests here, developmental science is centrally concerned with stability and change in the child, the environment, and relations between child and environment over the life course (Bornstein, Putnick, & Esposito, 2017).

This chapter focuses on time and fleshes out three developmental perspectives on time: the chronosystem from the bioecological systems framework, transaction, and specificity. Time, as we see, fits integrally into each developmental perspective. Each perspective is multidimensional; this chapter could elaborate on each constituent of each perspective, but the chapter stresses the role of time in each.

Bioecological Systems

As Elder and Cox and Schoon and Bynner (this volume) observe, human lives are shaped by ongoing interactions between a developing individual and socio-historically changing contexts. Bioecological systems theory characterizes development as a joint function of process, person, context, and *time* (Bronfenbrenner & Morris, 2006). Briefly, processes refer to dynamic interactions that the developing individual experiences. Characteristics and qualities of the developing individual (age, gender, temperament, and intellect) influence the nature and structure of developmental outcomes. In everyday life, developing individuals are exposed to multiple contexts that shape development (Greenfield, this volume). The contexts that envelop the developing individual are hierarchical. At the most proximal and innermost level, the microsystem encompasses patterns of activities, roles, and interpersonal relationships, which the developing individual experiences in face-to-face settings, including immediate social milieux (parents, siblings) and physical environments (objects, places). Mesosystems constitute links between two or more microsystems, when the same developing individual participates in two or more settings, such as a peer group and school. The exosystem encompasses linkages between aspects of the environment the developing individual does not directly encounter, but which influence development through lower-level systems. Macrosystem patterns of beliefs, values, customs, and living conditions (culture, religion, the socioeconomic organization) permeate and color exo-, meso-, and micro-systems. Lower-level more proximal contexts nest within and channel higher-level more distal contexts. Understanding the meaning and impact of proximal influences on the developing individual often requires placing them within the broader systems in which they occur (Bornstein, 1995).

Crosscutting all of these systems is the chronosystem. Effective time frames in development range from moment-to-moment processes (micro-time) to periodicities over days, weeks, or years but within a generation (macro-time) to time frames of the life course or historical eras across generations (historical time). The chronosystem is usually studied in the bioecological systems framework as age, often with regard to the questions of the unique salience of experiences at one or another time for later development. Chronosystem-microsystem links are manifest when proximal processes occur at different ages and vary in their comparative salience; sensitivity of the developing brain to biological and psychosocial stimulation varies depending on the stages and rates of development of different parts of the brain (sensitive periods; Bornstein, 1989). Chronosystem-macrosystem links occur when people of different ages encounter macrosystem events, such as the Great Recession (Schoon & Bynner, this volume) or the Great Depression (Elder & Cox, this volume). Developmental-ecological researchers need to "unpackage" time so as to identify specific underlying mechanisms driving chronosystem associations.

Developmental Transactions

Characteristics of individuals shape their experiences, and reciprocally experiences shape characteristics of individuals, through *time*; this is the principle of transaction in development (Bornstein, 2009). Children influence which experiences they will be exposed to, and they interpret those experiences and so determine how those experiences will affect them. By virtue of their unique characteristics and propensities children actively contribute, through their interactions with their parents, to their own development. Child and parent bring distinctive characteristics to, and each changes as a result of, every interaction; both then enter the next round of interaction as changed individuals. Transactions in parent–child dyads are an everyday affair. A paradox in development, highlighted by transactional analyses, is that child, parent, and experience/environment are simultaneously consistent and inconsistent through time.

Like ecological systems, transactions consist of several separable constituents: individual variation, stability and continuity, parent effects and child effects, as well as temporal relations among them. Human beings vary dramatically on every psychological construct, structure, function, or process (CSFP). Individual differences in some CSFPs are fleeting, whereas others are relatively consistent through time. Developmental science is centrally concerned with temporal consistency in CSFPs, and it is instructive to distinguish individual order consistency (stability) and group mean level consistency (continuity), which are conceptually and empirically independent (Bornstein et al., 2017). Temporal consistency in development depends on the CSFP, the age of the developing individual when the CSFP is assessed, the frequency or duration of the CSFP assessment, the temporal interval between assessments of the CSFP, and whether assessments of a CSFP are made across the same or different contexts. Temporal consistency is important for several reasons. First, some CSFPs require consistency – physical, chemical, psychological, and environmental – to survive. Second, consistency provides basic information about the overall developmental course of a given CSFP. Third, it is generally assumed that to be meaningful, a CSFP should show (substantial) consistency across time. Fourth, consistency affects the environment as interactants often adjust to consistent CSFPs in one another. Of course, developmental science equally (or more so) emphasizes inconsistency through time. The lifespan perspective in development asserts that human beings are open systems, whose plastic nature ensures that people exhibit both temporal consistencies and inconsistencies in CSFPs. Consistency and inconsistency in a CSFP are attributable to genetic or biological factors in the individual and emerge through the developing individual's experiences and environments.

The transactional model of development asserts that parents affect their children (parent effects) and that children affect their parents (child effects) through time. With each child advance, parenting changes in some corresponding ways: Longitudinal cross-cultural study shows that mothers of younger children from the United States, France, Argentina, and Japan use more affect-laden speech, but that as children achieve more sophisticated levels of motor exploration and cognitive comprehension, mothers increasingly orient, comment, and prepare children for the world outside the dyad by increasing information in their speech to reference the environment to orient, comment, and prepare infants for the world outside the dyad (Bornstein et al., 1992). Multiple-term transactions define temporal dynamics in which the child changes the parent who in turn changes the child who in turn changes the parent … and vice-versa. Multiple-term transactions are common in everyday life.

Bates, Pettit, and Dodge (1995) found that harsh parental reactions to four-year-olds who were identified in infancy as temperamentally difficult enhanced externalizing behavior in adolescence. In a transaction, two people interact such that the intentions or actions of one reciprocally affect the intentions or actions of the other through time. The transaction principle acknowledges that a developing individual's characteristics shape his or her experiences, and reciprocally, experiences shape the characteristics of the developing individual through time.

Specificity

Understanding lifespan human development depends critically on what is studied in whom, how, and *when* (Bornstein, 2015). Thus, specific CSFPs in specific individuals are affected by specific experiences in specific ways at specific times. This is the Specificity Principle in lifespan human development. Specificity contrasts with many common developmental assumptions, for example, that overall level of stimulation influences overall development. It is not the case that a global shared experience affects performance in particular areas or compensates for selective deficiencies. Familial love, financial well-being, or a stimulating environment do not guarantee, or even speak to, lifespan development of specific characteristics, such as healthy eating habits, an empathic personality, verbal competence, sports prowess, or religious affiliation. Rather, contemporary developmental science indicates that specificities are normally at play.

As with ecological systems and transaction, specificity is characterized by multiple constituents. Operative settings and experiences in life represent specific exposures and social and physical environments. Schoon and Bynner (this volume) demonstrate how young people on the cusp of adulthood during the Great Recession of 2008 varied depending on whether they lived in the United Kingdom, Germany, or the United States based on similarities and differences in education systems, variations in access to the labor market, and support systems that scaffolded youth transitions to independence. Masten, Motti-Stefanidi, and Rahl-Brigman (this volume) point out how experience of the "Dutch Hunger Winter" (which was confined to certain regions of the Netherlands and not others) affected life-long health of children only in the affected regions.

Characteristics of both the person subject to an experience and the person providing that experience moderate development. Since Heisenberg, science has acknowledged that no experience affects every individual the same way, as experiences are not perceived, interpreted, or responded to by all individuals identically. To the extent that individuals differ in age, gender, temperament, ethnic identity, or the like ("stratifiers" in Schoon & Bynner, this volume), effects are moderated – that is, the same experiences can have different effects on different people. For example, Masten and colleagues (this volume) point out that children might experience less direct exposure to the horrors of war or disaster, in part because they lack full understanding of the situation or are sheltered by adults, whereas adolescents in similar circumstances may suffer more because they are enlisted to help or fight, have greater understanding of situations and future consequences, and are more connected to other people who may be harmed. Which experiences people have, as well as the meaning and impact of those experiences, are also influenced by who provides those experiences. Specific people of specific genders and so forth emphasize different experiences. European-American mothers expect early mastery of verbal competence and self-expression in their children, whereas Japanese mothers expect early mastery of emotional maturity, self-control, and social courtesy in theirs.

Developmental science has identified a limited number of different processes by which experiences might shape development. One general class of mechanism is socialization. A second is learning that is conditioning, reinforcement, and modeling. A third is cognition, including tuition, instruction, and scaffolding. The fourth focuses on opportunity structures, the number and types of situations provided to or encouraged for the individual. Leventhal et al. (this volume) posit that children living in disadvantaged neighborhoods are exposed to a wider array of cultural scripts and role models than their peers from more advantaged neighborhoods and hypothesize that the consequent diversity of opportunity in both mainstream and variant pathways creates confusion and presents the possibility for suboptimal or deviant choices.

Experience effects do not often or readily generalize across domains of development. Rather, different experiences in different people delivered via different processes can be expected to affect different specific outcomes in development. Masten et al. (this volume) distinguish developmental tasks that are universal (learning to walk or speak the language of the family) from others that are unique to a context or historical period (such as learning to weave or hunt for food). Greenfield (this volume) examines effects of having a laptop on children's cognition: Children with laptops outperform children without laptops on two abstract reasoning tests (analogies and categories), but laptops do not improve school performance. Marks, Woolverton, and Garcia Coll (this volume) show how pre-migration, settlement, and post-migration contexts and experiences differentially shape immigrant children's developmental trajectories.

Finally, time has multiple construals in specificity: age, duration, generation, and history. Some experiences need occur only at one or another particular time in life to be effective where, to be equally effective, other experiences need to recur on a fairly regular basis or over extended periods of time. In developmental science, the relative importance of early versus later experiences has been a long-standing issue. Some early experiences are special because they exert lasting effects on development over and above stability in the individual and later experience. Philosophers, theoreticians, and scientists from psychoanalysis to ethology to epigenetics have pointed to the special importance of early experiences, suggesting, on the one hand, that the ways young children are treated establish lifelong personality traits and, on the other, that organisms develop relationships to objects they first experience. Crosnoe (this volume) points to econometric evidence that investments in early childhood interventions bring greater long-term returns in the form of adult outcomes (e.g., more education, higher earnings, lower odds of criminal justice contact) than human capital interventions that target older youth. Similarly, Leventhal and colleagues (this volume) report that neighborhood affluence in early childhood is associated with children's superior achievement 15 years on. Early sensitivities may exist because childhood is a period of rapid developmental changes, and environmental inputs at that time may set developmental trajectories that carry forward.

Some antecedent effects may not persist, however, or they may be altered or supplanted by subsequent experiences that are more consequential. That is, concurrent experiences may be more potent than antecedent ones in determining development. Phenomena such as the recovery of function after early deprivation provide empirical support for a contemporary effects model as do failures of some early interventions to sustain. Elder and Cox (this volume) point to periods later in life when defense and stress systems are open to recalibration by experience. In early and contemporary temporal effects models, specific relationships and contexts exert unique effects on development at a specific time, consonant with a sensitive period interpretation of developmental effects.

Still other developmental effects answer only to consistent experiences through time. A cumulative effects model contends that an experience at any one time may not necessarily be effective, but meaningful longitudinal relations are structured by similar experiences repeating and aggregating through time. Thus, seemingly small consistent differences in opportunity at school can be compounded over time into large end-of-school outcomes, and those end-of-school outcomes in turn have a hefty impact on the transition into higher education (Crosnoe, this volume). Another line of longitudinal research links children's cumulative exposure to neighborhood socioeconomic conditions to their developmental outcomes (Leventhal et al., this volume): The Panel Study of Income Dynamics showed that cumulative exposure to neighborhood poverty from birth was more strongly associated with high school dropout and early childbearing than a single point-in-time estimate. Bronfenbrenner and Morris (2006) emphasized as essential the stability of proximal processes over time for establishing long-term developmental pathways. As exposure to stable developmentally facilitative ecosystem factors cumulate over time the probability of influence over developmental trajectories increases. Cumulative exposures can influence children's perceptions of the world they live in and how they evaluate their future insofar as, for example, children who experience time-limited trauma can be reassured of an eventual return to normalcy, whereas such reassurance is moot for children experiencing chronic trauma as those continually confronted with uncontrollable and unpredictable events come to view the world as a threatening place with little trust.

In a nutshell, a given relationship or context experience may exert an effect on development at one (early) or another (late) time in life or it may need to persist through the life course to be effective.

Duration of experience is another specific temporal factor. Child soldiers who were with the armed group RENAMO in Mozambique for less than six months described themselves as victims of RENAMO, whereas those with the armed group for a year or longer viewed themselves as members of RENAMO (see Masten et al., this volume).

Yet a different construal of time is generation. As Greenfield (this volume) reports, from the generation born between 1970 and 1990 who watched Mr. Rogers (an empathic TV character) as young children to a generation of children born in the 2010s, a decade after Mr. Rogers's Neighborhood went off the air, a significant decrease occurred in cooperating and obeying parents. Adolescent Arab girls of northern Israel were the first generation to have mobile technologies during their teenage years; they value female independence and egalitarian gender roles more than their mothers or grandmothers (see Greenfield, this volume).

Finally, historical time holds sway over many aspects of development. As reported in Marks et al. (this volume), during the Great Depression mass unemployment in the US caused immigration from Mexico to the US to wane; in the years following the Depression widespread demand for labor in the US resulted in temporary but not permanent migration of Mexican nationals to the US; then after World War II in a decade of economic prosperity, restrictions on permanent immigration were largely unenforced and migration from Mexico waxed again. Parke (this volume) reports a startling decline in the nuclear family form as the guiding template for the organization of family life: In 1975 only 34 percent of mothers with preschool children participated in the labor force, but by 2013 this number jumped to 61 percent.

The Specificity Principle advances a theory of development as particularistic in nature such that development depends on several separate factors, including the experience involved, who experiences and who generates the experience, how the experience occurs, the domain of development affected, and when in the developing individual's lifecourse the experience occurs. The Specificity Principle asserts that development is multiply moderated. As life proceeds, advantages and disadvantages aggregate to amplify heterogeneity of developing individuals' experiences with the inevitable consequences that, in essence, variability in the population, and specificity for the individual, increase. Specificity unveils a picture of human lifespan development painted by what is studied in whom, how, and when (Bornstein, 2015, 2017).

Research and Policy in Time

Issues of time in lifespan developmental science speak to contemporary concerns of researchers and policy makers. For example, fulsome incorporation of the chronosystem in the thinking of developmental scientists broadens the scope of understanding processes of development that are time limited versus universal. Understanding the nature of transactions places proper weight on contributions of child and parent, experience and environment, in development. Likewise, specificity helps to explain observations, reconcile discrepancies, and expose existing gaps in the literature as it has implications for sampling, design, measurement, and analysis. Lifespan theoreticians and researchers today concern themselves with understanding which experiences affect which aspects of which person's development how and when: "what works for whom." To explore determinants of development and promote well-being it is necessary and desirable to incorporate time in systems, transactions, and specificity.

Majoritarian positions traditionally (and mistakenly) drive most policy recommendations, yet specificity, for example, implies that experience effects are conditional and not absolute (true for all people under all conditions and so forth). Specificity informs programs and policies in ways that productively meet the specific needs of specific peoples in specific ways at specific times. Probing transactions uncovers strategic points of profitable intervention. Systems, transactions, and specificity help policy makers to better appreciate why "one-size-fits-all" interventions often fail – why some individuals benefit from some intervention experiences but others do not, and how best to choose profitable directions for future attention.

Conclusion

Children's development is dynamic, multifaceted, and complex, and it is multi-determined such that the contributions of person and environment, while necessary are, by themselves, not sufficient to explicate development. Rather than studying just individual or environment, there needs to be simultaneous appreciation of both person and environment in *time*. Failing to value the many forces that affect development has impeded our understanding of children and childhood. These lessons are critical to producing research that informs policies and practices to improve health and well-being. Time plays vital roles in all major perspectives on child development, as consistency and inconsistency over time in the individual, in the environment, and in relations between individual and environment constitute the norm.

References

Bates, J. E., Pettit, G. S., & Dodge, K. A. (1995) Family and child factors in stability and change in children's aggressiveness in elementary school. In J. McCord (Ed.), *Coercion and Punishment in Long-Term Perspectives* (pp. 124–138). New York: Cambridge University Press.

Bornstein, M. H. (1989). Sensitive periods in development: Structural characteristics and causal interpretations. *Psychological Bulletin, 105*, 179–197.

(1995). Form and function: Implications for studies of culture and human development. *Culture & Psychology, 1*, 123–137.

(2015). Children's parents. In M. H. Bornstein & T. Leventhal (Eds.), *Ecological Settings and Processes in Developmental Systems, Vol. 4: Handbook of Child Psychology and Developmental Science* (7th ed., pp. 55–132). Editor-in-Chief: R. M. Lerner. Hoboken, NJ: Wiley.

(2017). The specificity principle in acculturation science. *Perspectives on Psychological Science, 12*, 3–45.

Bornstein, M. H., Putnick, D. L., & Esposito, G. (2017). Continuity and stability in development. *Child Development Perspectives, 11*, 113–119.

Bornstein, M. H., Tal, J., Rahn, C., Galperín, C. Z., Pêcheux, M.-G., Lamour, M., Azuma, H., Toda, S., Ogino, M., & Tamis-LeMonda, C. S. (1992). Functional analysis of the contents of maternal speech to infants of 5 and 13 months in four cultures: Argentina, France, Japan, and the United States. *Developmental Psychology, 28*, 593–603.

Bronfenbrenner, U. & Morris, P. A. (2006). The bioecological model of human development. In R. M. Lerner (Ed.), W. Damon (Series Ed.), *Handbook of Child Psychology, Vol. 1: Theoretical Models of Human Development* (6th ed., pp. 793–828). Hoboken, NJ: Wiley.

Elder, G. H., Shanahan, M. J., & Jennings, J. A. (2015). Human development in time and place. In M. H. Bornstein & T. Leventhal (Eds.), *Ecological Settings and Processes in Developmental Systems* (Vol. 4, pp. 6–54). Hoboken, NJ: Wiley.

11   A Sociologist's Perspective: The Historic Specificity of Development and Resilience in the Face of Increasingly Ominous Futures

Jeylan T. Mortimer

In this sequel to the now-classic *Children in Time and Place: Developmental and Historical Insights* (1993), Parke and Elder have brought together a group of scholars representing diverse social science disciplines to examine the impacts of dramatic societal changes during the past quarter century on children and families. The editors sought fresh theoretical thinking and new insights, drawn from socio-cultural, historical, and life course perspectives, and recent empirical findings based on state-of-the-art methods. They have remarkably succeeded. This timely collection forges into new territory in its consideration of some of the most pressing challenges facing children and families in our time, including severe economic turbulence in the global economy, war, mass migration, climate change, disintegration in third world countries, mounting crises in the US (e.g., poverty, racial/ethnic segregation), technological transformations, and the concurrent responses of major institutions. In this short commentary, I highlight three themes that pervade the volume: human development as an historically-specific phenomenon, ominous trends toward an increasingly bleak and challenging future, and the countervailing capacity for resilience in families and children.

Development is Historically Specific

In their introductory chapter, Parke and Elder lay out the book's conceptual framework, drawing on Bronfenbrenner's systems perspective, including socio-cultural exosystemic contexts, the institutional "mesosystem," and the proximal contexts (e.g., family, school) directly impinging on the child, conceived as a biological, psychological, and social entity. As Greenfield points out, historical change transforms phenomena at all these levels, altering the systemic contexts, the learning environment of the child, and the expression of human genetic potentials.

In doing so, the very character of development is altered. Even the way we conceive the developing organism changes historically, as it affects the very "stages of life" that are recognized; the age-graded life course is a preeminently historically specific construct (Mortimer & Moen, 2016). But because much work in the developmental sciences remains firmly rooted in the here and now, Parke and Elder sought a group of scholars who would seriously explore the implications of recent historical change for developmental processes.

Elder and Cox take on this challenge, posing an overarching question – when do historical upheavals, and their ramifications in individual and family lives, have the more detrimental developmental outcomes? That is, is it more harmful to experience highly adverse circumstances, often attendant on rapid social change, early or later? Drawing on Elder's pathbreaking study of children in the Berkeley and Oakland cohorts who experienced depression hardship in childhood or adolescence, respectively, they make the case, consistent with much work in developmental psychology, that adversity early on has the most detrimental effects. Indeed, the experiences of adolescent boys in the Oakland cohort whose families suffered severe income loss were developmentally favorable, providing opportunities to enact positive behaviors, as they helped their families cope with financial troubles. Whereas military service (World War II, the Korean War), higher education (promoted by the GI Bill) and movement into a rapidly expanding economy helped the Berkeley cohort overcome childhood disadvantages, the societal contexts that promoted such positive "turning points" were quite historically specific.

Supporting the hypothesis of early vulnerability, Leventhal, Anastasio, and Dupere cite evidence that exposure to neighborhood poverty has more negative impacts on development and achievement among younger children. However, the debates surrounding timing continue. Schoon and Bynner suggest that the more recent "Great Recession," has had more detrimental psychological implications for older youth (age 18–25) than for adolescents, who were largely shielded from economic hardship by their families and schools. During the Great Recession those at the cusp of adulthood were especially hard hit as they tried to enter a labor force plagued by high rates of youth and minority unemployment.

Schoon and Bynner emphasize that historically-specific national contexts of school-to-work transition fundamentally alter the experience of entry to the labor force in both good and poor economic times, providing relatively smooth transition pathways where there are strong institutional bridges between school and the labor force (as in Germany, Austria, and the Netherlands), but particularly difficult transitions where these connections are weak (as in Britain and the United States).

Their analysis provides a sound explanation as to why the prospects of older youth entering the labor force in the recent US recessionary downturn were especially poor. Unlike the booming post-World War II US economy, which drew in job-seekers despite the absence of school-to-work connections, growth after the Great Recession has been relatively anemic.

Marks, Woolverton, and Garcia Coll examine the developmental importance of historical conditions that make societies more or less receptive to immigrants. Families and children who arrive in destination countries at times of high unemployment are likely to face resentment from natives who see them as competitors for jobs; those arriving in times of labor shortage may instead be welcomed as helping to resolve severe economic problems. Marks et al. also describe the historically shifting stances of developmental scientists who, in an earlier period, favored "assimilationist" approaches, whereby immigrants were expected to relinquish the cultural values and practices of their origin countries in favor of rapid uptake of the new host societal culture. They note that contemporary scholars now recognize the advantages of biculturalism for adjustment and health. (Similarly, Masten, Motti-Stefanidi and Rahl-Brigman refer to "intercultural competence" as essential for adaptation today in pluralistic societies among both immigrants and host populations.)

Though Marks et al. imply that the earlier "assimilationist" perspective was mistaken one might entertain an arguably plausible alternative point of view based on Elder and Cox's stress on the historically specific character of development. Perhaps an assimilationist stance was indeed more adaptive in earlier periods of mass migration (e.g., from the turn of the twentieth century to the 1960s, for example) when the host society was less welcoming of diversity. As Masten et al. point out, "destination communities vary in their attitudes and support of cultural practices brought to the host country by refugees." The upheavals of the 1960s, increasing promotion of minority civil rights and recognition of the value of diversity, could have made bi- or multi-culturalism both increasingly frequent and more developmentally advantageous in contemporary diverse populations.

The historically-specific character of human development is clearly manifest in Greenfield's overview of the evolution of communication technologies from the Middle Ages (with the invention and rapid diffusion of the printing press) to modern transformations brought about by television, the internet, videogames, laptops, smartphones, social media, etc. Each new innovation, moving away from oral communication to more impersonal, mediated styles, led to greater separation of children and parents and erosion of familial authority, thereby altering the character of the socialization environment. These historical changes have altered the character of development, as they have been accompanied by increases in the capacity for cognitive abstraction and value shifts toward individualism and materialism, at the expense of collectivism and benevolence. Children are increasingly drawn into large circles of non-intimate communication partners, with numbers of "followers" and "likes" having strong implications for self-esteem. Unfortunately, downsides of these technological developments are also apparent: increases in loneliness, poor mental health, and declining intimacy.

The Future is Bleak

Taken together, the chapters in this volume paint a bleak picture of the present circumstances of children and youth, and some ominously predict even greater difficulties, if recent trends continue, in the future. Mounting inequality in the United States, with a similar though less extreme tendency in Europe, has contributed to very different and unequal family structures and processes, with distinct consequences for children. As Parke points out, the most disadvantaged families are characterized by cohabitation (as an alternative rather than a prelude to marriage), early parenthood, union instability, and serial child-bearing (with multiple fathers); more advantaged couples marry and bear children at later ages after they complete education and become economically self-sufficient, and they are at less risk of dissolution. Affluent and college-educated parents shower their children with investments – material, social, cultural, etc.; this "concerted cultivation" prepares children to succeed in school and acquire the credentials necessary for the acquisition of professional and managerial employment. Since the more disadvantaged families lack the resources to transmit these forms of human capital, this divergence ensures the reproduction of advantage across generations. And because of the "hollowing of the middle class," described by Crosnoe, more families are sinking into the disadvantaged group as the ranks of the precariat, who suffer employment instability and economic hardship, grow.

As Crosnoe explains, shifts in the economy – including the decline of the manufacturing sector, and the growth of poorly paid service jobs – place a premium on college degrees as tickets to the upper stratum. A continued steady stream of accomplishment is necessary to achieve this goal in the increasingly cumulative and highly differentiated educational system. Children whose schooling is interrupted for whatever reason will be greatly disadvantaged in such a regime, and the occasions for such disruptions appear to be increasing (with the rise of the "precariat," homelessness, migration, etc.).

Leventhal, Anastasio, and Dupere, in their chapter on the Urban World of Minority and Majority Children, continue in this vein. The trend toward increasing inequality has been accompanied by increased economic and racial segregation in US cities in recent decades. Research documents the double-whammy of poor children whose well-being and achievement suffer not only from the detrimental impacts of their own families' circumstances, but also from being surrounded by other poor children in their neighborhoods and schools.

Similarly, Marks, Woolverton and Garcia Coll paint a very bleak picture of the impacts of migration on the adjustment of children and families. Due to persistent wars, economic dislocation, crime, environmental disasters and other negative conditions in their countries of origin, ever more people are moving within their countries or crossing national boundaries to seek a better life (or to preserve life itself) for themselves and their children. The sheer numbers of recent refugees (e.g., from the Syrian War) and asylum seekers are outpacing the capacity of host countries to support and assimilate them. Masten, Motti-Stefanidi and Rahl-Brigman report that 68.5 million people were displaced in 2017 alone, and more than half the refugees are children. Initial receptivity toward refugees in the European Union, and especially Germany, has given way to increasing hostility and suspicion. The emotional toll on refugee children can lead to long-term trauma, post-traumatic stress disorder, and behavioral maladjustment.

Masten et al. point out that the ramifications of acute climate events (e.g., tornados, floods, wildfires, etc.) as well as more chronic, slow-moving problems (e.g., droughts, rising sea levels, and temperatures) are likely to produce mass movements of populations unlike any heretofore seen. Increasingly frequent wars over declining resources will prompt families to escape the violence and turmoil. Youth become soldiers in war, voluntarily or not, witnessing and often perpetrating acts of violence and genocide. I return to the implications of climate change, arguably the most serious and historic potential disrupter of developmental processes, later in this chapter.

Finally, Greenfield notes the rise in many childhood and adolescent problems that has occurred along with technological advances and the distractions (what she calls "technoference") that they produce. One can only surmise that the trends observed in regions where the youth population is already saturated with videogames, laptops, tablets, and smart phones – that is, increases in internalizing and externalizing problems, desensitization to aggression and suffering, disinhibition of racist and sexist comments, cyberbulling, increased use of pornography and depersonalized sex, etc. – will only spread as these advanced communication technologies become more available elsewhere.

The Resilience of Families and Children

A third overarching theme of this volume, offering somewhat of a coun-
terpoint to the second, is the remarkable resilience of children and families in the face of seemingly insurmountable difficulties. In Chapter 4,
Masten et al. define resilience as "the capacity for adapting successfully
to challenges that threaten adaptive function, survival, or future development." Their comprehensive synthesis of research describes the unique
developmental challenges faced by migrant children who endure calamities of all kinds (e.g., violence and war, famine, extreme poverty, loss of
parents, persecution, and the witnessing of atrocities). Despite the highly
traumatic character of these events, most recover over a period of time.

Consistent with the ecological multi-level systems framework of this
volume, in explaining resilient processes Masten et al. stress the importance of both adaptive individual child characteristics (self-regulation,
cognitive flexibility, executive functioning, bilingualism, academic confidence, immunological functioning, etc.) and the web of interpersonal
relationships and structures that promote mental health and behavioral adjustment. These may account for the "immigrant paradox,"
the successful adaptation of first-generation children noted in US and
Canadian studies. But highlighting the importance of historically and
nationally specific conditions, Masten et al. also cite a meta-analysis
showing that immigrant youth exhibit poorer adjustment in Europe.

Critical in the aftermath of disaster is the maintenance (or quick restoration) of supportive structures that foster the healthy development of
all children. That is, much of the psychological harm following episodes
of war, genocide, natural disasters, and other events results from the disruption of families; relationships with friends and spiritual leaders; loss
of familiar routines and rituals that provide a sense of normalcy, and
interruption of school attendance. This observation is important as it
underlines the potential for interventions, especially if they are rapid and
multifaceted, to enhance resilience.

Masten et al. do not directly weigh in on the question of timing –
whether circumstances that produce trauma have more or less lasting
consequences depending on the child's age. Very young children do not
understand what is happening and may be sheltered by parents and other
adults, but at the same time they are more vulnerable when their caregiving is disrupted. Disruption of secure attachment, which occurs (or
not) in the early years, can have life-long consequences. Adolescents will
often have a more accurate comprehension of the disastrous character of
the situation and they may be forced to join rebel armies. They are also
more likely than younger children to migrate alone, suffering terrible

vicissitudes along the way. But like the Oakland children described by Elder and Cox, they may experience growth and resilience if they are able to help their families and others endure the crisis.

In Chapter 8, Parke provides a comprehensive overview of the dramatic increases in what were previously considered "alternative" family forms. Shifts away from the dominance of the nuclear family, through the historic "second demographic transition" have led to a proliferation of family types, including single parent families (mostly headed by women, but increasingly by men), cohabiting families, single sex families, step-families (including those "blending" children from each spouse), adoptive families, families with children produced by in vitro fertilization and other techniques, and various combinations thereof (e.g., single parent families with adopted children). This increasing diversity allows more people to experience the benefits of marriage (e.g., homosexual couples) and children (e.g., infertile couples).

However, the emergence of highly diverse contexts for the socialization and development of children has caused so much societal alarm that they may be less conducive than "traditional" nuclear families to healthy child development. Parke draws on a large body of recent research to argue that function and process are far more important than structural form in producing healthy, well-adjusted children. That is, children who experience warm and supportive relationships with their parent(s), positive interactions, consistent discipline, etc., will prosper irrespective of their family's form. Societal concerns may, in fact, lead parents in non-nuclear families to compensate for any deficiencies that may result from their particular family structure (for example, the absence of two adults to provide monitoring and discipline), just as dual worker families have adjusted their time budgets to spend more time with children (with less time devoted to seemingly less important functions, like cleaning the house).

All this is good news, as it highlights the potential for many family forms to be positive contexts for child development and resilience. I offer one caveat. Although process may well trump form, children growing up in most of the alternative family forms tend to be in less favorable economic circumstances than children who grow up in nuclear families. Indeed, as noted above, marriage, the timing of children, and family stability are highly class differentiated. Single mother families are far more likely to be poor than married couple families, and this places children at risk for all the developmental disadvantages associated with poverty. (The phenomenon of "selective fathering" among men in poverty raise questions about the development of those children not so selected.) As long as non-nuclear families have fewer economic resources, children will be disadvantaged accordingly. Moreover, persistent concerns about "normalcy" in an era that still upholds the nuclear family form as the ideal, may lead to continuing discrimination (e.g., against homosexual couples who have children) and stigmatization.

Ways Forward and Final Thoughts

Surely, the chapters in this volume point to the need for research to fully understand the consequences of the societal transformations under scrutiny for families and children. In their chapter on urban worlds, Leventhal et al. provide a superb overview of the challenges confronting those who wish to study the impacts of context on child development, due to the ever-present specter of selection effects. That is, families choose to live, or are constrained from living, in neighborhoods with particular characteristics; people with different attitudes enter into cohabiting relationships and legal marriages, etc. The authors describe a range of methods to overcome these challenges (e.g., controlled social experiments, like Moving to Opportunity and similar demonstration projects; propensity score matching; fixed effects modeling; instrumental variables, etc.).

To fully understand the implications of changing cultural and structural contexts for children in this rapidly changing world, developmental scientists need to be ready to abandon traditional areas of research to make room for the investigation of new questions (e.g., the implications of mass migration) and to adopt new methodological approaches best suited to address them. The impacts of social media and other forms of digital communication technology have been neglected by developmental scientists, as they have difficulty keeping up with the rapid changes in these forms of communication. Greenfield's comprehensive review shows that this situation is changing, but we need to know much more about what the shifting time allocation of children means for developmental processes. Of course, abstract relativistic thinking and technological intelligence are clearly needed in modern post-industrial economies. How can the positive consequences of modern communication technologies be preserved, while reducing its costs? As Greenfield points out, "Research is desperately needed to counteract the dehumanizing aspects of expanded communication technologies and reduce the costs to well-being and social closeness, without losing the benefits of efficiency and connection with those at a distance."

The chapters in this volume call for shifts in policy. As Marks, Woolverton and Garcia Coll point out, the migration of families and children across borders is a growing phenomenon around the world. It is in each country's interests to settle migrants quickly, not only for the sake of children's mental health and adjustment, but for the future of nation states themselves. Particularly in rapidly aging societies, healthy children, destined to become successful adults, are needed to populate the labor force, support economically dependent elders, and assure continued institutional stability. Children are the hope of aging societies, particularly in circumstances, as in the United States, where fertility is declining below replacement levels among native-born populations.

Just as individual children are embedded in circles of increasingly distal contexts, policy may be fruitfully directed to several targets. Crosnoe advocates the reduction of economic segregation (while at the same time lessening ethnic/racial segregation) in schools. He highlights the merits of educational "intensification" with de-differentiated curricula, allowing less choice, to bring all children up to sufficient standards to enable them to become full members of the labor force and economically self-supporting. In contrast, for the past several decades secondary schools have been allowing greater choice among alternative courses whose implications for long-term educational attainment may be little understood by students or their parents. Developmental scientists interested in education may find the experience of Japan particularly instructive. Late in the twentieth century, Japan moved in the other direction, away from a highly structured educational curriculum to enable greater choice, and suffered greater class-based inequality of achievement as a result (Kariya & Rosenbaum, 2003).

Leventhal et al. note two viable approaches to policy – a focus on communities (investing in neighborhood institutions like schools, day care centers, parks and recreation facilities, health clinics, etc.), or a focus on families (moving them out of high poverty areas to neighborhoods where contexts may be more conducive to healthy child development). Support of families, and keeping parents and children together, are especially important in times of crisis and disaster (Masten et al.). At the individual level, interventions that support student "growth mindsets" (Crosnoe), confidence, and children's hope for the future (Masten et al.) are needed.

Whereas these and other suggestions are well taken, this reader comes away with a sense that even more radical, macrostructural changes are needed to fully address the challenges of the future. If global, technological (automation, digitization) and other changes are producing economic contexts that cannot provide stable livelihoods for families and children, whether nuclear or "alternative," we need to be seriously considering ways of supporting those left behind, transiently (e.g., due to migration, loss of employment, health problems, etc.) or permanently. Already, a patchwork of policies is in place to help a growing precariat in the United States – housing subsidies (Section 8 vouchers), TANF,

Medicaid, Food Stamps, and other programs. If we are to assure stable contextual conditions for all of our youth – immigrants and native-born, residents of affluent suburbs and inner cities, minorities and majorities, children in intact nuclear and "alternative families," etc. – we need to enhance and integrate these programs and remove the stigma now attached to them.

Finally, developmental scientists must come to grips with the specter of climate change. Masten and her colleagues correctly point out that "the most ominous long-term threat to human life on the planet is gradual climate change." World heat records continue to be broken year after year, accompanied by historic wildfires, floods, droughts, and disruptions linked to these events. As sea levels rise, large coastal populations will be displaced; the melting of ice caps in China, India, and elsewhere will deprive large populations of water, needed for agricultural production, livestock, and human consumption; and drought in the Sub-Saharan region will increase famine. Indeed, scientists predict that if climate change is not mitigated (by drastic reduction in the use of fossil fuels) increasing areas of the earth itself may become uninhabitable.

Probably because the degree of dislocation and threat to future generations is unthinkable, developmental scientists have not fully grasped the implications of climate change for children and youth. More attention should be paid to the challenges and potentially catastrophic consequences for development. Illustrative questions to be considered: How have recent severe weather events in the US (e.g., fires in California, droughts in the Western states, torrential rains on the East coast) and in other countries impacted children? Is the threat of climate change affecting the capacity of youth to envision stable and promising futures? Are youth beginning to re-evaluate the benefits and costs of economic growth, family size, energy conservation, life styles, and living arrangements? Are they becoming attracted to social movements advocating governmental and individual ameliorative action, or are they increasingly acknowledging dystopian futures, assuming a fatalistic stance, and turning inward?

One might ask, will societies of the future have the resources both to address the dislocations caused by weather events (e.g., floods, wildfires, etc.), and to maintain the institutional structures (schools, health clinics, public universities, etc.) needed to scaffold children and youth as they move toward adulthood? Indeed, the severe threat of climate change argues for supra-national interventions to lessen the frequency of climate-related disasters and migratory pressures. The future of our children is at stake.

References

Kariya, T. & Rosenbaum, J. E. (2003). Stratified incentives and life course behaviors. In Mortimer, J. T. & Shanahan, M. J. (eds.), *Handbook of the Life Course* (Vol. 1, pp. 51–78). New York: Springer.

Mortimer, J. T. & Moen, P. (2016). The changing social construction of age and the life course: Precarious identity and enactment of "early" and "encore" stages of adulthood. In Shanahan, M. J., Mortimer, J. T., & Johnson, M. K. (eds.), *Handbook of the Life Course* (Vol. 2, pp. 111–129). New York: Springer.

Author Index

Amato, P. R., 209, 210–211
Anderson, C. A., 246–247, 248
Ashton, D., 60
Austin, B., 52–53

Bailyn, L., 243–244
Beck, U., 66
Bem, S. L., 209
Berry, J.W., 94, 120
Betancourt, T.S., 90
Blair, C., 32, 35
Blossfeld, P., 63, 73
Bornstein, M. H., 33, 94
Boudon, R., 142
Bowlby, J., 199–200
Braga, L. W., 71
Bronfenbrenner, U., 5, 6, 86, 118, 169, 278, 287
Brooks-Gunn, J., 5, 179
Brown, S., 11, 195, 197, 204
Bynner, J., 57, 278, 281

Cahn, N., 222
Calvert, S. L., 8, 246
Caspi, A., 45
Cherlin, A. J., 206
Cicchetti, D., 86
Cohen, L., 71
Conger, R., 33, 172
Cox, M. J., 14, 278
Crosnoe, R., 64, 71, 153, 173
Cundiff, K., 71

Danzinger, S., 71
Dehaene, S., 71, 241–242
Dill, K. E., 246–247, 248
Duncan, G. J., 31, 142, 170
Dupere, V., 182
Dweck, C. S., 154

Eccles, J., 136
Edin, K., 11, 196, 203

Elder, G. H., 10, 14, 28, 29, 32, 33, 37, 45, 60, 62, 76, 85, 200, 278, 287
Emerson, P. E., 200
Epstein, J. L., 152
Evans, G.W., 35, 66

Filho, G. N., 71
Furstenberg, F., 195

Garbarino, J., 89
Garcia Coll, C., 92, 114
Garmezy, N., 85
Glaeser, E., 52–53
Goldberg, A.E., 218
Goldin, C., 133
Golombok, S., 199, 221
Granger, D. A., 35
Greenberg, M. T., 35
Greenfield, P., 9, 239, 259
Gunnar, M. R., 35, 37

Hareven, T., 48, 52
Harlow, H. F., 200
Heckman, J., 145
Hetherington, E. M., 210, 211
Huston, A. C., 32

Jackson, M., 142
Jobert, A, 71
Jones, H. E., 27

Katz, L., 133
Kelly, J., 211
Kennedy, S., 209
Kivlighan, K. T., 35

Laub, J., 46
Leccardi, C., 67–68
Lerner, R. M., 5, 169
Lesthaeghe, R., 195t8.1
Leventhal, T., 5, 176
Livingstone, S., 243

Subject Index